CW01506970

ATTENTION SEEKER

Also by Amber Medland

Wild Pets

ATTENTION SEEKER

The Truth About ADHD

Amber Medland

dialogue books

DIALOGUE BOOKS

First published in Great Britain in 2025 by Dialogue Books
An imprint of John Murray Press

1

A CIP catalogue record for this book
is available from the British Library.

Hardback ISBN 978-0-3497-0413-5

Typeset in Sabon by M Rules
Printed and bound in Great Britain by
Clays Ltd, Elcograf S.p.A

John Murray policy is to use papers that are natural, renewable and
recyclable products and made from wood grown in sustainable forests.
The logging and manufacturing processes are expected to conform to the
environmental regulations of the country of origin.

Carmelite House
50 Victoria Embankment
London EC4Y 0DZ

The authorised representative
in the EEA is
Hachette Ireland
8 Castlecourt Centre
Dublin 15, D15 XTP3, Ireland
(email: info@hbgi.ie)

www.dialoguebooks.co.uk

John Murray Press, part of Hodder & Stoughton Limited
An Hachette UK company

For the parents who wanted to understand but had nowhere to turn, and the children who needed to be seen. This is the book I wish we'd had.

Contents

A Note on Language

As a writer, words are everything. But prioritising the surface of language over its substance can sometimes stand in the way of deeper understanding. Language is inherently flawed, fluid, evolving. It matters, yet it isn't everything.

In this book, you'll find 'people with ADHD' used more often than 'ADHD people', but I use both interchangeably. My priority was to create something everyone could access and enjoy – so I leaned towards brevity where I could. Like the autistic community's advocacy for language that reflects individual experience, choosing your own words is part of shaping your narrative. Variety and cadence also count in writing, so I've used both terms for flow and readability.

Prologue

A few years ago at a party, I was off on some tangent when a man – who had been assessing the value of everyone present – interrupted, looking relieved to have figured me out: 'You're like an information tube, taking everything in – even the useless stuff – and just saying it all at once.' He barked a satisfied laugh and walked off.

His remark stung because he wasn't wrong. Difficulty filtering and prioritising information is part of attention deficit hyperactivity disorder (ADHD), which I was diagnosed with at fifteen.

ADHD is a neurodevelopmental disorder marked by inattention, hyperactivity and impulsivity. People often notice only the behaviours which disrupt the status quo – the gap between neurotypical norms and our more haphazard reality. Their curiosity rarely extends beyond the traits they can readily identify with to the messier lived experience.

Due to low dopamine, external rewards don't motivate people with ADHD, so I've spent years rigging my own reward systems and budgeting attention. I've learned so much by observing and imitating neurotypical people. But now, more than ever, everybody could benefit from the skills ADHD people have developed out of necessity. My attention is mine to spend as I choose. In the current attention economy, where we are all competing for clicks and impressions, this is a manifesto for everyone.

This book moves beyond articles by neurotypical writers who reduce ADHD to a social trend or downright deny its existence, diverting focus from our lived reality. Instead, it explains what ADHD truly is and how it impacts all areas of life: personal, social and political. Right now, only those with first-hand experience or those who have witnessed its effects on loved ones take ADHD seriously. I want to change that.

ADHD is a lifelong neurobiological disorder, backed by decades of research, involving imbalances in dopamine and noradrenaline that affect motivation and reward systems. ADHD brains mature more slowly and have disrupted connectivity, leading to challenges with executive function, emotional regulation, time perception, planning, decision-making and organisation.

In the UK and US, ADHD is legally recognised as a disability. This label doesn't mean ADHD is entirely negative (that's ableist). Whether or not we choose to use it ourselves, having ADHD has a serious negative impact on functioning in a world designed for neurotypicals.

ADHD is deeply intersectional, exposing biases embedded in education, employment and society at large – understanding it empowers everyone. When ADHD is reduced to a casual metaphor for feeling overwhelmed or helpless, it robs both neurodivergent and neurotypical people of dignity and agency.

The degree to which having ADHD fucks up your life depends on its severity, which is often compounded by co-existing conditions including mental health problems (e.g. anxiety, depression) and learning disorders (e.g. dyslexia, dyspraxia). I have all of these, which is common.

Substance misuse, executive function challenges, lack of support, and systemic discrimination can further amplify its impact. Support and socio-economic status can determine whether ADHD becomes disabling. Someone with ADHD who has access to therapy, medication and a supportive workplace is far less likely to experience it as a disability.

Not everyone with ADHD-like symptoms has ADHD, and many won't seek diagnosis. The current discourse risks distracting people from the real causes of their struggles while invalidating those with ADHD. The widespread misconceptions about ADHD harm everyone.

This Book Is for You If

... You're newly diagnosed or love someone who is

You may feel relief, excitement, grief for what could have been different, or worry about medication. You might be forgiving yourself and others, feeling understood for the first time. You may be feeling all of the things!

For some people – especially those who've been undiagnosed for years, labelled lazy or stupid, or as 'ditsy' girls in the 1990s – ADHD is an identity. Lost jobs, friendships and relationships make any positive description a relief, replacing shame with understanding. For me, ADHD is a neurotype – part of my life's context – it enriches my identity, but it's not who I am.

'ADHD is an identity!'

- » Validation and Belonging: provides community and shared understanding.
- » Reframes Experience: shifts perception from personal failure to neurodivergence.
- » Empowerment: encourages self-advocacy and destigmatises struggles.
- » Solidarity: connects individuals facing similar challenges.
- » Self-Awareness: helps individuals understand their behaviour and needs.

'ADHD is *not* an identity!'

- » Complexity Reduction: risks oversimplifying multifaceted human experience.
- » Label Limitation: can confine people to a single aspect of themselves.
- » Structural Overshadowing: focuses on individuals, potentially neglecting systemic issues.
- » Self-Surveillance: may reinforce neoliberal tendencies towards self-branding and measurement.

» Identity Overload: risks prioritising diagnosis over holistic identity.

Whether or not ADHD is your identity is up to you, and only you.

... You have ADHD, diagnosed or undiagnosed, or love someone who does

Maybe you feel relief at the growing awareness, frustration at hit pieces, or irritation at parts of the discourse. When I started writing this book, I wasn't an advocate – being a writer let me acknowledge an awkward truth: not everyone who suspects they have ADHD does. Advocates tend to avoid saying this for good reason – it risks opening a can of worms. But through researching and writing, I became both a writer and an advocate, able to hold both truths: not everyone who suspects they have ADHD is right, but we should still take them seriously. The same applies to OCD or tennis elbow – I've thought I had Lyme disease more than once. Late-diagnosed individuals, especially women, often struggle with imposter syndrome, worsened by difficult diagnoses. Crucially, just because some people are mistaken doesn't mean ADHD isn't real. Unless you're a doctor, you can't judge the 'functional impairment' happening behind the scenes.

... You vaguely suspect you have ADHD

You're anxious, overwhelmed, forgetful, struggling at work, comparing yourself unfavourably to friends. These are valid feelings. You may indeed have ADHD, but keep an open mind. Many conditions – anxiety, depression, PTSD, long Covid – can mimic ADHD and need to be ruled out.

Why is ADHD appealing? When I was a teenager, ADHD had no social capital; it was stigmatised as a working-class problem. Recently, however, it's been linked online to creativity and entrepreneurial spirit. ADHD has become a signifier of 'kooky' cool.

Today, when some people talk about ADHD, they are not actually describing the symptoms that can derail every aspect of a person's life. Rather, they're expressing a broader anxiety – the impossibility of keeping pace with the demands of hustle culture, deteriorating mental health and a lack of resources. In this context, 'pandemic brain' emerged as the perfect shorthand for our collective unravelling: a foggy, restless dysfunction that looks like ADHD. But what if it wasn't ADHD at all? What if it was simply the natural response to a cascade of crises from late capitalism to a global pandemic?

Labelling people instead of addressing structural issues shifts focus and resources away from the real problems affecting us all. This book asks what happens when the language of neurodevelopmental disorders collides with cultural burnout – and what we can do about it.

… You're sympathetic towards ADHD but think it was overdiagnosed during the pandemic

Surely not everyone can have ADHD, right? The 400 per cent spike in adult diagnoses post-2020 – plus celebrity cases – is just unrealistic. But during the pandemic, the loss of structure and routine exposed undiagnosed ADHD. Most research focuses on men, meaning ADHD has been underdiagnosed in everyone except white men. Expanding awareness means more diagnoses.

ADHD voices are loud and driven by dopamine-seeking behaviour, which is why we're overrepresented online. But more visibility doesn't mean we're taking over or that it's a trend. Like the increase in left-handedness when schools stopped forcing right-hand use, ADHD numbers shoot up with recognition, then level out. Hypervisibility shouldn't dismiss ADHD; it signals long-overdue recognition. For every person who is vocal about ADHD, thousands stay silent, internalising labels like 'lazy' or 'stupid'.

If you get diagnosed with ADHD, you're offered medication, but its full impact on life is rarely explained. This isn't unique to ADHD, but it deepens the already superficial understanding of the condition. For me, describing ADHD is like trying to describe the colour of my internal wallpaper. Only talking with others made me realise how many of my behaviours are coping strategies, developed to survive a neurotypical world.

Crucially, unlike many other books about ADHD, this will be written in a way that people with ADHD can actually read.

People with ADHD often find it hard to focus while reading.

We tend to skip details and struggle to comprehend and retain information. This causes anxiety.

This book will be packed full of juicy things that people with ADHD can remember.

There's no 'right' way to read it – no pressure to finish it or go chronologically. In fact, if you have ADHD, I suggest picking whichever chapter you find most interesting from each section – you can follow the link from self, to society, to attention economy, without getting stuck in the drier chapters.

Each unit stands alone, so it will make sense wherever you start, and you can always turn to the glossary.

Between chapters are ARCADES.

By ARCADES, I mean pages full of things that release dopamine, like VIDEO-GAME ARCADES do.

The arcades will structurally enact the ADHD preference for transition between activities.

If you're neurotypical, you have enough dopamine in your brain to focus. If you have ADHD, dopamine production only kicks in when you're interested. As their name suggests, ARCADES will be full of easy dopamine hits – lists, exercises, drawings by Rubyetc, games – amusing diversions for neurotypical readers, which will help people like me to focus.

Low dopamine means inconsistent attention. We're often understimulated (bored, lethargic) or overstimulated (hyperactive, overwhelmed). Engaging multiple senses can help keep dopamine levels up, so some chapters will include suggested snacks and movements.

Unlike the books written on how parents/teachers/spouses should handle us, this book is written by someone with ADHD for readers with ADHD or those who truly want to understand and experience what it is like inside our brains.

Glossary

Autism Spectrum Disorder (ASD): a neurodevelopmental difference affecting communication, social interaction and behaviour. People with ASD often have unique ways of learning, moving or paying attention, alongside sensory sensitivities and focused interests or routines. The term 'spectrum' reflects the wide range of abilities and challenges, from highly independent individuals to those needing significant daily support.

Attention Economy: a market system where human attention is treated as a finite, valuable resource, with companies competing to capture and monetise it through ads, content and algorithms.

Attention Regulation: the ability to direct and sustain focus on specific tasks or stimuli.

Cognitive Flexibility: a key executive function, which involves adapting when plans change or new information arises. It's the brain's ability to pivot and shift perspective. For ADHD brains, this can feel like turning a ship – it takes more time to adjust when things go off course. Though sometimes excluded from the main list of executive functions, it is crucial for handling life's curveballs.

Crip Time: a term that refers to the flexible approach to time management that accommodates disability and neurodivergence.

Comorbidities: additional mental health or learning disorders often present alongside ADHD, such as anxiety or dyslexia.

Dopamine: a neurotransmitter involved in motivation and reward, often deficient or imbalanced in people with ADHD.

Dopamine-seeking Behaviour: actions that stimulate dopamine production to maintain interest.

Executive Function: think of it as your brain's control centre – the mental tools you use to manage everyday life. With ADHD, those tools get glitchy:

1. Working Memory: remembering details and holding information while using it; e.g. remembering: 'What was I just doing?'; holding: 'What do I need to keep in mind right now?'
2. Task Initiation: starting tasks without delay; e.g. starting: 'How do I begin this?'; activating: 'What's the first step to get moving?'
3. Planning and Prioritising: organising steps and deciding what matters most; e.g. organising: 'How do I arrange these tasks?'; sequencing: 'Where do I start? What next?'; prioritising: 'Which of these is the most important?'
4. Focus: concentrating on one task without getting distracted; e.g. concentrating: 'How do I stay focused on this?'; filtering: 'What distractions can I block out?'
5. Emotional Regulation: managing emotions so they fit the situation; e.g. managing: 'How can I control my feelings right now?'; tempering: 'Am I reacting too strongly?'
6. Self-Monitoring: evaluating your progress and adjusting in real-time; e.g. evaluating: 'How am I doing so far?'; adjusting: 'Do I need to change anything right now?'
7. Inhibition: stopping impulses and pausing before reacting; e.g. stopping: 'Should I hold off on this?'; pausing: 'Is this the right time to act?'

8. Cognitive Flexibility: adapting when plans or perspectives change; e.g. shifting: 'How can I switch my approach?; switching: 'What's another way to think about this?'

Hyperactivity: a symptom of ADHD characterised by restless, excessive activity.

Hyperfocus: a state of intense, narrowing concentration on a specific task, often to the exclusion of everything else, common in ADHD (and ASD) but usually triggered by personal interest rather than obligation.

Interoception: the ability to sense internal bodily states, like hunger, thirst or how full your bladder is. ADHD can affect awareness of these signals, making it easier to ignore or misinterpret them.

Masking: the practice of concealing or suppressing ADHD (or ASD) symptoms to conform to neurotypical expectations.

Neurodivergent (ND): refers to people whose brain functions differ from what society considers 'typical'. This includes those with ADHD, dyslexia, dyspraxia, dyscalculia, Tourette's syndrome and auditory processing disorder (APD), among others. Definitions of neurodivergence vary across professionals, advocates and individuals.

Neurodiversity: the idea that everyone experiences and interacts with the world differently, with no single 'correct' way to think, learn or behave. These differences aren't deficits but natural variations of humanity.

Neurodiversity Movement: a social justice movement advocating for civil rights, equality, respect and full inclusion of neurodivergent people in society.

Neurotypical (NT): describes people whose cognitive functioning aligns with what society expects as 'typical'. In this book, when

I say 'neurotypical', I'm specifically referring to people without ASD or ADHD.

Object Permanence: a concept from developmental psychology about understanding that things still exist even when you can't see them – something that TikTok often links to ADHD. But ADHD doesn't mean you lack object permanence; it's about working memory. Your brain's so overloaded it files important stuff (like dinner plans) next to 'Am I emotionally ready for a puppy?'

Persuasive Design: a design approach used in apps and technology to subtly influence your behaviour, like endless scrolling or notifications engineered to make you stay online longer.

Rejection Sensitive Dysphoria (RSD): an intense emotional response to perceived criticism or rejection, common in ADHD. Worrying about someone 'wanting a chat' isn't paranoia if your brain has learned to recognise the pattern – it's the result of a lifetime spent feeling in trouble for things you didn't even realise you did wrong.

Reward System: the brain mechanism responsible for motivating behaviour, often dysregulated in ADHD.

Surveillance Capitalism: a system where companies collect and analyse personal data to predict and influence our behaviour, turning our private lives into profit. Instead of selling products to us, they sell us – our attention, habits and desires – to advertisers.

Time Blindness: difficulty perceiving the passage of time – a common issue for people with ADHD.

Transitions: the process of switching from one task or activity to another, which is often challenging for those with ADHD.

Working Memory: a cognitive function that holds and processes information temporarily, like a mental whiteboard – often smaller or less reliable in people with ADHD.

Introduction

ADHD in the British Media

Having read every article about ADHD published in the UK over the last thirty years, I got hung up on the phrase 'taking responsibility', which cropped up in every op-ed. 'Taking responsibility,' I murmured, fighting a comb through my tangled hair. I muttered it again as I stepped out of the shower, dripping wet, having forgotten my towel. 'Taking ... ?' I glanced at my pillbox, unsure if I'd already taken my ADHD medication, then looked to my boyfriend, who shrugged to remind me that he's not my keeper. In the context of neurodevelopmental disorders, what does 'taking responsibility' actually mean?

ADHD diagnosis remains controversial partly because the NHS lacks centralised data on how many adults or children seek or obtain diagnoses. Meanwhile, in the UK media, the conversation around ADHD has always been tangled up with talk of responsibility – who takes it and who doesn't.

For individuals, taking responsibility for ADHD involves managing it through diagnosis, accommodations, strategies, holistic treatment, self-care and awareness. But when the press talks about responsibility, it often means finding someone to blame. This chapter provides a chronological overview of how the media has influenced public perception of ADHD, highlighting how cultural views have evolved.

Brace yourself for a barrage of headlines.* In recent years, ADHD has been swept up in the attention economy, reshaped by Covid and amplified through social media. But the story began long before it became a trending topic. Think of this chapter as a pressure washer, blasting away the glossy sheen of current media narratives to reveal how today's ADHD conversations were first shaped in newspaper headlines decades ago.

Our understanding of ADHD is intertwined with broader political perspectives on individual versus societal roles. One view holds that society thrives when individuals take full responsibility for themselves – society as a by-product of self-reliance. The other argues that society should support individuals and recognise that some may need more help than others, but that assisting them benefits everyone collectively in the long run.

Nowhere is this tension more pronounced than in the realm of ADHD and mental health. Some believe those with ADHD should 'try harder' or 'pull themselves up by their bootstraps' – a nineteenth-century expression to describe an impossible task. (Try lifting yourself off the ground by pulling on your boots to grasp the absurdity of this phrase underpinning a political ideology.) Others argue that people with ADHD are already 'trying harder' by default, and society must do more to support them.

In March 2024 Work and Pensions Secretary Mel Stride claimed that 'mental health culture' had 'gone too far'. A year earlier, Tory Deputy Chair Lee Anderson blamed ADHD on 'bad parenting', suggesting that the meagre benefits available only harmed young people with ADHD. He added, 'Sometimes we've got to be a little bit braver and say to those young people, "You are not disabled, you can go to work ... we're going to support you."' – without detailing what that support might entail.

Given that this tension reflects a left–right political divide, ADHD can't be discussed in a vacuum. Any understanding must include the political context shaping its perception. The period I cover is a political sandwich: two large slices of right-wing Conservative Party rule with thirteen years of centre-left Labour filling.

---

* Media sources for headlines referenced in this chapter, as well as all sources and references throughout the book, are listed in the endnotes.

If I didn't have ADHD, or know anyone who did, my understanding of the condition would hinge entirely on which newspaper I read. Scanning the last thirty years of headlines, I might come away thinking ADHD was fiction. This narrative is extremely damaging. When science is distorted, hazy or dismissed, the media doesn't merely mirror society's beliefs, it defines them. In this chapter we'll dive into some of the most misleading headlines from the 1990s onwards, and dissect the forces at play beneath the surface.

Successive governments have dismissed ADHD for various reasons, making it a kind of social litmus test. Initially, it served as a class marker to disparage 'yobs'. Today, UK media portrayals have at least diversified – some now see us as superheroes. Framing ADHD as a 'superpower' began as advocacy, intended as a positive and empowering rhetorical shift. But countless celebrities claiming ADHD as their 'superpower' complicate things for those experiencing it as a disability, often without privilege or support to seek help.

Over the past two years, referrals to specialists and self-diagnoses have spiked, with the reported 400 per cent increase in adults seeking diagnoses since 2020. Here's a graph of Google searches for ADHD in the UK over the last five years.

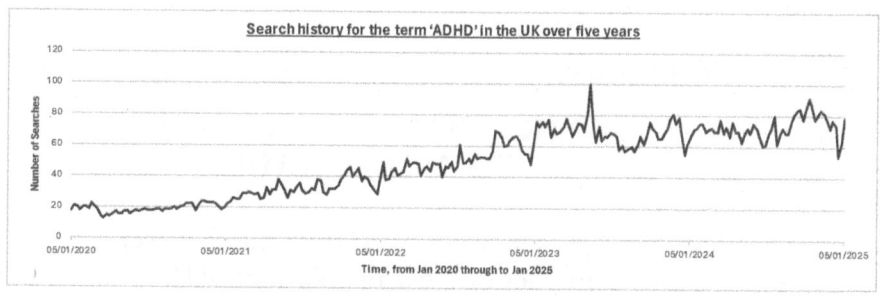

Google-generated graph from Google Trends. Keyword: ADHD.

I'll confess that after reading all these headlines, even I got sick of seeing the acronym. It tasted like sour grapes. I felt frustrated with the newly diagnosed, envious of how much more support and understanding they had compared to what I experienced twenty years ago. *When I was your age we had*

Parallel timeline

to walk ten miles to school in the snow! But it would be stingy to begrudge others the diagnosis that changed my life – I was bothered by my own frustration. I eventually realised that I resented the newly diagnosed for not knowing the rules of the playground: if you make yourself bigger, people will throw things at you, then me, then all of us. With the historical context in mind, I knew what would come next: a media backlash, potentially hurtling us back to where things stood in 1987, when ADHD first entered the American Psychiatric Association's handbook *The Diagnostic and Statistical Manual of Mental Disorders* (DSM).

1987
The Simpsons premieres.

Oh, *this* timeline? This chapter speeds through ADHD's history as it unfolded, within its political context. ADHD memory often links more to personal hooks than dates – for example, I don't remember the date Princess Diana died, but I know the Spice Girls were topping the charts around the same time – so this timeline includes those hooks – pop culture, news events – to make the chapter more accessible. Feel free to add your own dates.

1988
Section 28 enacted: teachers banned from 'promoting [talking about] homosexuality'.

The Nineties

I THOUGHT I'D GIVEN BIRTH TO A DEVIL CHILD

Media representation of ADHD has a direct negative impact on how people with ADHD are treated and how they see themselves. In 1991, for the first time, a five-year-old boy successfully sued the *Sun* for libel. The paper had branded him the 'worst brat in Britain' in a 1989 article that began: 'Terror Tot Jonathan Hunt was last night dubbed Britain's naughtiest kid after wrecking his parents' home, cutting off his own ear, and

killing the cat.' The *Sun* neglected to mention that
Jonathan was registered as disabled. The court
found the journalist had portrayed him as 'wilfully
naughty', and implied his mother was complicit in
encouraging his behaviour. Also, those colourful
details (the ear, the cat) were complete fiction. The
family received substantial compensation.

Back then, journalists wrote as though ADHD
kids heralded the downfall of humanity. Parents in
newspaper photos clutched their heads in despair.
Their spawn were depicted as airborne, zombie-
eyed, screaming and running so fast they blurred.
Headlines cautioned of 'The Criminal Gene', and
articles warned, 'Children with Attention Disorders
Can Destroy a Family.'

The media's sensationalism mirrored the
shortcomings of Tory policies like the 1981 Education
Act, which aimed to integrate children with special
needs into regular schools but often exacerbated
educational gaps due to inadequate support. Stigma
remained high, fuelled by negative portrayals.

The Margaret Thatcher years (the 1980s) were all
about self-reliance. They left little room for systemic
support in mental health, laying the groundwork for
later administrations to either challenge or uphold
these views on conditions like ADHD.

The John Major years (1990–1997) saw at least
a shift in perspective. He recognised that ADHD
wasn't just 'bad behaviour' but a misunderstood
condition needing more research and better
educational resources. Despite his push for improved
training and resources in schools, the gap between
policy intentions and real-world impact persisted,
leaving families feeling unheard.

Reflecting on my own irritation with flippant
mentions of ADHD in today's media, I realise it
stems from a deep-seated awareness of historical
struggles – and a fear that without nuanced

Parallel timeline

1989
Twenty million
viewers watch
'dirty Den' leave
Eastenders.

1990
Margaret Thatcher
resigns.

Parallel timeline

reporting, we could regress to the full-blown sensationalism of the extremely recent past.

MOTHER'S HYPER HELPER

Parents who chose to medicate their children for diagnosed ADHD were judged harshly by the press. Ritalin was nicknamed 'mother's hyper helper' (a play on Prozac: 'mother's little helper'), implying the decision to medicate was self-serving. Articles about Ritalin's proven safety and efficacy were rare; disaster stories were published monthly. Headlines like 'My Son was "Like a Cabbage"'and 'Ritalin Made My Son a Demon' dominated the narrative.

Let me be clear: Ritalin is a serious medication and should be treated as such. It's not a mood booster; like all drugs, it comes with side effects. For some, it may cause a slight dulling effect, and if side effects like mood shifts become too challenging, there are alternatives. That's why doctors should take time to find the right medication. For many, me included, the benefits of ADHD medication far outweigh the downsides. Everyone's decision is personal, but the effect of these headlines was to induce fear.

ADHD medication was treated with suspicion from the start. Opinion pieces polarised ADHD kids into being either 'ill' or 'naughty', 'sick' or 'bad', with medication presented as another binary – either a 'wonder drug' or a 'chemical cosh'. The children were always photographed but never interviewed or asked how they felt.

I was left with the impression that, from the beginning, the UK press disproportionately emphasised the dangers of ADHD medication. When rare Ritalin-related deaths occurred, the media cemented a causal link in the public imagination. Misuse of stimulants as recreational drugs was

1991
Nirvana releases
Nevermind.

1992
Beauty and the Beast nominated for Best Picture Oscar.

often conflated with controlled use as prescribed by doctors. Reports breezed past evidence of the drug's efficacy, highlighting stories like the first 'Ritalin-linked death', only to clarify later that Lucas Lawson, a nineteen-year-old American, had died after crushing and snorting pills. Most Ritalin-related deaths were due to misuse by neurotypical people or children accessing improperly stored medication, similar to accidents involving paracetamol.

CHILDREN'S DRUG IS MORE POTENT THAN COCAINE

Time and again, ADHD medication was likened to class-A substances, ignoring the differences in how the substances affect the brain. 'Children's Drug is More Potent Than Cocaine' proclaimed the *Observer*, as if the parents themselves were racking up lines.

As early as 1996 the *Daily Mail* described ADHD as a 'fashionable' disorder, with stories of kids trading pills dubbed 'Vitamin R' in playgrounds.

Over the next decade, articles focused on dismissing ADHD as a convenient fiction. They claimed a diagnosis was an excuse for working-class families to avoid taking responsibility for their 'inevitable' poverty. They bemoaned that terms like 'lazy' and 'incompetent' had been phased out by a culture too soft for personal failings. One columnist even wrote, 'Have you come to accept the fact that your work ambitions and dreams may never be realised?', suggesting that ADHD was merely an alibi for personal failure. These narratives often seemed designed to provoke outrage, allowing journalists to thrive in an attention economy that rewards divisive and sensational takes.

These columns were often cynical and they reinforced the idea that ADHD was a ruse for

Parallel timeline

1993
The *X-Files* debuts, fuelling UK appetite for conspiracies.

1994
Friends debuts.

Parallel timeline

exploiting the welfare system. ADHD became shorthand for idleness and dependency, a convenient excuse for living off benefits. This rhetoric reinforced societal biases, casting ADHD as a moral failure of the working class.

The Noughties

The New Labour Years (1997–2010)

1995
Colin Firth's wet shirt in the BBC's adaptation of *Pride and Prejudice*.

Under Tony Blair's New Labour, ADHD was recognised as a valid diagnosis by paediatricians, and the first National Institute for Health and Care Excellence (NICE) report on ADHD emerged. The government promoted early diagnosis and educational support and there was a public shift in attitude to mental healthcare. But with the introduction of Antisocial Behavioural Orders (ASBOs) – explored in the chapter on prisons – ADHD's link to crime crystallised, deepening the stigma. On ADHD, New Labour's messaging was muddled at best.

1996
Trainspotting hits cinemas. Dolly the sheep is cloned. The Spice Girls' 'Wannabe' is a global anthem.

With increased awareness came a backlash of articles like 'Are We Creating a Generation of Addicts?' ADHD was seemingly painted as a weakening of 'British moral character', invoking imperial-era ideals of discipline, stoicism and self-control. Such 'values' were used to justify and sustain the imperial mission, suggesting that British culture was morally superior and thus deserved to rule. When ADHD deniers frame ADHD as a weakening of this character, they're invoking our colonial past and playing on nostalgia for Victorian children – seen, not heard.

ADHD was also mistrusted as an 'American import' or 'infection', a result of additives, lax discipline and too much TV in American life. Such arguments were laced with the appearance of cultural elitism and xenophobia, where ADHD's increasing recognition was scapegoated as a sign of cultural decay rather than a medical condition needing care and empathy. Critics' rhetoric helped to fuel culture wars, linking ADHD to larger societal shifts many disapproved of, like single mothers, the decline of the nuclear family, and, more recently, trans people. As early as 2012, the *Daily Mail* lumped ADHD with 'trans issues', appearing to mock both as symptoms of 'politically correct' overreach and dismissing ADHD as a 'modern malady' born of indulgent parenting.

ARE WE TURNING CHILDREN INTO DRUGGED ZOMBIES?

Sensational pieces framing ADHD medication as a form of 'mind control' which turns kids into 'zombies' hit immigrant and non-white families hardest, tapping into deep, historically justified mistrust of the health system (a mistrust later laid bare by the widespread rejection of the Covid vaccine). ADHD studies and medication rates have largely ignored non-white communities, creating a gap in understanding how treatments affect diverse groups. Decades of medical exploitation and discrimination have only cemented this wariness, shaping choices around treatment. Parents feared that diagnosis and medication would pile onto their children's existing barriers, with racial prejudice adding weight to their concerns. In some communities, there are persistent fears that ADHD medication acts as sedation, leaving you vulnerable, less 'on', and unable to protect yourself.

Though corporal punishment was banned in UK state schools in 1986, some newspapers seemed to yearn for its return, publishing earnest letters explicitly putting ADHD forward as an opportunity to ask,

Parallel timeline

1997
Princess Diana's tragic death.

1998
Google launches.
Tamagotchi craze reaches its peak.
Then Furbies.

Parallel timeline

'Should We Let Teachers Smack?' Op-eds were written about France, where parents do, and children sit nicely at the table, whereas in England we've gone soft and children run wild and throw chips.

NOBODY IS CALLED BAD ANY MORE. OR A BIT THICK. THEY HAVE ADHD OR MILD BEEFBURGER'S SYNDROME ...

'These diagnoses give parents an excuse for failed parenting', wrote Paul Routledge in the *Daily Mirror*, where he repeatedly returned to this argument over the years. In one column, he recalled his father's belief that the 'medical intervention' needed for behaviour problems was 'a bloody good hiding'. Such commentary not only dismissed ADHD but also reinforced outdated and harmful attitudes towards discipline, resonating with readers nostalgic for a harsher, less understanding past.

Psychologist Aric Sigman once called for a return to smacking, blaming ADHD on working mothers and daycare. He even advocated threatening a child with a frozen salmon down the trousers, arguing that kids 'enjoy seeing justice served'. In his view, 'the medicalising of civil disorders ... deflects any apportionment of blame', effectively reducing ADHD to poor parenting rather than a neurodevelopmental condition. This conflation of discipline with diagnosis muddles cause and effect.

The underlying message is that hitting your child equates to 'taking responsibility', thereby absolving parents of guilt. It reframes accountability as a quick-fix punishment rather than addressing the structural causes of challenging behaviours. In reality, though, ADHD management – routine, holistic care and supervised medication – demands an ongoing commitment these commentators seldom acknowledge.

1999
The Matrix is released.
Millenium bug panic – people brace for Y2K meltdown.

2000
Big Brother UK airs its first episode, popularising reality TV.
The Sims is released.

Consider, for example, a letter to the *Daily Mail* titled 'SIX OF THE BEST', which extolled a 'herbal remedy' from the 'Far East'. Headmasters, the writer claimed, would hang dried branches of this plant on their doors to 'cure most outbreaks of ADHD' by swiping a child's outstretched palm or backside. The letter concluded, tongue-in-cheek, that ADHD only emerged in medical journals after such practices were banned. Like Sigman's stance, this nostalgic vision for corporal punishment overshadows the substantial research confirming ADHD's neurodevelopmental basis.

ARE THESE CHILDREN REALLY ILL OR ARE THEY JUST NAUGHTY?

This question is perfect for churning out endless media content and showcases the mechanisms of the attention economy. It perpetuates controversy and keeps audiences hooked. The loop of cul-de-sac debates – is ADHD real? (yes) Is Ritalin safe? (yes) – feeds a cycle of sustained attention and interaction, the true currency of today's media landscape.

The *Daily Mail* seemed hellbent on whipping up the menace of unstoppable children, demonising them with headlines like '£10,000 Wrecking Spree of the Little Devil Aged Four' and descriptions of ADHD medication as 'the chemical cosh'. Why? Presumably because the ADHD narrative tapped into societal anxieties about unruly children and the perceived loss of control, fears the *Daily Mail* used to stoke public outrage. Under sensational banners like 'The Curse of Kids' Cocaine', articles contained misinformation, claiming Ritalin was addictive, required ever-increasing doses and led to suicide. They harped on about the uncertainty of long-term side effects – standard for any new drug – with little evidence. Statements like 'one in seven children will

Parallel timeline

2001
9/11 attacks reshape global politics and UK security measures.

2002
The Queen Mother passes aged one hundred and one. David Beckham's sarong challenges traditional masculinity.

Parallel timeline

2003
Love Actually
released.
Iraq war begins -
subsequent protests
bring millions to
the streets.

be on such behaviour-controlling medication as
Ritalin by 2007' were unattributed, recycled and
eventually treated as fact.

Parents faced blame from both sides: for their
child's ADHD behaviour; and, if they chose
medication, for shirking responsibility. Amid the
scare stories were 'success' tales of mothers who
'took control' by weaning their kids off Ritalin
and embracing additive-free diets, exercise plans
or supplements like iron and zinc. Only omega-3
fatty acids have shown even mild effectiveness
in alleviating ADHD symptoms, particularly
hyperactivity and inattentiveness, but the benefits
are modest and over time come with a hefty
price tag.

FAT MUMS ARE LINKED TO HYPER KIDS

Mothers were warned that nearly anything they
did during pregnancy could cause ADHD: stress;
sunbathing; taking paracetamol; exposure to lead,
pesticides and cigarette smoke; eating farmed
fish; experiencing a lack of green space; taking
antibiotics; or having a non-'natural' birth – all
could be culpable. Every few years articles linked
ADHD to caesarean sections, suggesting that
swabbing a child with vaginal fluid reduces their
ADHD risk. But headlines like 'Fat Mums Linked
to Hyper Kids', or claims that women who 'Load
Up on Candy and Burgers', seemed to suggest that
ADHD was caused by maternal choices.

Even when the focus was on sympathy for the
children themselves, the stigma remained: 'Disease
Behind the Tantrums' declared one headline,
turning childhood meltdowns into pathology. It's
easier for the media to portray ADHD as a ticking
time bomb in kids rather than addressing the lack of
actual support available. ADHD is treated as a fault

line dividing 'good' and 'bad' parents, the media simultaneously trivialising the condition and hinting that it's inevitable if parents don't get it right. Meanwhile, in 2004, NICE reported that 1 per cent of children aged six to sixteen – 69,000 kids – had severe ADHD. About 48,000 of them didn't take Ritalin, but this went largely unmentioned, with headlines leaving the impression of an ever-growing ADHD 'epidemic' feeding the public's fears.

For many families, the decision to medicate children with ADHD is complicated by more than just medical advice. Parents are often navigating layers of stigma and systemic barriers:

> Stigma around single-parenting + stigma around poverty + limited access to resources + racial bias in healthcare + cultural stigma around mental health + mistrust of doctors
>
> =
>
> Parents too afraid to medicate children with severe ADHD, even when it could support them alongside holistic treatment.

ADHD ADVICE SECRETLY PAID FOR BY DRUG COMPANIES

Part of the backlash against ADHD and amphetamine medications is rooted in a deep scepticism of America – its pharmaceutical aggressiveness and profit-driven drug marketing. Remember Felicity Huffman in *Desperate Housewives* stealing her son's medication for an all-nighter to make Halloween costumes? Media and pop culture buzzed with fear of Big Pharma. Eleven years after *Prozac Nation* hit the shelves in 1994, the *Sunday Telegraph* ran a piece titled 'Ritalin Nation'.

Parallel timeline

2004
Facebook launches but only in universities. UK smoking ban: no more smoke-filled pubs. England's Euro exit on penalties confirms national football curse.

Parallel timeline

2005
Live 8 Concerts.
Doctor Who returns.
YouTube launches.
Tom Cruise jumps
on Oprah's couch
to declare love for
Katie Holmes.

Yet, with ideas of enhancement surfacing, there was an aspirational glint to some of these articles: 'Would You Rather Be Smarter, Sexier and More Successful? Soon, Wonder Drugs Could Transform You into the Person You Really Want to Be.'

CHILDREN BEHAVING BADLY ARE RAKING IN £170M A YEAR

ADHD support seekers often appeared demonised: 'How the Culture of Blame Has Made Victims of Us All'. Doctors like the still active Dr Sami Timimi of Lincolnshire NHS Trust were quoted stating that ADHD does not exist, which was then used to argue that many working-class parents were gaming the system. Headlines such as 'We Want a Mansion Say Family of Ten on £32,600 in Benefits' omitted to mention that £32,600 isn't much for ten people, and later revealed that £300 per month was for one ADHD child. ADHD parents faced accusations of claiming 'up to £10,000 a year'. Stories like 'Kicked Out of School 38 Times (But, Guess What, it's Not His Fault)' followed a similar pattern. The boy's mother, a single parent of five working in a factory, was portrayed in the *Daily Mail* in stark contrast to middle-class women who were lauded for refusing medication and trying diets. Medication was often represented as parental failure.

Media coverage of ADHD often linked it to benefit scroungers and ASBO recipients, framing it as a drain on society. 'Gratification culture' became a stand-in for ADHD, tied to low-income families and giro cheques. The subtext was clear: the state already gives you too much, and now you've found an excuse to demand more.

Take the article 'Gun Yob at Play' in the *Daily Mirror*: Ross, labelled a 'yob', was photographed rolling what 'appeared to be a marijuana joint'. The article included a photo of one friend holding a BB gun and another holding a rock behind his back, captioned: 'Yob: Mate Hides Rock Behind Back.' While Ross's actions – such as pointing a BB gun at a stranger – are serious, the article to my mind sensationalises these events, sidelining crucial context. It notes Ross's ADHD diagnosis and mentions the closure of his residential school – where he'd spent five years and was working on eleven GCSEs – leaving him without support. But these details took a back seat to caricature: Ross is framed as a 'yob' in 'trademark Adidas three stripe sports trousers' with 'hoodie friends', while the structural neglect that informed his circumstances is downplayed. ADHD becomes a footnote, not a meaningful lens for understanding his behaviour or the wider institutional failures at play.

IT'S NOW A CASE OF RULE BRATANNIA

Full-page spreads claiming '£20,000 Benefits So This Father of Seven Can Keep His Children in Video Games ... and Pay His Huge Booze Bill', as well as headlines like 'Scrounger Mum on £20,000 Wants More', had the effect of normalising talking about ADHD like this, but also the public adopting the same dismissive tone:

Parallel timeline

2006
Twitter emerges, but the UK remains largely indifferent. 'Chav' moral panic at its height; Vicky Pollard from *Little Britain* as cultural shorthand. Topshop reigns, and Kate Moss is its crowned icon.

Parallel timeline

> Little Johnny is never badly behaved. He has Attention Deficit Hyperactivity Disorder.
>
> I do not believe ADHD exists. It's a medical fake, nothing more than a cloak for inadequate parenting. Little Johnny runs riot because his mum (and his dad, in the unlikely event that he is around) does not give him the firm environment in which to grow.

THE BOY THEY CALL CHUCKY

2007
Final *Harry Potter* book released and millennials queue.

Media coverage presented ADHD as either biological (sparking debate over medication) or psychosocial (blaming parenting). The latter dominated, often portraying parents as having lost control. Headlines like 'Surviving Teens from Hell' told tales of sons mugging their mothers with knives, while 'The Boy They Call Chucky' likened a freckled boy in a football cap to a killer doll, with his mother weeping in the accompanying photo and the line 'I fear my son could kill me'. Even when ADHD was acknowledged as neurobiological, titles like 'The Scourge of ADHD' continued to appear. The vulnerability of ADHD families was largely ignored, as was sensitivity to how children might feel being publicly described as monstrous, typified by the grotesque cruelty of 'My ADHD Son Is Out of Control. If He Was a Dog I'd Put Him Down.'

2008
Financial crisis plunges UK into recession; austerity looms.

I was diagnosed in 2005, aged fifteen, a year when pieces like the above filled the press. Each is a rich text. I was acutely aware of how ADHD – or just being myself – affected my family, but only as an adult did I come to understand the media atmosphere that formed the context of my diagnosis. For my divorced parents, it tangled with widely published studies linking ADHD and divorce – studies often based on small sample sizes or overlooking key factors like socioeconomic status, parental mental health and family dynamics. These claims oversimplified complex issues, framing correlation as causation. My Indian mother wasn't thrilled. She worried about medication and what it said about her parenting. How had she missed the signs? With hindsight, I understand her reaction better, especially after talking to other Black and brown kids with similar experiences.

The media made ADHD shameful. Nearly two decades on from my diagnosis I asked my mother if she'd worried about what people thought. She reminded me that, at my competitive school, ADHD was associated with better grades. I was the first girl diagnosed in a school of more than a thousand students, and I got side-eye because ADHD medication meant better results, but I was 'weird' rather than typically disruptive.

ADHD wasn't taken seriously in UK schools back then. We didn't tell my Indian grandparents, but my teachers knew. None of them changed how they treated me – I changed. Medication meant fewer breakdowns, fewer classes sitting by the teacher. I went from crying every day to just a few times a week.

CHEMICAL STRAITJACKET

Since 2003, you often undergo an ECG and regular blood pressure tests before being prescribed ADHD medication. Ritalin had been licensed before 2007, when new regulations required warning labels for cardiovascular risks and potential psychiatric side effects like hallucinations or mania – standard for psychoactive drugs. In 2007, after a ten-year-old boy died while on Ritalin and Prozac, Theresa May, then just an MP, reportedly expressed concern on the radio about the overprescription of Ritalin, suggesting it was being used as a 'chemical

Parallel timeline

2009
Launch of Spotify.

2010
Sherlock featuring
Benedict
Cumberbatch
premieres.
BP oil spill – the
worst ever.

Parallel timeline

babysitter' and that parents were not doing enough to manage their children's energy levels. The state's failure to support these children was ignored; the blame fell squarely on parents.

One article cited a 'Conservative Party study' claiming Ritalin was overprescribed, even to children under a year old – evidence I haven't been able to find. The media tied Ritalin to junk food and TV, branding it a 'chemical straitjacket'. Tragic stories of young boys' suicides helped to build a terrifying narrative, often focusing on the supposed dangers of the medication. Reports would point to cases of teenagers found dead after years on Ritalin, often omitting or sidelining critical details like recent dosage changes or wider mental health struggles. These omissions painted a simplistic cause-and-effect picture, overlooking the fact that adverse effects, if caused by Ritalin, would likely emerge shortly after starting treatment, or significantly increasing dosage, rather than after years of stable use.

ADHD medication isn't risk-free – but neither is paracetamol. But medication alone, without education or holistic treatment, falls short. ADHD is incurable, and its comorbidities mean managing it requires more than a pill.

2011
London riots erupt following the police shooting of Mark Duggan. *News of the World* folds amid a phone-hacking scandal.

SCHOOLCHILDREN COULD BE GIVEN 'SMART DRUGS' IN A BID TO BOOST BRAINPOWER

In 2008, to my mother's dismay, NICE finally published its report on adult ADHD. Until then, the assumption was that people outgrew it. At university I had to switch GPs twice because they treated me like a drug-seeker and wouldn't refill my prescription. As fear of American Big Pharma grew, the media ran stories like, 'Parents Give

2012
London Olympics: opening ceremony directed by Danny Boyle. 'Gangnam Style' goes viral.

Parallel timeline

Children Ritalin at Exam Time'. Stories like these, which to my mind falsely implied that ADHD medication enhances long-term learning, seemed to appear with increasing regularity: 'Fear for Smart Pill Generation', 'Schoolchildren Could Be Given "Smart Drugs" in a Bid to Boost Brainpower'. These headlines reinforced the misconception that Ritalin is a shortcut to academic success.

Simultaneously, another genre of articles criminalised parents for medicating their children while suggesting ADHD could be 'cured' by a walk, a healthy stew, or a bedtime story. The subtext was clear – middle-class parents care; working-class parents look for alibis – and reflected the uniquely British obsession with class and behaviour, where working-class struggles are cast as moral failings, and ADHD is another excuse. The narrative reinforces a national tendency to equate virtue with self-reliance, and failure with a lack of discipline, leaving no room for systemic empathy.

The Twenty-Tens

The Cameron Years (2010–16)

IT'S NOT ADHD, SIR, IT'S IN MY GENES

In 2010, as austerity took hold under David Cameron's government, studies linking ADHD to genetics made headlines. The *Telegraph*: 'ADHD "Caused By Genetic Faults"'. Shortly after that, another headline quipped: 'It's Not ADHD, Sir, it's in My Genes'. The *Daily Express* chimed in with 'Naughty Boy Syndrome Is Genetic'. While acknowledging genetics doesn't absolve responsibility – most conditions have genetic roots – the narrative often leaned into scepticism. Some ADHD detractors appeared to cling to their

2013
Frozen frenzy begins – no one can 'Let It Go'.

2014
Ice Bucket Challenge goes viral. Scotland votes 'no' in independence referendum. Kim Kardashian tries to 'break the internet'.

Parallel timeline

2015
'The Dress' breaks the internet - is it blue and black or white and gold?

2016
Brexit vote. *Pokémon Go* launches and people go outside.

disbelief, railing against accommodations like theme parks allowing children with severe ADHD to skip hours-long queues. Journalist Paul Routledge stated, 'If further research provides conclusive proof of these findings, I will believe it is a brain disorder ... Until then, I will continue to believe that bad parenting is to blame.' Such scepticism wasn't confined to tabloids; a judge dismissed ADHD claims from a defendant, saying: 'Everyone under nineteen seems to have ADHD. It seems to be infectious.'

In a grudging shift, a *Daily Express* headline posed above a photo of Winston Churchill queried: 'Did Our Greatest PM Have ADHD?' ADHD began to be viewed as less of a moral failing, but back when Rory Bremner described his 'butterfly brain' in 2011, admitting to ADHD still attracted curiosity and scepticism, like confessing belief in UFOs.

Headlines leaned on alliteration and recycling catchy critiques: 'Kids Don't Need Pills, They Need Parenting'; 'Hyperactive or Just Hype'; 'Doctors Too Ready to Diagnose ADHD'. By 2014, Richard Saul's *ADHD Does Not Exist* grabbed front pages and was reviewed in every major outlet (twice in *The Times*). The book's title was a stunt. Saul acknowledged ADHD's existence, but most of the press, in summarising the book, ran with the provocation. His argument hinged on the idea that ADHD was overdiagnosed and better understood as a cluster of other underlying conditions, which he claimed were often missed in diagnosis.

During the David Cameron years (2010–16), austerity measures strained mental health services, overshadowing ADHD in broader discussions. Under Theresa May (2016–19), these services continued to buckle, especially in special education. Under Boris Johnson (2019–22) neurodivergence occasionally surfaced in policies like the National Disability

Strategy, which aimed to improve access to public services, but critics called it scattershot with little appetite for addressing entrenched social inequalities.

In the Conservative imagination, neurodivergence often translates to untapped economic potential, acknowledged only when it can boost productivity. Symbolic gestures, like nodding to World Autism Awareness Day, masked Johnson's superficial engagement with ADHD or autism.

Fear-mongering around Ritalin persisted, with media flare-ups over trends like fidget spinners. The *Daily Mirror* hyped them one month, then warned of 'bladed fidget spinners' the next, testing them on pork skin and tomatoes as stand-ins for human flesh and eyes.

The pandemic, however, was a game-changer, prompting widespread self-recognition of ADHD-like symptoms. Media coverage mirrored the past but with a twist: an acknowledgement that women have ADHD too, or advocating the therapeutic benefits of activities like ping-pong. Headlines like 'ADHD is a brain disorder, not a label for poor parenting, say scientists' were still newsworthy in 2017, but publications like the *Daily Mail* published:

FORGETTING WHERE YOU'VE PARKED YOUR CAR COULD MEAN YOU HAVE ADHD

IS YOUR WARDROBE CRAMMED? IT COULD BE A SIGN YOU'VE GOT A NEW MEDICAL DISORDER

In the 2010s, explanations for ADHD expanded to new scapegoats: younger children seeming developmentally behind their older classmates, or the effects of social media overload. This 'blame-shifting' narrative was a media staple.

Parallel timeline

2017
The Grenfell Tower fire exposes systemic neglect.
#MeToo movement gains momentum in the UK.
Stormzy's Glastonbury set.

2018
Love Island fever peaks.
Theresa May's dance moves in Africa become fodder for memes and critique.

Parallel timeline

Then things became very Jekyll and Hyde. On the one hand, ADHD was attributed to geniuses – from Leonardo da Vinci to Beethoven – while, on the other, it was often demonised in crime reports ('Brother's an Evil Monster'). Whenever Ritalin was involved in a violent crime, it made headlines: 'Twisted Bruv & Sis Couple Get 35 Years' – a story of an incestuous couple who murdered their children opened with their use of ADHD meds as an attempted method.

The Twenties

2019
Brexit: Britain leaves the EU.

Today, most people in Britain know someone with ADHD, or suspect they have it themselves. Yet, while demand for diagnoses overwhelms the NHS – with waiting lists stretching up to ten years in some areas – articles centring ADHD dominate public discourse. Lockdown triggered a surge in self-diagnoses and referrals, fuelling endless headlines: 'Reading this Column May Be a Sign You Have ADHD'; 'Why Do So Many Comedians Have ADHD?' and 'Number of People Seeking ADHD Diagnosis Soars Since Lockdown'. Meanwhile, the media churned out clickbait like, 'The ADHD Self-Diagnosis "Industry" Offering a Quick Fix That Doesn't Exist' and 'No, You Don't Have ADHD'. *Love Island* contestants broke down in tears over their diagnoses, and TikToks claiming to diagnose people in seconds went viral.

2020
Covid-19 pandemic: lockdowns begin.
Tiger King.

Despite this frenzy, news stories by people with ADHD remain rare. Instead, ADHD experiences are often conflated with those of overwhelmed neurotypical people. It's like when thin people judge those with obesity, believing sheer willpower keeps them slim. The argument – such as it is – goes: 'I'm overstimulated by my phone too, so you probably don't have ADHD.'

In 2021 the narrative started to shift. Realising ADHD affected more than just 'problem kids', journalists published more empathetic, personal and confessional stories. Headlines like *The Times*'s triptych – 'I Can't Persuade My ADHD Son to Stop Smoking Cannabis'; 'I Was Diagnosed with ADHD at 47. I Cried from Relief'; 'I Was Diagnosed with ADHD at 37. This Is My Story' – signalled a growing recognition of ADHD's impact – but only up to a point.

The empathy in these stories is always personal and does not appear to extend beyond the interviewee to the larger community of those with ADHD. Too often, it seems that the interviewee has to bleed to earn empathy – we're expected to bare our deepest wounds to access even a shred of public sympathy. ADHD is humanised as an individual's unique burden, not a systemic issue. This is empathy with limits – selectively granted to those who fit a certain profile and who narrate their struggle in a way that's digestible and familiar. It comforts readers but doesn't challenge the structures that make life harder for those without a similar platform or appeal.

By 2022 the first parliamentary debate on ADHD assessment hinted at growing recognition, with politicians acknowledging the 'lack of understanding about what ADHD actually is' and the 'complete lack of data on ADHD care'. Still, despite these signs of progress, media outlets often cling to outdated frames of reference, trivialising ADHD as a 'snowflake' condition.

Reading pandemic-era articles, ADHD felt like it had become a right-wing dog whistle – lumped together with grievances about trans identities, queer people and food intolerances. At first I thought I might be overreacting, but after reading every British press article on ADHD from 1987 to

Parallel timeline

2021
England reach the Euro 2020 finals. Britney's conservatorship ends #FreeBritney.

2022
The Queen dies. The Lionesses win the Euros! Matt Hancock goes on *I'm a Celebrity*.

Parallel timeline

2023
AI technologies, like ChatGPT, dominate headlines.
Cost of living crisis deepens; food banks become lifelines for many.

2024
Keir Starmer becomes prime minister, ending fourteen years of Tory rule.
Taylor Swift's *Eras* Tour.

2023, the pattern was undeniable. (This chapter contains roughly half the headlines surveyed.) Seeing the *Spectator* allow Julie Burchill to plead 'Please ... No Adult ADHD Diagnoses' was a gut punch. She equated ADHD with 'late-onset allergies' and 'gender reveals', seemingly dismissing them as 'luxury maladies'. My father developed a shellfish allergy in his forties and nearly died; hardly a trivial indulgence.

This kind of dismissal is a conservative sleight of hand – appearing to recast genuine health needs as whims which stoke culture wars and spread misinformation, which in turn can deflect from real issues. Burchill even tossed 'self-harm' and 'transing' [*sic*] into the 'attention-seeking' bin, reducing what I consider the deeply personal and painful experiences of countless people to frivolous or manipulative cries for attention. Framing ADHD as identity politics trivialises the need for accessible care. The same reductive rhetoric that has long been weaponised against LGBT people now often targets neurodivergence, treating difference as a threat to traditional values.

The ADHD medication shortage that started in 2023 shifted some media conversations. NHS England launched a taskforce to address rising demand and supply issues. The *Guardian* called for reform; the *Daily Mail* used the task force as proof of overdiagnosis – everyone printed headlines.

One thing is clear: ADHD thrives in the attention economy. Whether it's Joe Wicks blaming ultra-processed food, or *The Times* recycling contagion-theory debates, ADHD remains a hot topic. It makes people trend. So we have to ask: why is this debate so lucrative?

Chapter 1

Beyond the Headlines: The Realities of Diagnosing ADHD

In March 2023 popular trauma specialist Gabor Maté diagnosed Prince Harry with ADHD during a live-streamed therapy session. The internet erupted, fuelled by ADHD denialism and culture-war rhetoric. Within ninety minutes, Maté also 'diagnosed' Harry with anxiety, PTSD and substance misuse – but the ADHD diagnosis grabbed headlines. With the King's coronation looming and the recent release of Netflix documentary *Harry & Meghan*, the diagnosis was catnip for columnists. Both Prince Harry and ADHD were seen as overexposed, privileged and millennial – fair game for ridicule. Critics called Maté's approach 'reckless', pointing out it wasn't a real diagnosis. But the damage was done, leaving ADHD as tabloid fodder yet again.

If you or someone you love hasn't sought an ADHD diagnosis, your view is likely guided by this kind of media spectacle. Those of us with first-hand experience cringed, knowing it would only fuel stigma. Misinformation has real consequences: it makes people doubt their diagnosis, hesitate to pursue one, or lose confidence in advocating for a child. For Black and brown parents already facing cultural stigma, it adds yet another barrier.

I was lucky to be diagnosed with ADHD aged fifteen. Before that, I was seen as simply having an 'attitude problem'. In computing class, I wasn't allowed a spinning chair like everyone else because I'd whirl around. I had to sit by the teacher in some classes; in others, I'd burst ink cartridges just so I'd be allowed to leave and wash my hands. Finally, the teacher who usually sent me to detention referred me to an educational psychologist. We'd had to colour in a diagram and I couldn't keep within the lines (not a metaphor). Around half of ADHD kids struggle with fine motor control – using scissors, joined-up writing, tying shoelaces. This first led to a dyspraxia diagnosis, but, more importantly, it introduced me to Mr Hopf, the first adult who truly listened.

Before my diagnosis and medication, my memories are vivid, high-octane and blurred by an overwhelming sense of injustice. I did well in writing-heavy subjects but was constantly in detention – for being late, skipping class, talking or breaking pointless rules. I even had my own bin in lost property. No one believed I was trying. At my privileged school in Kent, surrounded by guardrails and green fields, I still managed to get into trouble. If a child feels crushing despair most days, they're not coping.

During his session with Prince Harry, Maté claimed ADHD was both curable and a 'normal response to normal stress'. ADHD isn't curable, but its symptoms can be managed, depending on privilege, support and co-occurring disorders. People often ask if I'd opt out of ADHD, given the choice. It's a strange question. How else would I be? I only know that *undiagnosed* ADHD made me question whether life was for me.

The Stakes of Getting it Right: Why Accurate Diagnosis Matters

ADHD is underdiagnosed and undertreated, with debilitating effects. People with ADHD are at higher risk of chronic underachievement in school, relationships and work. Many with undiagnosed ADHD turn to self-medication through substance misuse, which can spiral into addiction and incarceration. Failing to diagnose ADHD comes at a huge cost – human, social and financial.

Despite three decades of media coverage, ADHD remains largely misunderstood. As advocates have tried to shift the narrative positively, ADHD has become a culture-war issue. The backlash is driven by the attention economy: media coverage seeks engagement, not understanding. The tragedy is that ADHD treatment is highly effective, affordable and safe, with fewer side effects than most mental health treatments. Yet outlandish headlines reinforce stigma, ignoring that untreated ADHD raises the risk of severe mental health challenges – ADHD adults are five times more likely to attempt suicide, with one in four women considered at such risk. Accurate media representation is vital to support public understanding and access to diagnosis and treatment.

From Symptoms to Diagnosis: How ADHD is Evaluated

In that conversation with Prince Harry, Maté casually said, 'I think you have ADHD,' as if diagnosing someone's personality over coffee. He skipped the basic screening questions: Are the symptoms present? Severe? How long have they lasted? Do they affect daily life across multiple settings – home, school, work? Were they present in childhood? Could trauma or substance misuse be influencing the picture? Proper ADHD diagnosis requires trained professionals to ask these questions, as well as conducting thorough clinical and psychosocial assessments.

Medical professionals don't diagnose ADHD in public. They follow the *DSM-V* criteria, refer patients to mental health specialists and rule out other possible causes. A full ADHD diagnosis involves input from multiple sources, like parents and teachers, and uses standardised assessment tools to build a comprehensive understanding. Integrating all this information takes clinical expertise; symptoms must disrupt multiple areas over time – otherwise, it's not ADHD. This is why self-diagnosis, while often necessary as a first step (and sometimes the only one available), isn't enough on its own.

NHS ADHD Diagnosis Process	Gabor Maté's ADHD Diagnosis of Prince Harry
» Referral (from GP to Specialist)	» Public Discussion with Prince Harry
» Clinical Interview	» General Observations
» Use of Assessment Tools	» Personal Opinion
» Observation in Different Settings	
» History Gathering (Family, Childhood, etc.)	
» Rule Out Other Conditions	
» NICE Guidelines for ADHD Diagnosis	
» Multidisciplinary Team Assessment	
» Diagnostic Criteria	
» Post-Diagnosis Treatment Plan	
» Follow-up and Monitoring	

Getting Clear on ADHD: A Definition

Attention deficit hyperactivity disorder (ADHD) is a neurodevelopmental disorder characterised by persistent patterns of inattention, hyperactivity and impulsivity that interfere with daily life and functioning.

Barkley Versus Maté: The ADHD Debate that Keeps on Giving

Russell Barkley, dubbed the 'father of ADHD', has spent decades researching the condition's neurobiological and genetic roots. His evidence-based work contrasts sharply with Gabor Maté's theory that ADHD is a result of environmental stress and emotional wounds – a view largely sidelined in scientific circles.

Barkley describes ADHD as a developmental impairment of

brain-based executive functions like working memory, self-control and emotional regulation. As he puts it, 'ADHD is not a disorder of knowing what to do; it's a disorder of doing what you know.'

Brain Wiring, Not Excuses: The Neurobiological Roots of ADHD

» Research reveals that ADHD isn't a single attention deficit but a fluctuation in performance, compounded by issues with inhibition, motivation and self-regulation.
» Brain-imaging scans show fewer dopamine receptors in areas responsible for processing rewards and controlling movement, hinting at an innate lack of reward sensitivity.
» Genes linked to brain development connect ADHD with schizophrenia, bipolar disorder and autism.
» The way these genes express over time, combined with environments that either support or hinder self-regulation, shapes how these conditions unfold.

Why ADHD Often Gets Misclassified

ADHD is often mistaken for a mental health disorder because its behaviours – like excessive talking – seem mentally driven. Furthermore, it's technically classified as a mental health disorder in diagnostic manuals. Roughly 80 per cent of ADHD people have at least one additional mental health condition, such as major depressive disorder, bipolar disorder or PTSD. Half of us have an anxiety disorder. Some symptoms of poor mental health – like anxious people speaking quickly – overlap with ADHD.

But thinking of ADHD as a mental health disorder is like assuming whales are fish just because they swim. Whales are actually mammals, and ADHD, likewise, is a neurodevelopmental disorder – not a mental health condition. This distinction matters because understanding ADHD in this way changes how we treat it and view ourselves. Recognising ADHD as a neurodevelopmental condition, like ASD, emphasises that it is chronic and shows up differently throughout life, opening the door to legal protections and educational support.

If we abandon the neurodevelopmental framework, we're left trying to control ADHD behaviours in isolation. This leads to an endless game of emotional whack-a-mole, where the goal is simply to avoid being 'too much'. If ADHD is a fire, that approach is kerosene. Understanding the biological basis – the differences in brain structure and neurotransmitter function – reminds us that ADHD isn't a character flaw or a lack of effort. It quietens the self-blame.

The real casualty of ADHD misinformation is that those who need diagnosis and treatment most miss out. Without a diagnosis, you're flying blind in a world not designed for your brain. While psychosocial interventions like therapy help with mental health issues, without a diagnosis there's no access to the medications that target ADHD's neurobiological core.

TL;DR? 🔑 Takeaways:

» Gabor Maté channelled Dr Phil and casually 'diagnosed' Prince Harry with ADHD live on air, kicking off a media storm.

» Real ADHD diagnosis is way more thorough, and way less clickbait-y.

» ADHD is still underdiagnosed and undertreated, and missing it can have severe real-world consequences.

Understanding the Diagnostic Criteria

The diagnostic criteria for ADHD have evolved as our understanding of the condition has grown. Originally dubbed 'Hyperkinetic Reaction of Childhood' in the *DSM-II*, it focused solely on hyperactivity.

In **1980**, the *DSM-III* introduced the term attention deficit disorder (ADD), recognising both inattention and hyperactivity, and allowing for diagnoses with or without hyperactivity. Then, in **1987**, the

DSM-III-R refined these criteria, stressing that symptoms needed to appear across different settings. By **1994** the *DSM-IV* expanded ADHD into three subtypes – predominantly inattentive, predominantly hyperactive, and impulsive – adding nuance to the diagnosis. The *DSM-V* (**2013**) raised the age for the onset of symptoms from seven to twelve and finally recognised ADHD in adults, acknowledging the lifespan view of ADHD. The latest update, in **2022**, continues to classify ADHD as a neurobiological condition, not just a behavioural one – emphasising its developmental nature.

Today, ADHD diagnosis involves three main symptom categories:

> **Inattention** (e.g., making careless mistakes, struggling to sustain focus, appearing not to listen when spoken to directly).
> **Hyperactivity** (e.g., fidgeting, needing to move when it's inappropriate to do so, feeling restless).
> **Impulsivity** (e.g., blurting out answers, having trouble waiting, interrupting others).

Some doctors question the usefulness of ADHD subtypes, noting that symptoms can shift over time. Still, these categories help structure diagnosis.

Traits or Symptoms? The Fine Line in ADHD Assessment

ADHD symptoms are rooted in fundamental brain-wiring differences, yet ADHD-like behaviours can result from many factors, like stress or anxiety. Inattention, hyperactivity and impulsivity are, after all, part of being human. Everyone gets distracted, forgets to pay a bill, or can't find their keys. Talking fast with friends doesn't make you hyperactive, and suddenly *needing* to move when you hear Taylor Swift doesn't make you impulsive. Drunk-dialling doesn't mean you have a persistent pattern of impulsivity.

ADHD can be hard to diagnose because other issues can cause similar traits. Professionals need to rule out other medical causes, like PTSD or thyroid issues. Long Covid, with its 'brain fog' and executive function struggles, can also mimic ADHD, making diagnosis even trickier. Specialists look for persistent patterns that show up in multiple areas of life over time. They also have to consider environment: struggling with sleep because of a 3 a.m. email from your psychopath boss isn't ADHD; being consistently still up at 3 a.m. despite good sleep habits might be.

Other factors, like a stressful home environment, or malnutrition, have to be ruled out too. Even if it's not ADHD, ADHD-like traits deserve attention. As one headline put it: 'Think you've got ADHD? You might not, but you may still need help.'

The Tangled Web of Comorbidities

'Comorbid' sounds grim, like two people dying at once, but it just means people with ADHD often have one or more additional disorders – commonly: sleep issues, substance misuse or learning disorders. ADHD has high rates of overlap with both neurodevelopmental and mental health conditions – 90 per cent of adults with ADHD also have a psychiatric disorder. These combined conditions can amplify each other, causing shame and the feeling that something is always 'wrong'.

Some people seek help for these secondary conditions and discover they have ADHD. But ADHD often flies under the radar due to stigma and bias – especially for women, where it's often mistaken for anxiety. Untreated ADHD can lead people to self-medicate, most with alcohol, sometimes worsening the anxiety and impulsivity linked to ADHD. Diagnosing ADHD first is key since treating secondary disorders alone isn't effective. For example, taking antidepressants alone won't pull you out of ADHD-fuelled depression. Managing ADHD without medication is like trying to build walls before you've laid the foundation.

Why Early Diagnosis Matters

Back in 2005 when I was diagnosed with ADHD doctors still thought kids outgrew it. ADHD symptoms shift with age, showing up differently at eleven, eighteen and twenty-five. But in the UK, once you turn eighteen, care 'transitions' from child to adult services – a turbulent shift for anyone with mental health disorders. ADHD students are especially likely to drop out of university because their symptoms clash with new environments, and many lose access to support systems just as life's demands intensify.

The Complexities of Late Diagnosis

Most ADHD diagnoses in the UK still happen in childhood, which gives those kids a head start with early support and accommodations, and ideally collaboration with teachers. Those of us diagnosed young have had more time to learn strategies, build systems, and manage medication.

Diagnosing ADHD in adulthood is tougher – symptoms must have been present since childhood, not acquired through illness, injury or trauma. Without evidence of behaviour from primary school, some adults are denied referrals. ADHD has a hereditary aspect, too, so having a parent diagnosed can help confirm your case. Unfortunately, for those with complicated family or care dynamics, getting this 'proof' can be difficult. Increasing public awareness around ADHD in schools is crucial, especially for kids facing family breakdown or estrangement.

> TL;DR? 🔑 Takeaways:
> » ADHD has been through a few rebrands – from 'Hyperactive Kid Disorder' in the 1960s to today's nuanced subtypes.
> » Diagnosis is complicated: symptoms often overlap with everyday behaviours, and ADHD rarely turns up alone – it usually arrives with a messy entourage of other conditions.
> » The real issue isn't overdiagnosis; it's an underfunded NHS creating a postcode lottery, forcing many to rely on expensive private clinics.

Who Gets Diagnosed? The Impact of Bias

Most of the research into ADHD used white men as its subjects, shaping diagnostic criteria around their experiences. This historically skewed focus led to the belief that ADHD was four times more common in men. Today, anyone outside that demographic – women, people of colour – is less likely to be diagnosed. Medical biases still influence how doctors apply diagnostic criteria. A Cambridge-based consultant psychiatrist, who had her own delayed diagnosis, highlights how hormone shifts make it easy for doctors to dismiss ADHD symptoms in women. She is among many clinicians advocating urgently for research into how hormonal fluctuations affect ADHD diagnosis and treatment.

Adam Bond (London, 34), a trans man, was well placed to observe how his gender impacted his experience with ADHD and the medical system. Diagnosed prior to coming out, his ADHD symptoms were initially downplayed; later, as a man, the same system took his experiences more seriously – a stark example of how gender bias in ADHD diagnosis can dismiss symptoms based on outdated stereotypes.

Cultural norms can affect how ADHD is diagnosed too. In the US, only 2 per cent of Asian American children are diagnosed, but studies in Asian countries show ADHD rates closer to 6 per cent. This disparity exists because ADHD behaviours can be culturally influenced. For example, an Asian child might appear 'less disruptive' to an American doctor, masking their symptoms. Race further complicates diagnosis – Black boys are often labelled as 'disruptive' rather than accurately diagnosed. ADHD is often overdiagnosed in white children and underdiagnosed in children of colour due to biased, white-centred diagnostic models.

Marsha Martin, founder of Black SEN Mamas, a UK-based support group and informational hub (that assists Black mothers of children with special educational needs and disabilities [SEND]) explains how cultural stigma around neurodivergence can lead to children's behaviours being misinterpreted as disrespect. As a Black autistic parent of three neurodivergent kids, she faces added barriers, with her advocacy mistaken for aggression. 'Culturally,' she says, 'the expectation is punitive rather than supportive.' Martin works to spread awareness around the intersection of race and neurodiversity because her advocacy is often met with less empathy than that of non-Black parents.

Gatekeeping in ADHD Diagnosis

Getting an ADHD referral can feel like navigating a minefield. GPs are supposed to refer patients they suspect have ADHD, but they can also refuse, often letting biases about socioeconomic background or family dynamics get in the way. Working-class parents and single-parent families frequently report being dismissed, as if seeking a diagnosis were a shortcut.

For those who don't fit the 'typical' ADHD criteria, getting a diagnosis is a tightrope walk. Headlines that paint ADHD as a trend, or as something only 'faddy women' seek, deepen stigma, leading many women to second-guess their symptoms and hesitate to advocate for themselves – especially when the treatment involves amphetamines. After years of feeling dismissed, pursuing a diagnosis is exhausting. Women are frequently misdiagnosed with anxiety, depression or burnout, or told to take Evening Primrose Oil for their hormones. Hormonal changes eventually make compensating for ADHD impossible, amplifying symptoms so that they can't be ignored, pushing many women to advocate more fiercely and refuse dismissal.

Some doctors are trying to change this. A Sheffield-based GP, who struggled with her own diagnosis, calls for improved ADHD education for GPs. After twenty-three years on SSRIs (selective serotonin reuptake inhibitors) for anxiety and depression that never helped, she was finally diagnosed with ADHD: 'My frustration with diagnosis access for my patients is tempered by shame that I didn't spot it in myself.' GPs receive little ADHD education. As they explain, 'We fail to recognise it, fail to refer, and when we do, we don't properly assess risk.' Even once diagnosed, NHS patients often get no support beyond medication. Counselling, coaching and work adjustments are left up to the individual – many don't know where to start.

If you're not white, male, able-bodied and without a history of mental health issues, your ADHD symptoms might not match what doctors expect. I was lucky to be diagnosed before I accumulated other labels. The system relies heavily on making the 'right impression' on the right people. Since then, my diagnosis has been confirmed multiple times, most recently

in Hackney, north-east London, where my GP and the local
ADHD clinic were excellent. By then, I knew what to expect and
was confident I'd be believed, because the doctor would have to
contradict several other doctors. Expecting to be believed is a
privilege.

TL;DR? 🔑 Takeaways:

» ADHD diagnostic criteria were built around white men,
  leaving everyone else at a disadvantage.
» Women get dismissed as hormonal, high-achievers don't
  'look like' they have ADHD, and Black and Asian kids are
  mislabelled as 'troublemakers' or 'quiet'.
» Diagnosis is shaped by cultural bias at every level.

Privilege, Persistence and Postcode Lotteries

Access to a proper ADHD diagnosis and treatment – a disability
affecting every part of life – should be a right, not a privilege.
But, in reality, the system favours those with time, money
and persistence. Since 2010, austerity measures have slashed
healthcare funding, including mental health services, just as
demand was soaring. ADHD assessments are now a postcode
lottery.

Funding cuts to GPs and ADHD clinics mean that whether
you're referred – and whether a clinic can see you within months,
or years – depends on factors well outside of your control. A
Black girl in Wales, for instance, is less likely to be diagnosed
than a middle-aged white man in Kent, even if her symptoms are
more disruptive. Society often overlooks her lost potential as less
of an issue.

GPs, clinics and schools often find themselves stuck in a
system without the resources to handle all referrals. Overworked
teachers, already battling for funding and support, might nudge
GPs for a referral. GPs, facing their own limitations, can refer
only a select few to ADHD clinics. Many adults and children
are dismissed without explanation, as clinics are under pressure
to reduce waiting lists. In theory, patients in England have the
'right to choose' their mental healthcare provider if wait times

are excessive, but charity ADHD UK notes that this policy, introduced in 2018, is still 'relatively new' and poorly understood by GPs and patients alike.

Private Diagnosis: A Leaky Lifeline

In March 2023 – possibly while Gabor Maté was making headlines with his public diagnosis – North Yorkshire and York Health and Care Partnership launched a pilot scheme removing access to autism and ADHD assessments for adults, citing the need to 'stem the flow' of referrals. Those at immediate risk of harm or facing urgent court decisions would be referred. Everyone else was given a self-report questionnaire – useless for medication or disability benefits. Even the two thousand already waiting for assessments faced delays of up to two years. At the time of writing, specific details about the permanent changes post-pilot have not been fully disclosed. Unfortunately, this isn't a one-off situation.

Many people turn to private diagnoses due to these long NHS waiting lists, but private diagnosis isn't affordable for everyone, creating a two-tier healthcare system. Diagnosis isn't a one-off – follow-ups, check-ups and prescriptions pile up fast. But equally, framing private diagnosis as undermining the NHS ignores the reality: it's like using a leaky bucket to bail out a sinking ship. The NHS simply can't handle the recent spike in ADHD diagnoses, with waiting lists stretching up to ten years according to ADHD UK. Covid-19 sparked a new awareness of ADHD, but simultaneously strained the resources needed to treat it.

Exposing Private Clinics: The *Panorama* 'Investigation'

Two months after Gabor Maté's 'diagnosis' of Prince Harry, the BBC's *Panorama* aired *Private ADHD Clinics Exposed*, hitting every tired trope that frames ADHD as a controversy rather than a serious condition. The programme followed an undercover journalist, a white man previously told by an NHS doctor he didn't have ADHD, as he secured diagnoses from three private clinics via Zoom. Suspenseful music and dramatic rain-soaked car shots heightened the theatrics, while the real issues – barriers to NHS treatment and the realities of ADHD care – were ignored. For many ADHD advocates, the problem wasn't the diagnoses themselves (white men are statistically more likely to be diagnosed) but his apparent 'cosplaying' of ADHD, turning our struggles into props to discredit the condition.

More importantly, the programme dodged the real issue: healthcare privatisation. It portrayed ADHD patients as a threat to the system, conflating those seeking genuine care with individuals misusing the process to obtain amphetamine medication. This flawed logic unfairly blames people with ADHD, who already face significant barriers, for the system's vulnerabilities. Take other controlled medications, like sleeping tablets or benzodiazepines – though addictive, and with street value, they're prescribed when appropriate and monitored by the NHS rather than denied to the people who need them most. Even the opioid crisis in America didn't prompt questions about the reality of pain or the drug's legitimate use in surgery.

NHS psychiatrist Mike Smith, who participated in the *Panorama* documentary, later acknowledged its damaging fallout. As a clinician in Leeds with over three thousand patients on his waiting list, he saw first-hand how the episode sowed doubt – patients feared GPs would question their legitimate diagnoses or even began doubting themselves. Yet Smith argues the real issue isn't overdiagnosis, but decades of underdiagnosis and an NHS system designed before ADHD was properly understood.

In response to the backlash, advocacy groups criticised *Panorama* for failing to consult people with ADHD or address chronic NHS underfunding. They also pushed back against its misleading portrayal of a three-hour NHS consultation as typical – it isn't. The episode became the most complained-about *Panorama* broadcast in history, even surpassing the one about Princess Diana.

In May 2023, the BBC defended the documentary, claiming it followed editorial guidelines – it said that it did not seek to question the legitimacy of the condition or its impact but believed that it sparked vital debates on private ADHD diagnoses and care standards, and was clearly in the public interest.

But Smith's post-documentary recommendations were far more constructive than his participation in it. He called for updated NICE guidelines, as current ones require only an 'appropriate, qualified practitioner' without defining a minimum training standard. He also pushed for national ADHD wait time targets and dedicated funding. ADHD isn't 'rising' – it's finally being recognised. As Smith put it, 'A tiny fraction of people in the UK take stimulant medication, the gold standard treatment – far fewer than the 2–4 per cent of adults who likely have the condition.'

TL;DR? 🔑 Takeaways:

» *Panorama* stirred controversy by showing an undercover journalist collecting diagnoses like Pokémon, but NHS psychiatrist Mike Smith had the real takeaways.

» He called for updated NICE guidelines, national wait time targets and proper funding for ADHD services.

» ADHD isn't on the rise, we're just finally acknowledging it. Most people who need treatment still aren't getting it.

The Diagnosis Debate

When people say 'ADHD is overdiagnosed', they're usually just parroting headlines. What they really mean is that they're hearing about it more or that there's no 'objective' test. But that's true for most neurodevelopmental and mental health conditions – schizophrenia, bipolar disorder, anxiety, dyslexia, dyspraxia – none have a definitive blood test. Like these, ADHD is diagnosed through observable behaviours, cognitive assessments and medical history because it reflects a brain wired differently from the neurotypical one.

The demand for a single, conclusive test makes no sense. Even with advanced brain imaging, mental health diagnoses remain largely observational. We can understand the chemistry better, but that doesn't generate a neat, binary diagnosis. Validating someone's experience shouldn't hinge on an elusive marker.

When I see columns dismissing ADHD screening as 'box-ticking exercises', I wonder how these writers reached middle age without ever filling in an NHS depression questionnaire. Nobody questions those, because no one wants to have depression, whereas some assume people want an ADHD diagnosis. That's a whole other conversation. As one former NHS GP put it, 'You can't "overdiagnose" a condition. What you can do is misdiagnose it – mood disorders can mimic ADHD, or they may actually be secondary to undiagnosed ADHD.'

Misdiagnosis: The Process of Elimination in Real Time

At various points, doctors suspected I might have thyroid issues, polycystic ovary syndrome (PCOS) or bipolar disorder. Misdiagnosis is part of the process, even for conditions with clear biological markers like cancer. Diagnosis isn't a one-time 'discovery' but a process of eliminating possibilities. For conditions like ADHD, where research is still developing, the 'best story' based on the information available changes as we learn more.

Most of the time, the media's take on ADHD boils down to: 'But what about neurotypical people?' Misdiagnosis isn't the worst-case scenario. Nobody is frog-marched into diagnosis. Even if someone is misdiagnosed, short-term treatment can be stopped, and its effects are reversible. The real danger is for those undiagnosed left to struggle with anxiety, depression, addiction and even suicidality.

The True Purpose of Diagnosis: Self-Compassion and Accountability

A proper ADHD diagnosis unlocks effective treatment and access to services, protections and accommodations under the Equality Act of 2010. It's a foundation for understanding ourselves and, for some, even if medication isn't the choice, it helps make sense of our experience – like adding subtitles to a foreign film.

Diagnosis also gives us a shared language to talk about these conditions, which neurotypical people sometimes find alienating.

But if I say, 'I have asthma,' it's reasonable to assume that nobody will yell, 'Stop making excuses. You're just wheezy.' (Unless they've had the pleasure of teaching me PE, in which case, fair enough.) If, however, I say that I have ADHD, I often have to justify that it's real.

Accountability, ADHD-Style: Redefining Responsibility for Real Life

ADHD stigma stems from the suspicion that we're using it as an excuse to dodge responsibility. 'Taking responsibility' is a politically loaded phrase. When it gets used, we're often talking about power and who has the ability to direct their own destiny. A real understanding of responsibility involves accountability for what we can control – and knowing where that ends.

In my experience, ADHD people aren't dodging responsibility any more than anyone else – our fuck-ups are just more routine. Responsibility with ADHD can look like therapy, exploring medication, or setting up organisational systems to catch us before we fall. I'd expect the same from a neurotypical friend with bad time management. The truth is, people with ADHD are hyperaware of when it's being used as an excuse and tend to police themselves. Unless you're carrying out deep surveillance, you have no idea how hard anyone is trying, especially as most ADHD people mask the effort it takes to carry out simple tasks – like wearing matching socks – out of shame.

People with ADHD shouldn't be expected to achieve perfection by neurotypical standards any more than someone with a physical disability should be expected to run in the Olympics rather than the Paralympics. I still try, but I'm learning not to judge myself so harshly when I fall short. By twelve, the average ADHD kid has heard twenty thousand more negative remarks than their neurotypical peers. I still berate myself over things like being late or interrupting people – things others barely notice. A friend once said, 'You try harder than any-one I know at calendars and organisation.' It sounded a bit sad, but she was right: I burn through a huge amount of energy attempting tasks neurotypicals barely think about. Not having to worry about those 'small' actions is a privilege, like not having to choose between taking the bus or the train because of money. ADHD is like taking the longest route and banging your knees on every obstacle along the way.

The idea that ADHD is just an 'excuse' doesn't hold up. First, it'd be a pretty useless excuse because the world doesn't cut us much slack. The journalist in the *Panorama* documentary couldn't even imagine our reality. He shook his head, baffled, saying, 'Everyone finds laundry hard.' Maybe, but it's not normal to wear clothes that smell or itch because you can't make yourself do the laundry, or to wear clothes visibly covered in barbecue sauce. It's like life has become so challenging that acknowledging a treatable difficulty feels like 'skipping the line'. Trust me – it's not.

Responsibility with ADHD is about empowering self-awareness, not self-pity. If I'm late and someone's waiting in the rain, my response should be, 'I'm sorry I was late; I'll set a timer next time.' We'd all benefit from giving each other some grace, especially when the effort and intention are there, even if the result sometimes falls short.

Diagnosis means different things to us individually than it does socially. Personal ADHD stories and the rights we're entitled to – like employment protections or legal accommodations – can fuel culture wars. But at its core, diagnosis is about self-compassion and creating a personal system of accountability grounded in self-respect. ADHD won't protect you from labels like 'lazy' or 'attention-seeking', but it does help you understand that you deserve compassion. By recalibrating expectations to suit our brains, we can begin to reimagine responsibility in a way that acknowledges who we truly are, rather than trying to meet the demands of the majority neurotypical population.

TL;DR? 🔑 Takeaways:
- » No, there's no blood test for ADHD – just like there isn't one for depression or bipolar disorder.
- » Diagnosis isn't instant; it's a process of elimination, not a one-and-done test.
- » The real risk isn't overdiagnosis, it's missing ADHD, leading to mental health struggles, addiction and burnout.

» Diagnosis is about understanding yourself, getting the right support and building a life that works for your brain, not against it.

UNDERSTANDING

OH MY GOD I'M Sooo ADHD!

ADHD REALITY

Many people have ADHD-like traits or behaviours, but they're not ADHD symptoms unless they meet diagnostic criteria: persistent, impairing and pervasive. For instance, eating the same lunch daily or reboiling a kettle isn't ADHD – it's just being human.

Chapter 2

The Attention Economy

In today's world, focus isn't just a verb – it's the hottest commodity on the market. Every scroll and swipe pads someone else's pocket as Big Tech perfects the art of keeping us hooked. ADHD feels more relevant now not because it's better understood, but because neurotypicals are getting a taste of the shattered concentration we've dealt with all our lives. The surge in ADHD discourse isn't just about increased awareness: it's neurotypical people scrambling for words to describe their own fragmented experience.

ADHD was discussed as a pathology of late capitalism in 2011, seen as a by-product of hypermediated consumer culture by some cultural theorists and critics. But like most people with ADHD, I reject that. ADHD isn't just capitalism's collateral damage – it's a complex neurodevelopmental disorder that exists outside of the systems that amplify its effects. Using stigmatised disorders as metaphors for broader experience isn't new: Fredric Jameson did so when he called 1980s postmodern culture 'schizophrenic', reducing a serious mental health condition to an abstract critique of identity fragmentation.

Neurotypicals tend to co-opt ADHD as a metaphor for distraction, flattening our lived reality into a shorthand. Almost every book on attention throws in a section on ADHD, as if by word association. ADHD isn't just an errant subset of attention;

it's not 'me no focus'. When neurotypicals casually borrow our neurology to explain themselves, they erase the real challenges we face.

For those of us managing ADHD, attention becomes a form of self-defence – something we tend to like a garden, knowing its limits. If I moved through the world with neurotypical carelessness, I can't imagine ever having an engaged conversation or finishing a book. Many don't. Whether or not you're conscious of it, we are operating in an economy that slips past our defences, fractures attention, burns through priorities, and profits from the wreckage.

Patricia Lockwood wrote, 'Your attention is holy, it is the soil seeding itself.' I believe our attention is the most precious thing we will ever have. Just as I've had to manage mine consciously, society now grapples with its commodification. While capitalism might amplify 'ADHD-like' symptoms in neurotypicals, it distracts from a larger truth: we live in a late-capitalist system that devalues human wellbeing by taking our focus hostage, steering it towards profit rather than meaning.

I'll trace the history of the attention economy – from Big Tech and surveillance capitalism to social media (covered later). But I write in the spirit of liberation. This isn't about resisting the attention economy to make more money; it's about resisting with stubborn gladness, for a richer, more meaningful experience of your finite time on earth.

Redefining Value in the Information Age

The attention economy, as we know it, exploded with late capitalism. Economist Herbert A. Simon pointed out in 1971 that in an information-rich world, the real scarcity is attention: 'What information consumes is rather obvious: it consumes

the attention of its recipients.' Twenty-six years later, cultural
theorist Michael Goldhaber popularised the term, declaring
attention more valuable than money in the digital age. But how
do we judge value? Traditional economic frameworks measure
productivity, output and profit – metrics that ignore joy, flow,
friendships, community and the realisation that you've wasted
your life at your desk. Some frameworks try to bridge this gap,
including metrics like the happiness index, but they remain
fringe.

Economist Mariana Mazzucato calls for a radical re-
evaluation of how we define and measure value. She critiques
the financial sector's obsession with *value extraction* and argues
for a system that appreciates *value creation* instead. Imagine the
economy as a gourmet kitchen. We've praised private-sector chefs
for their flashy garnishes, ignoring the public sector that preps
the essential ingredients – stocks, sauces – vital to every dish.
Mazzucato reminds us that innovations like the internet and GPS
weren't profit-driven but born from public initiatives. Shifting
focus to what truly sustains us benefits everyone, not just those
obsessed with extracting profit.

The ADHD experience, with its non-linear, fragmented
attention, subverts the capitalist obsession with optimisation.
We show that human value can't be distilled into neat economic
terms. Creative, intuitive, relational thinking holds equal (if
not greater) value. As I'll explain in the later chapter 'Unlikely
Prophets', our presence in these systems exposes their limitations.
It's not ADHD that needs fixing but the societal models that
define value.

The attention economy holds us hostage. The victors are
companies that 'capture' and 'retain' our 'eyeballs', stringing
them on necklaces. Their algorithms feed us personalised content
with micro-targeted ads, while every scroll leaves us drained. As
information sources multiply, attention becomes more valuable,
but we don't see the benefits. How did our attention become
so thoroughly commodified? By examining the internet's shift
from idealistic beginnings to data-driven empires, we'll see how
surveillance capitalism took root.

Surveillance Capitalism: They Know What You Ate

The attention economy became inevitable when Big Tech embraced surveillance capitalism during the early internet years. They realised that user data was worth more than direct payments. Companies used our attention as bait to extract this data, which they turned into a commodity to be sold and exploited.

Cookies are the foot soldiers of surveillance capitalism. Imagine walking into a café, where you're given a free cookie which tracks what you like and follows you, offering you your favourite drink when you return. Online cookies do the same – part helpful assistant, part creepy AF.

If something is free, you're the product. You hear mattress ads on 'free' podcasts, and then you're stalked by those mattresses on 'free' articles. Even CAPTCHA tests, which verify human users by solving puzzles, harvest data to train AI, embedding us deeper into surveillance without compensation.

At every stage of the attention economy, we've accepted trade-offs for convenience, seduced by the illusion that we're getting something for free. Surveillance capitalism has built an architecture that encroaches on our autonomy, monetising every view and click. The utopian vision of the internet as a democratic space for knowledge is dead – now, engagement and profit drive the system. Platforms like Twitter/X, Facebook and Instagram don't just capture attention – they control it. Their ad models turn our 'data exhaust' into powerful tools to sway decisions and even undermine democracy. If users are commodities, so are citizens.

Attention: From Novels to Notifications

The history of the attention economy is one of alienating and reselling our focus. Social media, TV and a trillion flashing visuals constantly vie for our attention. Cultural panic about distraction has existed since the days of Saint Augustine. Even nineteenth-century novels were feared to promote 'superficial' and 'debased' attention.

Mechanisms have evolved, though. In the 1930s, OG data

geek Arthur Charles Nielsen paid families to install 'black boxes' in their homes to track what they tuned into on the radio – much like today's cookies. The data he collected became the Nielsen radio ratings, a product he sold to broadcasters eager to know their audience's habits. This innovation quantified and monetised attention in ways never seen before.

No one wants to watch ads – except movie trailers – but we're bombarded daily by thousands of them (though probably not the 'ten thousand' figure that's now internet folklore). Even basic brain reflexes, like reacting to loud noises, are hijacked. Recognising these triggers – animated icons, jingles, clickbait – is the first step to regaining control. These forces are not neutral. They are capitalism in strobing forms, stealing our attention and converting it into profit. In the attention economy, what we notice and react to becomes the basis of exchange. Engagement is for sale. Late capitalism isn't about goods or services any more – it's about capturing attention long enough to cash in, forcing experiences to grow more outlandish, and content to trend extreme. It's a race to outdo the last spectacle.

Safeguarding Our Focus

In our attention-trap world, deep focus is rare for everyone, neurodivergent and neurotypical alike, which makes it a political issue. Those of us with ADHD, who start with diminished self-regulation, pay the price first.

UK GDPR and cookie laws have given us more control over digital privacy, but for many with ADHD, vigilance becomes just another challenge. The industry constantly finds ways around these rules (like with native ads that blend in and are hard to spot, especially for the neurodivergent). These regulations help, but they can't dismantle the surveillance machine that powers the attention economy. The issue is systemic, requiring more than individual resistance. Without taking on sole responsibility for resisting a deliberately addictive system, anyone concerned about guarding their bandwidth can take practical steps:

» Use an ad-blocker and privacy tools to block trackers.
» Regularly adjust privacy settings on devices and social media.
» Be cautious about app permissions, especially location access.
» Set screen-time limits.
» Support organisations that regulate data collection.
» Stay informed about the mechanics of surveillance capitalism and share knowledge – it's a form of communal care.

Collective action can lead to change, protecting privacy and reclaiming our attention. But larger shifts are necessary to fully address these challenges. Even as we push for systemic reforms, the market finds ways to commodify our struggles – and ADHD is no exception.

Brand ADHD: Cashing in on the Chaos

For those of us with ADHD, diagnosis offers a lifeline. But medication alone doesn't teach us how to live with it. We're left figuring out how to 'do life' with anxiety, depression and our ADHD brains – often without access to therapy or meaningful support.

ADHD has become a commodity, marketed to hyperstimulated neurotypicals. Social media simplifies ADHD, blending advocacy with profit-driven narratives that target isolated symptoms and create a billion-dollar industry. 'Treatment' products, many pushing self-diagnosis, target a vulnerable group.

Over the last year, I've burned through my phone's memory with screenshots of ADHD-targeted ads: supplements, nootropics, self-help courses. Many ADHD people know their danger zones (e.g. eBay) and avoid them, but aggressive advertising is all over 'free' social media. One such ad claims, 'ADHD: Replace doom-scrolling with micro-learning,' alongside a girl face-planting on her bed next to an empty pizza box. It promotes *The 4-Hour Work Week* by Tim Ferriss, a book

unrelated to ADHD yet often recommended by NTs who
conflate their time-management struggles with the realities
of ADHD. To me, it's a stellar example of toxic positivity,
focusing on individual hustle over systemic challenges – a
mindset particularly damaging for neurodivergent people. Ferriss
popularised the mantra, 'we all have the same twenty-four
hours in a day,' a phrase parroted by influencers like Molly-Mae
Hague, who faced backlash for ignoring systemic inequality.
In my misguided youth, I bought *The 4-Hour Work Week* and
spent a year eating black beans for breakfast – this didn't cure
my ADHD, but then the book doesn't mention it – so why was
the ad marketing it to those with ADHD? Even so, that kind of
misplaced optimism feels almost quaint compared to the outright
exploitative tactics of newer ADHD-targeted solutions.

Effecto: The Absolute Worst?

Effecto is an app which has been widely criticised for luring
users into a quiz designed to make sure everyone scores high on
ADHD traits – there's no 'none' option. Then they're funnelled
to a subscription page, baited with discounts and bombarded
with spam once their data is sold off. ADHD people struggle
to resist predatory marketing tactics, like the relentless emails
demanding IMMEDIATE action, or fake scarcity alerts. The
app's $90 price tag plays on the assumption that high cost equals
value. By the time users realise it's a glorified mood tracker,
cancellation is neither quick nor easy. Plus, their website doesn't
give you the option to click on their privacy policy to consent,
meaning you can't object, opt out or change your mind.

AI visuals exploit known ADHD vulnerabilities, like eating
disorders, pulled from enough #ADHD content to push all the
right buttons (tagline: 'Transform your body by transforming
your ADHD'). Other taglines, like 'Reach your potential', salt
the wounds many of us carry from school, where 'unfulfilled
promise' was the best praise we got.

Effecto has been accused of reducing ADHD diagnosis to a
Myers-Briggs personality test for productivity bros, preying on
ADHD people's impulsivity and tendency to forget to cancel

subscriptions. A recent ad offers quizzes about 'limbic' and 'ring of fire' ADHD types. As one Reddit commenter put it, this is 'the modern equivalent of snake oil salesmen' exploiting a vulnerable audience.

The tactics Effecto has been criticised for using are just the latest iteration of strategies that have commodified attention, from the rise of newspapers to today's digital landscape. These are the 'attention merchants' that legal scholar and author Tim Wu warns us against. They've always thrived on manipulation – but how did they get so good at it?

Stages in the Evolution of the Attention Economy

Newspapers. In 1833 Benjamin Day's *New York Sun* revolutionised newspapers by selling them cheap and relying on ad revenue. Readers fancied themselves as consumers – but they were the product. Sensationalism became a core strategy to capture attention, starting the 'race to the bottom of the brainstem'. Day's circulation skyrocketed after he published a fake story about life on the moon, replete with unicorns and horny man-bats.

Posters. By the 1860s, posters in Paris grabbed attention with bold designs. Artists like Henri de Toulouse-Lautrec made them famous, but authorities eventually reined in the craze over concerns about aesthetics and invasiveness. Posters showed how public attention could be commodified.

Patent Medicines. In the late nineteenth century, hucksters like Claude C. Hopkins sold miracle cures using early direct mail campaigns – the precursor to today's spam. These ads thrived until consumer protections exposed their fraud. The 'snake oil' once peddled in the streets is now marketed differently by modern-day attention merchants like Caroline Calloway. Writer and self-styled celebrity, Calloway now sells skincare explicitly branded 'Snake Oil' in a playful nod to her grifter reputation, cleverly repackaged for the attention economy.

Propaganda. Before the First World War, governments rarely advertised, but during the war, propaganda campaigns like 'Your King and Country Need You' turned attention into service, with thirty thousand British men signing up daily. Captured attention was converted into action.

Advertising. By the 1920s, advertisers pivoted from making wild promises to creating problems consumers didn't know they had. Companies like Listerine planted anxieties with slogans like 'Halitosis Makes You Unpopular', using behaviourist psychology to shape behaviour.

Radio. Radio brought attention capture into homes, and wartime propaganda used this to devastating effect. Figures like Joseph Goebbels harnessed the collective attention of Nazi Germany, with radio listeners growing 'from 4.5 to over 16 million households' by 1942.

TV. By the 1950s, television became a household staple in the US. Increasingly through the decade, shows served as gaps between commercials, and cheaper formats like quiz shows dominated. Attention became the currency advertisers relied on, sparking cultural critiques about TV's impact on society. Orson Welles quipped, 'I hate television. I hate it as much as peanuts. But I can't stop eating peanuts.'

Over time, we've only got better at squeezing profit from attention. Each evolution in the attention economy has scaled up, from Nielsen ratings to platforms like Meta and TikTok, which now allow misleading ads that commodify ADHD and exploit those who identify with it. Instead of blaming self-diagnoses, we need tighter regulations to protect vulnerable groups from these increasingly manipulative practices. Yet, with every new twist in attention-harvesting methods, our capacity to shield ourselves falls further behind, tipping us into a state of perpetual overload.

Information Overload

Since psychologist William James's work in 1890, our understanding of attention has evolved, but the core problem remains: how do we navigate a deluge of information without drowning in it? 'Without selective interest, experience is an utter chaos,' James wrote.

Humans have a finite capacity for focus. Our brains haven't adapted to the flood of information we now face. The more we're bombarded with, the less attention we can give to each piece. Former Google employee James Williams likened the problem to 'information velocity' in *Tetris*: the challenge isn't the number of blocks but the ever-increasing speed at which they fall, overwhelming your ability to keep up.

Unpacking Persuasive Design

Platforms like Facebook, Instagram and Twitter/X aren't neutral – they're built on persuasive design, turning our cognitive habits into revenue streams for tech companies. They exploit vulnerabilities by manipulating dopamine responses and emotional triggers to keep us hooked. Persuasive design taps into our brain's reward systems. Neurotypicals may not notice it as acutely, but those of us with ADHD have long critiqued how the attention economy hijacks focus. Our experience puts us in a unique position to expose its dangers – something I'll revisit later. As Nir Eyal, behavioural expert, bluntly explained, 'Technologists build products meant to persuade people to do what we want them to do ... we call these people "users", and, even if we don't say it aloud, we secretly wish every one of them would become fiendishly hooked.'

Smart Tech, Sneaky Tactics: How They Hook You

Big Tech weaponises persuasive design to exploit vulnerabilities in the ADHD brain. Low dopamine makes instant gratification irresistible, and social media is built to capitalise on this, heightening addiction risks. To resist, we need to understand how these billion-dollar tools hook us, and channel our frustration towards those pulling the strings. Here are some of their main tactics:

Variable Rewards. The most potent reinforcement encourages repeated behaviour and compulsion. Tinder's roulette principle – unpredictable likes – keeps users engaged. Randomised rewards fuel addictive cycles, where intermittent access to something – whether drugs or attention – makes us crave more.

Neuroscience Manipulation. Billions are spent making it harder for us to resist. Even small details, like Gmail's red notification, tap into our hard-wired instincts, making it harder to ignore.

Friction-Free Interaction. Because checking emails or social media only takes seconds, it feels harmless, but those seconds add up, especially when an occasional satisfying message reinforces the habit.

Social Vulnerabilities. 'Contagious media' (Buzzfeed, et al.) is simple, pleasurable and provokes an immediate need to share. Sharing equals clicks, which equals profit. Platforms encourage sharing without thought, turning engagement into revenue.

Emotional Manipulation. They let you customise your profile like decorating your own space. But like decorating a rented flat, the illusion of control is fleeting. You've invested time, effort and identity into something that isn't really yours, pressuring you to stay engaged.

Gamification. Remember Clippy, the Microsoft Office assistant? Turning mundane tasks into games gives users a dopamine hit, something ADHD brains crave. Apps like Duolingo award badges and encourage you to maintain streaks, drawing you back for that small thrill of accomplishment – I stayed solely for the little owl's champagne tracksuit.

The Illusion of Free Entertainment. Google's doodles, like their thirtieth-anniversary playable *Pac-Man* logo, are prime examples of distraction disguised as free fun. That one logo drew more than a billion players, turning nostalgia into engagement while keeping users tethered to the platform.

> *1-2-3-4, We're Not Little Alberts Any More!*
> *5-6-7-8, Resist Big Tech's Click and Bait!*

Behaviourist psychology reduces us all to Pavlov's dogs, twitching in response to stimuli. It treats us like Little Albert, the infant at the heart of a famous 1920s experiment. Psychologist John Watson conditioned baby Albert to fear rats by striking a metal bar behind his head whenever one appeared. Eventually, whenever Albert saw a rat, he screeched. Watson bragged that soon the baby would be terrified of everything furry and white – even Santa Claus. Big Tech uses the same methods, making us fear missing out and compelling constant engagement.

This same thinking led American psychologist B. F. Skinner – a true creep – to fantasise about humans as programmable machines, entirely conditioned by rewards. In one experiment, he placed a hungry pigeon in a 'Skinner box'. The pigeon accidentally pressed on a button that released food. Guess what happened next? The pigeon pressed and pressed. Today's digital spaces use the same tricks.

Tristan Harris, a Big Tech whistleblower, was trained in these behaviourist principles while attending Stanford's Persuasive Technologies Lab, a class taught by B. J. Fogg – a Mormon behavioural scientist who sounds like *The Secret History*'s Julian Morrow, except in tech. He didn't just teach algorithms, but how to build profiles, mapping user anxieties and stress triggers to build behaviour loops.

Instagram's top creators were in that class too. There they mastered the art of real-time reinforcement, using 'visible likes' and instant feedback to create compulsive engagement. The goal wasn't to make users happy – it was to keep them endlessly scrolling, feeding the machine. As we move from understanding these manipulative tactics to examining the so-called remedies offered by insiders, it's worth asking: can the same system that engineered our addictions genuinely provide meaningful reform?

Is Ethical Tech the New Ethical Non-Monogamy?

Whenever I see the word 'ethical' tacked onto something, I get suspicious. It's like when a guy claims to be in an 'ethical non-monogamous' relationship – cool story, but does your girlfriend know? Slapping 'ethical' in front of anything is often a rebranding trick, duct-taping a halo on the same old power dynamics. BP's 2004 'carbon footprint' campaign comes to mind: ordinary people were made to feel guilty as climate villains while the real polluters kept cashing in. Corporate responsibility, it turns out, is as easy to outsource as blame.

Big Tech has perfected this move. Instead of dismantling surveillance capitalism, they flog digital 'detoxes' and certifications as moral solutions, redirecting our attention inward so we don't question the system they built. It's basically a bartender offering a miracle hangover cure after plying you with lethal cocktails all night.

A few repentant insiders have tried to reform. James Williams, a former Google strategist, now pitches himself as a 'tech ethicist' and co-founded the Time Well Spent movement, promoting technology that respects users' attention. Former Facebook executives admit the platform was engineered to exploit human psychology for profit. Their proposed solutions – a detox here, a nod to 'ethical tech' there – sound enlightened, but don't go far enough or have enough impact: a juice cleanse for the soul while the factory keeps churning out junk food.

This approach creates a personal austerity plan: tighten your screen-time belt, focus on 'well-being' and accept responsibility for self-regulation. As American writer Grafton Tanner notes, these strategies shift blame from platforms back onto users, reinforcing the neoliberal ideals that fuel the runaway growth of the attention economy and prioritise individual responsibility over systemic change. For those of us with ADHD, these so-called solutions feel especially hollow.

Even Time Well Spent certifications, which reward less

mind-melting tech, follow the same top-down logic. They risk creating new inequalities while leaving the core issue untouched: technology's relentless drive to control our attention. These solutions reward those privileged enough to unplug or pay for premium 'less addictive' options. Meanwhile, the kid mining cobalt for your phone battery isn't part of the moral equation. The entire ecosystem still revolves around extraction – of minerals, data and attention.

Take Tim Ferriss's *The 4-Hour Work Week*. At first glance, it sells the dream of liberation – only on reading does it become clear that this dream hinges on outsourcing tasks to lower-cost labour markets and relying on global wage disparities, much like how 'ethical tech' solutions rely on exploitative systems. Both perpetuate neoliberal ideals, where comfort at the top depends on invisible margins of exploitation. The ethical tech crowd rarely acknowledges this dynamic – or the surveillance capitalism and data privacy issues that trap us in the systems we're told to manage better. During the pandemic, companies even monitored remote workers' keyboard strokes to gauge productivity – productivity, as defined by Big Tech.

Ultimately, the ethical tech crowd may want to reform the industry, but they're still invested in the same system. Their pivot to ethical tech feels like a rebrand to stay relevant, like nineties pop stars going slutty. The goal – mastery – remains.

Attention, Please: The Battle We Share

In the digital attention economy, neurotypicals are now starting to experience the kind of fractured focus ADHD people have long lived with – feeling like everything is vying for attention, yet nothing gets done. This might explain why neurotypicals co-opt ADHD traits to understand their struggles.

Reading James Williams's book, *Stand Out of My Light*, I couldn't shake the sense that his fear is becoming 'ADHD-adjacent', which reeks of 'lesser mind' bias. Research shows empathy dims when people think about marginalised groups like the homeless. But add a specific detail – like a homeless person enjoying carrots – and suddenly empathy lights back up, as if now they can relate. There's a whiff of ableism in the tech-bro panic over cognitive offloading – using reminders or audio GPS to help with executive function. Some of us need these tools. Depending on them isn't a personal failure.

One silver lining in our collectively frazzled state could be an alliance built on compassion and solidarity. We're all in this together. But stop treating ADHD traits as something that makes us less human. Don't cherry-pick ADHD traits that resonate with you while dismissing 'lack of motivation' as laziness.

James Williams hasn't got the memo yet. He claims tech 'undermines our capacities for reflection and self-regulation', framing what he sees as neurotypical weaknesses – traits which are also symptoms of ADHD – with a heavy dose of moral judgement. His idea of 'epistemic distraction' reads like a roll call of ADHD traits. He says it leads to 'impulsivity' and 'wantonness'. I like being called 'wanton' as much as the next girl, but I flinched at his idea that this distraction means we're less capable of knowing ourselves or the world. Without this reflection, Williams says, we lose autonomy, dignity, and what makes us human. He doesn't appear to have considered the neurodivergent. Does this mean those of us with ADHD are less human?

To me, humanity goes beyond a deliberative pause – a pause an AI could mimic. The tech bros reduce attention to a basic cognitive function, sharpened by 'willpower' and 'discipline'. But I'm more intrigued by attention as a devotional practice, something that fuels creativity and resists easy measurement.

We ADHD folk live with levels of distraction neurotypicals are just now beginning to understand. This makes us the distracteds' village elders. We've earned our wisdom through hard-won experience and deserve respect for the insights we bring to the attention economy.

NOT DOING: LOW EXECUTIVE FUNCTION

Low executive function makes even basic tasks – like feeding yourself – feel impossible. Being told to 'just make something simple' and handed a five-ingredient recipe is maddening. If bread feels like the only option, anything requiring a pan is off the table. My go-to meals? Snack plates, pre-cooked lentils, Greek yoghurt with toppings, endless spinach and feta salads with pepitas. If you're neurotypical and dealing with long Covid or fatigue illness, stuck on what you can realistically prepare, ask your ADHD friends – they'll have quick answers.

Making a meal plan where you cook a vat of dal on your hero days and live off it is a game-changer. So are sauces – they can turn any rice, lentils or beans into a hit.

Low-Mid Executive Function Meals – All with Sriracha

Avocado Toast Deluxe: Smash half an avocado on toast, sprinkle with salt and pepper, maybe chilli flakes if you're feeling bold. Cherry tomatoes on the side if they're within reach.

One-Pan Egg Mess: Toss in a handful of spinach or frozen veggies, crack a couple of eggs right on top and let it all cook together. Minimum effort, max satisfaction. Pour boiling water on the pan afterwards.

Lazy Pasta: Boil pasta, drain and add olive oil, a pre-grated handful of cheese and cherry tomatoes (don't bother chopping).

Snack Plate ('girl dinner'): A bit of cheese, deli meat or equivalent, crackers, maybe an apple or some nuts thrown in. Charcuterie vibes.

Microwave Sweet Potato Supreme: Nuke a sweet potato till soft, slice it open, add canned black beans (a feast in themselves) and top with salsa if it's around.

Hummus, pitta, carrots.

Chapter 3

Education: What Is School For?

Covid-19 Shuts Schools: When Classrooms Went Silent

In March 2020 Prime Minister Boris Johnson shut down schools across England as the pandemic took hold. Overnight, nine million children were expected to transition to remote learning on untested digital platforms. Teachers scrambled to adapt, while parents became reluctant overseers. Schools briefly reopened in June, only to close again after the Omicron surge in December. By April 2021, students had missed over half of their scheduled classroom days.

The government focused on 'lost learning', treating students like malfunctioning machines in need of recalibration, but failed to address why so many never fully returned. By summer 2022, the number of 'severely absent' children – those missing more than half their school days – had doubled. Unsurprisingly, those with disabilities, special educational needs and mental health challenges worsened by the pandemic were most likely to stay away. **The pandemic didn't just disrupt education; it spotlighted and deepened the system's existing inequities.**

ADHD Kids in Lockdown: Freedom or Frustration?

As ADHD kids need high stimulation and novelty to focus, lockdown presented unique challenges. The government failed to provide additional learning support or accommodations, like more outdoor exercise. Restricting movement to a single walk per day was, for many, borderline cruel.

While COVID was incredibly challenging for many, studies reveal that some students – particularly those with ADHD – benefited from the flexibility of remote learning. Freed from rigid school structures, they could move, fidget, and adapt their surroundings to suit their needs. Lockdown stripped away the relentless exam prep, social anxiety, bullying and pressure to conform – staples of the neurotypical classroom. **Given the chance to work on their own terms, many excelled.** Over a third reported improved performance in reading, writing and mathematics; a quarter even noted better relationships with family and peers. This raises a crucial question: why should they return to a system that stifles them?

Time for a Rethink: Don't Rebuild a Broken System

We all want children in school – those who don't attend face higher risks of legal trouble later on – but pushing them back into a broken system is a missed opportunity. The pandemic offered a glimpse of what's possible: flexible, digital learning models. Historical precedents, like the 2011 earthquake in Christchurch, New Zealand, showed that expected learning loss doesn't always materialise. In some cases, students even made gains. **With environmental unpredictability on the rise, future-proofing our education system should be common sense. The current model fails a third of students. Pushing kids back into a broken system misses the chance to embrace flexible, future-ready education that serves all students, not just the privileged few.**

Attention Metrics: The Misuse of Data in Education

The attention economy has infiltrated education. In the US, advertisements are everywhere in schools – even plastered on lunch trays and bathroom walls. In the UK, the obsession manifests as a relentless focus on measurable outcomes over meaningful learning. **Standardised testing is the academic equivalent of social media's 'likes' and 'shares': superficial metrics that replace real engagement.**

This approach sacrifices curiosity and critical thinking for short-term cramming and compliance.

Philosopher Yves Citton critiques this outdated passive-absorption model, arguing that it disengages students – particularly neurodivergent ones who often find the material irrelevant. **Citton advocates for an 'attention ecology', where learning is interactive and collaborative, turning classrooms into dynamic networks of shared information.** Our fixation on grades and numbers creates the illusion that high statistics will translate into economic growth. But these numbers don't reflect genuine understanding or sustained curiosity; they reward memorisation and obedience.

William Davies, a sociologist and political economist, notes that twentieth-century education crushed spontaneity in favour of discipline. Today, anxiety has replaced submission as the dominant emotional response – heightened by the constant feedback loops of technology. Attendance metrics, for example, reward able-bodied children while publicly shaming those with chronic illness or disabilities. Attendance apps and EdTech systems turn every moment of a child's school day into a data point, feeding stress, especially for neurodivergent students. **While we know intrinsic motivation drives deep learning, we've created systems addicted to extrinsic rewards, leaving children in a state of perpetual anticipation – not of discovery, but of judgement.**

When post-pandemic absenteeism spiked, the government responded by doubling down on tests, reducing breaks and sticking to a rote curriculum. **This deficit-focused approach threatens to disengage students further – especially ADHD** students – by ignoring warning signs and pushing them further into a failing system.

'Pay Attention!': Unpacking ADHD in the Classroom

Attention problems are increasing, and our education system hasn't adapted. In his TED Talk, Sir Ken Robinson, educational theorist, criticised how schools separate the 'academic' from the 'non-academic'. Standardised, one-size-fits-all curricula and high-stakes testing crush creativity, stifle individual talent and exacerbate attention issues.

Robinson's critique is valuable, but he oversimplifies ADHD by conflating general attention problems with the specific challenges of neurodivergent students. **In doing so, he risks reframing ADHD as a catch-all explanation for broader systemic failings.** The RSA animation accompanying that TED Talk visualised a child drugged on Ritalin, reduced to a zombie amid a hyperstimulating reality of screens and distractions. While highlighting the danger of forcing neurotypical children through an outdated industrial education model is valid, it overlooks how deeply harmful this system is to those with ADHD who need the medication to function.

When you hear complaints about an 'ADHD epidemic' without reference to those actually diagnosed, ask yourself what's really being argued. **ADHD is not merely a metaphor for societal stress; it's a neurotype that magnifies the flaws of our educational system.**

Andy Hargreaves: Wisdom from an ADHD Insider

Educational expert Andy Hargreaves, diagnosed with ADHD as an adult, gently reminded me that many of these ideas aren't new. By the 1980s, a three-tiered intervention model existed for special needs students:

Classroom support first.
External assistance second.
Specialised schooling if necessary.

The inclusion movement, which gained momentum in 2000, recognised that what was essential for children with special needs could benefit all students. The focus shifted to equity – narrowing achievement gaps by supporting diverse learning needs.

Hargreaves and I commiserated over the gap between being 'accomplished on paper' and the terrifying breakdowns that happen behind closed doors due to the invisible struggles of ADHD. He spoke of his anxiety around managing spreadsheets – not out of laziness, but fear of mistakes. Delegating tasks can be misinterpreted as exploitation, adding complexity to ADHD management in professional settings. 'Some people will understand, some won't – and when they don't, you have to manage it,' he said.

How ADHD Students Feel

Children with ADHD are particularly vulnerable in today's education system, often facing compounded challenges like dyslexia and dyspraxia (about half of those diagnosed with ADHD have both). Lacking the resources to properly support these students, schools frequently resort to exclusions or part-time timetables – strategies that function more as blame than as support. Designed around neurotypical norms, schools fail to help ADHD students build their potential or establish healthy social relationships. Internalising negative messages from teachers and peers, they often struggle with the transition to higher education, leading to higher dropout rates and reduced career opportunities. The statistics are staggering:

» Children with ADHD are a hundred times more likely to be permanently excluded from school than their neurotypical peers.
» In the UK, 46 per cent of excluded students have ADHD, and nearly half of ADHD students have been excluded at least once.
» These exclusions increase their risk of criminal behaviour – 49 per cent of male and 33 per cent of female prisoners were once excluded from school.

Excluding ADHD students doesn't fix problems; it pushes vulnerable kids further into the margins, compounding their struggles. So-called 'bad behaviour' in these students is often misunderstood. What looks like 'acting out' is often the result of overwhelming emotions and a lack of language to express them. Many experience extreme psychological and emotional distress when demands are placed upon them which do not make sense – 'Because I said so,' doesn't wash. **Neurodivergent children need support to navigate a system that prioritises compliance over understanding – a system that neurotypical children may manage to endure, but at the cost of creativity, curiosity and critical thinking. Just because they can bend to its demands doesn't mean they should.**

Pathological Demand Avoidance: When 'Just Do It' Doesn't Work

Originally associated with autism, Pathological Demand Avoidance is increasingly recognised in ADHD. Defined by extreme avoidance of everyday demands, coupled with high anxiety, PDA makes classrooms especially difficult to navigate. **Traditional discipline fails students with PDA; they need personalised support that reduces pressure, not adds to it.** They need strategies that promote autonomy, but the high-stakes, test-driven nature of schools amplifies their avoidance behaviours.

Neurodivergent Norms: Breaking Rules to Survive

Neurodivergent students – especially those with PDA – need to operate on their own terms. I've unconsciously rejected many neurotypical norms myself. When cursive writing didn't stick, I switched to printing, a habit I've kept to this day. Detentions became routine for minor infractions, like undoing my top button for comfort, until I eventually cut them off altogether – leading to more trouble. Assignments go unfinished, verbal instructions are hard to follow, and students struggle to organise their thoughts in neurotypical ways. We answer hastily without thinking and rarely wait our turn. Fidgeting disrupts the classroom atmosphere. What seems small fare to neurotypicals – like keeping study materials organised – presents major barriers for neurodivergents. During exams, we miss key details or can't recall what we've learned, fuelling cycles of underachievement. **Over time, these struggles drain our enthusiasm for learning, leaving us feeling trapped in a loop of 'doing multiple things' urgently, but unable to manage any of them effectively.**

Stigma by Default: Race and Class

Class and race compound the challenges neurodivergent children face. Concerns about medication interfering with brain development persist in some communities; **for many students of colour, an ADHD diagnosis leads to stigma and harsher punishment, not support.** This makes many parents of colour hesitant to pursue an ADHD label, rightly fearing that ADHD diagnoses might reinforce negative biases.

Race on the Agenda (ROTA) ran seminars across London, gathering insights from five hundred participants from communities of colour. The findings were damning: ADHD labels were often used to excuse poor behaviour and academic underperformance, reinforcing low expectations and allowing schools to sidestep providing proper educational support. Some young people felt their ADHD label was used opportunistically, only to later regret the unexpected lasting impact it had on their academic progress. **They wished schools had responded to their educational needs instead of simply labelling them.** A diagnosis should be a call for support, not dismissal. Yet many parents worry that schools will take the easy way out – giving up on their children instead of advocating for the help they need.

The Support Gap: Why Wealth Matters in ADHD Outcomes

When I asked Andy Hargreaves whether working-class children face harsher punishment for ADHD-related behaviours than their middle-class peers, his answer was revealing. While kids across all social classes get into trouble, what differs is the support that follows. Middle-class parents often have the means to hire lawyers, secure therapy or find alternative solutions. '**The inequity isn't in who takes drugs or not,**' Hargreaves said. '**It's in the kind of support available afterwards.**'

The same is true for ADHD: wealthier parents are better equipped to navigate the system, advocate for their child, and access services. In Nova Scotia, Hargreaves has looked at how the system created 'parent navigators' to help parents from all backgrounds understand and manage the complexities of supporting their children.

Between Patience and Panic: Parenting

Shame is a constant companion for parents of children with ADHD, though it has no place in education. The UK-based Not Fine in School Facebook group, with seventy-one thousand members, paints a heartbreaking picture. After the 2023 GCSE results, the structural ableism of the school system became even more evident, punishing children who don't fit into neurotypical norms. Even when parents fight for an education, health and care plan (EHCP) or get Child and Adolescent Mental Health Services (CAMHS) reports stating their child needs specialist support, councils often insist mainstream education will suffice. Parents are told to drag their children to school, sometimes literally in their pyjamas, despite their panic attacks when they return home.

Unlike the old days of sending kids home with a note pinned to their jumper (which ADHD kids would lose anyway), schools now measure compliance through bells, grades and punishment systems. ADHD diagnoses often stem from escalating school complaints rather than a parent's 'light-bulb moment'. Teachers blame parents, parents blame teachers – there's enough blame to go around.

My former English teacher, Stuart MacAlpine, emphasised how negative emails home can cause enormous stress for parents. He advocates for a partnership where the centred child takes an active role in advocating for themselves, fostering a transformative dynamic between parents and teachers. **But here's the catch: parents can't get their child medication without a diagnosis, and diagnosis often means battling NHS waiting lists so long that a child referred at age twelve might be sitting GCSEs before they're diagnosed. Private healthcare is out of reach for many families.**

Teachers on the Brink: Burnout Meets ADHD

The most important factor in a student's success is the quality of their teacher. But what happens when teachers are underpaid and completely burned out? Sixty-nine per cent of primary and 78 per cent of secondary school teachers find their workloads unmanageable. Over half say their job has a negative effect on their mental or physical health. **Overcrowded classrooms and limited resources make ADHD-related disruptions feel like just another nuisance in an already chaotic day. It's easy to see why overwhelmed teachers might see ADHD students as troublemakers rather than anxious, overstressed kids.**

Teacher training barely covers how to support neurodivergent students. The few resources that did exist were gutted by austerity measures. Meanwhile, schools are under immense pressure to deliver results and teach to the test. There's little room for experimentation or figuring out how to make education work for neurodiverse students when everyone is hyperfocused on a school's OFSTED ranking.

Overwhelmed and unsupported teachers often fail to recognise that ADHD students are bombarded by challenges to their attention, organisation and social skills. Transitions – moving from one activity to another – are especially stressful because they disrupt the small sense of control ADHD students have. Punishing them only makes things worse. Research shows ADHD students lag 30 per cent behind in self-regulation and executive function – the mental skills needed to plan, focus and manage tasks, yet the refrain of 'rules are rules' persists, often followed by, 'Do you think you're special?' This was the standard response to my asking to do things differently. I wasn't asserting that I was a magic unicorn, or asking to try less, but to try *differently*.

A Classroom That Works: Lessons from Mr MacAlpine

In English class Stuart MacAlpine created a rare environment where I could actually focus. He seemed uniquely interested in what we, the pupils, had to say. I remember him reading Sylvia Plath's poem 'You' in our first class and tearing up in front of us. It was the first time I'd seen a teacher be emotionally present like that. Whenever I started talking too much in class, he would tap the desk gently to remind me, which, surprisingly, worked. Once, I asked him how he got students, especially those with ADHD, to behave in a way that promoted learning. His response was simple: '**They have to feel safe and in control of their environment. Once they do, "love is a better master than duty" – always.**'

Too many exhausted teachers lose sight of ADHD's positive traits: creativity, empathy, originality and energy. Low morale and lack of support make it harder for them to meet students' needs. Like most teachers, Stuart figured things out on the job. Over time, some strategies became clear:

- » Movement breaks
- » Standing desks
- » Fidget tools
- » Short-term goals
- » Regular check-ins
- » Positive reinforcement

He realised that ADHD students need frequent emotional payoffs. Intrinsic motivation sounds great, but these kids need regular boosts. Something as simple as reading anonymous excerpts from the best essays made a huge difference. These students work hard for a good relationship, not just for a grade.

When students feel safe and valued, they engage. Emotional connection is key. Proper training for teachers to manage classroom dynamics and understand student feedback improves the whole classroom.

Red Pens and Broken Spirits: the Need to Be Heard

ADHD kids tell sad stories about red pens. What they really want is to feel heard. According to one book, students with ADHD want to 'be treasured for the gifts they bring to the classroom, not demeaned for failing to do things the same way as everyone else'. If the word 'treasured' makes you cringe, I get it – but ADHD kids do want to be challenged. **What they don't want is to be asked to do the impossible and then made to feel terrible when they fail.** Once a child realises they'll always be seen as stupid, or a lost cause, they stop trying. We've all done this at some point, especially after a teacher made us feel worthless. Luckily, most of us have also had a teacher who made us feel like it was worth trying again.

I used to remind myself that no adult I respected had a great time in high school. Still, wellbeing isn't just about enjoyment – it's a prerequisite for learning. I reached a point where, no matter how hard I tried, I couldn't succeed in certain subjects, so I stopped trying. I only did my homework in detention because I was going to end up there anyway. In my mind, this meant I won. I eventually realised that you could only lose one point for forgetting to write your name or the date. So, I did what I liked and resigned myself to an occasional explosion at parents' evenings.

Personalised Support Versus Classroom Pacing

Maintaining an engaged classroom where every student gets equal attention is difficult. In larger classes, it's nearly impossible to balance individualised support for ADHD students with the pacing of lessons for everyone else. **But personalised teaching works because students pay attention when the information resonates with them.**

Small classes make personalised attention easier, but the real issue in larger classes isn't just size. The system, designed for uniformity, puts immense pressure on everyone involved, from students to teachers. Stuart's approach was eye-opening. He once told me that one particular student thrived because he knew Stuart would 'rather die than let him down'. That level of care makes all the difference. **Building confidence, focusing on small gains, and showing students that what they're good at matters – that's the key.** When students value one skill, they can learn others. Stuart helped his students see their potential, step by step.

The ADHD Alarm Bell: System Failure Exposed

ADHD students don't just highlight individual struggles – they expose the deeper systemic failures of an outdated, one-size-fits-all education system. They're the clearest example of how the system fails to meet diverse needs. **If the education system doesn't work for ADHD students, it doesn't work for anyone.**

In over a decade of Tory rule, we had ten different education secretaries, none of whom delivered a cohesive education plan. Education spending has increased by only 3 per cent since 2010, while austerity measures led to lay-offs, overcrowded classrooms, and cuts to extracurricular programmes. These cuts hit ADHD students hardest. Former education secretary Michael Gove's suggestion to withdraw child benefits from children who 'truanted' reflects the system's knee-jerk reaction to punish rather than understand. Meanwhile, Dr Tony Sewell, head of the commission on race that declared racism 'over', was nominated as head of OFSTED – despite his school's notorious use of isolation booths, which became more common under Tory rule.

Isolation booths are a form of solitary confinement in schools. Rather than addressing the real causes of behavioural issues, these booths create a hostile environment, increasing anxiety, shame and disengagement. **For students with ADHD – who are disproportionately subjected to them – these booths deepen feelings of alienation and being broken.**

Pandemic Spotlight: Cracks in the Educational Foundation

The pandemic was like flipping on a fluorescent light in a dingy room, revealing glaring cracks in the education system. Many neurodivergent students didn't even have laptops or reliable Wi-Fi, further widening the digital divide. While some students thrived with the flexibility of remote learning, those without parental support to fill the gaps were left behind. The rigid structure of standardised exams and the lack of focus on life skills or individualised support only worsened things for ADHD students, who floundered without adaptation.

Schools obsess over whether students are physically present or ticking the behavioural boxes, but they ignore the more important aspects – cognitive and emotional engagement. **ADHD students, whose minds don't align with traditional teaching, aren't just misbehaving – they're checked out.** Even if their bodies are there, their attention isn't. If the system doesn't connect with them, why should they connect with it?

Enter SLANT: A Dystopian Tool

SLANT is a behavioural management tool turning UK classrooms into low-level panopticons. SLANT commands students to:

Sit up
Lean forward
Ask and answer questions
Nod
Track the speaker

It's enough to make anyone anxious, let alone a child whose brain is wired for spontaneity, not micromanaged body language. **SLANT is punitive and, to my mind, creepy, reducing students to robotic performers rather than fostering genuine engagement.** For ADHD students, who can't simply flip a switch to focus, this forced performance of attention is farcical. As long as they appear to be paying attention, the system pretends they're learning.

If I had been forced to sit like that, all my mental energy would have gone into co-ordinating those actions, leaving none for actual learning. For autistic students, forced eye contact would be intolerable; for dyspraxic students, the physical co-ordination SLANT demands would be overwhelming.

In this system, ADHD students are set up to fail – not because they lack ability, but because success is defined by conformity. Classrooms should accommodate neurodivergence, not force everyone into the same narrow behavioural expectations. Learning comes from curiosity and connection, not compliance.

Fake it Till You Make it: The Illusion of Engagement

For ADHD students, learning often feels like battling an environment that doesn't fit how they process information. Hargreaves compares it to his childhood swimming lessons, where the teacher would shout in a thick Scottish accent, 'SWIM! SWIM!' but he and his classmates, unable to swim, crouched in the shallow end, performing swimming motions. 'The tragedy was, as long as we gave the appearance of swimming, he was prepared to accept it,' Hargreaves recalls. This is much like the education system today – as long as students appear engaged, the system is satisfied, without addressing the real problems. If you're dyslexic and can't read, or if you have ADHD and can't remember what the teacher said, one way to cope is by skiving.

Robots and Redemption: Creativity Reignites Learning

After Covid, Hargreaves helped launch a network of schools in Canada focused on play-based learning for vulnerable students. He told me about a boy who rarely attended school until his teachers involved him in a creative project using tiny robots 'half the size of a pencil' called Ozobots. These robots followed trails drawn with a pen and performed actions based on the colour coding of the trails. The students dressed them in costumes and narrated stories as the robots moved along their paths, like 'tiny Daleks'. One part of the project required building a bridge, which was assigned to the boy who had been a chronic non-attender. Remarkably, he consistently showed up on days when the project was in progress. This creative, inclusive approach reintegrated him into school life, helping him build relationships with other students while improving his literacy and storytelling skills. **This example shows how creative learning can re-engage neurodivergent students, while rigid, traditional models drive them away.**

ADHD students are like canaries in the coal mine, warning us of the consequences of policies like SLANT. Their neurology makes it nearly impossible to learn in environments designed for passive consumption. **This should be a wake-up call confirming that we all learn differently. Instead of forcing ADHD students to conform, we should embrace how they challenge our outdated systems.**

As Stuart said, 'Interest can't just be turned on.' While neurotypical students may be able to focus with a flip of a switch, ADHD students need the material to be compelling. Our transmission model of education – where information is delivered to passive learners – doesn't work for them, and frankly, it doesn't work well for anyone.

Both the Organisation for Economic Co-operation and Development (OECD) and the World Bank have called for a reimagining of education, one that focuses on genuine learning rather than just passing exams. In Finland, kids don't start formal reading until they're seven, with early education centred on play – the love of learning this creates leads to high literacy rates. Similarly, Estonia's education system, rated the best in Europe by the OECD, emphasises problem-solving, critical thinking and digital literacy from an early age, integrating technology like robotics and virtual reality into the curriculum. Yet in the UK we're still stuck preparing students for standardised tests, failing to prepare them for real life. **The system isn't working, but bureaucratic inertia, risk aversion and a neoliberal obsession with performance metrics keep us trapped in outdated practices.**

Unity in Diversity: Rethinking Learning Differences

Focusing on ADHD means focusing on learning diversity, period. The system isn't just failing neurodivergent students; it's failing many others as well – those who can't read, don't speak English at home or are dealing with poverty and complicated home environments. **We need to cultivate kinship between all students who don't fit traditional moulds. If the education system doesn't work for ADHD students, it doesn't work for anyone.**

The Times Education Commission only recently recommended that all schools have a counsellor. ADHD students, often dealing with comorbid conditions like anxiety or depression, are prime examples of why this is desperately needed. But their experience speaks to a larger crisis. **How we treat neurodivergent students reflects what we value in education. Do we want a system that prizes compliance, or one that cares about curiosity? Do we want teachers who teach children to think, or simply to regurgitate facts?**

Wasting Potential: When Curiosity Gets Crushed

We're squandering the neuroplasticity of childhood – the crucial period when children can learn to think critically, problem-solve and engage with the world in ways that later become harder to access. Instead of fostering these skills, we're stuffing their heads with irrelevant facts. For ADHD kids, whose brains crave novelty and interest, the traditional education model is particularly ineffective. Project-based learning – hands-on, dynamic and aligned with their interests – offers a solution, not just for ADHD students but for all.

Dreams Deferred: ADHD's University Struggle

Without proper support, even successful ADHD students can hit a wall in higher education, revealing systemic failures. One woman I spoke to, diagnosed with ADHD in her twenties, spiralled into anxiety and depression during her first term. She had masked her ADHD all through school, but university pushed her to breaking point – she couldn't function and had to pause her studies. Like many women, she hit a wall of panic attacks, exhaustion and a body that said, 'Enough.' Trying harder – through planners, caffeine and pulling all-nighters – only made things worse. She described the experience like a slow-motion plane crash: knowing she was going to crash no matter how hard she fought. Luckily, she had supportive parents, but found the thought of those left to navigate this alone, without proper diagnosis or access to medication, harrowing. ADHD, especially when undiagnosed, can destroy a person's ability to function, and the system's failure to support these students is unacceptable.

Blueprint for Change: Learning from ADHD in Schools

Our education system fails students with ADHD, and we should take that as a warning – they aren't the only ones suffering. **Addressing the difficulties faced by ADHD students will benefit all students.** Progressive educators argue that every child needs project-based learning in the classroom. ADHD students, with their dopamine-deficient, interest-driven brains, need purpose and agency to learn. And don't we want all students to have that same vitality?

Before exams, we normalise children having breakdowns, and parents reassure them by saying, 'Exams aren't everything.' If that's true, why does our entire education system hinge on them?

Meaningful Learning: The Power of Projects

In a low-income community, Andy Hargreaves came across a student who'd been excluded for fighting. The school got involved in a healthy eating and sustainability project, building a six-foot grow tower for indoor food production. When the student saw the $1,200 price tag on the tower, he told his teachers that he and his father could build one for a fraction of the cost. Encouraged, he did just that, leading his peers in the project using bits of old wood, with help from the local hardware store. This project didn't just bring him back into school life; it addressed the real cause of his exclusion: disengagement. It gave him a reason to show up.

We need more of this – real-world, hands-on learning that reignites students' interest. ADHD students struggle with passive learning, but meaningful projects can transform their engagement. Progressive educators argue that project-based learning benefits all students. When subjects resonate with their interests, motivation and retention skyrocket. What do we have to lose by embracing it?

Invest in Teachers: The Real Architects of Change

Children with ADHD teach us an essential lesson: relationships between teachers and students matter. ADHD students work harder when they feel seen and supported by their teachers. A learning environment where they feel they matter has a more significant impact on them than punishments or rewards. Their wellbeing, in turn, improves their teachers' wellbeing.

Andy Hargreaves emphasises that learning, especially for marginalised and vulnerable children, doesn't happen without quality teaching. He argues for investing in the 'professional capital' of teachers – building trust, collaboration and emotional wellbeing – for both students and educators.

Effective education systems recognise that teaching is an emotional practice, where the wellbeing of students and teachers is intertwined. During Covid, teachers were forced back into schools under threat of sanction. One described it as 'a slow walk to madness or death'. No wonder students are struggling – teachers need to be valued and supported, not burdened with compliance-based directives.

Homework Versus AI: Flip the Script

Human beings rarely change unless forced to. Much like the pandemic proving remote work possible after years of resistance: change happens when there's no other choice.

Now, we must face the fact that AI has blown up traditional homework. Cheating is undetectable and free. But, honestly, who was homework serving? It burns out teachers, and research shows it deepens inequities – wealthier kids get help, often from tutors. **If AI can outsmart homework, maybe it's time to rethink homework itself and focus on meaningful, in-class learning.** AI shouldn't be able to answer every question we want students to think critically about.

Flipping the classroom is a better approach. In this model, students do 'homework' in class – solving problems or collaborating – then watch instructional videos or read at home. This takes the pressure off real-time performance, letting students learn at their own pace.

Blended learning became common during the pandemic, but flipping the classroom is the next step. It doesn't mean more tech and less in-person engagement – it aims for the opposite. Shifting lectures and note-taking (passive learning) to the home frees class time for problem-solving and active engagement. Instead of zoning out in long lectures, ADHD students can pause, rewind or clarify content in a space that works for them. Then, during face-to-face time, they can focus on applying what they've learned, working with peers and building real understanding. This model champions deeper, more meaningful learning by letting teachers spend less time delivering content and more time interacting with students directly. Teachers can focus on higher-order thinking instead of just delivering information. AI becomes a tool for personalised learning, not a shortcut for cheating.

Arguments for keeping homework – like 'kids need practice' or 'they need to learn time management' – overlook that these skills can be part of pre-class learning. Nightly reading isn't 'busy work' but practice. And the idea that kids need to do things they don't want to do? Kids do that all day, every day. Forcing endless homework in a time of global upheaval is less like playing the violin on the *Titanic* and more like demanding every child take their recorder seriously while the ship is at 90 degrees.

Playing to ADHD Strengths: Aligning Digital Learning

Research suggests the digital world may actually align with ADHD attention styles. Curiosity, quick attention shifts and rapid yet shallow bursts of cognitive focus might suit digital settings. Digital learning lets ADHD students control their environment, making it therapeutic in some ways. But the same vast content that captivates them can also distract and overwhelm. The challenge is ensuring AI doesn't become a crutch for shallow learning but deepens understanding. In a flipped classroom, ADHD students could thrive by balancing flexibility with guided focus and task completion.

Roots and Wi-Fi: Balancing Tech with the Outdoors

A key to transforming education is getting students out of classrooms and into nature. Research shows that children with ADHD have reduced hyperactivity outdoors, and studies support the idea that learning in natural environments benefits physical and mental health. Outdoor play fosters resilience, confidence, memory, problem-solving skills and creativity – qualities students need now more than ever.

Blending digital learning with outdoor experiences creates balance. Post-pandemic, education must be more digital to stay accessible, but nature should offset this. **Reducing screen time in isolation won't work. Teacher training should include outdoor teaching methods, and curriculums should feature outdoor learning to reconnect students with the planet while promoting environmental responsibility.** Indigenous activists often argue that recognising ourselves as part of nature is crucial to our sense of meaning and saving the planet. Environmental responsibility must be integrated into education.

By incorporating outdoor learning we help students become well-rounded, thoughtful citizens. Digital learning is crucial for accessibility, but nature provides a calming counterbalance, especially for ADHD students who are overwhelmed by constant digital engagement.

Big Questions, Bigger Answers: Making Learning Relevant

Our education system forces students to jump through hoops. Much of the curriculum is pointless beyond progression along a rigid path. It doesn't just need to accommodate ADHD; it needs to accommodate the future. We're preparing students to take tests, not live thoughtful lives. Where's the focus on emotional wellbeing or environmental stewardship? Why did we learn every step of Italian unification but nothing about Britain's colonial history? **If we want engaged students, we must make learning relevant to their world.**

The curriculum needs to evolve from rote learning to real-world application. Project-based learning, flipped classrooms and outdoor education are part of this shift. Students should build skills that matter – whether that's learning a trade or developing critical thinking. Learning to problem-solve, collaborate and ask meaningful questions should be the core of education.

For ADHD students, low dopamine disrupts the current system. This should push us to create a dynamic curriculum that aligns with the lives young people will inherit. To make learning relevant, we should 'centre lessons around broad understandings and essential questions – ones that transcend specific topics and tie learning together'. Education should spark curiosity and uncover a subject's richness, beyond surface-level answers. Instead of asking, 'What is the symbolism of *The Great Gatsby*?' why not ask, 'What makes a book great?' Rather than assigning routine maths exercises, why not ask, 'How does estimation affect real-life decisions?' Why teach trigonometry but skip over how to budget for a mortgage?

I asked my chemistry teacher if the colourful CGP revision guides had all the GCSE answers. I was tired of feeling stupid. No matter how hard I tried, I couldn't remember anything said in class except odd details. My notes were illegible. After my ADHD diagnosis, I got a laptop, but difficulty sorting relevant from irrelevant information led to chaotic notes, triggering meltdowns during revision. Pulling all-nighters before exams helped me cram, but the knowledge disappeared the next day. My teacher admitted the CGP books had everything – bullet points, cartoons, memory tricks. So I stopped taking notes and went on autopilot.

Beyond the Test: Cultivating Lifelong Learners

Even high-achieving students often crash after university because
they've been conditioned to focus on high marks, not real-world
challenges. **What happens when there are no more tests?**

As careers become fluid and unpredictable, the ability to adapt
and self-motivate is critical. Intrinsic motivation – driven by
interest and autonomy – leads to long-term success, especially
in creative fields. But self-directed learning habits don't emerge
overnight. Motivation thrives when engaging tasks are paired
with autonomy.

Project-based learning, already successful in parts of Canada
and the US, encourages students to engage actively with material
while teachers act as guides. This approach fosters lifelong
learning, preparing students for an uncertain future. Personalised
learning plans, co-created by students and teachers, offer a path
forwards by empowering students to pursue education that
resonates with them while benefiting from direct instruction and
support.

Tiny Tweaks, Big Impact: Practical Teaching Changes

I want to yell, 'BURN IT ALL DOWN!' But as we push for
structural reforms, we need to be pragmatic. ADHD awareness
is growing, and simple accommodations – like regular breaks,
short-term goals, and self-advocacy strategies – are becoming
more common. Teachers are recognising that small adjustments –
like allowing non-disruptive fidgeting, or using music to ease
transitions – can help ADHD students focus.

These accommodations must be empowering, not punitive.
Without them, children with ADHD often struggle with peer
relationships, loneliness and bullying. My best friend's report
cards regularly labelled me as a 'bad influence' and encouraged
her parents to separate us. Yes, I talked incessantly and passed
notes that she mostly ignored. But she was incredibly shy, and
I was her closest friend – we both did better in class sitting
together.

Redefining Success: It's Not All About Grades

Neurodivergent students often struggle with interoception, which means they have difficulty recognising their own internal states. Visual reminders to hydrate or take breaks can help everyone, not just ADHD students. Regular movement breaks, large fonts for written work, and recording assignments in audio formats can transform learning experiences.

For instance, if I had been allowed to wear noise-cancelling headphones (which revolutionised my adult life) during 'silent work' my school career might have been entirely different. Now, in-ear noise-cancelling devices are available. Simple tools like break cards, which students can use to signal they need a brief timeout, could have helped me manage emotions without missing entire classes.

Education works better when students understand they're being prepared for real life, not just jumping through hoops. Authentic experiences, where students apply their learning in ways that mirror real-world tasks, are what make education meaningful. Scientists don't just read chapters and answer questions – they develop hypotheses, set up experiments, and test their ideas. Likewise, ADHD students need relevant, hands-on experiences that engage their strengths.

Closing the Loop: ADHD as a Catalyst for Change

ADHD isn't just a set of behaviours – it's a way of processing information and understanding the world. Traditional punitive measures, like withholding break time, don't teach accountability. They demotivate students, much like the dunce cap of old. I often felt like I was wearing one. **Refusing to mark late work only teaches ADHD students to stop turning it in altogether.**

Sensitivity, empathy and responsiveness are far more effective in helping ADHD students succeed. Adapting lesson plans to promote understanding – not rote memorisation – isn't difficult. I could memorise definitions without truly understanding them. But if a student finishes two maths exercises (instead of ten) because of processing speed, they've still grasped the concepts.

These lessons extend beyond neurodivergent classrooms. ADHD students teach us that success lies not in their conformity but in the system's flexibility. When movement breaks and project-based learning become the norm, they stop being accommodations and become prototypes for a better way to educate everyone. The challenge isn't to make them fit the system but to reshape the system so that it fits all of us.

NOT LISTENING

'Think before you speak!'
'Stop making excuses.'
'You'd lose your head if it wasn't screwed on!'
'You just need to try harder.'
'Pay attention!'
'Why can't you ever finish anything?'
'Are you even listening to me?'
'You're just being lazy.'
'You're forgetting on purpose!'
'If you cared, you would remember.'
'Why can't you be more like your brother.'
'You can do it when you want to.'
'You're acting like a child.'
'How many times do I have to tell you the same thing?'
'Everyone else can do it, why can't you?'

Chapter 4

Gendered Expectations: 'Maybe You Should Try Harder'

The Invisible Struggles of Women with ADHD

While writing this chapter, I caught Covid for the third time. When my temperature hit 40 degrees, I perversely felt a sliver of satisfaction and sent photos of the thermometer to friends. Sure, my head felt like a glass orb full of hot candyfloss, my eyelids ached, but I had proof of my suffering: sweaty objective facts.

As a woman, I've learned that facts are the holy grail. Living with ADHD, an invisible disability, you're constantly proving your experience, as if life is a hypothesis needing validation. Since childhood I've been told I'm not trying when I am, and accused of being dramatic due to the operatic scope of my emotions. There's always been a disconnect between my inner reality and how I am judged. Over half of UK women report that their pain is dismissed by GPs, leaving them questioning their own reality.

I kept my ADHD diagnosis private for years. When I finally shared it, I noticed a sharp gender divide: men responded with scepticism or statistics, while women offered empathy but quickly shared their own organisational struggles as if to say, 'Welcome to the club.'

Society sends women a clear message: life is supposed to be hard. Overwork is the price of entry into the sisterhood, and suggesting it's uniquely hard for you risks isolation. For women with ADHD, it's not just the volume of tasks that's overwhelming – it's the way our brains refuse to juggle them all. As Dr Zoë Ayres put it, 'A high-functioning, overachieving woman, constantly bordering on burnout, was seen as fine. As long as I didn't burn out, no one cared that maybe I was functioning but not fine.'

Lost Girls: Why is Female ADHD Diagnosed So Late?

Until 1979 there was no research specifically on women with ADHD. Early studies suggested ADHD was five times more common in boys, but this gap was inflated by bias and misunderstanding. Diagnostic criteria focused on hyperactivity – more common in boys – while inattentive ADHD, often seen in girls, was overlooked. Girls are typically diagnosed around age seventeen, a full nine years later than boys, contributing to chronic underachievement and a high risk of mental health issues that configure their futures. This delay also affects autistic women, making dual diagnoses particularly complicated.

Since 2018, guidelines have flagged that ADHD is underrecognised in girls and women, who are referred for assessment less often and more frequently receive misdiagnoses. **Teachers tend to refer boys for support when they exhibit ADHD-like behaviours, reflecting societal expectations: boys' symptoms are flagged, while girls' symptoms – often showing up as anxiety or physical complaints such as headaches – are dismissed.**

Women often remain undiagnosed until life pressures, such as motherhood, make their symptoms unmanageable. In the UK, ADHD is underdiagnosed in girls, who are three times less likely than boys to receive a diagnosis despite comparable prevalence. Early diagnosis is crucial for reducing risks such as substance abuse, poverty (twice as high in ADHD women), chronic pain, insomnia and anxiety. The risk of attempting suicide is high for all people with ADHD and jumps to one in four among women.

There is little research on ADHD in women, and even less on transgender and non-binary experiences. When I use 'woman' or 'female' in this chapter, I include trans women and those who identify as women while acknowledging that gendered pressures for trans women with ADHD differ from those of cisgender women like myself. These experiences deserve representation in both medical research and media.

Why Women Wait: Barriers to Seeking an ADHD Diagnosis

Seeking an ADHD diagnosis is fraught with doubt and systemic barriers. Common refrains I hear from women questioning if they should seek help include:

» I'm sick of having to prove myself to doctors.
» Everyone struggles with organisation ... it's not that I think I'm special.
» I don't want to seem like I'm jumping on a bandwagon.
» I've got by so far ... so maybe I'm fine?
» I'm too old.
» NHS waiting lists are SO long.
» Private diagnoses are expensive and don't guarantee prescriptions.

The Weight of Expectation: ADHD and the 'Good Girl' Ideal

After a year of wading through self-help books and essays, I wondered: why is the combination of womanhood and ADHD so uniquely fraught? Are neurotypical women hesitant to validate ADHD struggles, fearing their own difficulties will be drowned out? Does dismissing ADHD in women act as a form of 'punching down'? Society's interest in neurodiversity often revolves around its 'unlockable potential' – does the lack of research into ADHD in women imply that society assumes women have less to offer?

My womanhood is filtered through ADHD, then twisted by society's responses to it. Many women I spoke to described feeling like they were constantly failing to meet social expectations. There's no 'right' way to be a woman with ADHD, and no productivity hack will assist us to 'girl-boss' our way through it, though you can certainly burn a lot of cash trying.

Shame sits at the molten core of the female ADHD experience. Society expects women to excel at tasks that 'shouldn't require much thought' – self-care, routines, tidiness. With low executive function, these 'simple' tasks often feel impossible. For example, 'laundry' isn't just one task. It's task-switching (remembering it needs doing), planning (finding time), organising (sorting colours), working memory (keeping track of steps), self-monitoring (not letting it sit in the machine) and impulse control (folding instead of doom-scrolling). And don't get me started on putting it away. We're trained to interpret finding these tasks difficult as laziness or even moral failure. As a result, failure at something basic doesn't just create frustration; it sends us spiralling, doubling down on attempts to fix ourselves, overpersisting in tasks we can't complete, trapping ourselves in a cycle of chaos and shame.

Girls are socialised to be compliant, thus internalising problems and masking ADHD. Society romanticises inattentive ADHD as a gauzy, twirly femininity – daydreaming, forgetful, 'off with the fairies'. As long as girls remain quiet, their struggles stay invisible. Unlike boys, who are typically more disruptive and prompt quicker intervention, girls' symptoms often fly under the radar, only surfacing when life pressures overwhelm their internal coping mechanisms.

This social conditioning fosters an external locus of control in many women with ADHD. Life feels like it's happening to you – good things are chalked up to sheer luck, while the bad are somehow your fault. Over time, this mindset erodes confidence and creates a pattern of maladaptive coping strategies that can leave us vulnerable to abusive situations or, at the very least, relationships that mimic our own harsh self-assessment.

The lack of control extends to our energy and mood. One day we're lethargic; the next, so animated we appear manic. Feedback is equally erratic – one person praises our insight, while the next critiques our incompetence. This whiplash breeds a sense of instability and deep self-doubt. In my research, I spoke to women who felt caught in this turbulent state, as if they were unravelling. Many had experienced shame on a generational scale. As one woman put it, 'It's not the ADHD that caused my shame; it was the confusion of not knowing what was going on. I wasn't ashamed of ADHD; I was ashamed of not being the "good girl" I thought I should be. My shame wasn't about ADHD; it was about me.'

Societal Expectations and Structural Shame

For women with ADHD, societal expectations around femininity, self-control and domesticity create a constant, unspoken pressure to embody qualities that don't come naturally, which leads to isolation and higher rates of anxiety and mood disorders.

ADHD symptoms often conflict with these gendered ideals, eroding self-esteem and reinforcing a sense of inadequacy that begins in childhood. The neurotypical world repeatedly tells us that we're inadequate at fulfilling our 'primary social role' as women – a message reinforced by societal archetypes of perfection, tidiness and emotional self-management. As Judith Butler theorised, gender is a construct – a performance repeated until it feels natural and creates an illusion of a stable identity. But for women with ADHD that performance often falters, leaving us out of step.

The shame women with ADHD experience isn't merely personal – it's structural. Society equates womanhood with care-giving and domesticity, tasks that demand the very executive functioning many women with ADHD struggle to maintain. Falling short doesn't feel like a small failure; it feels like failing at the core of 'womanhood'. For mothers, the load becomes heavier, as they're often expected to take on the 'mental load' of parenting – an expectation that can feel relentless. Without understanding or support from healthcare and mental health services, which often overlook ADHD in women, this structural shame is compounded, making it harder to feel competent or capable.

Even after receiving a diagnosis, women with ADHD are frequently seen as unreliable narrators of their own experiences, often dismissed as 'quirky' or infantilised rather than taken seriously. Society's limited archetypes for 'successful' women rarely account for those of us who exist outside their bounds, leaving us categorised as eccentric or the 'manic pixie dream girl', complete with messy charm but little agency. This infantilisation undermines our experiences, forcing us to continuously defend our right to exist as we are.

Diagnosis can be transformative, offering a framework for understanding and validating our struggles, preventing us from spending our lives feeling 'different', 'stupid' or 'lazy.' Yet these challenges remain because structural failures in healthcare, education and research leave many without effective treatment options. Without adequate representation in studies or diagnostic tools that reflect our experiences, we're left in cycles of anxiety, self-blame and shame. For women who are already trying to navigate a world that resists our realities, the systems that fail us only deepen that shame, leaving us to manage lives within structures that continually overlook our needs.

Invisible Burdens: Executive Function and the Mental Load

Women with ADHD often carry a mental load that requires relentless executive function, and this burden disproportionately falls on them in traditional roles. Consider the endless to-do lists, meal planning, remembering dates, social commitments and housekeeping tasks that add up like layers of emotional sediment. Each small responsibility demands initiation, planning, organisation – an unbroken chain of mental effort that ADHD routinely interrupts.

ADHD coach and mother Dusty Chipura observes, 'Women with ADHD aren't the organised yoga moms with the cute diaper bags. They're the ones who forget the birthday present or pick up their kid late.' Women with ADHD work harder just to maintain a baseline, a process that grinds away at self-esteem and makes them question their worth as mothers. Her advice? Learn to be gentle on yourself, ask for help even when it's uncomfortable, and connect with others who truly understand. For ADHD mothers the weight of self-criticism runs deep because it's layered with both societal expectations and personal desires to excel.

Social Killer Butterflies: Female Friendships with ADHD

Social situations pose unique challenges for women with ADHD, especially those that rely on small talk and fluid group dynamics. In high school, girls with ADHD are bullied more often than their neurotypical peers, not only physically but socially and online. For girls, breaking social norms invites punishment; ADHD amplifies this by introducing behavioural quirks that challenge the delicate balance of adolescent social hierarchies.

It's difficult to recognise ADHD in yourself when you've never met another woman with it. For me, meeting writer Elissa Schappell (New York, 60) at twenty-three was a revelation. After ten minutes, she said, 'I recognise your brain – I have the same, but mine's in dark blue.' With Elissa, I didn't have to second-guess myself. The aural marginalia heckling in my head quietened down. She described her diagnosis as a shrug: 'This is the kind of animal I've always been. I'm a writer, an artist. I won't wear a bathrobe, I won't get in a hammock, I don't like kites, I can't concentrate. Being diagnosed just made me go: "Oh, OK."' She showed me a self-portrait she'd drawn as a Siamese cat.

Elissa's feline aspirations were not unique. Many ADHD women describe feeling like 'aliens' pretending to be real people, or like a different species entirely. It is as if their experiences are so far removed from their own bodily comprehension that they anthropomorphise creatures to explain them.

The 'attention seeker' label often sticks to us, even when we're naturally shy. Imagine calling a man an attention seeker – society would see his confidence as assertiveness, not vanity. It's a subtle, strangely sexualising but powerful way of diminishing women's agency, reducing our expressions to mere bids for attention. Elissa experienced something similar: 'I was always auditioning to be everybody's favourite person in the classroom, but I should've known: sit down, cat girl, you're not even in the running.'

Hormones on High: The Rollercoaster of ADHD and PMDD

Nearly half of women with ADHD also experience premenstrual dysphoric disorder (PMDD), a severe, clinically recognised mood disorder distinct from PMS. I didn't discover this connection until I was twenty-three, having by then lost five days each month to a crushing depression. Not informing teenage girls about the hormonal impact on ADHD isn't just negligent, it's cruel. Treatment for PMDD was life-changing for me, yet I had to research and advocate for it myself – five days of Prozac before my period starts.

Hormonal shifts worsen ADHD symptoms, with dopamine and noradrenaline levels fluctuating wildly. The week before menstruation, progesterone spikes while dopamine drops, often triggering a crash for those already operating with lower dopamine levels. Despite this, the medical field rarely considers hormones in treatment plans, leaving women especially vulnerable at key life stages. Doctors are just beginning to acknowledge that ADHD medication loses effectiveness before menstruation, making even basic activities – like driving, which is already risky for those with ADHD – more hazardous.

The need for research on these interactions is urgent. Sari Solden, a leading voice on ADHD in women, observes that many of us 'just border on coping' until we reach perimenopause or menopause. By then, the symptoms can be so disruptive that some women, myself included, have asked doctors if early-onset Alzheimer's might be to blame – a question I found myself asking as young as thirteen, when hormones began to make themselves known.

Motherhood: Embracing 'Good Enough' Over Perfection

First, there's pregnancy: no clear guidance exists on taking ADHD medication. The typical advice, like with SSRIs, is to continue if not taking them would cause more harm. This leaves women with the weight of tough choices backed up by little data. Personally, I'd hesitate to be pregnant on ADHD meds, but I'll have to – without them, I'd risk severe mental health issues – and loss of income. Many women I spoke to share this anxiety, finding little reassurance from doctors due to the lack of research.

Motherhood is challenging for anyone, but for women with ADHD the endless demands of parenting can feel insurmountable. Tasks don't 'end' – they diffuse into an unending cycle that wears down executive function. Partly as a result, many ADHD mothers are haunted by the ideal they think they should be. Child psychiatrist Donald Winnicott may be the patron saint of ADHD mothers with his 1950s concept of the 'good enough mother'. Instead of aiming for flawlessness, the 'good enough' mother creates a space where the child can play freely, safely tethered to reality. She responds to needs, and allows children to handle manageable frustrations. This compassionate approach teaches resilience and releases ADHD mothers from impossible standards.

ADHD mothers can excel but often need to redefine 'good' on their terms. Society's perfectionist expectations hit mothers hardest. We may achieve as much as neurotypical women, but may take different paths and use more sequins. As Elissa put it, 'Someone else might go from A to B to C, but I'll do a little bit of this and a little of that, and we both get there by the end of the day ... it's more like being a spider than an ant.'

After taking her son to a neurologist, Elissa was surprised when the focus shifted to her own potential ADHD. It hadn't crossed her mind – ADHD in girls wasn't recognised when she was young. Her first experience with medication was a revelation: 'I never knew people could think one thing at a time: what? You're not always going on multiple tracks? Wow, I guess everyone is sitting in their seats now.' She was hesitant to medicate her son, but when he came home excited about finally being able to sit on the rug, she was glad for him – even if the implied conformity rankled her riot-grrrl heart, which muttered silently, 'Never sit on the rug.'

Motherhood was especially tough for Sarah (Cambridge, 30). She expected an instant bond with her daughter, but confronted an enduring taboo when she felt an overwhelming sense of burden instead. Already struggling with self-care, she thought the connection would come naturally. Her isolation deepened as she misread her mother-in-law's offers to help as criticism. She cried daily for seven months: 'When you have ADHD, sometimes you don't even want to leave the bed; brushing your teeth feels like a struggle – and now this baby needs breastfeeding.'

The intense demands of motherhood heightened her demand avoidance. When I shared about a friend who refused to breastfeed despite midwife pressure, Sarah smiled, calling it 'wisdom'. She was surprised by how rigidly gender expectations around motherhood were imposed on her. Breastfeeding, compounded by her sensitivities, became unbearable, so she switched to formula milk after a year. Her daughter's own sensitivities – like not wanting to be held close – triggered Sarah's rejection sensitivity, making her feel unchosen: 'If she's not happy in my arms, I feel rejected, and that makes me angry at her. Why don't you want me?'

The Intimacy Paradox: ADHD, Relationships and Desire

For many women with ADHD, navigating relationships feels like a high-wire act, balancing between connection and self-doubt. Physical intimacy, in particular, requires sustained attention, sensory regulation and presence – all things ADHD complicates. Sex becomes another task on the checklist, often weighed down by low self-esteem, impulsivity and sometimes trauma from chaotic or unsupportive environments.

The disconnect between desire and execution is common: the mind is willing, but the body can't keep up. The guilt of not meeting expectations – both internal and external – only heightens this tension. Research shows that women with ADHD often struggle to maintain intimacy, form close relationships, and share emotions without losing themselves. Emotional dysregulation can lead to frequent outbursts, leaving partners feeling alienated or helpless. We're inclined to merge our identities with our partners', orbiting around them until that sense of alignment inevitably collapses.

Impulsivity might sound sexy, but it's not. Mine involves eating and drinking everything, oversharing and turning over enough new leaves to fill a tree. Then cutting down the tree. In the sexual arena, impulsivity can lead to increased one-night stands and risky behaviour. Women with ADHD are four times more likely to become pregnant as teenagers and more vulnerable to toxic relationships, confusing emotional highs and lows with passion. Our craving for dopamine can draw us into chaotic partnerships, mistaking the instability for excitement. Manipulative partners can exploit our need for stimulation, keeping us on an emotional rollercoaster that feeds our dopamine-starved brains.

There's an urban legend that women with ADHD are crazy in bed, which likely began by conflating 'lacking impulse control' with 'lacking inhibition'. Being uninhibited may lead to great sex; being impulsive is more likely to lead to a poorly made costume. While some women with ADHD might be more sexually adventurous, they also report lower sexual desire and fewer orgasms – a contradiction that underscores how ADHD can create paradoxes in even the most personal spaces.

Gender Defiance

ADHD doesn't just disrupt daily routines, it also questions our social roles. Neurodivergent children are more likely to defy traditional gender roles, often mixing up pronouns. Many women I spoke to described their gender as something they wear lightly, like an itchy jacket they might toss aside at any moment. Often neurodivergent people disrupt the norm unintentionally, and then end up embracing it.

Kit (Margate, 34) when asked about her pronouns, responded with, 'gender greedy'. Although she identifies as a 'totally fluid human' she often feels at odds with femininity. Her sense of womanhood remains steady, even though her outward presentation prompts others to perceive her as masculine.

For Kit, embracing a 'visibly gender-queer' presentation provided relief from the trap of conventional beauty standards. Conforming – long hair, make-up, all that performance – felt like punishment disguised as success: 'I always felt like I was failing, and when I did feel sexy, society punished me anyway.' What matters to Kit isn't fitting into a category, beyond 'bloody queer' as the acceptance of her vast internal world: 'I've long accepted that no single person outside will get more than a glimmer of it. They don't need to. I don't need to be understood to be loved. If we slept together, you'd get a bit more than a glimmer, but words are trash.'

Comorbidities and Coping Mechanisms

Women with ADHD are more prone to comorbid conditions – especially depression and eating disorders – compared to men, which creates an additional layer of complexity in diagnosis and treatment. Many girls with ADHD are first treated for symptoms of other conditions, and it's not uncommon for them to be prescribed antidepressants before ever being evaluated for ADHD. Misdiagnosis doesn't just mean the wrong medication – it's about being robbed of an explanation for your life and a chance to move forwards with self-understanding.

Many girls with ADHD develop maladaptive coping strategies like self-harm. They're also four times more likely to develop eating disorders than their neurotypical peers. Our dopamine inconsistencies, combined with heightened sensory sensitivity, can make food a battleground. Hyperfocus and impulsivity drive crash diets or restricting eating as a way to gain control. It's easy to develop maladaptive coping strategies, and the line between pushing ourselves and harming ourselves becomes blurry.

For me, practising 'the pause' feels like tightrope walking. Learning to sit with urges is harder than it sounds. People with ADHD are often hypersensitive to taste or texture and prone to misinterpret bodily cues, like mistaking thirst for hunger or failing to recognise physical discomfort until it's severe. At the same time, low dopamine creates a chemical need for stimulation, and can drive eating to escape boredom or blunt anxiety.

For many, starvation becomes a way to self-soothe, to impose one constant to create an artificial sense of control. Mary (London, 44), diagnosed with ADHD later in life, recalls dieting as young as eight after her mother took her to Weight

Watchers. 'I wasn't even overweight,' she says. 'Now I know it was the constant trips to the fridge, searching for dopamine hits.'

She tried Overeaters Anonymous, which she describes as 'horrific. Talking about fixating on someone else's plate – it felt like ruining food the way AA ruins booze.' She sees her relationship with food as a 'form of self-harm'. She's knows the health risks, but she's also a single mother of young children and exhausted 'because trying so hard to think straight wears my brain out'.

Vulnerable Appetites: Cravings and Validation

The isolation of adolescence, combined with a hunger for validation, makes teenage girls with ADHD particularly vulnerable to 'perceived exhibitionism' – from sexting to posting nudes. Despite sex-positivity movements, double standards persist. Promiscuity might enhance male reputations but often damages female ones. Girls with ADHD who break norms around female sexuality are met with greater social rejection, which feeds into the cycle of shame and isolation.

Teenage girls with ADHD are particularly susceptible to grooming and coercive relationships. When you've been criticised your entire life, the first middle-aged loon who says, 'They don't understand you,' is a *Romeo + Juliet*-era DiCaprio. It's like shooting fish in a barrel. This vulnerability is part of a larger pattern – a by-product of stigma, loneliness and the quest for belonging.

Romantic or sexual attention provides a potent dopamine boost, creating a feedback loop that doesn't diminish with age. Mary, now sober, warns her daughter about the dangers of making a man her 'higher power', borrowing language from AA. She advises, 'Don't lose your friendships. Don't make him your breakfast, lunch and dinner. He should be your dessert.'

Mary's parenting style, shaped by her own experiences, centres on open dialogue about control, boundaries and manipulation. Mary endured abuse as a toddler and spent years believing it was her fault – because she was 'kissy-kissy and affectionate' she internalised the blame. Her history of coercive relationships left deep scars, reinforcing the idea that girls need explicit education on recognising unhealthy dynamics. Therapy helped her establish boundaries she'd never had before, and she's now adamant about giving her daughter the tools she lacked.

When Mary became pregnant unexpectedly at university, she wasn't ready. 'ADHD got me into that situation because I wasn't thinking straight,' she says. Misdiagnosed with infertility due to PCOS, she'd impulsively stopped the pill. While she partied, others helped care for her baby. Now, her daughter is eighteen, and Mary says, 'I feel like she's got the gene, and I don't want her to go off the rails.' Understanding how ADHD inflected her choices means she can support her child, like helping her get a coil fitted to prevent impulsivity from leading to unintended consequences.

Mary's deep understanding of her children – who also have ADHD – makes her an exceptional mother. She doesn't yell but supports them proactively. 'Last week, my daughter lost her key three times. I was at work, and she had to wait in the rain,' Mary recalls. She uses the same calm approach with her youngest, a high-energy five-year-old: 'Sometimes she gets into such a tizz she starts shouting. I ask, "Do you want a hug?" and she says, "Yes." That's all she needs.' When teachers mistake her youngest's ADHD for misbehaviour, Mary advocates firmly. When a teacher explained that other children were expected to count to twenty, while her daughter's goal was simply to sit on the mat for ten minutes, Mary pushed back: 'That's not an educational target. That's for your benefit so you can manage the class better. Would you say that to a mother with a child in a wheelchair?'

Media Backlash: Diagnosing ADHD in Women as 'Fad'

WOMEN IN THEIR 20S AND 30S DRIVE RECORD SURGE IN ADHD PRESCRIPTIONS AMID ROW OVER WHETHER CONDITION IS BEING OVER-DIAGNOSED

In recent years, women with ADHD have become the tabloids' favourite target. Headlines accuse us of 'jumping on a trend' and paint women with ADHD as gullible, attention-seeking and overdiagnosed. Meanwhile, men with ADHD are portrayed as quirky geniuses, their diagnoses cast as badges of honour. When Richard Branson discusses his ADHD and dyslexia, it's framed as part of his 'exceptionality' not his 'disability'.

The diagnosis double standard is glaring. While men's late-in-life diagnoses are presented as revelations, women's experiences are recast as fads. When Nadia Sawalha went public with her ADHD diagnosis, the story focused on her tears, not her insight. Non-white women are erased from the conversation altogether. ADHD coverage remains thin, reduced to recycled headlines about 'Signs You Shouldn't Ignore', trivialising the condition for clicks rather than fostering understanding.

The stigma cuts deep. ADHD in women was ignored in medical research for decades, yet now, seeking help brands us as hysterics or neurotic consumers. The irony is infuriating: we were left out, and now we're criticised for catching up.

The Loveliness Factor: Executive Function as Performance

Women observe each other differently – we're trained to. I've always been captivated by women with what I call 'the loveliness factor'. For a long time, I didn't question why. The loveliness factor applies if more than one of the following is true for you: you can casually throw together a supper for six. You cook recipes with more than five ingredients just for yourself. Being alone prompts you to light candles for ambiance rather than shame-eat in the dark. You always have a birthday card or small gift on hand. Your skincare routine is called 'simple' but involves more than three steps. You view your hair as an asset rather than a wild beast to tame. You do things you don't want to without swearing.

The role of 'woman' requires a high level of executive

function, and it starts early. By the time they hit puberty, boys are expected to brush their teeth and put on clean clothes. It's a different story for girls: skincare routines; managing menstruation; hair care; clothing choices that aren't to do with 'Does this smell?' I'm in my thirties, and I still haven't figured out a way to keep socks from going rogue. The 'sock bag' isn't it.

Many of us try to compensate for our ADHD with complex, rigid systems, which only fuels the cycle of perfectionism and falling apart. This makes us hyperaware of things going wrong, which means we're the first to notice, reinforcing the belief that nobody else will step in – a process that can be exacerbated by a 'helpless' partner, creating a fast track to burnout.

I remember becoming fascinated with how people spent their time alone when I was a teenager. It wasn't voyeurism; it was an instinctive recognition that my way of functioning wasn't 'normal'. Reading Miranda July's *The First Bad Man* was a revelation. The narrator uses one bowl and one spoon to minimise her choices, to manage daily life without being overwhelmed. When I excitedly told a doctor friend, he flatly remarked, 'That's a symptom of mental illness.'

Even after twenty-five years of managing ADHD, I find myself questioning it. Recently, after yet another wave of media scepticism, I asked my best friend if I really had ADHD. 'Maybe,' I proposed, 'I am simply a kook!' She pointed out that we started talking about how to *be*, how to get through the day, when we were eleven.

'Always Be Optimising': The Pressure of ADHD Productivity

Managing ADHD is often about the basics – making it through the day intact. But the ads targeting women with ADHD tell a different story. They urge us to 'optimise' ourselves and 'harness our explosive energy', promising a quick route to better productivity. The implication? We're failing at being women because we're failing to juggle life's demands.

These ads are relentless, pushing productivity apps, audiobooks and coaching services that promise to make us more efficient. They prey on our insecurities, playing on the idea that neurotypical women are somehow 'slaying' it all. In reality, most of us – neurotypical or otherwise – are barely keeping up. Yet these ads insist we'd thrive if only we rose at dawn, used our jade roller, drank our lemon water, green tea *and* green juice, and 'invested in' the right tools.

But real self-care, as Audre Lorde put it, is self-preservation and political warfare. It's resisting a system of endless productivity and reclaiming self-care as a radical act, not a commercialised checklist of products to buy, and it's certainly not meant to be an additional source of guilt.

The push towards productivity isn't new. It's hustle culture, repackaged for women who are already exhausted. In the 1950s and 1960s amphetamines were marketed to women as 'pep pills' to help them keep up with domestic duties. Millions became dependent on speed in the name of being good wives and mothers and, as one scholar put it, 'Given access to enough amphetamine, any rat, monkey, or man would eventually self-destruct.' Today's ADHD apps and tools echo this history, promising us better lives while reinforcing the idea that we're never enough. In an ad for the app Effecto, a girl in a sports bra pauses her run to gaze dreamily at the sea: 'My bf didn't want me to lose weight,' the caption reads. 'All he wanted was to help me manage ADHD.'

The Invisible Labour Tax: Emotional Work and Mental Clutter

For women with ADHD, emotional labour – anticipating, managing and responding to everyone else's needs – is an unspoken tax, draining our executive function reserves before our own day even begins. While men might be praised for carrying out occasional tasks, women with ADHD often feel as though they're carrying a mental burden for everyone in their lives – their executive function is taxed with holding the activities of family members in relation and motion.

Even in supposedly equal relationships, women often end up shouldering the bulk of emotional labour, quietly managing tasks no one notices until they're undone. Wedding planning is peak gendered labour – especially for ADHD women, where the nightmare is made worse because we're told it's a daydream. Every checklist and timeline highlights our executive dysfunction against the fantasy of the 'effortless bride'. Weddings reinforce traditional gender norms, assigning women the organisational burdens as part of performing femininity. Marketed as the happiest day of your life, they instead become a societal stress test, demanding project-management perfection. Several ADHD women described masking and deploying coping strategies, only to discover that once invitations went out, they became the default point person for every logistical question, while their partners stayed out of the storm. Social media only exacerbates this, showing us carefully curated lives where everything is managed, perfectly in place. We can't help but compare our messy realities to these polished snapshots, fuelling our sense of inadequacy.

It's easier for men to capitalise on the richness of having ADHD because they're expected to do less. The eccentric male professor who can't cook because he's too busy being brilliant is always a man. The female equivalent – a woman who forgets to eat and relies on her husband to bring her sandwiches – isn't quite myth yet, though some feminist authors are working to get it enshrined.

Shame and Radical Acceptance: Redefining Success on Our Own Terms

The shame that comes with ADHD, especially for women, is profound. We're taught that our worth is measured by how well we manage the basics – tidy homes, organised schedules, seamless lives. The problem arises when these 'basics' elude us, and what should be minor failures – missing an appointment, forgetting a birthday – become overwhelming sources of shame.

Our culture's fixation on productivity makes it harder to accept ourselves as we are. The expectation to constantly 'do more' is toxic for women with ADHD, who already feel stretched to their limits. The reality is that few people genuinely enjoy 'women's work' – the invisible, emotional and logistical labour society expects of us. For us, this labour includes not just our daily to-do list but also the weight of our own internalised expectations, amplified by years of judgement and self-doubt.

The danger comes when we fail at something seemingly trivial, and that failure becomes sharp and jagged, and then we double down. We engage in self-destructive behaviours meant to soothe us – behaviours that are often far more damaging than the thing we failed to do, like obsessively ruminating over tasks undone. As Sari Solden points out, 'It goes from "I have a messy desk" to "I'm messy" to "I'm bad and that means I shouldn't let myself go out into the world."' Many of us retreat from social situations to avoid being judged, amplifying our sense of isolation.

Shame blooms in the dark. After years of being told we're not 'normal' we hide the ways we cope, taking extraordinary measures to avoid social judgement. Many ADHD women avoid having friends over, because we're judged on the state of our homes. Hiding creates intense isolation. Every time we feel the need to conceal how we function, we tell ourselves we're broken. Over time, that message builds chronic stress and a profound sense of inadequacy. For many of us, this comes from repeating the negative messages we've received all our lives – from people we love and respect – back to ourselves in the dark, locking us into a state of stress.

The answer isn't to change ourselves to fit neurotypical standards. Instead, it's to embrace radical acceptance, a concept psychologist Tara Brach describes as acknowledging the reality of our experience without judgement. For ADHD women, this means redefining success on our terms, rejecting the notion that competence in every domain is the goal. We need to move through the shame that arises from living in a world structured around gendered expectations that don't fit us. Acceptance doesn't mean giving up; it means freeing ourselves from the tyranny of 'normal'.

Equity over Equality: Building Support Systems that Work for Us

An ex-housemate once told a friend that I 'get a lot of help'. It stung, but today I'm not ashamed of it. I get a lot of help because I give a lot of help. For women with ADHD, building mutual support systems is essential. We create a network where everyone does what they're naturally good at, pooling resources and sharing the load in ways that work for us. Equality is like giving everyone the same size shoes and saying, 'Here, wear these!' Equity is more like asking, 'What size do you wear? Let's find you a pair that fits so you don't walk around like a bad clown.'

Take, for example, a friend of mine who sincerely loves Excel and does my taxes. In exchange, I'm there for her in any emotional or practical crisis. It is in no way quid pro quo, but she knows I'd show up in the dead of night, no questions asked. This isn't about equality – where everyone gets the same. It's about equity, recognising that we don't all have the same strengths. In this way, managing ADHD becomes less about 'fixing' ourselves and more about accepting that we are interrelated and interdependent, and, as such, accepting help isn't a sign of weakness.

Celebrating Difference: The Freedom to Be Ourselves

As women with ADHD, we disrupt social patterns just by existing. Our very presence challenges the rigid gender roles and structures society has constructed. The more we try to conform, the more miserable we become. Instead, we should focus on doing things in ways that work for us, cultivating our agency and self-efficacy in the process.

This requires a shift in how we see ourselves. Society tells us that difference is a liability – especially for women – something to be minimised. But on my strongest days I'm profoundly grateful that ADHD makes conformity impossible. Why would I want to conform to a society that isn't interested in difference?

Life might be easier if we were neurotypical, but it wouldn't necessarily be better. ADHD forces you to choose what really matters. It liberates us from the expectation of automatic functionality, allowing us to create lives that reflect our true values. It means rejecting the notion that doing things simply because it's our job as women is desirable. We don't need to juggle everything. Not all hobbies need to become side-hustles! We don't need more stuff – as it is, women with ADHD often feel oppressed by both the mental clutter in their heads and the literal physical objects around them which seem to rise up like a tide. Living well with ADHD means ruthlessly prioritising what we care about and cutting out the noise.

Instead of punishing ourselves for failing to meet impossible expectations in a sexist world – in which case ADHD is a barrier – I choose to see it as a filter, a way to cut through society's demands and focus on what's meaningful. After all, who decided that a woman's floor must always be clean, especially if it means constantly tidying up after everyone else?

EATING

Eating with ADHD is a rollercoaster. Here are some common experiences:

» Feeling out of control around food, leading to obsessive restriction or over-controlling habits that cycle back into binging.
» Forgetting to eat all day while hyperfocused on something, then overeating late at night.
» Mindless overeating while distracted, without realising how much has been consumed.
» Snacking constantly for dopamine but never feeling satisfied, followed by punitively skipping meals.
» Struggling to plan meals, leading to last-minute junk food or defaulting to 'pizza, I guess'.
» Feeling overwhelmed by cooking or meal prep, so skipping meals entirely.
» Eating the same few 'safe' foods on repeat because decision-making feels exhausting.
» Avoiding grocery shopping until the last possible moment, making balanced meals even harder to manage.
» Relying on ultra-processed foods for convenience, then feeling hungry/guilty afterward.
» Losing track of what's in the fridge, leading to wasted food or missing ingredients.

In the past, my relationship with food was exactly what you'd expect from a girl raised in the 90s – complicated. These days, I'm not about rules, but as someone with ADHD, here's what keeps me sane around food:

» Add, don't restrict: I focus on throwing in easy extras like greens instead of obsessing over what to avoid.
» As women, many of us have been culturally trained to fuse food and movement into 'diet and exercise'. Prying them apart makes both much nicer. I forget this weekly (okay, daily), but life with ADHD is easier when movement is casual, joyful and entirely separate from food.
» Find your structure: I meal plan once a week – not prep, because that's too much – but having a go-to formula of grain + protein + veggie + sauce keeps meals simple.

Sensory Mood Food

Snack break! Grab a dopamine snack.
Think high-contrast, like:

» Apple slices + crunchy peanut-butter
» Warm cookie + cold ice-cream
» Frozen raspberries + melted white chocolate
» Mint chewing gum + hot tea
» Cucumber slices + chilli oil + sesame oil

- » Salted popcorn + chocolate buttons
- » Pretzels with sharp cheddar and honey, for dipping

ADHD brains thrive on novelty and pairing surprising textures or temperatures creates satisfying bursts of stimulation, banishing restlessness and helping your mind refocus.

Chapter 5

Family Dynamics: Reimagining What Family Can Be

The conversation around ADHD in families has long been defined by stigma and blame. Historically, ADHD was the purview of 'broken homes'. Studies show that couples with a child with ADHD are almost twice as likely to split before their child turns eight. Tabloid headlines of the nineties reinforced this link, with both ADHD and divorce framed as personal failings rather than complex realities.

When I was diagnosed, ADHD-like behaviours were often seen as a child's response to divorce trauma – the idea was fresh in my divorced parents' minds. ADHD became another tool for blame: the child was 'broken' by the family rupture, or one parent was blamed for faulty genes or behaviour. As divorce rates rose and no-fault divorce became more common, the blame shifted to the ADHD child. ADHD behaviours are difficult to live with, ergo ADHD causes divorce. Parenting books profited by playing on the fear that if ADHD behaviours weren't controlled, the unruly child would tear the family apart. People often attribute ADHD behaviours to either faulty genes or bad parenting. The latter view presents ADHD as a case of 'you reap what you sow'. But the truth is, nobody knows exactly what causes ADHD.

THE UNICORN

THE SCAPEGOAT

Root causes might intrigue researchers, but families live with realities, not theories. How does ADHD affect those who have it and the people who love them? Key questions emerge: how does ADHD change family dynamics? Do siblings feel overshadowed? Is the ADHD child the 'squeaky wheel'?

While bad parenting doesn't cause ADHD, it can intensify problematic behaviours. Effective parenting – calm, responsive, firm – leads to better outcomes than confrontation. The focus should shift from blame to creating a supportive home and seeking appropriate treatment.

By the end of this chapter, I want to have conveyed three ideas: first, ADHD doesn't happen to just one person – it shifts the entire family dynamic. Second, ADHD must be understood within the broader context of family and care systems. Finally, when we stop using ADHD to interrogate a family's past and focus on how it shapes the present, diagnosis becomes the first step towards strengthening family bonds and creating kinder, more compassionate members of society.

The Unicorn and the Scapegoat: How ADHD Warps the Family Orbit

Family structures often warp around the ADHD child. In an unconscious act of homeostasis, the child is either scapegoated or coddled. Parenting books typically offer two prototypes: the *Unicorn*, around whom the family orbits, with everyone else forced into secondary roles to accommodate their needs. And the *Scapegoat*, whose behaviour is blamed for the family's dysfunction. I propose a third way: recognising the ADHD child's sensitivities as an opportunity to consider the needs of all family members.

Take the Phalanges – a family simmering with unspoken tension. The father's alcoholism and the mother's anxiety go unaddressed. Their younger daughter, Regina, has undiagnosed ADHD. At 8 a.m. the family waits for her to get in the car for the school run. Her mother woke her, her sister checked on her, and her father made breakfast, but Regina chooses that moment to reorganise the cutlery drawer. The car is a powder keg. By the time she shambles along, it's her lateness that triggers an explosion. Her father's hangover and mother's anxiety remain unnoticed. In this dynamic,

Regina becomes the scapegoat, absorbing the family's frustration while everyone else's issues go ignored.

Now meet the Puddingfoots. Mrs Puddingfoot quit her job to meet the needs of her son Ben, who has ADHD. Meanwhile, his dyslexic older sister is left to fend for herself. Ben, now seven, co-sleeps with his mother, while his father heads to work early. At 8 a.m. Ben is buckled into the front seat with a bacon sandwich, coaxed through the morning routine. Mrs Puddingfoot doesn't notice her daughter sulking, needing help with homework, because she's busy repeating 'please don't' as Ben kicks the dashboard – following a psychologist's advice to use fewer words to avoid stressing him. Coddling an ADHD child disempowers them, fostering dependence and learned helplessness that harms both the child and the family.

The Work of Parenting an ADHD Child

Raising a child with ADHD can make neurotypical parents dislike themselves. Studies show ADHD kids view their parents as 'demanding and power-hungry', while parents feel 'more power-assertive and less warm'. Mothers, especially, report more 'stressful', 'demanding' and 'exhausting' interactions. Over time, ADHD behaviours erode parents' confidence, amplifying frustration and helplessness, worsened by the lack of support from social programmes and benefits. The relentless scrutiny parents face isn't limited to the home – it extends into public discourse.

Mumsnet: A Chorus of 'Relentless'

ADHD is the first acronym on the Mumsnet glossary (alphabetical, but still). For the uninitiated, here's a sample of the user's guide:

AIBU	Am I Being Unreasonable?
BC	Before Children
CC	Controlled Crying
YABU	You Are Being Unreasonable
YANBU	You Are Not Being Unreasonable

In the first six months of 2023, 8,750 posts tagged 'ADHD' appeared – a rich text of ADHD discourse. The word most often used to describe parenting a child with ADHD? 'Relentless.' A post on the AIBU forum captures the frustration of parenting a child with ADHD. One parent vented about the constant need to remind their eleven-year-old to do basic tasks like brushing their teeth or flushing the toilet, despite their age. They wrote, 'I sometimes feel like there's all this chatter about ADHD and how to help people with it ... but no acknowledgement' of the 'frazzled' neurotypical parents who must guide every step of the day. This sentiment highlights a gap in ADHD discourse: the challenges faced by caregivers trying to support their children while maintaining their own lives.

Scrolling through Mumsnet reveals a common theme: parents expressing fatigue, frustration and isolation, with some venting about husbands who likely have undiagnosed ADHD. A much-needed reminder from someone with ADHD appeared: '**ADHD doesn't make someone an arsehole. Only arseholes do that.**'

Despite this, the site can devolve into snippy infighting, where mothers police each other's behaviour, enforcing the assumption that mothers of ADHD children must be saints. One user snaps, 'Have you taken him off all fortified foods?' Another responds incredulously, 'You're frazzled by reminders? Really? Believe me, life could be much worse. I wish that's all I had to do.'

Parenting Books: Aspirational Nonsense

My mother never read a parenting book, or one about ADHD. Her approach was part Indian, part generational, part instinct. She ensured I had extra time in exams and allowed me medication despite her gut-level mistrust of the pharmaceutical industry, which still surprises me. When I asked her what it was like raising me with so little information, she said, 'You feel like you've failed, you feel alone. You say, "Pick up your books," or "Shut the drawer," until you're screaming.' She wasn't alone in her frustration.

ADHD parenting books from the 1980s and 1990s emphasised 'structured parenting' – which meant discipline above all. Then came the start-up jargon: connect, support, unleash potential, harness 'explosive' energy. More recent titles focus on unlocking ADHD 'superpowers', which, like calling children 'gifted', is unhelpful. Not all ADHD kids are gifted – many drop out of school. Telling kids they're gifted encourages a fixed mindset, which discourages trying new things. ADHD kids, who fail more often than their neurotypical peers, need grit and a growth mindset. I don't dwell on fuck-ups; I focus on recovery and going again. A parenting book called *Mediocre but Eager* would be more realistic, though probably not a bestseller.

The Worst Parenting Book I've Ever Read

Some books go further, framing ADHD behaviours as deliberate attention-seeking. One such book from 2012 – *Parenting Your Child with ADHD: A No-Nonsense Guide for Nurturing Self-Reliance and Cooperation* – advocates reinforcement theory, an approach that has been widely critiqued and fallen out of favour in recent years. Catchily, the book boils these secondary gains down to 'the Five As': Attention, Accommodation, Avoidance, Acquisition and Antagonising.

> Your child's ADHD behaviour may have any of the following beneficial effects: it may garner Attention for her; it may get others to make Accommodations for her; it may help her Avoid certain situations; it may help her Acquire something she wants; and it may Antagonise others for doing things she does not like. Any one of the five As can increase the frequency of ADHD behaviour.

One friend summed it up best: 'Also, your daughter is a little bitch!' Given how harsh traditional parenting advice can be, newer models offer a more empathetic alternative.

Gentle Parenting Meets Emotional Regulation

The newer trend of 'gentle parenting' emphasises empathy and emotional regulation, both crucial for managing ADHD.

Emotional regulation teaches children how to tolerate emotions rather than avoid them. If your kid drops an ice cream and screams, and you scream back, no one deserves the ice cream.

For most, emotions are manageable ups and downs, like a typical rollercoaster. For someone with ADHD, it's more like a rollercoaster designed by a squirrel on amphetamines – full of wild, unpredictable loops. Emotional regulation means learning to ride out the chaos and come out intact. Emotional regulation isn't automatic; it grows out of connection.

Attunement: The Parent-Child Dance

Attunement is the precursor to emotional regulation. It's how a child's sense of self develops through interaction with a responsive caregiver. It helps them recognise their emotional cues and later form secure attachments.

Without attunement, children are left vulnerable to overwhelming emotions they don't know they can survive. The brain's self-regulation systems develop through the emotional connection with a caregiver, which requires that the mother be in a non-stressed, non-anxious, non-depressed state. Reading about its sanctity, I wondered how mothers with their own mental health struggles transform into Madonna-like figures.

Gabor Maté warns that infants whose caregivers are too stressed to provide attunement may grow up feeling chronically alone with their emotions. He suggests that ADHD may originate from disruptions in this emotional connection, leading to disordered brain circuitry.

Maté might be right, and lack of attunement may trigger a genetic predisposition to ADHD, but what good does it do to focus on causes beyond a mother's control, like postpartum depression? Given the UK's lack of postpartum support and childcare, focusing on these causes can feel like misplaced blame. Parents can learn emotional regulation alongside their children. The best teachers are learners, and nobody is born knowing how to regulate emotions – it's a learned skill. At some point, we all have to learn to parent ourselves.

The 'Secure Attachment Versus Obedience' Dilemma

In *Scattered Minds*, Gabor Maté emphasises the importance of building ADHD children's self-esteem through 'unconditional positive regard' – essentially, unconditional love. Maté focuses on 'long-term development' over 'short-term obedience', suggesting that self-regulation can be nurtured by prioritising a child's wellbeing over behavioural goals. He states, 'The cost of getting a child to school on time is secure attachment ... the world will teach her the necessary lessons if she is helped to become open to learning.'

However, in contexts where obedience is tied to survival, especially for Black and brown families who face state violence, Maté's perspective can feel naïve. For many parents, obedience is a matter of safety. The stakes are higher for kids who aren't white. ADHD stigma in many communities runs deep, tangled up in cultural and systemic biases. Mental health is often seen as a moral failing rather than a medical issue, and ADHD gets dismissed as laziness or bad parenting. For families dealing with systemic racism or economic precarity, it's often seen as a 'luxury problem' compared to the real work of survival. Distrust in schools and healthcare – thanks to centuries of discrimination –doesn't help. Add religious interpretations, like advocate Rachel Idowu (London, 29) being told to 'pray on it': passages from scripture convinced her that everyone struggled with ADHD traits, e.g., 'Better a patient person than a warrior, one with self-control than one who takes a city.' Diagnosis and treatment, when they're even an option, are expensive, and ADHD research still centres white, Western experiences. It's no wonder that for many, ADHD doesn't look like a condition – it looks like something you're supposed to grit your teeth and handle.

Maté's narrative is both alluring and dangerous. It works if you're privileged enough to view ADHD as an enriching wild card, but it rests on an oversimplification. He argues ADHD arises largely from early nurturing, overlooking the scientific consensus on genetics. Both nature and nurture matter.

Cultural differences deeply influence how we talk about ADHD and our parents. Non-acceptance of ADHD often reflects a different cultural lens – where neurodevelopmental disorders and mental health discussions aren't mainstream – rather than a lack of love. For some, the idea of nurturing through adversity makes less sense when survival demands toughness. My mother didn't cut me any slack, and I wouldn't trade the resilience she instilled. I learned early to work with what I had.

Vivienne Isebor, founder of ADHD Babes – a community for Black women and non-binary people of African Caribbean descent – emphasises how language shapes understanding. She avoids jargon and explains ADHD in ways that reduce stigma, especially within communities already navigating systemic racism and ableism.

The most exciting part of the recent advocacy surge is that we're finally hearing voices previously silenced. On TikTok, comedian @AsherGlean shares how his African parents dismissed his ADHD as stupidity. When his school raised suspicions about his condition, his mother beat him because she believed he was misbehaving rather than neurodivergent. Several male friends in the video nodded in recognition; one wiped a tear away. Schools can't get medication for children if their parents don't consent. Asher was helped by an individual, his deputy headteacher, Mrs Burrows, rather than the system. In year eleven, she got him support. To stop him getting into fights, she set him up with boxing lessons in the gym with her husband. Later, at university, having started medication, he realised the lost possibilities. 'If my parents had kind of collaborated with her . . .' Asher shook his head, 'If they try to understand you, that's all that needs to happen,' he said.

Growing up with ADHD

Undergraduates with ADHD often describe their childhoods as filled with feelings of 'difference', 'isolation' and a 'craving for understanding'. School, designed for compliance, becomes a battleground. Family life can either protect or shatter self-esteem. For ADHD kids, daily tasks that others breeze through feel impossible, eroding confidence. The most common descriptors for their experience are: 'stupid', 'lazy', 'useless', 'selfish' and 'broken', leaving them feeling that their 'real' selves are persistently 'bad'.

Stupid, Lazy and Useless? Nope, Just Dopamine-Challenged

Dopamine, often thought of as the 'pleasure neurotransmitter', is central to motivation. What looks like laziness often stems from dopamine inefficiency. Neurotypical people don't need toys or stimulants to kick-start their motivation because their brains motivate them to act in accordance with what they deem important, but ADHD kids can't will themselves to change, leading to cycles of self-hatred.

Rejection Sensitive Dysphoria

All children perceive their parents' anger as oversized, but ADHD kids experience this more intensely due to rejection sensitive dysphoria (RSD). Even mild criticism can feel like overwhelming rejection. This is why ADHD kids might plead, 'Stop shouting!' when no one is raising their voice. Frustration from family members only amplifies the feeling of being the family disappointment.

How parents talk to, hold and describe their ADHD children in the company of others is the raw data from which they learn whether they are lovable, likeable and of worth. A child who feels like a constant source of distress may seek validation in all the wrong places, leaving them vulnerable to bad influences.

Poor Working Memory

Dopamine inefficiency disrupts working memory, making it impossible for ADHD kids to hold on to tasks. Forgetting isn't laziness; it's biology. Attention happens, or it doesn't.

For me, memory issues have been one of the most painful parts of ADHD. Even with medication, my memory feels like a cluttered table rather than a filing cabinet. Think of short-term memory like RAM – temporary computer memory holding what you're actively using. Long-term memory is more like a hard drive – you can store information there permanently, but it's harder to access.

For neurotypical people, information moves from short-term to long-term memory when deemed important, clearing space for new info. For ADHD people, information may not register in short-term memory at all. Even if it does, it might not get stored in the long-term memory, or might get filed in the wrong place, making retrieval nearly impossible.

Parents: Caught Between a Rock and a Hard Place

Parents of ADHD kids are under immense pressure to respect their child's individuality while ensuring they don't disrupt society. For hyperactive children, stillness can feel physically painful, leaving parents to choose between forcing compliance or risking accusations of poor parenting. Their child is more likely to get into trouble, self-harm or misuse substances. Keeping them safe feels like constant vigilance, but kids don't perceive intentions, only actions. If they hear more criticism than praise – even when 'deserved' by neurotypical standards – they grow up thinking they're unlovable or bad.

ADHD behaviours like impulsivity and recklessness are often mistaken for 'naughtiness', leading to judgement from society. These kids are four times more likely to have accidents, lie, steal or fight, which further fuels the stigma. ADHD parents must manage their child's fragile self-esteem, their own frustrations, and public scepticism that ADHD is even 'real'.

The flavour of stigma depends on the intersection of class, income and race. Upper-middle-class parents may be accused of doping up their kids to boost grades, while working-class parents are accused of sedating theirs for convenience. The judgement is always there, like an unwelcome relative.

ADHD's inattention makes life harder for everyone. According to a NICE report, 91 per cent of parents of ADHD kids feel stressed or worried about their child's life, and over 60 per cent say family activities are disrupted. Siblings might resent that ADHD seems like a free pass. Or maybe they're thrust into the 'grown-up' role, pulling double duty by becoming unofficial caregivers. They may end up running interference, or doing extra chores. Even when they know ADHD is to blame, it's hard to accept when their sibling spends hours hyperfocused on video games.

ADHD involves a 'pronounced attentional bias' – our attention gets pulled towards certain stimuli. Hyperfocus sounds magical but comes with drawbacks. It can feel like 'flow' – both immersive states render time irrelevant – but where flow is creative and expansive, hyperfocus narrows attention at the expense of basic needs like forgetting to pee. Transitioning between tasks becomes a struggle, making everyday activities, like car rides, stressful for everyone.

When families don't understand ADHD, they often mistake the child's wandering attention for a lack of interest. The glassy eyes or distracted chatter seem like signs of disregard when, in reality, it's a dopamine-driven shift in focus.

Siblings are left to watch as the ADHD child swings between overarousal (dopamine chasing) and underarousal (boredom). Without understanding dopamine inefficiency, how ADHD warps attention and behaviour, these mood shifts can be seen as selfishness.

Executive Dysfunction and Emotional Dysregulation

Executive dysfunction means ADHD kids often do less around the house, or need more reminders, leading to family tension. Big emotions flood the working memory, making it impossible for ADHD kids to distinguish relevant from irrelevant details – and leaving siblings to tiptoe around emotional outbursts. One interviewee said, 'I wish I got to have Big Feelings sometimes.'

Good Consistent Habits

Inconsistency is part of the disability. ADHD means that routines inevitably crumble, but for children, it's even harder. A child may navigate their routine smoothly one day; the next, all hell breaks loose. They don't yet understand the causal links between their actions and feelings, so even when they try to stick to a routine, the lack of understanding – and the inconsistency inherent in ADHD – makes it fall apart. As a child, I felt like a cartoon character, constantly running just to stay in place.

Inconsistency leads to struggles with self-care. ADHD kids often experience 'self-neglect' – the opposite of self-care – where basic tasks take longer to master. Explaining why you can't perform these tasks often sounds like making excuses, feeding into cycles of shame. When I was a child, my thick hair became a haven for lice. Everyone at school had them, but I was ashamed. My mother treated my head, but I ignored signs that they were still there. I vividly remember scratching my head in class, getting a little body stuck under my nail, and flicking it away. Weeks later, I was unusually keen to get my hair cut. I'm not sure what my grand plan was – presumably to ask them to shave it off. The hairdresser tied the robe round my neck, took one look and called my mother to complain about bringing in a lice-ridden child. But my mother didn't know. I had been too ashamed to tell her.

ADHD people also struggle with falling and staying asleep. Many have autonomic nerves, a result of an overactive nervous system, and complain about random shifting pains and 'restless legs'. I still kick my feet in my sleep like I'm wearing flippers. This too effects everyone; exercise has to be factored in to make sleep more likely; siblings are kept awake.

Time Blindness: Stress and Misunderstanding

Time feels different for people with ADHD – it's more fluid, harder to grasp, and this disconnection creates friction within families. ADHD children often haven't developed coping mechanisms to manage their altered sense of time, leading to missed appointments and disrupted schedules.

Every full-blown fight I've had with my boyfriend has happened while getting ready for a party. I'd start returning ASOS parcels while he'd get increasingly agitated, hovering. Recognising that if we were in separate rooms before a party we were in different time zones allowed us to laugh about it; a big source of tension was dispersed by simply getting ready in the same room.

All too often ADHD kids find understanding not in their biological families but in chosen families. After playing the roles of scapegoat or unicorn, they can become the black sheep, the ruiner, the fuck-up. ADHD adults face major challenges maintaining stable employment and mental health, often leading to isolation or even homelessness.

Even with an early diagnosis, support dwindles after secondary education. In care systems, where ADHD rates are high, the transition to adult services is messy, with many slipping through the cracks. For those without a strong family network to lean on, educating the existing family becomes critical. It shapes how ADHD people see themselves and how they deserve to be treated by the world. A family's understanding and handling of ADHD can provide grit – or reinforce feelings of shame and inadequacy.

Parents with ADHD: Double the Challenge

Parents diagnosed with ADHD may empathise more with their children's struggles and share helpful tools, but they face a much harder job. ADHD often runs in families – if a parent has ADHD, their child's risk increases threefold. Yet ADHD remains underdiagnosed in adults, especially women, leaving many parents unaware they have it, managing multiple demands with reduced executive function and time blindness, making phases like teething feel endless, worsened by sleep deprivation and stress.

ADHD parents may experience their child's needs as urgent and rejections as personal and devastating, while being told they must stay calm for attunement. They often feel 'touched out', leading to a loss of intimacy in relationships. Hyperfocus on the newborn can leave partners feeling neglected.

If a parent doesn't believe in ADHD, they may repeat harsh discipline patterns from their childhoods. Low emotional regulation increases the likelihood of screaming rows. When children are diagnosed, some parents seek their own diagnosis; others remain in denial. The latter group normalise ADHD behaviours as things that 'everyone does', leaving the condition untreated for years. In such cases, maladaptive coping

strategies – commonly alcohol and substance misuse – are passed
down through generations.

Parenting a child with ADHD is an ultra-marathon. It requires
understanding and patience but brings higher stress, exhaustion
and increased risks of anxiety and depression. Raising a child
with ADHD can also be expensive, thanks to the 'ADHD tax' of
replacing lost items.

Generations of parents have raised ADHD children without
realising they have it themselves, which takes a toll on the whole
family. Many feel guilty for not noticing sooner, uncertain if
ADHD is real or if they caused it, while grappling with public
stigma around medicating children. Confronting this judgement
takes strength. To avoid burnout, ADHD parents need to
practise self-compassion and self-care while balancing many
unpaid roles – collaborators with teachers, advocates in a hostile
media environment, and cheerleaders for small wins.

The Joy ADHD Can Bring

ADHD is like a hard-to-unwrap gift – difficult without privilege
or support, but full of unexpected treasures. Easy things may
bring temporary happiness, but they lack the texture of real joy.
ADHD disrupts routine, offering friction, sparks and moments
of surprise that remind us we're alive.

When was the last time you felt so much that you thought the
roof of your head would blow off? Shouldn't childhood be full of
mystery, discovery, even a touch of anarchy? Do we really want
childhood to become sanitised, time-bound, screen-bound? Or do
we want it, at least sometimes, to be messy and playful and free?

ADHD kids may be creative and spontaneous, but it's often the
challenging parts that teach families deep-rooted joy. Emotional
outbursts clear simmering resentment. Life may have given us
lemons, but neurotypicals can learn a lot from watching us make
lemonade. ADHD guarantees a rate of failure which necessitates
living with a sense of humour and giving yourself grace. We are
far more resilient than neurotypical people. We have to be. For
family members participating in the process of unwrapping the
gift, of learning grit, self-compassion and a healthy appreciation

of the absurd, these things are bonus skills. But beyond managing differences, ADHD teaches families empathy.

Families as Proto-Societies: Cultivating Empathy

Families aren't necessarily about shared genetic material any more. They're proto societies, in which parents model how to treat people. ADHD in the family pushes everyone to respect diverse thinking styles, supporting children who aren't yet fully responsible for the impact of their actions.

Language Lessons: Speak Their Colourful Dialect

People with ADHD often get weird with language, twisting it and spraying it neon to reflect their internal experience. Telling someone with ADHD to 'focus' is as unhelpful as telling a depressed person to 'be more positive' or asking a dyslexic to spell better or demanding that a colour-blind person do better at identifying green. Instead, ask your child how they feel. You may realise your own language needs a lick of paint.

Active Listening: Simple Acknowledgements Matter

Talking to someone with ADHD means talking consciously. It's how we tend to recognise each other in the wild: sudden swerves, tangents, audible parentheses. ADHD conversations are shot through with distraction and often veer into oversharing and attempts to re-knit lost context. These tics worsen if we feel judged. The ADHD person risks getting stranded on a very lonely tangent, but that doesn't mean we aren't listening – it just means we have a different style.

Conversations with ADHD kids invite associative listening – interruptions and tangents don't mean we aren't listening but reflect a different conversational style, one full of animated marginalia, like a conversation overlaid with marching bands and radios. Talking with ADHD kids teaches others to be attentive and empathetic listeners. 'I missed that – can you go back?' shows genuine interest and invites ADHD kids to keep engaging without feeling judged. Active listening and gentle nudges create a safe space where they feel heard.

Many ADHD people try to listen actively, something you can't always assume from glazed-over neurotypical listeners. When my boyfriend tells me about his day and I interrupt with something random, he kindly repeats himself after my tangent. It's not a reprimand, just a gentle nudge. He knows I want to hear him – he assumes good intentions, which makes all the difference.

Creative Parenting Hacks: Turning Chaos into Connection

For ADHD kids, standard parenting hacks often need a twist. Here's how some parents turn everyday routines into fun challenges:

- » Reframe chores as quests: tidy the living room? No, you're reclaiming the 'Mysterious Land of Lost Socks'.
- » The Countdown Dance: use a timer when leaving the house, and do a silly dance every time it beeps.
- » The Timer Game: challenge your child to clean a room before the timer goes off – it feels like a race, even if the room takes longer.
- » Reverse Psychology Bedtime: tell your child, 'I bet you can't fall asleep in less than ten minutes.' Works wonders with competitive kids.
- » Hula Hoop Focus Zones: place a hula hoop around your child's desk. Anything outside the hoop doesn't exist – creates a 'focus bubble'.

Knowing the one-size-fits-all approach won't work, often out of sheer desperation, parents are forced to get to know their kids as they are and meet them where they're at.

The Five Cs of ADHD Parenting

Psychologist Dr Sharon Saline's 'Five Cs' – self-Control, Consistency, Compassion, Collaboration and Celebration – are parenting essentials for ADHD families.

The most important thing is ensuring the ADHD child isn't ashamed of who they are. In both the 'scapegoat' and 'unicorn' models, the ADHD child becomes isolated within the family system – problems are pinned on them, and solutions focus on them alone.

A whole-family approach, on the other hand, works because what helps ADHD children thrive also benefits neurotypical ones. ADHD kids may require extra effort, but that work enriches everyone. Parents just need to be a little extra: extra curious, extra flexible, extra compassionate.

Embracing the Chaos: Turning Challenges into Opportunities

ADHD is like a carnival breaking out at a tea party. Between wild outbursts, bright lights and escaped tigers, things will get messy. ADHD forces the emergence of a positive framework. Fortunately, while ADHD kids are sensitive to negativity, they're equally responsive to positive changes. Here are a few suggestions to help families nudge ADHD kids towards a happier life:

Educate the family. Understanding ADHD reduces frustration and reminds everyone that difficult behaviours aren't personal. Don't just read – listen to your child's unique experience.

Check yourself. What looks like attention-seeking is often anxiety or compensating for an underaroused nervous system. Just be there.

Define justice. Fairness isn't about equal treatment, it's about meeting each person's unique needs. The ADHD child may require more attention, but remind siblings that love is neither conditional nor finite.

Create flexible habits. Structure is vital for ADHD kids, but so is flexibility. Building positive habits starts in childhood. Still, inconsistency is the disability. Habits will follow a boom–bust cycle, so when things fall apart, empathy goes a long way.

Be realistic. Plan for inevitable forgetfulness. Help your child ADHD-proof their lives in terms of minimising the effects, rather than denying their neurotype. Buy bright phone covers, keep spare chargers, and use apps like 'Find My Phone' without shame. Have a charger, a snack and medication in every port.

Redefine strength. Teach your child that asking for help is a strength, not a weakness. Encourage them to play to their strengths.

Teach reframes. Help your child understand that challenges are things to manage, not signs of personal failure. Celebrate their strengths rather than dwelling on weaknesses. Pobody's nerfect.

Validate low executive function. If your child hasn't started their homework after being asked five times, ask why. They might genuinely not know how to begin. Encourage small steps, like doing just five minutes to get started.

Adopt a growth mindset. Focus on effort, not outcomes. ADHD kids experience more failure, so building resilience and grit is key.

Redirect Rejection Sensitivity Dysphoria (RSD). Help your child navigate emotional rejection by distracting them with something positive – a hug, a funny video, a change in scenery.

Handling hyperfocus. Breaking someone out of hyperfocus is like throwing ice water on a sleeping person. Teach family members to approach it gently and understand that hyperfocus isn't always deliberate or pleasant. Siblings should be armed with helpful mantras to remind ADHD kids, like, 'I feel like this now, but I won't feel like this for ever.'

Give them a head-start. Since ADHD kids develop more slowly, help them practise essential skills early. Set up a credit card to build credit and teach them simple tasks, like cooking one-pan meals, so they can manage low-executive function days in a low-pressure environment.

Teach self-trust. Children who often 'flake' on plans lose self-trust. Encourage them to set small, realistic goals to build confidence and reliability. Help them see that self-trust comes from steady, consistent effort and small successes, not grand gestures or perfection.

Rig your reward systems. Gamify everything! Building personalised reward systems which continue to give a dopamine payoff is an art. Take advantage of your child's neuroplasticity by changing the rewards so that they don't get bored. Soon after moving in with me, my boyfriend said, somewhat grumpily, 'You can't have a reward for everything.' But, guess what? I do. Why not? It works for me. I rig the whole system. And I think you should too.

Be on their side. ADHD children will hear 75,000 more negative comments than their neurotypical peers, so they need to know their family has their back. Choose your battles. If you do need to criticise, be constructive and specific. This is particularly important for ADHD teenagers who are far more likely to engage in impulsive risky behaviours; if they get in trouble, you want them to feel safe coming to you.

ADHD Tools for All Parents: Integrate, Don't Just Contain

Like all kids, ADHD kids need homes where technology isn't central, perfection isn't worshipped or expected, and play is a priority. Families that truly integrate (rather than simply contain) people with ADHD will prioritise habits that benefit everyone. Intuitive eating and movement as a family can help. While 'pills don't teach skills', the skills families learn are transferable. For example, taking a non-reactive stance in the moment when someone is yelling, then discussing things later is always a good idea.

Tools designed for parents of ADHD kids help all parents. These could include: adapting to structureless summer holidays by picking a theme; praising kids within earshot of others so that they hear positive conversation about themselves; recruiting your child's attention before you talk to them by establishing eye-contact rather than yelling between rooms.

Modelling Self-Care: Breaking Shame Cycles

Children who don't learn how to stop judging themselves will become adults like me who can't admit to a dentist that it's been five years, or to a doctor that they scratched an infection, or to a landlord that they ignored a flying-ant infestation, or to their friend that they've been unable to force themselves to sweep up the hundreds of brittle flying-ant carcasses. But the truth is, nobody wants to sit in a flying-ant graveyard. This is the kind of shame that shrinks you. It stops people asking for help.

No parent is perfect. On the twentieth thing that goes wrong in a day, even the calmest parent might lose their cool. To support their ADHD child, parents must help themselves first. Self-care isn't selfish – it makes you more present as a parent. In self-parenting it's important to be consistent with boundaries, but it's also important to cut yourself some slack.

What's better than your child seeing you learn? Parents can practise tools alongside their children: naming big emotions, recognising warning signs like a racing heart, using calming techniques like deep breathing, exercising and journalling. When you have a full-blown argument, sit with your child afterwards and help them reframe self-judgement like 'I ruin everything' into 'I'm learning to express my feelings better'. You might not be the one to break the cycle, but with your help, maybe they will be.

A Space for Discovery

When Dolly Parton said, 'Find out who you are and do it on purpose,' she could easily have been talking to ADHD kids. The job of the family is to create a space where that act of discovery is both safe and possible. Without shifting focus away from neurotypical expectations, family life will become a constant telling off and daily wrangling of cats. ADHD children take different routes, but they get there in the end.

ADHD forces families to work harder, think weirder and get

creative in ways that benefit everyone. Managed well, ADHD can be a good thing for the family as a whole. Having a child with ADHD is an opportunity – an urgent one, perhaps – to build a family that not only tolerates but thrives on difference and which only worries about things that *actually* matter. Sure, there's chaos, but the effort put into fostering understanding can strengthen the family and teach resilience.

Confronting Family Truths

ADHD forces families to confront the truth about their home life. Children with two or more ACEs (adverse childhood experiences) are twice as likely to be diagnosed with ADHD. ACEs include abuse, substance misuse, mental illness, incarceration, domestic violence or losing a parent. The strongest link is between a parent's mental illness and a child with ADHD. While the focus here is on ADHD's effect on family life, recognising these correlations often pushes families to assess their environment honestly.

Feeling unsafe or financially insecure shatters attention. Hypervigilance, which might be a necessary survival tool in some situations, can mimic ADHD. There may be other explanations for a child constantly jumping up, or being unable to finish a sentence. For a family dealing with ACEs, the explanation of ADHD may seem neater, but if ADHD-like symptoms are danger flares, or pleas for help, diagnosis and medication won't work. It's essential to assess the whole picture. Instead of clinging to outdated family ideals, we must accept and work with the families we have. Radical honesty can turn every family situation into an opportunity for a new beginning.

LOVING

Maintaining friendships with ADHD can easily lead to a shame spiral.

THE SHAME SPIRAL

» Struggling to balance between obsessively messaging friends (What's the plan? When am I seeing you next!) and 'out of sight, out of mind' tendencies.
» Procrastinating on replying to messages or forgetting entirely, leading to a cycle of overwhelm and avoidance.
» Hiding from the phone, going into a shame spiral, and feeling stuck in a loop of guilt and inaction.
» Making plans but getting distracted mid-process or forgetting to follow through.
» Rapidly shifting interests that sometimes cause drifting apart from friends.
» With friends, navigating social anxiety, poor time management, inconsistent communication and rejection sensitive dysphoria (leading to fears they secretly hate you).

ADHD Bingo square card

NB: Frazzled NTs might do some of these things sometimes too.

Rearranged the entire room instead of doing the thing I was supposed to	Left my phone in the fridge	Bought all the stuff I needed for a new craft and never did it	Lost my keys while holding them
Went to get something, forgot what it was, left with snacks	Replied to a message in my head (and hit send ... never)	Slept in yesterday's clothes (hey, it happens)	Set five alarms and slept through all of them
Got distracted while taking a shower and forgot to rinse out the conditioner	Set up a complex organisation system I will never actually use	Found fifteen tabs open for the same topic on my browser	Fell into a YouTube rabbit hole and ended up watching 'how pencils are made' videos
Realised I was wearing two different shoes halfway through the day	Bought a planner, used it for two days, and now it's somewhere under my bed	Had to re-read the same paragraph five times	Watched a stranger's eyes glaze over as I told them about my best new subject

Chapter 6

The Neurodivergent Alliance: Autism and ADHD

Double Diagnosis: AuADHD

ADHD and autism share significant overlap in traits and diagnoses. Until 2013 the *DSM* didn't allow dual diagnoses, even though many people showed traits of both – then finally, the *DSM-V* update recognised AuADHD. The numbers at a glance:

> Roughly 3 to 4 per cent of the general population has ADHD.
> But, within the autistic community, 40 per cent to 70 per cent also meet ADHD criteria.
> Similarly, 20 per cent to 50 per cent of those with ADHD meet the criteria for autism.

But this overlap isn't just statistical, it gestures towards the underlying relation between the two conditions.

Shared Biology: The Deeper Connection

ADHD and autism might seem like cousins at the family reunion, sitting at opposite ends of the table, but they share the same genetic secret handshake. Both have genetic markers influencing focus and behaviour, along with neurotransmitter glitches in dopamine and serotonin affecting mood and attention. Brain structure tweaks – especially in the prefrontal cortex and basal ganglia – play havoc with executive function and social processing. Then there's the gut–brain connection, where messed-up gut flora tinkers with brain development and stirs up neuro-inflammation. Even their retinas are in on it, with altered visual processing suggesting unique neurological twists. These biological connections haven't made recognition easier, and misdiagnoses and stigma have only added to the challenges faced by both groups.

Misdiagnosis, Marginalisation and Advocacy

ADHD and autism have long been dismissed as childhood quirks to be ironed out through discipline, leading to misdiagnoses, mistreatment and even institutionalisation. These systemic failures paved the way for a modern fight – not to 'fix' neurodivergence but to gain recognition and support. Together, ADHD and autism are part of a broader narrative defined by stigma and, ultimately, revolution.

Autism's Fraught Legacy

This wild thing happened in the 1940s: Leo Kanner, an Austrian American psychiatrist, labelled autism 'a rare form of childhood psychosis'. He believed it was something children might grow out of, effectively ignoring its lifelong impact and leaving countless autistic adults to slip through the cracks.

Meanwhile, across the Atlantic in Nazi-occupied Vienna, Hans Asperger was taking a completely different approach. He described autism in terms of a range of behaviours and focused on children's strengths. But here's where it gets dark: Asperger's legacy is deeply tainted by his Nazi-era affiliations. In a 1938 speech to an audience of Hitler super-fans, Asperger claimed, 'Not everything that steps out of line or is unusual is inferior,' which sounds noble – until you realise he selectively showcased so-called 'promising' children to align with Nazi ideals of racial purity. His advocacy for gifted children also introduced harmful 'high-functioning' and low-functioning' labels which endure today, though many autistic people reject them as oversimplifying the context-dependent nature of their support needs.

The recognition of autism as a spectrum wasn't immediate. In 1994, the *DSM-IV* officially included 'Asperger's Syndrome', reflecting British psychiatrist Lorna Wing's work to expand the definition of autism into something broader and more 'elastic'. In 2013, the *DSM-V* folded Asperger's into autism spectrum disorder aiming to remove hierarchies but simultaneously sparking debate over the loss of a label that had brought clarity and community for some. Historians like Steve Silberman (*NeuroTribes*) and Edith Sheffer (*Asperger's Children*) have unpacked Asperger's morally complicated role, suggesting that he saved the children he could while working within a regime that devalued many lives. However, after those books were published, documents surfaced showing Asperger directly referred children to euthanasia programs where they were killed.

Under Nazi rule, human worth was tied to economic output, with disabled people dehumanised as 'life unworthy of life'. Children with autism, epilepsy and most likely ADHD became test subjects for mass extermination. The eugenic obsession with productivity didn't die with the Nazis. It persists in capitalist frameworks that devalue disabled lives, with modern stereotypes about ADHD people as 'lazy' or 'unmotivated' reflecting the same harmful fixation on worth as conformity to arbitrary standards. The mindset that worth must be 'earned' still informs how society views neurodivergent people. Advocacy must not only fight these perceptions but dismantle them entirely – neurodivergent people have worth simply because they exist.

My boyfriend often asks, 'How relevant can the Nazis be?' when I bring them up in my writing. But the rise of populism and the power of propaganda in today's attention economy make their relevance disturbingly clear. If Holocaust education is meant to prevent systemic violence, the erasure of disabled people's suffering – past and present – must be addressed.

Media and Culture Wars: Shaping Neurodivergent Identities

Public perception of ADHD and autism has been defined by distorted media narratives. Big Tech screams, 'Not today, Satan!' at ADHD and autism, echoing old-school eugenics by framing us as evolutionary backslides. Until relatively recently, doctors weren't much better – making parents feel hopeless by likening the condition to 'terminal illnesses' and comparing autistic children to 'animals'. The media didn't miss a beat, doubling down with grim metaphors. In 1989, Asperger's Syndrome was first described in an English-speaking newspaper, the *Toronto Star*, which compared autistic people to 'stroke victims', while the *Sydney Morning Herald* declared autism 'the plague of those unable to feel'.

When parents are blamed, children's behaviour becomes something to eradicate, often through harsh methods. As autism became seen as a neurodevelopmental condition, rather than a parental failing, empathy increased. Autism had a head start; ADHD still lags behind. Then, in the 1990s, the neurodiversity movement flipped its hair and declared that being 'wired differently' wasn't a glitch to be fixed but a language to be learned. Of course, no revelation comes without drama. In 1987 expanded diagnostic criteria had whipped up panic about an 'autism epidemic': a dress rehearsal for the full ADHD freak-out when it got its spotlight in the *DSM-III*. (Expanded diagnostic criteria for both autism and ADHD have a shared history of triggering moral panics, casting them as modern scourges despite their longstanding existence.)

The rise in diagnoses divided opinion. Some celebrated increased awareness, with films like *Rain Man* bringing adult autism into the mainstream. Others blamed external factors like lead exposure or environmental toxins. And, of course, we can't ignore the vaccine controversy. Though the *Lancet* paper linking

vaccines to autism was retracted and its author exposed as a
fraud, the conspiracy stuck.

But the rise in diagnoses wasn't due to some sinister force,
rather heightened awareness. Yet we need more advocates to
push for a world that adapts to neurodivergence, rather than
fixating on finding causes or cures.

Complex Identities: Beyond Binary Perspectives

ADHD debates are full of divisive questions: superpower or
disability? Genetic or environmental? Medication or natural
treatments? Self-diagnosis or gatekeeping? Disorder or identity?
We can fight like alley cats, but it's a fool's game. Each
neurodivergent person exists within a unique context, and
what works for one may not work for another. Getting stuck in
binaries doesn't serve our community. Still, I've spent a lot of time
mulling these questions. I can't speak for everyone, but ADHD
colours everything in my life – although it's not my identity. But
for some it is, reshaping emotions, decisions, perceptions and
community. Embracing it moves us from deficit to diversity.

Labels can feel like clutter – they create a false simplicity,
when life is anything but. As someone who lives at several
intersections – I'm mixed race, bisexual and multiply
neurodivergent – this is the first time I'm declaring these things so
directly. I shy away from singular identities. None of those labels
defines me. They're just stories that help me understand myself,
but I change, often, and in a world obsessed with identities,
I reserve the right to evolve. Also, in a world of hashtags and
curated personas, strongly identifying with one label can reduce a
person to a brand. Conversationally, labels kill vibes.

Depending on the season, I pass as vaguely exotic white. But
my heritage as half-Indian, with grandparents who fled Lahore
during Partition, is in my family's DNA. It altered how I was
raised. My ADHD is likely more visible, but identity isn't just
about how others see you – it's how you see yourself. Labels, no
matter how loudly announced, can't control how they're received.

I didn't realise how much internalised stigma kept me quiet
about ADHD. Talking about it showed me how helpful it could

be for others – even friends who've known me for years had no idea. But why would they know what it's like to live inside my head? Have you ever looked deeply into a friend's eyes and described how you personally experience time?

ADHD is the most common neurodivergent comorbidity in the UK, yet neurotypicals and neurodivergents talk about it differently. That's why neurodivergent advocacy must be collective, addressing challenges in education, legal systems and work accommodations.

Bonded in Overlap: Neurodivergent Kinship

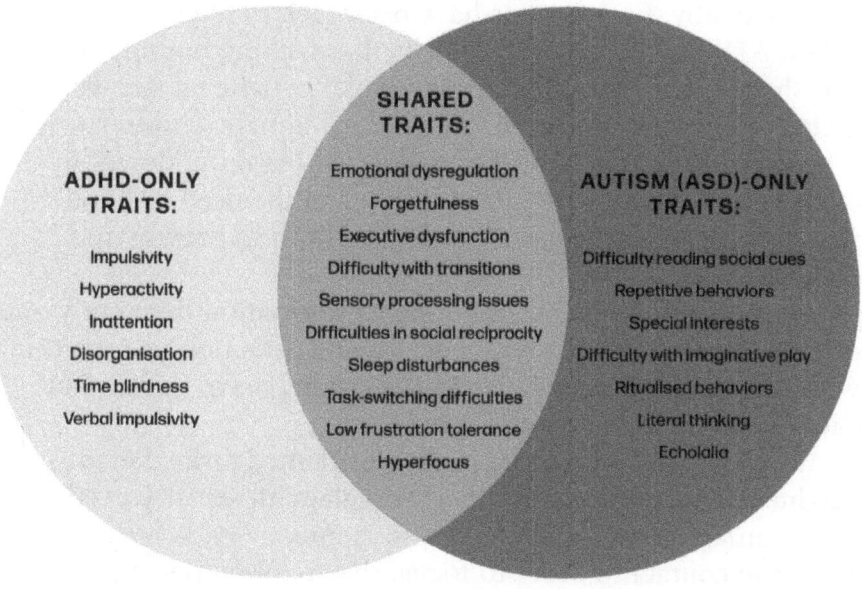

ADHD-ONLY TRAITS:

Impulsivity
Hyperactivity
Inattention
Disorganisation
Time blindness
Verbal impulsivity

SHARED TRAITS:

Emotional dysregulation
Forgetfulness
Executive dysfunction
Difficulty with transitions
Sensory processing issues
Difficulties in social reciprocity
Sleep disturbances
Task-switching difficulties
Low frustration tolerance
Hyperfocus

AUTISM (ASD)-ONLY TRAITS:

Difficulty reading social cues
Repetitive behaviors
Special interests
Difficulty with imaginative play
Ritualised behaviors
Literal thinking
Echolalia

ADHD and autism share enough traits for instant recognition, like catching someone else's frequency at a party, pulling you away from the big light and small talk. We struggle with similar mismatches in neurotypical spaces. Autistic people might fumble social cues; ADHD folks often miss them completely. But we both vibrate in a world that's too loud and too fast, and there's comfort in the overlap.

We often feel like our 'insides don't match our outsides' and struggle to translate our inner worlds for others. I've unintentionally dated more neurodivergent people than neurotypicals – maybe because of the complementary strengths. There's electricity in the ADHD-autism match.

Autistic people aren't antisocial; they just engage differently. When ADHD people are together, nobody – or everybody – is disruptive. Tangents aren't tangents – they're just angles in a conversation.

Autistic people thrive on routine, appealing to ADHD's love–hate relationship with structure. Their deep, specialised interests match ADHD's ability to hyperfocus. I'm hypersensitive and emotional – which is culturally frowned upon – but talking to an autistic person is relaxing because I always know where I stand.

Historically, both groups have been seen as having strange edges. ADHD people were described as lacking boundaries – oversharing with 'no filter'. Meanwhile, autistic people were seen as 'shells': unreachable. Mothers of autistic children said, 'I can see her in there,' as if a wall needs breaking down. By contrast, mothers of ADHD children feel the need to build walls around their oversensitive kids – both to protect and contain them.

Neurodivergent people often filter information differently out of necessity. I am obsessive – but if I paid attention to everything with the same intensity I give to the bright, sharp things that catch my eye, I don't think I'd survive.

Autistic people may excel in detail-oriented tasks due to heightened perception but often struggle with sensory overload. Neuro-imaging shows altered brain connectivity. While they may avoid eye contact in order to focus, they're often paying closer attention than the neurotypical person grinning into your face.

Neurotypical people smile to make others comfortable, and say things like, 'Uh-huh,' to show they're listening. In neurodivergent conversations, you lose this validation in favour of substance. If we're still talking, we're truly engaged. And let's kill the myth: autistic people are funny. Their dry, deadpan humour is often missed because it lacks sarcasm or irony – both of which involve 'not saying what you mean'.

Redefining Neurodivergence

The shift from seeing neurodivergence as pathology to recognising it as human diversity has been monumental. Early autism advocacy focused on 'cures', treating autistic children as burdens to be normalised, not understood. This push for conformity suppressed natural behaviours and reinforced the idea that neurodivergent people needed to be 'fixed'. This may be why the autistic community developed a new language around neurodiversity more quickly.

Redefining 'neurodiversity' meant coining terms like 'neurotypical' (thanks to pioneering advocates like Neurodivergent K and sociologist Judy Singer in 1998) to challenge the idea that the majority defines 'normal'. It amuses me when neurotypical people bristle at being called 'neurotypical'. One friend thought I was calling her 'neurologically basic'. But there's no hierarchy here – in a neurodiverse world, we are simply different, not lesser. The eugenics-stained language falls away.

A stranger online told me that using terms like 'disorder' and taking medication meant I was using 'the master's tools'. I appreciated the Audre Lorde reference but, for me, medication is about agency. Without it, I couldn't pay my rent. ADHD medication doesn't endorse the pathology model – it helps me manage symptoms and improves my quality of life. For many, medications support rather than negate identity, allowing us to balance ADHD challenges and even enjoy the strengths.

ADHD makes life difficult, but difficulty doesn't mean broken. Life is hard – most worthwhile things are. Rejecting the pathology model isn't about rejecting treatment; it's about advocating for a world that accommodates all cognitive styles, not just 'normal'.

Advocacy Lessons From Autism: Cross-Pollinating Insights

The autistic community's history of advocacy can serve as a playbook for ADHD. Decades of grassroots organisation have shown that effective advocacy depends on self-representation.

Yet, despite its influence, US organisation Autism Speaks often
fails the community it claims to represent. By framing autism
as a condition to be cured, it diverts resources away from
supporting autistic people in their lives, focusing instead on
'eradicating' autism.

A key example of this tension lies in applied behaviour
analysis (ABA), a therapy rooted in B. F. Skinner's behaviourism.
You might remember Skinner from the attention economy
chapter – it's no coincidence that his ideas underpinned ABA,
a system originally designed to programme behaviour in
animals. Developed in the 1960s by clinical psychologist Ole
Ivar Løvaas, ABA aimed to suppress autistic traits by enforcing
'normal' behaviours through harsh methods. Løvaas broke down
complex tasks like tooth-brushing into simple actions drilled
into the brain through repetition, resorting to hitting, starving
and electro-shocking children. One institution in America – the
Judge Rotenberg Educational Center in Massachusetts – still uses
electric shocks in ABA therapy.

The goal of Løvaas's ABA was to reduce stigma by making
autistic children less 'embarrassing' for parents and more
'comfortable' for others. But many advocates, like Amy
Sequenzia, have spoken out against ABA's focus on forcing
autistic children to pass as neurotypical. Sequenzia, who
'flunked' ABA, said, 'The "experts'" explanation for failing to
make me a "tidy", "appropriate", "good girl", obedient and
compliant Autistic was my severe impairment, low IQ, my
inability to learn, or, as Løvaas might have said (and something
a doctor actually said), my lack of human dignity.'

While modern ABA has evolved, with some programmes
focusing on independent living skills rather than erasing
autistic traits, the debate remains fierce. Some parents say ABA
helped their children communicate and navigate life without
harming themselves, while others argue it forces children to
perform neurotypicality at the expense of their wellbeing.
Tiffany Hammond, an American autistic writer and activist,
critiques this binary view, arguing that some anti-ABA voices
reduce autism to a 'quirk' by dismissing the genuine challenges
faced by people like her son. Though she eventually pulled him

from ABA, Hammond believes nuanced advocacy is needed – particularly for young Black men, who face additional risks in a 'compliance-based society'.

The backlash against ABA reminds us: advocacy isn't just about what we fight against but what we fight for. Debates around ABA echo those in ADHD treatments, where rigid behavioural programmes can prioritise enforcing neurotypical norms over adapting environments to neurodivergent needs. Both highlight a bigger issue: should therapy focus on 'fixing' individuals or dismantling the structures that marginalise them? ADHD campaigns can take a cue, advocating for supportive structures that honour our differences rather than erasing them.

Neurodivergent advocacy doesn't exist in silos. Epilepsy, like ADHD, is a common comorbidity for autism, affecting nearly a third of autistic people. ADHD advocacy could be where neurodivergence intersects, providing a foundation for collective action, which has historically advanced progress. Advocacy for one group benefits the whole.

Neurodivergence and Climate Activism: A Collective Strength

One of the hardest parts of being neurodivergent is the ambient confusion – being baffled by things that neurotypicals either don't notice or dismiss but which tie us in knots. It's uncomfortable, but that discomfort can be a compass. If we channel it, ask why something feels off and trace its root, we often uncover assumptions worth questioning. This ability to see what others overlook is a rare strength, one that neurodivergent people have brought to global issues like climate change. Greta Thunberg's autism, OCD and selective mutism fuel her activism. Where others detached, she couldn't let go of plastic-choked oceans. She couldn't just conform to the defeatist logic of 'this is just how things are'.

Chris Packham, another autistic activist, says many fellow campaigners share traits of autism, 'with an aggravated sense of injustice and a deep desire to tell the absolute truth'. In a world of detachment and distraction, neurodivergent people's ability to fixate and continue feeling that urgency and still function is key to driving societal change.

Thunberg exemplifies this – her empathy sharpens into focus. She doesn't numb out or give up. Where neurotypicals might see despair, she sees purpose. Her literal thinking cuts through the noise, rejecting the euphemisms of 'sustainable growth' to demand real, systemic change. Neurodivergent traits like literal thinking, pattern recognition and a relentless ability to pursue solutions – even in the face of overwhelming odds – make activists like Thunberg invaluable. She credits her way of thinking to her diagnosis: 'If the emissions have to stop, then we must stop the emissions. To me that is black or white. There are no grey areas when it comes to survival.'

At the same time, these traits highlight the vulnerabilities neurodivergent people face, particularly with the mental health challenges that climate anxiety exacerbates. For people like Thunberg, activism isn't a choice – it's essential for maintaining mental health during crises. As Packham and others note, our allergy to injustice, which often makes traditional systems like school or work unbearable, equips us with the audacity to challenge the status quo, reframing what's possible for the planet. Neurodivergence doesn't just push us to demand change; it insists that change is non-negotiable.

What Society Needs to Unlearn

Autistic advocates have spent decades reframing neurodivergence, shifting public understanding with nuance and depth. ADHD, by contrast, is still fighting to move beyond clichés of laziness and chaos, to show how our minds truly think, create and flourish.

As more ADHD people and autistic people recognise our similarities, our collective challenge to narrow definitions of 'normal' gains momentum. But advocacy is about more than individual narratives; it's about challenging the systems that enforce narrow definitions of productivity, intelligence and worth. When society demands that neurodivergent people adapt to a world not built for us, it reveals the cracks in its foundations. Advocacy must reframe the narrative: not what neurodivergence needs to fix, but what society needs to unlearn.

What neurotypicals call 'confusing' is often logical in our world. My style of talking has been called childish, intense, emotional, and confusing – but only by those who think they're in charge. To people like me, I make perfect sense. And isn't that the real challenge? Not just to make sense to ourselves, but to show the world that maybe their version of 'normal' was never quite enough.

RECOGNISING EACH OTHER

* VERY LONG, INTRICATE EXPLANATION OF SOMETHING I'VE BEEN RESEARCHING AND HAVE DEVELOPED A PROFOUND INTEREST IN BUT IN QUITE A TANGENTIAL WAY*

DOES THAT MAKE SENSE?

YES, IT MAKES NO SENSE...

... AND FOR THAT REASON IT IS **PERFECT.**

NOW, I HAVE SEVERAL THOUSAND THOUGHTS...

How Neurodivergent People Recognise Each Other

» Frequent self-interruption or abruptly changing topics mid-sentence.
» Overexplaining or info-dumping on favourite topics.
» Rapid switching between high and low energy levels.
» Struggling to regulate speaking volume or pace.
» Unusual eye contact – avoiding it entirely or making it overly intense.
» Fidgeting, stimming or unintentionally making noises (e.g. humming, whispering aloud).
» Sensory friendly clothing, uniform dressing (wearing the same thing every day), or a tendency towards quirky personal style ('we all dress like big kids').
» Frequent apologies for minor social mistakes or self-perceived awkwardness.
» Self-checking ('Does that make sense?' or 'Am I boring you?').
» Frequent accidental oversharing of vulnerability during casual conversations.
» Expressive body language, or exaggerated facial expressions.

How NTs and NDs Can Actually Help Each Other

» **Listen like you mean it:** You don't have to fully 'get it' to validate someone's experience.
» **Ask clarifying questions:** Neurotypicals often find the volume of clarifying questions from NDs perplexing, but our sense of clarity is more detailed. If you're thrown by our eerie specificity, show genuine interest by asking simple, direct questions like, 'What do you mean by that?' or 'How does that feel for you?'
» **Address the gaps:** Clashes often happen when either side assumes shared knowledge or experience that isn't there. Requests for clarity should always be met with reassurance – they're an attempt to build understanding, not a critique.

- » **Adjust your pace:** Both neurotypes benefit from intentional communication. Tangential loops don't have to be awkward – people process information differently. Pauses create space for reflection and alignment.
- » **Ditch the need to agree:** Mutual respect hits harder than consensus. Understanding grows from shared curiosity, not matching opinions.

Memory Game

The next chapter is an extremely detailed tangent, so if you feel yourself checking out, pause and try this mini-exercise:

Close your eyes and remember three items within reach. Open your eyes – can you name them? Move one item slightly to signal you're ready to continue.

This simple trick briefly anchors your attention, interrupting anxious spirals or sensory overload. For ADHD readers especially, it's a dopamine-friendly nudge towards intentional calm.

Chapter 7

Cultural Mythology: Amphetamines and the American Dream

In the UK, ADHD medication isn't something you hear about every day. Unlike the US, where drugs like Adderall fuel college all-nighters and propel careers, the British approach is more restrained, guarded by the cautious machinery of the NHS. Yet much of our ADHD discourse is imported from the States, where Big Pharma profits from healthcare. To untangle the messy cultural myths around ADHD that have crossed the Atlantic, we need to understand the American experience.

Full disclosure: neurotypical amphetamine use has absolutely nothing to do with ADHD, but the history behind it explains our cultural obsession. The association between amphetamines and ADHD persists in the US and, thanks to our shared cultural feedbag, the UK because of how neurotypicals misuse amphetamines. Recognising this distinction – between ADHD and amphetamines – helps reduce the stigma that blocks access to treatment. I geeked out hard, so if you'd rather absorb your history as soundscape, or if you just fancy some music, try this:

Side-quest: Scan the QR code and listen out for the amphetamine-charged lyric in each song. These tracks capture how amphetamines have shaped cultural narratives – glamorised, satirised and criticised across decades. From fuelling hustle culture to embodying rebellion and excess, these lyrics reflect society's complicated relationship with productivity, escape and control.

To see how amphetamines got tangled with the American Dream, let's rewind to their earliest promise of 'pep', and how that shaped an entire culture.

The Pep in America's Step

Since the 1930s, amphetamines have been part of American life, first as mood-lifters and later as antidepressants. Their promise of 'pep' aligned with American cultural values, those in which productivity defines worth. They fuel the ragged pursuit of the 'American Dream', the belief that hard work is a moral virtue and guarantees success – even though only half of Americans born in 1980 earn as much as their parents. Amphetamines sustain the illusion: no matter your background, work unholy hours wired on stimulants and ceilings will become floors.

Who doesn't want more pep? Post-war consumerism turned amphetamines into pastel-coloured symbols of progress, sold as solutions to everything from mild depression to weight loss. Doctors medicalised societal pressures, shifting responsibility onto individuals rather than questioning the systems that created those struggles. The result was a blurring of personal failure and systemic flaws, as amphetamines slotted neatly into the demands of soldiers, students, truck drivers and dieters alike.

When I taught at Columbia University I banned 'the American Dream' as an essay topic – too many earnest, irony-free takes. My students' fixation introduced me to the cultural mythology linking productivity, success and amphetamines. It wasn't surprising that Nathan, a bright student, struggled with Adderall addiction, though I didn't know it then. On American campuses, neurotypical amphetamine misuse is normalised. 'Everyone did it around mid-terms and finals,' Nathan told me; athletes used cranberry juice to beat drug tests.

Each generation repurposes amphetamines, revealing its priorities. ADHD medications like Adderall, Dexedrine and Vyvanse share their core – amphetamine, a central nervous stimulant – with illegal drugs like meth, complicating public perception of ADHD. Meanwhile, Ritalin, the UK's most prescribed ADHD medication, isn't an amphetamine at all.

Next, let's explore how these same stimulants turned into the medical mainstay for ADHD and the fierce controversies that followed.

Amphetamines as ADHD Medication

The argument that amphetamines shouldn't treat ADHD because they are misused is flawed; the backlash against ADHD has always been about amphetamine misuse among neurotypicals.

There's now scientific consensus on why amphetamines help with ADHD symptoms, though not on why responses vary or the long-term effects. They boost dopamine and norardrenaline – neurotransmitters ADHD brains often lack in the prefrontal cortex, key for focus and impulse control. Amphetamines block reuptake, promote release and slow breakdown, while Ritalin focuses on blocking reuptake. For ADHD brains, this reduces distractibility and hyperfocus – both modes of dopamine-seeking – and allows for a more controlled, shallow focus. Essentially, they help us 'look before we leap', calming hyperactivity and improving attention. For neurotypicals, amphetamines can feel like speeding up because their baseline dopamine levels aren't low to begin with.

I've been prescribed Ritalin, Concerta and Dexedrine in the UK; in New York, it was Adderall, rarely prescribed here. In the US, where private healthcare dominates, Adderall is readily accessible, if you can pay. This contrast says more about different cultural priorities than about ADHD.

Amid media fear-mongering, let's clear the decks: ADHD medications work for about 80 per cent of those diagnosed. Many choose not to take them, or use them selectively. Used under medical supervision, these meds don't lead to addiction. In fact, untreated ADHD increases the risk of substance misuse. Crucially, people with ADHD generally don't need escalating doses – my dosage has remained the same for nearly twenty years. The UK's recent medication shortage, beginning in September 2023, mirrors a crisis I saw unfold in the US. The NHS attributed it to 'manufacturing issues and increased global demand,' but the reality felt more complicated. ADHD diagnoses have risen, supply hasn't kept up, and manufacturers prioritise larger, more profitable markets like the US. It left many of those who rely on these medications, including me, feeling helpless.

But not everyone taking these pills is managing ADHD and a parallel story of misuse has shaped public perception even more.

Amphetamines as Neurotypical Drugs

Neurotypicals use amphetamines to get high, lose weight, or neck them under the illusion of increased productivity, but they don't act as 'smart pills'. There's no evidence amphetamines enhance creativity or complex understanding; instead, they provide a sense of wellbeing, vigilance, and sometimes a cocky attitude. They owe their reputation as 'study drugs' to keeping people awake – they're also prescribed for narcolepsy – and increasing perseverance, not intellect. At best, some students retain material short-term. The drugs give dull tasks an inexplicable sheen, often leading to obsessive behaviours like overplucking eyebrows or obsessively cleaning.

Amphetamines don't make neurotypicals better at their primary tasks. Dosed-up soldiers charge into battle, but rates of friendly fire skyrocket. Joan Didion's use lent amphetamines a certain glamour, but she was the exception. Swathes of bad writing has been done – very fast – on speed. Dieters were early targets for pharmaceutical companies, but the drugs' appetite-suppressing effect fades quickly.

Despite corporate America's dreams, humans aren't machines, and treating them as such is dangerous. Amphetamines enable people to conform to societal norms, whether it benefits them or not – soldiers obey orders, women stay thin and compliant, and writers produce more, regardless of quality. Eventually, all three groups increase their dosage, leading to severe health issues like anxiety, heart attacks, seizures, addiction and psychosis.

That blur between genuine treatment and casual misuse became glaringly obvious during America's recent Adderall shortage.

America's Adderall Shortage (2022)

Track 1

Two years before the Adderall shortage, America's Ryan Haight Act was temporarily lifted, allowing telehealth providers to prescribe controlled substances without in-person appointments so that they could access medication safely during the pandemic. Telehealth, providing remote healthcare online or by phone, has become common in the US, where long waits and high costs for in-person care are the norm. Kyle Robertson, founder of Cerebral, a telehealth provider, in 2019, claimed his goal was to improve mental health access, but his eagerness to make Class II stimulants widely available raised questions. Cerebral's model, offering online therapy and meds for $30 a month, seemed appealing in America's privatised health-care system. Then former employees reported pressure to prescribe ADHD meds to thirty patients a day in ten-minute evaluations, bypassing proper diagnostic protocols like ruling out other conditions or trying non-stimulant options.

Fast forward a year, and Cerebral's valuation had soared to $4.8 billion, with more than two hundred thousand patients registered. Regulatory backlash followed: Robertson was ousted and Cerebral ceased prescribing stimulants. Investigations ensued. Max (Oregon, 25) a student who first tried Adderall in college, recalled slick ads from other telehealth companies too, with dystopian names like Done and Clarity, promising 'super easy ways' to get ADHD meds – his story doesn't end here. Cerebral became TikTok's third-largest advertiser, using marketing tactics straight out of Purdue Pharma's playbook – the company infamous for fuelling America's opioid crisis through aggressive promotion of OxyContin. In 2024, Cerebral agreed to a non-prosecution deal, paying a significant settlement for practices that encouraged the unauthorised distribution of controlled substances between 2019 and 2022.

Max recounted seeing an Instagram ad and, after a brief online call, was approved ninety pills of instant-release Adderall for $75, plus a $150 call fee. He referred friends to waive the fee. Two years later he hadn't used up the prescription, realising he didn't need it and regretting the purchase. 'It felt like a Faustian bargain,' he said, noting how easily companies preyed on vulnerable people. His friends shared his 'loose morals about the legality of drugs' but agreed it went too far.

Despite having a legal prescription, if I'd seen such ads years ago I might have clicked out of sheer impulse. These companies aren't just selling drugs – they sell the illusion of control to desperate people, much like filling an alcoholic's cart with booze.

While the demand for amphetamines in the US keeps rising, the supply of qualified doctors doesn't. There are fewer than ten doctors per hundred thousand young patients, and nearly half don't accept insurance, meaning that patients have to pay out of their own pocket. Previous shortages have highlighted this issue: in 2011, after record ADHD prescriptions, President Obama's FDA investigation led to increased stimulant quotas but not more trained professionals. Effective ADHD treatment requires more than medication; it demands holistic support for neurodivergent people.

The US government's Drug Enforcement Administration

has been cracking down on ADHD meds, and their aggressive marketing, especially given the opioid crisis. They aim to differentiate between necessary treatment and profit-driven excess. Although it's tempting to blame the tech cowboys responsible for overprescription via telehealth, the root causes of the shortage are more complex. Teva Pharmaceuticals, the largest US supplier of generic Adderall and other amphetamine-based ADHD medications, faced labour shortages in 2022. On top of that, the DEA's strict quotas on stimulant production haven't kept pace with rising demand – which has surged due to increased ADHD diagnoses and platforms like Cerebral. In a market dominated by Big Pharma, where just a handful of companies control supply, one faltering impacts the whole system. This disruption even reached the UK, where my medication, also made by Teva, became unavailable for months, highlighting the fragility of global reliance on US manufacturers.

Globally, ADHD affects about 5 per cent of the population, but in the US that figure is 10 per cent, with some states – Louisiana, Kentucky, Alabama, Mississippi, West Virginia – reporting rates closer to 15 per cent. ADHD is much more readily diagnosed and medicated in the US than in the UK, where teenagers are nearly fourteen times less likely to receive medication.

The medication shortage jeopardised the mental health of ADHD patients, as well as their jobs and relationships. On college campuses, low-income students faced pressure to sell their meds. Depriving ADHD patients of medication can have severe consequences; teens with ADHD are 62 per cent more likely than their peers to have car accidents within their first month of driving. Comorbid mental health conditions also can't be effectively treated until ADHD is managed.

Yet this 'overprescription versus real need' debate isn't new; it began almost a century ago, when amphetamine first went looking for a market.

Looking for a Problem: Amphetamine Goes Shopping (1920s and 30s)

Track 2

The stigma around ADHD traces back to its medication entering public consciousness before the disorder itself, as amphetamines were marketed for their effects long before ADHD was understood as a condition. Forty-six years after Lazăr Edeleanu synthesised amphetamine, Smith, Kline & French (SKF) – the precursor to GlaxoSmithKline – acquired and marketed it as Benzedrine Sulphate. While Edeleanu didn't see its potential, American chemist Gordon Alles did, synthesising it in 1929 and selling the patent to SKF. In hot pursuit of 'adrenaline-like effects' SKF distributed samples to doctors and funded research for its use in every condition imaginable.

For proto-Big Pharma the 1930s was a regulation-free era. New drugs only had to prove they were safe for treating symptoms before being advertised. While they were getting the safety nets in place, SKF focused on finding the best market for Benzedrine Sulphate. Amphetamines were lucrative from the start, without the need to 'invent' a disorder; they were continually repurposed for each generation's needs.

SKF's first big hit was the Benzedrine inhaler, sold over the counter for sinus issues. People soon discovered they could crack them open and chew the Benzedrine-soaked cotton for its stimulant effects. By 1936 SKF had released 10 mg amphetamine tablets. In 1937 Rhode Island psychiatrist Charles Bradley tested it on children with behavioural issues and noted a 'definite drive to accomplish as much as possible' and a 'subdued' emotional response in half of them. The use and misuse of amphetamines has never been clear cut, making the line between 'diagnosing' and 'selling' not only slippery, but lucratively so. The group benefiting from Bradley's research weren't sexy. SKF preferred results from doctors who tested Benzedrine on standardised tests with mainstream populations, aligning better with SKF's marketing goals.

PR issues loomed as early as 1937 when college students began using amphetamines to cram. Though the reputation for abuse emerged before true signs of abuse occurred, the idea of students gaining an unfair advantage deterred SKF from marketing Benzedrine as a neuroenhancer. Instead, they targeted issues like mild depression, influenced by studies like Abraham Myerson's 1920 book *The Nervous Housewife*, which argued that modern women's dissatisfaction stemmed from emotional strain rather than social inequality. Tests revealed amphetamine wasn't that useful for severe depression, but it gained approval for treating Parkinson's and narcolepsy.

Then, as the Second World War dawned, amphetamines found a new frontier in military use, with disastrous results.

War: Meth Mistakes and Military Madness (1939-45)

Track 3

With horrifying synchronicity, amphetamines became commercially available on an industrial scale just as the Second World War began. The Germans led in battlefield stimulant use, consuming 35 million methamphetamine tablets in the war's early months. They drove tanks for three days without sleeping. Terrified British troops sent home reports of 'heavily drugged, fearless and berserk' soldiers who marched until they dropped. The Nazis had rejected escapist drugs like psychedelics, but amphetamines better fit their ideology, fuelling notions of the 'Aryan race' and fascist superiority. After doping with Benzedrine in the 1936 Berlin Olympics, the Germans graduated to methamphetamine (Pervitin) for *Blitzkrieg*, their mechanised 'lightning war'. Sleep was weakness. As historian Peter Steinkamp puts it, '*Blitzkrieg* was guided by methamphetamine. If not to say that *Blitzkrieg* was founded on methamphetamine.'

However, soldiers soon faced severe side effects – chest pains, heart attacks. One SS infantry company surrendered to Russian forces after firing all their ammunition during a terrified mass hallucination. By 1940 meth use had dropped by 90 per cent. Soon, both meth and amphetamines were branded as addictive and only available by prescription.

As the Germans cut back, British and American troops began using 'go' pills. The Japanese dubbed theirs the 'drug to inspire the fighting spirits'. British experts theorised that methamphetamine allowed dive-bombing pilots to stay conscious against 'G-forces'. Horrified by Germany's rapid advances, Winston Churchill personally recommended Benzedrine for use by British military personnel. Though the US and UK knew it didn't grant superpowers, it created an emotional buffer of aggression and optimism.

The British, haunted by the First World War's shell shock, rebranded it as 'operational fatigue', suitable for amphetamine treatment. High doses made hypervigilance automatic. Inevitably, there were cautionary tales. Nicolas Rasmussen's authoritative history *On Speed* is full of case studies like that of the sailor who consumed five inhalers within forty-eight hours, didn't eat or sleep then hurled himself through a plate-glass window. Wary, the RAF limited usage to crisis points. A doctor noted that while Benzedrine made soldiers feel 'on top of things and able to carry on [their] duties without rest' really they were 'making all sorts of mistakes'.

The Americans, meanwhile, normalised meth use within their military. Post-war, SKF capitalised on Benzedrine's civilian potential – it was the first psychiatric drug for mood disorders – and flooded the market. It wasn't approved for weight loss, but diet companies matched SKF's production rates.

Rasmussen's research reveals how cultural priorities shaped reactions to amphetamines. Americans felt 'pepped up' and jittery, valuing ambition and assertiveness, in keeping with their respect for hustle. British subjects, however, found overt striving vulgar, described feeling 'right as rain' and appreciated sounding effortlessly clever – even if they were spouting 'flash gibberish'. In 1930s Germany, amphetamines were promoted to rejuvenate 'joy in work'. Rasmussen argues that each nation's values – wit in Britain; drive in the US; industriousness in Germany – shaped the subjective effects of the drug.

Peacetime didn't end the amphetamine story; it simply shifted from the battlefield to the stage.

Benzedrine Blues: From Judy Garland to Charlie Parker (Post-1945)

Track 4

After the Second World War, psychiatric care moved into the mainstream as psychiatrists treated soldiers whose minds bore the scars of battle. It proved good PR: with this shift came a new openness to diagnoses and pharmaceutical solutions. SKF capitalised, marketing Benzedrine as the sole approved antidepressant, and by 1947 sales had surged. As far back as 1939, 80 per cent of amphetamine prescriptions targeted women, capitalising on elastic definitions of 'obesity', a health crisis stretched to include everything from natural post-pregnancy weight gain to minor fluctuations. By 1947, SKF had approval to market Benzedrine and Dexedrine for weight control, framing even slight weight gain as 'pre-obesity'. If you were a pound or two overweight, Dexedrine could catch you on the brink.

Judy Garland, one of Benzedrine's early users, became hooked at the age of sixteen during filming of *The Wizard of Oz*. Her stage mum used it to keep her awake and sleeping pills to knock her out. Later, Benzedrine helped her meet the weight clause in her contract. Long-term, it ensured a corrosive cycle of disordered eating. By twenty-seven Garland was in a psychiatric hospital for amphetamine psychosis.

By the 1950s, pills had become the preferred medium, with housewives often prescribed Dexedrine and Valium cocktails to manage everyone's needs and stay peppy. SKF tapped into the cultural narrative, giving women what they were told they needed.

Then came the artists. Long before his heroin addiction, Charlie Parker was on Benzedrine inhalers – during his 1948 'health kick' the only toxins allowed were Benzedrine and beer. SKF distanced itself from counterculture associations with jazz, finding it bad for business.

Until the 1960s, amphetamines were seen as causing habituation, not addiction. Addiction was defined by severe withdrawal symptoms, unlike those seen with stimulants. SKF

cited a 1939 article by Assistant Surgeon General Lawrence
Kolb, arguing that stimulants weren't addictive because, unlike
cocaine, they were self-limiting: 'Artificial stimulation eventually
becomes unpleasant.'

But concerns grew as doping scandals surfaced – at the 1952
Winter Olympics, where speed-skaters fell ill, and the 1967
Tour de France, where English cyclist Tommy Simpson died.
Amphetamines mask the body's survival messages; fatigue
exists for a reason. Persisting beyond limits leads to increased
temperature and muscle breakdown. (Despite this, pieces like
'The Adderall Workout' published in *New York Magazine* in
2016 persist in glamorising their use.) SKF introduced a bitter-
tasting inhaler in California to deter misuse, but it failed. Inhalers
remained popular in the counterculture scene throughout the
1960s, even becoming the Beatles' first drug experience. Though
most were banned by the late sixties, one version remained until
1971, bearing a warning: 'For Inhalation Only!'

**By then, Benzedrine had moved beyond pharmacies, finding
new life in the hands of writers intent on enriching its cultural
mythology.**

Dexedrine Dreams: The Myth of Lucid Creativity

Track 5

Mention Benzedrine, and most people think of the Beats. Jack
Kerouac's first amphetamine high came from a Benzedrine
inhaler. In a taxi on the way to Times Square to score heroin,
a friend tipped the contents into the mouths of three soon-
to-be legends: William Burroughs, Joan Vollmer and Allen
Ginsberg. Vollmer was hit hardest, surviving multiple bouts of
amphetamine psychosis, ending up covered in sores she believed
were from radiation. Her son, Billy Burroughs, born dependent
on amphetamines, later wrote a book called *Speed*. For the
Beats, amphetamines sparked bursts of creativity and a fervent
hunt for magic, typified by the 'amphetamine-tinged stone-
collecting craze' that swept Greenwich Village.

It's hard to distinguish Kerouac's accelerating style from chemical speed. The rush is in the prose. In a letter to Ginsberg, he wrote, 'Benny has made me see a lot. The intensifying awareness naturally leads to an overflow of old notions, and voila, new material wells up like water, forming at the brim of consciousness. Brand new water!' *On the Road* was written on a 120-foot scroll, allegedly in three weeks while on 'Bennies'. Though later edited, the myth of spontaneous brilliance persisted.

How people think about ADHD tends to be coloured by a sense of literary daring. I was twenty when I first heard 'Dexedrine' sound illicit. My friend's boyfriend, who was writing a PhD on the poet Delmore Schwartz – who took hundreds of pills and saw angels, likely contributing to his fatal heart attack at fifty-two – introduced me to his world. I knew about Graham Greene and Jean-Paul Sartre's rumoured use, and W. H. Auden's morning Benzedrine ritual. Joan Didion wrote *Slouching Towards Bethlehem* with 'gin and hot water to blunt the pain and ... Dexedrine to blunt the gin'. This legacy of writers chasing lucidity amplifies the narrative that amphetamines can boost literary prowess.

As the 1960s dawned, society caught up with the downside of all this 'pep', fueling a regulatory crackdown on diet pills and dope alike.

Diet Pills, Dope and Disaster: The Road to Regulation (1960s)

Track 6

A 1960 UK study in Newcastle revealed that amphetamine prescriptions could have kept 1.5 per cent of the city's population taking two pills daily. About one-third were for weight loss, another third for psychiatric issues, and the rest for vague symptoms like tiredness. Eighty-five per cent of these patients were women aged between thirty-six and forty-five, mostly housewives, echoing the demographic targeted by American tranquillisers. As Betty Friedan noted in 1963 in *The*

Feminine Mystique, male doctors often pathologised women's dissatisfaction, prescribing pills instead of addressing systemic issues.

Amphetamines kept people going, whether it was in their best interests or not. They were cheap and effective, and other antidepressants didn't exist yet. Despite rising numbers of amphetamine users in emergency rooms, America ignored the warning signs. Britain paid attention. In 1943 it had become illegal to possess amphetamines without a prescription, giving police the right to raid clubs.

In 1968 the British Medical Association limited amphetamine use to narcolepsy, stating that for everything else they did more harm than good. After a brief spike in methamphetamine injections, the UK's amphetamine use began to decline. Meanwhile, illicit meth production surged in the US, leading to 'speedfreaks' injecting large quantities. By 1965 Papa Allen Ginsberg became an unlikely anti-speed campaigner: 'Speed is anti-social, paranoid-making . . . a plague in the whole dope industry.' Speedfreaks hit amphetamine psychosis faster and harder. Haight-Ashbury, the pacifist hippie haven, transformed during the 1967 Summer of Love as addicts flooded the scene.

On the day Andy Warhol was shot in 1968, he was on his way to pick up a prescription for Obetrol, a popular meth-based diet drug. It was candy at the Factory, keeping appetites down, energy up and numbness at bay. Warhol wasn't alone – JFK also partook, courtesy of Dr Feelgood, who dosed him during the Cuban Missile Crisis, spiking him with the liquid courage to play chicken with Khrushchev. When questioned, Kennedy snapped, 'I don't care if it's horse piss . . . it's the only thing that works.' By the mid-1960s, around one in twenty Americans had an amphetamine prescription, with nearly half also using illicit speed – around ten million people.

Nearly 10 per cent of American women were using amphetamines for weight control. Congressional action followed earlier hearings on military drug use in Vietnam, where soldiers returned addicted to heroin. One commando described taking Dexedrine: 'I turned into a pair of eyeballs and ears.' The collective fallout – dying dieters, speedfreaks and addicted veterans – had led to the Controlled Substances Act.

By the 1970s, stricter laws were in place, setting the stage for a new chapter in which ADHD diagnosis became big business.

Pills, Profits and Predicaments

Track 7

After other uses of amphetamines were outlawed, ADHD diagnostic criteria loosened. The *DSM-III* in the 1980s rebranded ADHD as ADD 'with or without hyperactivity' and prescriptions climbed. The *DSM-V* later raised the age for symptom onset, further widening the diagnostic pool. In the UK, the NHS's centralised approach ensures slower, stricter diagnostic processes, relying on both the *DSM-V* and ICD-10 (the World Health Organization's International Classification of Diseases). The US, however, lacks such centralised guidelines, creating loopholes for easier access – hence Max could legally acquire 2,000 mg of Adderall within twenty-four hours. Direct-to-consumer pharmaceutical advertising in the US also plays a role, making ADHD appear 'for sale'.

Social media in the UK now mimics American marketing, where productivity apps capitalise on Adderall's mythos. These platforms, though not offering the drug, sell the productivity fantasy and promote drug-seeking behaviour through proxy. While regulated telehealth services are important, controlled substances should not be marketed and awareness campaigns need to steer clear of backdoor drug promotion. The UK must avoid America's tangled web of ADHD research, advocacy and pharmaceutical profits – like the pharmaceutical sponsorship of the US's leading ADHD non-profit organisation (CHADD).

The consequences of this profit-driven approach are clear. Scandals and campaigns have punctuated the history of ADHD medication, revealing patterns of overprescription and systemic incentives to diagnose. In the 1950s, Swiss company CIBA developed Ritalin (a non-amphetamine stimulant). It boosted mood and reduced fatigue but flopped as an antidepressant in making people anxious. Eventually, it was prescribed for hyperkinetic reaction of childhood, ADHD's predecessor. However, reports revealed overmedication in US schools. In some, up to 10 per cent of children were on stimulants to 'make them easier to handle'. A congressional inquiry upheld that teachers' complaints were often enough for doctors to prescribe stimulants, thanks to drug company targeting. In 1988 the Church of Scientology's campaign against ADHD medication caused a 30 per cent drop in usage.

Then, in the 1990s, books like Richard DeGrandpre's *Ritalin Nation* and similar titles, fuelled concerns about overmedication. *The ADHD Explosion* (2014) offered a rare, nuanced view, highlighting the media's tendency to obsess over the dangers of drugging neurotypical kids while ignoring the benefits for those with ADHD. The authors argued US diagnosis rates were inflated, with insufficient exploration of alternative causes. Professional organisations set guidelines, but they lack enforcement. (Acts like 'No Child Left Behind' – a federal education reform – intensified this issue, tying funding – including teacher promotions – to test scores.) Special education diagnoses, including ADHD, excluded kids from test averages or provided services that improved scores – creating strong incentives for diagnoses.

When the government programme Medicaid started covering ADHD meds, diagnoses among low-income children rose. Improving access is crucial, but the sharp rise in diagnoses when accountability laws kicked in raised red flags. By 2007 ADHD diagnoses among poor children rose 59 per cent in states under No Child Left Behind, compared to under 10 per cent for wealthier children.

While increasing awareness naturally leads to more diagnoses, systemic factors have also inflated US rates. Advocacy groups funded by Big Pharma push the narrative. Extended-release (XR) meds designed to last the school day have become pricier. US doctors may be incentivised to diagnose, with prescriptions often being a quicker and cheaper solution for parents than therapy.

Before long, stimulants moved from the pediatrician's office to the dorm room, where high-achievers chased academic glory with a pill in hand.

Drugs: Ivy League Thrills

Track 8

Imagine the sheer volume of amphetamines that has passed through Columbia University's campus. In the Beat era, SKF colour-coded their pills to combat bootleggers: Dexedrine was yellow, Benzedrine pink and Dexamyl blue ('purple hearts' in Mod culture). Adderall is still pale azure. In the UK, prescribed ADHD medication comes as nondescript white pills. The American version is aestheticised.

At Columbia, the flimsy divide between those diagnosed with ADHD and those with Adderall prescriptions was a culture shock. Students who scorned recreational drugs embraced 'smart drugs'. The Beats, who sought to expand consciousness, would've been disgusted by the hustle culture aimed at bagging a McKinsey job.

Nathan (Brooklyn, 30) a former student diagnosed with ADHD in kindergarten – a diagnosis not allowed in the UK before the age of six – faced early struggles. He grew up in a small town, Hickory, North Carolina, with a life centred around church and sport, and he never felt accepted. His parents, dealing with alcohol addiction, were dismissive. By twelve, Nathan was on the highest dose of Adderall, escalating to 90 mg of Vyvanse daily by fifteen – far above the recommended maximum. His psychiatrist justified this on the grounds of Nathan's football-player size rather than following medical guidelines. At Columbia, the bureaucracy of disability services overwhelmed Nathan, and he missed out on support.

Initially, Adderall helped Nathan embody the behaviours authority figures expected, but he now questions its value. Where by twelve, he'd been doubling his doses unnoticed, by high school's end, he was taking over 180 mg of Vyvanse daily, resorting to stealing meds. Post-college, he sourced stimulants from the dark web. After losing his job and insurance, he quit cold turkey for nine months. Now, candid with a psychiatrist, he's on a reduced, monitored dose.

Nathan's addiction had profound physical and emotional issues, leaving him sceptical of Western psychiatry and its reliance on medication, yet he questions if he could do a desk job unless he loved it. His story shows how over-treatment can lead to rejecting not only medication but also the validity of an ADHD diagnosis itself, blurring the line between scepticism of treatment and denial of the condition.

Columbia is emblematic of widespread, culturally sanctioned amphetamine misuse on college campuses.

But hustling doesn't end at graduation; the campus mindset bleeds into work culture, where Adderall becomes currency for the daily grind.

Blue Pills and Big Ambitions

Track 9

After Sasha Obama was seen dancing to Popp Hunna's 'Adderall', the rapper issued a PSA against non-prescribed use. In the US the distinction between 'drugs' and 'study drugs' implies that use of Adderall carries less moral judgement because it boosts productivity. Students feel justified in taking these pills amid academic pressure, easy access, low stigma (after all, children take these pills daily) and minimal monitoring. Although ECGs are recommended before any stimulants are prescribed, they are often skipped. There's also a warped application of American values: 'If others can use these safe drugs to get ahead, why can't I?'

In the UK, tighter controls contrast with the US, where lax regulation lets students sell or share their meds without seeing themselves as dealers. Adderall is a sought-after commodity, with a lively bartering system. As Max put it, 'A rising tide lifts all boats.' During finals, Max noted that almost everyone he knew took a $5 pill, having started in high school. The prevalence of neurotypical misuse overshadows those genuinely needing medication.

Up to a third of US college students use stimulants to boost academic performance. The biohacking trend continues, with low awareness of the risks. A 2013 *Neuropharmacology* study showed students perceived Adderall as a performance enhancer, but actual cognitive benefits were minimal. This gap between perception and reality perpetuates the trend, reinforcing neuroenhancement without acknowledging its dangers.

Soon, you're juggling deadlines instead of exams, and the 'just get it done' ethos can morph into full-blown overdrive.

The Perils of Strategic Overdrive

Track 10

When I say I've never increased my dosage, I'm mostly telling the truth – except for one time, which I'm not proud of. I was twenty-three, deep in a depression where I stopped caring about roses and thought obsessively about death. Then, during a summer writing workshop, Joy Williams praised my short story. If you're not a big reader, this is the literary equivalent of Harry Styles proposing.

That summer, I test-drove the Adderall myth, obsessively taking 10 mg Instant Release (IR) pills and stretching my one decent short story into a novella filled with ellipses and diagrams about power dynamics. I became irritable, lashing out at my best friend. I got nasty. She still reminds me of the moment when I held up the empty prescription bottle, saying, 'They're all gone,' like there'd been a murder. When I mailed Joy the novella, she returned it with a note paraphrased as: 'It was better before.' So much for the experiment.

In the UK, I cut my medication into daily doses. I don't carry extra – not out of temptation (the thought makes me nauseous) but because with ADHD I sometimes forget if I've already taken it.

When people argue ADHD is overdiagnosed, they often refer

to students using it to boost performance. Professors see this
all the time – students faking symptoms, taking too many pills,
spiralling at the health centre. In the US, higher education is so
staggeringly expensive that the culture around it is different.
Students crave A grades as a return on their massive investment.
Columbia students say the stimulant culture is unavoidable: 'If
you don't take them, you're at a disadvantage.'

Max wasn't on the McKinsey track. He described his Adderall
use as a 'time function', reminding me of mathematician Norbert
Wiener, who later regretted his Benzedrine use: 'I tried to work
against time. More than once I computed all through the night
to meet some imaginary deadline which wasn't there.' Max
struck a different note: 'There was a ton of content to learn, and
I saw other people sit down for ten hours without moving or
seemingly breathing, and I wanted to try that shit.' He started
with occasional IR pills but soon developed a Sunday ritual:
cold brew, Oreos, a JUUL and locking himself in a classroom
for eight to twelve hours to do a week's homework 'with satanic
focus'. His friends joined him, earphones in, betting on NFL
games while they 'locked in' on Vyvanse.

Max was lucky. If he'd become dependent, he had the privilege
to be able to experiment, fuck up and recover. He's also smart:
he never upped his dose, avoided using it for parties, and stayed
strategic. Still, he noticed side effects: circulation problems, shaky
hands, inability to eat. He didn't realise the emotional toll until
he cut back. 'I broke up with my girlfriend right after one of those
big Sundays – did it too matter-of-factly. Not my best moment.'
He realised he was angrier, more biting, but so were his friends.

He was even luckier. When he decided he didn't like who
he became on Adderall, he was able to stop. He realised he
wasn't retaining information, and once his classes improved he
discovered he could work in two-hour bursts without the pills, a
structure he learned from IR amphetamines. This happens with
neurotypical friends who mirror my ADHD work habits. I'm
glad for them, but it's also infuriating.

Max's saving grace was self-awareness. He understood
Adderall was a 'sacrifice of learning and creativity just to
get shit done'. He realised he might ace tests on it, but true

understanding happened later, without them. Columbia's hustle culture made me question: are we even asking the right question? Instead of 'why misuse Adderall?' maybe it should be 'why does the system reward hollow productivity without engagement?'

Many neurotypicals speak of the wormholes they've been sucked down under Adderall-inspired hyperfocus; people with undiagnosed ADHD describe the same wormhole experience with self-loathing. Max's list of topics he became a short-term 'expert' in but remembers nothing about remains iconic:

Chess

Astronomy

Alan Watts

Particle accelerators

Mechanical oscillators

Car mechanics

Tank/Self-propelled gun

Orwell's *1984*

Wardenclyffe Tower

Tesla in every way

Garage Band

Rubik's Cube

Dante Machiavelli

Wim Hof

Faust

Colour psychology

Card games

Poker

Blackjack

Helicopter blades

Golf, physics of the swing

Giants pitcher with weird throw

Charlie-Gibbs fracture zone

Occam's Razor

Reverse magnetism

Electroplating

Tulip crisis

Cats' kidneys can process salt water

How tornados form

Barnum effect

Golden ratio

LEDs efficiency

Hoag's Object

Einstein-Rosen Bridges

Teleporting

Microscopically small means time moves slow meaning movement could be immediate and vice versa (time = energy of movement)

OODA systems

Sun Tzu

Heisenberg Uncertainty Principle

Brown noise

Anna Karenina

Chakras

TCM

The Magnus effect

Non fungible tokens

Facebook marketing (deep)

Gamma waves

Locksmith/ lockpick

Quantum computing

Fermi paradox

Mimetic theory

Interest rates

FACS – Facial Action Coding System

Blink

Malcolm Gladwell

Ship of Theseus

Rise and Grind: From Campus to Cubicle

Track 11

When college graduates like Max enter the workplace, the amphetamine habits formed in university become hard to break. Adderall use, already normalised for productivity, now comes with a pay cheque. ER visits in the US for non-medical amphetamine use tripled from 2005 to 2011, and rehab admissions for stimulant dependency rise annually. Publications like the *New York Times*, *Wired* and *Dazed* frequently feature pieces in which a neurotypical texts their dealer at 3 a.m. for Adderall, before eventually flushing the pills, only to reorder. These articles typically show a photo of a white handful of pills with captions like: 'Elizabeth, with her Adderall.' The cumulative effect of such stories reinforces the idea that amphetamine medication and misuse are inseparable.

Humans aren't built to code for ten hours straight. These stories always end with increased dosage, social pressure and deteriorating health: anxiety, hallucinations, addiction. One particular Elizabeth insists that abstaining from Adderall is like 'playing tennis with a wooden racket', calling it essential for high achievers. Such users wouldn't dare misuse a disabled parking permit, yet they feel justified in taking meds from those who genuinely need them – like diabetics struggling to access Ozempic, now a weight-loss trend. Simply put: there isn't enough Adderall for everyone.

Despite shortages and cautionary tales, pop culture keeps finding ways to turn Adderall into entertainment.

Pop Culture's Take

Track 12

How has pop culture's portrayal of amphetamines shaped public perception, either through glamorisation or mockery? *The Wolf of Wall Street* (2013) shows Leonardo DiCaprio's character popping Adderall to stay focused. In *White Lotus* (2021), it's part of the rich kid's stash. *Emily in Paris* (2022) jokes about needing it to manage multiple bosses. *Silicon Valley* (2014) features a coder who goes by the name of 'the Carver' and pulls twenty-four-hour work sprints thanks to Adderall.

The first time I saw Adderall onscreen was in *Desperate Housewives*. Felicity Huffman's character starts using her son's meds to manage the demands of suburban motherhood. After a fellow alpha mom tells her it's a secret weapon, Lynette nicks a pill, makes matching oak-tree costumes for her twin sons, and cleans her house with a toothbrush. It was depressing: the drug I'd just discovered that could help me stay in class was shown as a crutch for unrelenting domestic expectations.

Then there's the satire of 'zombie drugs'. *Unbreakable Kimmy Schmidt* (2015) shows boys on 'Dyziplen' walking like zombies. *The Simpsons* episode 'Brother's Little Helper' has Bart hallucinating after being put on 'Focusyn'. In *South Park*, a boy fakes ADHD and gets diagnosed by reading *The Great Gatsby* out loud, resulting in the entire class following suit and becoming zombies. Cartman hallucinates pink Christina Aguilera monsters and accidentally kills Kenny. They invent an antidote called 'Ritalout'; the bottle is marked MDMA. You get the picture. These portrayals suggest amphetamine meds are solely for neurotypical misuse or behaviour control, erasing those who need them.

From satire to starry-eyed veneration, these portrayals hint at a bigger question: do amphetamines really unlock brilliance, or just sell us the illusion?

The Illusion of Brilliance

Track 13

I won't claim I'd refuse a pill that promised to make me write like Joan Didion, though I hope I would. Even if it worked, I'd always know, which would be soul-destroying. Amphetamines offer only the illusion of improvement, not the real thing. They don't build the sturdy muscular work practice that allows brilliance to grow over time.

Jean Baudrillard called depression a 'passive rebellion against the competitive consumerist social order, the unconscious and private equivalent of the collective factory slowdown'. In the 1930s the pharmaceutical industry found a way to quell that rebellion with amphetamines, maintaining the status quo. It's impossible to disentangle amphetamines from their history of maintaining the social order. These drugs keep women flimsy, soldiers driven, and unruly children tamed. Neurotypical users chase false urgency, moving faster down narrow tracks. Amphetamines don't expand the mind; they make you jump hoops without questioning why.

Neurotypical misuse is about wanting to be the best at any cost, fearing what happens if they slow down. Swedish psychiatrist Gösta Rylander coined the word 'punding' for the compulsive, meaningless tasks amphetamine users engage in. Why have you taken apart your speakers? Do your skirting boards need dusting? If you're neurotypical, what do you care about when you take amphetamines? Analogies like marathon runners using wheelchairs or non-allergic people using EpiPens don't quite fit; they miss the neurotypical urge to gain an edge. Neurotypical misuse isn't about mocking disabilities but is still careless and predictable. Systems should protect against that.

I see neurotypicals misusing amphetamines as like talented writers handing their work to AI. They feel pressured to keep up. The result is faster but never truly theirs. Your atoms won't have recalibrated around creating it. Amphetamines can't synthesise the harmony and internal coherence that come with true creativity. Misuse provides a superficial shimmer, cheapens joy, offers fake flow, and eventually cripples the ability to enter a real flow state. Temporary output increases might appeal in a production-obsessed society but, in the end, you're stealing fire from the gods. Worse, you're a fool drawing diagrams you'll later fail to understand.

STIMULATING

Sensory Rest Menu - Ten Options

Why? Mini-sensory breaks refresh energy without fully disengaging from the reading experience.

For Instant Calm: Close your eyes and press your palms lightly over them, like you're covering your eyes to play hide-and-seek. The gentle pressure signals your nervous system to chill out, giving you a mini-sensory reset.

For a Brain Refresh: Try the 'smell wake-up'. Put a drop of peppermint oil on a tissue, take a quick whiff, and feel the zing wake up your mind. (If you don't have peppermint oil, coffee grounds can work too!)

For Anchoring Focus: Tap each finger to your thumb in slow succession – index, middle, ring, pinky – then go back the other way. Repeat a few rounds. This little finger dance is great for bringing you back when your mind's wandering. I do it all the time.

For a Mid-Read Energiser: Stand up and do a quick shake-out: shake your arms, hands and legs one at a time. Go faster with each shake until you feel like one of those inflatable tube dancers! It'll jolt your focus back to the page.

For Eye Refreshment: Give your eyes a break! Every fifteen minutes, look up from the page and focus on something far away for ten seconds. It's like a mini-vacation for your eyes.

For a Focused Break: Do a mini-foot massage. Grab a tennis ball or something round, put it under one foot, and roll it around. It's grounding and calming, and gives your brain a low-key reset before diving back into reading.

For a Little Rhythm: Pop on some quiet background music, like lo-fi beats or classical. Keep the volume low so it adds to focus without pulling your attention. Binaural beats really help too.

For Resetting Mental Energy: Do a quick wall push-up – just lean against a wall, push yourself away, and repeat five to ten times. It's a mini-move that gets your blood flowing without needing much space or time.

For Instant Clarity: Try a 'deep listening' moment. Close your eyes and listen to any sounds around you – distant chatter, birds, the hum of an appliance. Let your attention float from sound to sound; it's like a palate cleanser for your focus.

For Waking Up the Senses: Rub your earlobes gently with your thumbs and index fingers. The gentle pressure and movement can stimulate energy points that help boost focus.

Chapter 8

(Paid) Employment Versus (Invisible) Labour

On average, ADHD individuals earn 33 per cent less than their neurotypical peers. Driven by interest and novelty rather than high pay, ADHD brains are wired in a way that increases the risk of poor job outcomes and financial struggles. This chapter explores the realities of ADHD in the workplace: executive function deficits, impulsivity, task-switching and financial instability. While hyperfocus can occasionally be an asset, not everyone has it, and the difficulty with entry-level tasks – like organising meetings or managing details – often outweighs it.

Though social media sometimes glamorises ADHD as a source of entrepreneurial spirit and creative flair, the reality is a constant grind. Industries that attract ADHD individuals – those valuing creativity and flexibility – are often a necessity rather than a choice, as traditional roles rarely accommodate the way ADHD brains function.

A review by the Attention Deficit Disorder Association found that ADHD people are 60 per cent more likely to be fired, 30 per cent more likely to face ongoing job struggles, and three times more likely to quit impulsively. The traditional workplace often doesn't suit neurodivergent minds – fewer than 30 per cent of autistic people are employed. ADHD increases the risk of accidents and absenteeism due to comorbid conditions, worsening financial instability. Managing money is just as challenging: ADHD individuals are three times more likely to struggle with debt and four times more prone to impulsive spending, intensifying the risk of precarity.

In interviews conducted for this book, tears were common: employment struggles are often painful to revisit, sometimes causing more emotional distress than recounting experience of abuse or addiction. In a society where productivity defines worth, failing to hold a 'normal' job deepens isolation and stigma. What happens when the foundational concept of work becomes a constant source of failure and shame? While a neurotypical friend may worry about a single unexplained gap on a CV, mine looks like a crossbreed of several different animals – ADHD's organising principle is inconsistency, reflected in a jumble of jobs and experiences.

I remember once, during my first office job, my friend Oliver – newly employed as a consultant – told me with quiet certainty: 'You're being paid to be there, so it won't be a problem. Money changes everything.' At the time, his world-weary confidence was oddly comforting, even though I knew deep down that money wasn't going to fix the way my brain fought the urge to leave any room I was in out of sheer boredom. I'd fled classes, both as a teacher and student, and even exams. At a less supportive college, I'd have had to drop out. Oliver, on the other hand, was on a clear path – his existential angst didn't stop us both from knowing he'd be top of his field one day. His certainty about money as motivation seemed like common sense, but ADHD doesn't fit neatly into those trajectories.

The ADHD Tax

The 'ADHD tax' refers to the accumulation of overlooked costs: missed payments, wasted subscriptions and impulsive purchases. ADHD creates financial drag, where small mistakes – like forgetting a bill – snowball into larger problems. Impulse spending, driven by the need for novelty, plays directly into the hands of surveillance capitalism. The attention economy thrives on vulnerabilities like ADHD. Technology promises solutions but often intensifies the problem, trapping us in endless scrolling and spending. Ads and algorithms target us when we're seeking dopamine or escape, turning distraction into a financial hazard.

I avoid supermarkets unless under duress, bulk-buy everything – problematic in a tiny flat – and cancel every 'free trial' subscription immediately after opting in. I enter the advertising-saturated world wearing armour. This 'tax' isn't just monetary – it's emotional. Shame from financial mismanagement deepens self-blame, making it harder to seek help or accommodations.

The Invisible Labour of ADHD

Managing ADHD in a neurotypical world demands constant cognitive and emotional effort – *invisible labour.* Tasks like organising and time management, which neurotypicals take for granted, demand significant energy for people with ADHD. It's a second, unpaid job – mental gymnastics just to manage symptoms, regulate emotions and stay on task. It can feel like working twice as hard for half the recognition, and it consumes mental bandwidth, leaving little room for the 'real' work expected in professional environments.

ADHD, by its nature, is incompatible with the attention economy which is built on multitasking and information overload. Neurotypicals struggle in this environment; for us, it's like juggling chainsaws.

Success in the workplace is measured by neurotypical standards. The system rewards those who fit the mould, forcing ADHD people to overcompensate by performing extra cognitive and emotional labour just to keep up. You're considered successful in most environments if no one knows you have ADHD, which means masking – double-checking everything, putting in overtime, sneaking into the office to handle desk bonfires on weekends. It's exhausting, unsustainable and rarely acknowledged.

This invisible labour extends beyond work too. People with ADHD may do less contractual employment – which comes with pay cheques and legal protections – but we do much more unpaid labour: managing our homes, relationships and internal chaos. This work doesn't generate profit, so it's undervalued by capitalist standards.

The digital economy further exploits our distraction, capitalising on the very traits that make ADHD brains creative. Many ADHD people turn to freelance or gig work for flexibility, but these options come with instability, lack of benefits and increased financial risk – compounding the ADHD tax. Even in industries where we could excel, without support our strengths become liabilities, leading to burnout and missed opportunities. Creativity, rapid idea generation and the ability to hyperfocus in short bursts are valuable, but only if employers provide the right accommodations. These challenges aren't abstract – they affect real people, as the following stories show.

Case Studies: Personal Stories from the ADHD Workforce

Neurodivergent people tend to define themselves less by their jobs, probably because of the invisible labour they undertake just being themselves. These profiles offer windows into how the ADHD experience interacts with larger systems. Often, people are paying the ADHD tax in emotional, financial and personal terms. Their experiences are not isolated; they reflect a broader systemic critique of how labour is valued, how neurodivergent individuals are overlooked, and how those with ADHD are constantly working harder simply to keep up in a world that doesn't accommodate them.

Mike (Flint, North Wales, 60): The Cycle of Debt and Job Instability

At sixty Mike has faced the all-too-familiar ADHD struggle with employment. After years of battling debt, he's now declared personal bankruptcy. Housing stability has also been elusive – he's lived in twenty-two homes, averaging less than three years per place: 'When you consider I've spent the best part of a decade in some of them, you get the feeling that putting down roots hasn't happened for me.' He described his lifelong job cycle like this:

» Earn just enough to get by.
» Throw everything into a new career or hobby.
» Spend money and time on training courses.
» Get frustrated by lack of skill or imperfections.
» Get bored, lose focus, lose confidence.
» Give up at the first obstacle or criticism.
» Return to street performing.

This passionate start, followed by burnout and falling back on survival trades, is common for ADHD people. Street performing has remained a constant, despite Mike's double hernia. The financial cost is heavy, but the emotional toll of repeated failure weighs more. Consistency has always eluded him. His various gigs – web design, importing electronics, video editing, Forex trading, producing cabaret shows – never lasted: 'I thought I'd succeed if I just kept going, but when the passion died, I gave up.'

Talking to others with ADHD, Mike realised he wasn't alone: 'I thought my inability to stick to things was a character flaw, not brain chemistry. I felt like I'd failed at being good, at being successful, at finding my role in life. In my darkest moments, I told myself I'd failed at life itself.'

Now, he's aiming for self-acceptance: 'It's a challenge to undo a lifetime of bad habits and internal propaganda, but I'm giving it a real go this time. I'm sticking to a few things I love – and I'm embracing that busking will always be there for me. It's time to stop trying to be neurotypical. I've done OK at life. I'm going to just try to do it a little better from now on.'

Melanie (Edinburgh, 35): Unlocking the Brain

Before her diagnosis, Melanie was one of three people allowed into the office early to avoid open-plan distractions. Her routine was brutal: 5 a.m. wake-ups, modafinil (a stimulant) just to function, and late nights. Eventually, she burned out, leading to months off due to anxiety and depression.

One day, after breaking down during a Park Run, a friend offered her Ritalin. Melanie was desperate. That weekend, for the first time, she sat down for hours to write a job application, crying at the relief of finally finishing it. With medication, she sent several applications and received multiple job offers. 'It felt like I'd unlocked my brain,' she says. But frustration remains: 'What am I supposed to do while I wait four years for an NHS diagnosis?' After dipping into her savings for a private assessment, Melanie found a stable, remote job – ideal for raising a family. 'But managing without medication feels impossible. It's like a fucking minefield.'

Josh (Sussex, 36): Advocacy for Flexible Working

Josh has struggled with job stability and advocates for flexible work: 'Rigid systems are tragic for everyone, especially the neurodivergent. I can be explosively productive in bursts, but if you force me to a desk during a low-focus phase, I'm just fidgeting and hating myself. Who benefits from that?'

Josh thrives in high-pressure environments but struggles with consistency, leaving him in 'weird middle-class poverty'. His most successful role was as a psychedelic facilitator, leading mushroom retreats, where the intensity matched his need for stimulation. But when it didn't, he couldn't perform, almost failing his master's degree in primate biology, behaviour and conservation because he couldn't handle the data entry after doing 'amazingly at the "difficult" part, chasing monkeys through jungle ravines'.

Daisy (Cambridge, 31): Success in Academia

Daisy, a PhD student, has found that academia suits her ADHD, with the right support: 'A PhD lets me work with the ebb and flow of focus. No one questions my productivity day-to-day because I meet my long-term goals.' But she acknowledges the dangers of academia: overwork, heavy administrative burdens, and lack of clear job boundaries make it less ideal long-term.

Miles (Philadelphia, 26): Struggling with Invisible Labour

Miles spoke often of the 'labour of just being human'. Simple tasks like laundry or cleaning felt like mountains. 'Masculinity has changed,' he says. 'Now, taking care of your family isn't just about earning, it's day-to-day shit like dishes and scheduling. That's hard with ADHD.'

Miles doesn't share my problematic fantasy of being a writer who comes home to an adoring wife who shows me pretty new plates, cooks and tells me I'm a genius. He doesn't complain about the shift which demands men do more, but it adds pressure: 'Before, as long as you brought home the bacon, it didn't matter if you couldn't do the dishes and fold clothes. Now, you feel like a shitty husband if you can't manage both.'

Shauna (Norfolk, 56): Navigating Artistic Success

In an email, Shauna explained: 'Unfortunately, I'm not in a position to answer questions about the workplace – undiagnosed ADHD meant a lifetime on the periphery, finding my own ways to generate cash. Employment is not something I've properly experienced.'

At forty-two she won a rare £500,000 Arts Council commission. Managing the work was the 'best part' but the pressure of managing large sums of money led to intense stress and breakdowns. 'I felt like a banker in Monopoly,' terrified one mistake could lead to financial disaster. Despite the exposure from her commission, work dwindled, and Shauna still struggles to generate income: 'My exhausted brain is always in overdrive, trying to come up with the next idea or scheme.' Her reflection is bittersweet:

Apologies this has been so negative.

Obviously, it's not all bad. Indeed, I feel life is really good.

I live by the beach now, that brings its own calm and laid-back characters.

Unfortunately, for most of my life, ADHD has been a needless disability.

As you well know, with it come some amazing traits. I am optimistic that in time these traits are being recognised and will one day be harnessed.

That will be a great day for everybody.

James (Oxford, 34): The Job-Hopping Cycle

James cycled through thirty-six jobs between the ages of
fifteen and twenty, though he wasn't diagnosed until thirty-
one: 'Sometimes I'd be switched on, reacting positively to
tasks. Other times, I felt like a zombie, disconnected. Verbal
instructions would slip away, so I'd write everything down, but
that wasn't enough to combat my inattentiveness.' Boredom set
in. The initial high of a new job faded fast, leading him to quit
and chase something else, feeding the cycle: 'I didn't realise my
undiagnosed ADHD was driving it.'

Let's Be Reasonable: Understanding Workplace Adjustments

The debate around reasonable accommodations mirrors wider
discussions on diversity, inclusion and the clash between
individual rights and perceived 'entitlements'. Advocates see
accommodations as levelling the playing field, while detractors
view them as privileges that burden businesses.

In the UK, under the 2010 Equality Act ADHD individuals
who experience 'substantial' and 'long-term effects' are entitled
to accommodations to prevent workplace discrimination. But
ambiguity persists – ADHD isn't always seen as a disability, and
employers can't ask about it before making a job offer. What if
an employee discloses ADHD during a disciplinary hearing or is
still waiting for a diagnosis due to NHS backlogs?

A few months ago, I met my friend Oliver again, now a little
deeper into his career as a consultant. At the pub, he mentioned
a colleague who had disclosed ADHD and ASD after being
asked to attend an after-work event. My gut reaction was a
grimace – 'Bit much, right?' – a hangover from the culture we
both grew up in. I asked a few questions, relieved when there
were no obvious signs of this person struggling to cope at work.
I wanted Oliver's assumption – that his colleague was simply
making excuses – to be right, because he's a good person. But
later, I rethought the situation. The tiny minority who misuse
accommodations shouldn't undermine the essential frameworks
needed to support those of us who struggle in ways people don't
see. Perhaps the person panicked or felt there wasn't a clear

protocol for disclosure, and sensed Oliver's kindness, trusting him to understand. Knowing Oliver, I'm sure he'd follow any official protocol without hesitation, but I also know there'd be quiet, understated judgement, even if it wasn't visible on his face. Until ADHD is more widely understood, even the most understanding people – like Oliver – still face a learning curve when it comes to accommodating neurodivergence.

Examples of Reasonable Accommodations:

Written Instructions. Since ADHD brains struggle with working memory, providing written instructions via email can help with retention and task management.

Flexible Working Hours. ADHD-related time blindness can be managed by focusing on task completion rather than strict hours, allowing people to work to their own rhythms.

Noise-Cancelling Headphones. Many ADHD people have sensory issues, and reducing noise distractions helps with focus.

Private Rooms. Open-plan offices are overstimulating for ADHD brains; private rooms help minimise distractions.

Regular Check-ins and Smaller Deadlines. Breaking large tasks into smaller ones with frequent check-ins helps keep ADHD employees on track.

Awareness and Training. Educating managers and colleagues about ADHD beyond productivity metrics fosters a supportive environment.

One ADHD-diagnosed doctor described how the chaos of emergency medicine was stimulating, but when it came to admin tasks, 'Everything felt equally pressing and difficult to sort out.' After risking being struck off for not documenting her hours – despite having done the work – she applied for adjustments but found no clear guidance in her field.

ADHD advocate Dani Donovan offers a simple analogy: 'If I'm too short to reach something, I'll need a step. It's not about saying, "I'm short, so I can't."' Accommodations don't have to be

expensive or disruptive. Simple changes – like software updates
or noise management – boost productivity.

When I see TikToks about 'time blindness' and 'being late
isn't my fault' my gut reaction is to call 'Bullshit!' Fault isn't
really the issue, though – TikTok is for expressing how hard
it is. Demanding complete latitude for symptoms harms the
neurodivergent community and others managing disabilities. A
small minority who demand the right to be late make it look like
we're taking advantage.

That said, time blindness is real. Kobe (France, 34) explains:
'If you asked me when five minutes passed, I'd be way off.
Deadlines are hard because I can't estimate how long tasks will
take.' She sets alarms for everything. Clearly, Kobe is trying.
Much of the generational disdain for ADHD comes from the
misguided impression that people with it generally aren't. Hostile
work environments may push ADHD people to try harder, but
that frantic pace eventually leads to burnout.

With some articles claiming neurodivergent employees are a
burden, hiring us feels risky. Employment lawyers recommend
early disclosure, but it's a catch-22 situation as disclosure often
sinks our chances of being hired.

Employment Struggles: The Media Lens

Stories of ADHD work struggles get little sympathy. Many
people are undersupported and stuck in jobs they hate. With
austerity rhetoric focusing on the need to 'protect the public
purse', accommodations are often represented as special
privileges. Media narratives tend to focus on rare requests
for things like emotional support animals, which overshadow
common ones, such as flexible hours. Most common ADHD
accommodations benefit a wide range of people, from those with
chronic illnesses to caregivers. Without context, though, it's
easy to think, Why should they get allowances when I'm just as
exhausted, broke or anxious?

No Access to Work: Disability or Entitlement

In the culture wars, asking for accommodations is framed
as 'demanding special privileges', while claiming benefits is
labelled 'scrounging'. In reality, the benefits system is punitive,
shame-inducing, nearly impossible to navigate with ADHD, and
designed to make you feel less than human, as if the goal is to
humiliate you into choosing work over help.

The process is gruelling. ADHD UK reports that only 43
per cent of ADHD Personal Independence Payment (PIP)
claims succeed, compared to an overall average of 53 per cent.
Headlines like the *Daily Mail*'s '£300m Bill for Handouts' skew
reality, with inflammatory terms like 'handouts' implying deceit.
But these benefits are essential services, funded by taxpayers,
reflecting the long-overdue recognition of psychiatric disorders
and ADHD's frequent comorbidities – many claimants have
multiple disabilities.

Claiming PIP, like many benefits, is a form of unpaid labour.
Tory MP Mel Stride's Victorian notion that 'work is good for
your mental health' ignores the soul-crushing bureaucracy
involved. For people with ADHD, it's not a lack of work ethic –
it's the mind-numbing process of navigating endless forms. With
help from a social worker friend, I still struggled despite my
privileges: education, native English, no caregiving duties. I felt
like a burden on society – an inefficient cog in the machine.

The *Daily Mail* rails against so-called 'disability influencers'
for 'beating the system' but, in reality, these communities share
life-saving advice on navigating forms designed to trip you up. By
far the most helpful and often-given advice is to remember that
the interviewer is not your friend. ADHD applicants struggle
to convey impairments because symptoms fluctuate, and literal
thinking makes us less likely to push back when assessors say,
'That's fine, moving on.' Nobody wants to insist on detailing
everything they can't do repeatedly, in granular and humiliating
detail. The system favours visible disabilities over nuanced
context-dependent ones like ADHD.

The UK government's Access to Work scheme, meant to
support disabled employees, has been plagued by delays. In

early 2024 more than twenty thousand people were waiting for assistance, a number that quadrupled throughout the year: by December, the list had grown to 25,063.

I applied for Access to Work in January 2024, expecting to hear back within twelve weeks. By June, nothing. In July I finally spoke to someone – due to past experiences, expecting dismissal. To my surprise, they were helpful, and I was granted funds for tools – noise-cancelling headphones, transcription and mind-mapping software, and a wall planner.

This progress on available support is both surprising and exciting, but the process still exemplifies how wildly out of touch the system is with ADHD reality. The idea that people like us would 'take advantage' of this scheme is laughable. Most ADHD people don't even apply – they're too overwhelmed or afraid they'll never use the tools. I couldn't even afford to buy the tools I'd been granted until October. They weren't refunded until mid November. This alone makes this support inaccessible for many people with ADHD.

Nobody has ever signed on for a lark. As noted, Tory MP Lee Anderson, known for dismissing poverty as 'nonsense' and blaming hunger on people's inability to cook for 30p, believes ADHD is caused by 'bad parenting'. His solution? Force people off benefits so they 'don't grow up thinking they can't work'. He says, 'If you are not disabled, you can go to work,' claiming government support is there, but, in reality, it doesn't materialise. ADHD people are more likely to rely on benefits at some point, not because they don't want to work, but because they're disproportionately self-employed, lacking safety nets like workplace pensions, sick pay or holiday pay. These omissions compound over a lifetime.

Support Available for People with ADHD

> **PIP (Personal Independence Payment)**. Offers financial support for those whose condition affects daily living or mobility. It's difficult to navigate but can make a significant difference, especially with other disabilities.

> **Freedom Pass and Travel Discounts.** Provides free or discounted travel for those unable to drive or experiencing reduced income due to disability. Options include local authority Freedom Passes, Disabled Persons Railcards or regional equivalents, significantly reducing transport costs. **Access to Work.** Funds workplace accommodations such as assistive technology, noise-cancelling headphones or transportation. The application process is slow but worth it for long-term support. Make sure you pay your rent first – refunds can take a while.

These programmes offer necessary lifelines, but systemic barriers make them hard to access. Advocacy and shared resources are critical to navigating them successfully.

Why Traditional Work Clashes with ADHD

For people with ADHD, traditional work settings are full of obstacles. Without medication, deep engagement or urgency, low dopamine makes everything feel like a 'task'. Nothing is just an activity – *everything* is a task. While neurotypicals might describe a function of their job as 'liaising with corporate stakeholders', ADHD brains break things down into tasks that neurotypicals don't count: the commute, the email, meetings, phone-calls. ADHD brains struggle to hold and retrieve information under pressure. At my old workplace I had a script written on Post-it notes to help me get through calls, but my manager snatched it, leaving me floundering. If we're allowed our coping mechanisms, there are ways around these challenges.

Fear of Failure and People-Pleasing

Fear of failure means ADHD people often overcompensate, tolerating unacceptable behaviour to avoid confrontation or shame. When a previous boss was verbally abusive, I found it deeply upsetting, but I didn't complain or stand up for myself – I didn't realise it wasn't appropriate because it was a familiar experience. For many with ADHD, rejection sensitivity adds an extra layer: even the thought of displeasing someone can feel unbearable. Combined with low dopamine levels, which impair motivation and reward pathways, we often seek external validation to fill the gap. People-pleasing becomes a way to avoid perceived rejection and to gain a fleeting sense of accomplishment or connection. This dynamic makes it easy for others to waste our time, and we overextend ourselves to avoid conflict or disappointing others. In the long term, it leads to burnout, as we exhaust ourselves just to keep up.

Emotional Regulation Issues

Emotions can feel urgent and overwhelming, especially in stressful environments. ADHD individuals make great advocates for others, but intense emotions can strain workplace relationships. The emotional intensity may pass quickly, but colleagues often remember meltdowns or blow-ups, making it harder to form stable relationships.

Problems with Authority

ADHD people often struggle with authority, rooted in negative interactions since school. We thrive on accountability but chafe at being closely supervised, bristling at micromanagement and arbitrary rules. This may seem at odds with our tendency to people-please, but the distinction lies in context: while we avoid confrontation to sidestep rejection, rigid authority triggers a deeper frustration tied to fairness and autonomy. Inflexibility rubs up against our neurodivergent sense of justice, creating conflict. Gamifying tasks doesn't work in all offices, and replying 'done that' to every task can come off as obnoxious.

Constructive criticism is easier to handle when it's clear, but vague feedback can feel like a personal attack, leading to defensive reactions. When workplaces don't value different ways of working, it can be hard to explain the ADHD thought process behind an unexpected route to a solution, adding more invisible labour.

Novelty Seeking and Job Hopping

The modern job market suits ADHD brains, where frequent career changes keep us engaged. Some fields – like journalism or TV freelancing – offer the variety we need. Journalist Emma Mahoney thrived on deadlines and novelty, though mistakes led to job losses. James, a TV freelancer, thrived on short contracts but lost focus when stuck on one project too long, leading to being fired.

Job Search and Applications Struggles

Job applications demand high executive function and sustained attention – filling them out accurately and quickly is hard. ADHD people find it harder not to get stuck in the perfectionist loop.

Neurotypicals feel the sting of rejection, too, but they adjust and speed up the process. ADHD people keep reacting the same way, taking every rejection – especially for jobs we're not even qualified for – as a personal failure. I've racked up more than forty failed applications, throwing them about like a star-happy ninja, thwack into the wall. One recruiter laughed, asking, 'What did you think all this education would get you?'

Melanie gets it. She never applied for jobs while employed, only during mental health breaks, and found the process so gruelling it drove her to seek an ADHD diagnosis. Even with career coaching, she couldn't get applications out. Moving to a new city left her unemployed for six months, her brain unable to co-operate: 'I went to war with my laptop every day for weeks and weeks, trying until I was in tears, hating myself.'

Interviews test whether you can pass as neurotypical. I can't, and it's humiliating. I'd rather solve a Rubik's cube blindfolded with my feet. Once, after holding it together, I relaxed too soon after the interview, ranting about how weird the construct was – needless to say, I didn't get the job.

Succeeding in interviews means mastering unspoken neurotypical rules: making just enough eye contact, speaking clearly, staying on topic. If there's more than one interviewer, it gets harder: who do you direct your answers to? How do you divide eye contact? While some neurotypical people might overthink these situations, for many it's second nature – an invisible labour that's far more taxing for us.

Many neurodivergent people struggle to get past the absurdity. Where else in life are you expected to calmly recite a moment when you triumphed over adversity like it's no big deal?

In the attention economy, we value talking about doing things more than actually doing them. Task-based interviews would level the playing field for neurodivergent people. Let the person who can do the job get hired, rather than the one who dazzles in an interview. Some companies, like Specialisterne in Denmark, get it. They employ neurodivergent people in tech by letting them program Lego Mindstorm Robots, skipping traditional interviews and focusing on skills.

Media Representation Versus Workplace Reality

Discussions about neurodivergence in the workplace are almost always from a neurotypical perspective. Reactions range from wonder to a very British irritation – 'I'm fine with it, but do they have to talk about it all the time?' Advocacy groups push stories about neurodivergent strengths, but recruitment opportunities for these talents are few. Public awareness is growing, and some employers are asking how to accommodate ADHD employees. Recently, an *Irish Independent* advice column was asked about an employee who 'mentioned [. . .] he has ADHD' but doesn't have a diagnosis. 'I'm sceptical [but] ADHD might help explain the problems with his performance. What should I do?'

On the flip side, the *Daily Mail* published more stories about people using ADHD as a 'get-out-of-work-free card'. One article: 'Meet the Professional Victim Who's Made £35,000 from Over 100 Disability Complaints.' Amid this increasing paranoia, legal protections for ADHD are vague, and employers aren't compelled to take meaningful action.

Can ADHD Be an Asset in the Workplace?

Yes, but only with certain factors in play: socio-economic privilege, good cognitive skills, mental health support, and a strong support network. With these, ADHD strengths like creative thinking or rapid task-switching might provide an edge, but its strengths have tidal rhythms and they're hard to summon on demand. Some work environments make ADHD strengths easier to harness:

> **High-Pressure, Fast-Paced Environments.** Roles like traders, chefs, A & E doctors or athletes provide the urgency ADHD brains need to stay engaged.
> **Creative, Flexible Work.** Jobs in the arts, journalism and music allow bursts of hyperfocus and creativity, perfect for ADHD minds.
> **Clear Structure with Frequent Rewards.** Fields like coding, sales or real estate offer built-in feedback loops – frequent dopamine hits that keep motivation high.

ADHD people often gravitate towards entrepreneurship and tech because thinking differently can be a strength in such fields. But, even then, support and accommodations are key.

Finding Fit: Choosing the Right Sector

Take Miles. Diagnosed with ADHD at age eight, he struggled until finding work in recruitment – a fast-paced, task-oriented job that fits his need for constant activity and quick wins. At dinner, he checked his phone, worried about a no-show recruit, leaving a voicemail to ensure they kept the job if they turned up the next day, and I thought of how different his approach was from the recruitment consultants I've met. 'He wanted that job so bad,' Miles explained, as if apologising for caring so much.

Miles's journey wasn't always this smooth. Symptoms which had caused trouble in previous traditional roles found their perfect outlet in recruitment. 'I talk all the time. I'm never not doing something,' he says. 'It's constant tasks – emails, calls, texts – and every little hit of dopamine keeps me going.' There are fewer pockets of time to be sad and no downtime 'to be like, "What am I doing?" It's just: I *have* to call these people because I need a project supervisor.'

Similarly, Mary (London, 44) retrained in beauty therapy after quitting university and opened a small clinic. Her all-or-nothing approach has led her to qualify in multiple modules, DJ on the side, and dream of teaching creative writing in a recovery college. Now that she knows what works for her, she's unstoppable.

Dopamine on a Deadline: The ADHD Attraction to Crisis Jobs

Alice (London, 35) a late-diagnosed woman in her thirties, has always gravitated towards intense, high-stakes roles. First, supporting war correspondents covering conflicts in Syria and Ukraine, then working with trafficked women while doing a master's in genocide, and now supporting victims of sexual violence. 'I've only worked in dark, intense subjects,' she says. 'They're the only things that keep my attention.' For Alice, the high-octane, adrenaline-driven work gives her the dopamine she needs.

Her story echoes that of many ADHD people: drawn to danger and urgency, but at a cost. They don't choose trauma for focus, but high-stakes environments provide the structure and emotional intensity they need to stay engaged.

Melanie, another ADHD woman, thrived in high-risk social work cases, where intense situations helped her focus. 'When someone's telling me their story, I can focus like no other time,' she says. But social work turned into 80 per cent paperwork, draining her energy and leaving her feeling ineffective, as empathy and connection are what's most needed in these roles. By not supporting neurodivergent people like Melanie, the system is losing some of its most empathetic and skilled workers.

Being Brave Enough to Jump Ship

During my two-year spree of applying for 'real jobs', I toyed with advertising – enticed by that iconic Sony ad with bouncing colourful balls and José González's 'Heartbeats'. Kobe, who battles her time-blindness daily, started in advertising right out of university, and set me straight: 'Neurodiversity doesn't sell. They hire mainstream people because understanding the mainstream is key to making money.' Her tendency to 'call out naked emperors' (classic ADHD shorthand) didn't sit well either. She hated the cutthroat culture: 'Everyone's backstabbing, all double meanings and personal-brand messaging.'

Programming was different. 'ADHD helps in parts of my job,' Kobe explained. 'Hyperfocus, stubbornness for that dopamine hit when the test passes, thinking in slow-motion or jumping ahead – those are assets not all programmers have.' Her likability helped too: 'Most programmers are shy, so my no-filter attitude makes me seem extroverted, even though I'm not. It's useful in a room full of guys.'

She thrived by pairing with autistic colleagues, forming a neurodivergent alliance, a dynamic with immense potential, as as explored in Chapter 6. 'There's something special about ADHD and autism working together. I'm open, no social cues, they trust me. They usually have the right answers but not the loud voice to get them out. I champion them, and it works.' Still, being likeable sometimes clashed with earning the respect needed for promotion. Kobe also found that ADHD women often fit better in male-dominated fields, saying, 'Put me next to a neurotypical woman, I have less in common with her than a neurotypical guy. That's why I ended up in programming. ADHD women and men share that slow-developing frontal lobe thing.'

Writing

Unless you come from money, being a writer isn't a great career move unless you're prepared to tack on a bunch of prefixes – content writer, ghostwriter, copywriter, proofreader. Creative fields provide the novelty ADHD brains crave,

but it's a double-edged sword. Writing this book is the longest I've worked on one subject, and I've lost all sense of whether it's good. A friend with ADHD suggested that I consider a chapter finished once I'm bored with it.

Employers in the creative sector still expect neurotypical performance. After I casually took medication while typing for a well-known writer, I was fired the next day. It's hard to make amphetamines sound like a good thing. It's a juggling act: chasing creative satisfaction while also fitting into an industry that demands routine, deadlines and polished work. Every job you take is a balancing act between your love for the craft and the overwhelming weight of structure and expectations.

What an ADHD-Friendly Work Environment Could Look Like

Creating an ADHD-friendly workplace starts with reasonable accommodations: flexibility, understanding and support tailored to our needs.

> **Flexible Hours.** Josh sums it up: 'I just won't be able to concentrate for the full day. I work really hard, and I will exceed your expectations, but maybe I should leave at three instead of killing time eating biscuits and watching the clock.' The freedom to work when productive leads to better outcomes for everyone.
>
> **Task-Based Productivity.** Daisy pointed out that forcing herself to sit through a traditional workday increased stress and killed productivity. For ADHD employees, meeting goals is more important than staying at a desk all day. Managers need to understand that productivity looks different for people with ADHD; if we're meeting goals, micromanagement is counterproductive.
>
> **Noise-Cancelling Headphones.** Everyone I spoke to who disclosed their ADHD was allowed these at work, helping to reduce distractions and improve focus.
>
> **Awareness and Training.** Neurodiversity training could have prevented situations like Alice's. Overwhelmed, she froze and struggled to answer questions, turning what was supposed

to be a one-hour session into three. She became increasingly stressed and physically agitated, unknowingly banging the table with her hands and legs, but her colleagues only got angry. Neurodiversity training could have prevented that. Instead, five years later, she still tears up recalling the incident. **Acceptance.** Among neurodivergent people, things are simpler. When Melanie disclosed her ADHD to a new boss, he responded, 'That's fine, I'm dyslexic.' But disclosure is tricky – ADHD can feel like 50 per cent of your identity when you've only met someone twice. After hundreds of meetings, it's just a sliver.

Employment is where systemic change can make a meaningful difference to people with ADHD, yet many managers, while acknowledging ADHD, lack the training or resources to genuinely support neurodivergent employees. This gap reflects a deeper issue in modern work culture: the clash between the rigid demands of traditional workplaces and the dynamic, multitasking minds configured by the attention economy. Streamlining the process for accommodations and removing the need for repeated documentation would give ADHD workers the dignity to advocate for themselves without battling bureaucracy.

Too often, policies are created to shield companies rather than to genuinely uplift employees. A quiet room or checklist won't solve the deeper issue – the systemic underestimation of ADHD's invisible labour. The truth is, the future of work depends on building environments that don't just tolerate diverse ways of thinking but value them as essential to innovation and progress. We've seen how the attention economy profits from exploiting neurodivergent brains; now it's time for workplaces to harness that same creativity and adaptability in ways that support employees, not drain them.

Reasonable accommodations are meant to ensure fairness, not favouritism. They allow everyone, regardless of neurotype, to participate fully. Think of it as like having a wheelchair ramp to an exam hall: adjustments are made, but the result – whether three A grades with ADHD or without – should be equally earned. Accommodations don't lower the bar; they make the bar accessible to all.

SPENDING

Swiss Roll of Shame Ingredient List:

- » Late fees on bills or missed payments because you forgot the due date.
- » Buying replacements for lost items like keys, wallets or phones.
- » Paying for multiple subscriptions because you forgot to cancel the free trial.
- » Missed appointments that result in cancellation fees or losing the spot.
- » Ordering takeaways because you didn't plan meals or forgot groceries.
- » Parking tickets or fines for forgetting to move the car or feed the meter.
- » Buying duplicate items because you couldn't remember if you had them already.
- » Unworn clothing with tags that you bought impulsively but forgot to return.
- » Extra travel costs for missed flights, buses and trains due to poor time management.

Texture Check

Grab something textured nearby, like a cosy sweater, and feel it for a few seconds to reground your focus.

Why? It provides a physical way to reset and recentre in a quick, accessible way.

Chapter 9

Prison: Crime and ... Revenge?

Six years ago, a friend and I viewed a flat-share directly opposite
Brixton Prison. Set back from the main road and behind a layer
of security, it was unusually quiet because nothing was allowed
to happen there. Sensing my unease, the estate agent said, 'Relax,
you're safe – they're all locked up.' But prisons don't make us
safer.

In the last thirty years the UK prison population has risen by
80 per cent, giving us the largest in Western Europe without any
corresponding reduction in violent crime. Meanwhile, private
prisons profit from prison labour, and public prisons funnel
revenue to the private sector through contracts. Now, living
half a mile from HMP Brixton, I pass the bus stop 'Brixton
Prison/Jebb Avenue' daily, yet often forget that the prison itself
exists. As Angela Davis wrote, 'We take prisons for granted
but are often afraid to face the realities they produce.' Prisons
are both 'present' and 'absent', seemingly 'disconnected from
our own lives'. But the horror of UK prisons, as highlighted by
their failings during the pandemic, demand that we face their
realities – particularly for neurodivergent people – and ask what
this means for our carceral system as a whole.

Prisons don't work – especially for neurodivergent people.
They don't rehabilitate: over 40 per cent of adults are convicted
of another offence within a year; and for ADHD adults that

rate is one third higher. ADHD prevalence inside UK prisons is estimated as ten times higher than outside.

Calls for ADHD screening in the carceral system date back to 2009, with evidence since 2012 showing that treatment reduces criminal behaviour by 32 per cent in men and 41 per cent in women – yet little has changed. Untreated ADHD in prisons still costs the UK justice system £11.7 million annually.

Covid-19: Lockdown Within Lockdown

Speaking of handling a crisis with all the grace of a giraffe on roller skates, let's talk about the UK's treatment of ADHD in prisons during the Covid-19 pandemic. Neurodivergent people in prison received no extra support. Public discussion about the mental health impact of lockdown gave remarkably little attention to people living in prisons. From March 2020 until February 2021 85 per cent of people in UK prisons spent twenty-three hours a day locked in 3-metre-by-2-metre cells, meeting the UN definition of torture. Even before the pandemic, twenty-two-hour lockups were common. Restrictions were far slower to lift in prisons, with visits cancelled and rehabilitative programmes suspended for months. During lockdown 44 per cent of incarcerated people reported 'experiencing thoughts that they would "be better off dead"' or considered hurting themselves, with one in five experiencing these thoughts daily.

ADHD, often accompanied by other neurodivergent conditions (like ASD and dyslexia) and mental health disorders (like oppositional defiant disorder and borderline personality disorder) serves as a proxy to expose systemic failings. Studies show that half of people with ADHD have experienced depression and they're four times more likely to have generalised anxiety disorder. All of this was magnified by the experience of lockdown. The Prison Reform Trust gives some harrowing examples. One prisoner interviewed said: 'I also have ADHD, so the lockdown has affected that. I told them I was suicidal. The senior officer stood there when I slit myself, and instead of helping me, ran to get healthcare for himself because I had hepatitis at the time.'

The Tory government deflected criticism of its inadequate care during Covid-19 by promising reforms for neurodivergent people, but these vague commitments only served to justify expanding the harmful carceral system which harms them. The issues that surface when considering incarcerated people with ADHD highlight the injustices built into the carceral system and the ways in which prison is inhumane. ADHD symptoms – hyperactivity, insomnia, anxiety, emotional dysregulation and poor impulse control – are aggravated by being locked up. The carceral system 'penalises people whose condition is marked by failure to change when punished'. Punishment is ineffective in changing behaviours, as ADHD people tend to persist in whatever activity offers the most dopamine. One study suggests that 74 per cent of incarcerated people with ADHD have a substance misuse disorder characterised by persistence despite negative consequences.

Unmasking the Government

In July 2021 the Tory government published an independent review of neurodiversity in the criminal justice system (CJS), identifying ADHD as an area of high impact. It acknowledged some hard truths: around half of people entering prison are neurodivergent. Staff lack the awareness and systems to diagnose, manage or treat them. It promised specialist training and consultations with neurodivergent people. Yet by December 2021, when Deputy Prime Minister Dominic Raab presented the 'Prisons Strategy White Paper', the neurodiversity discussion was clearly a distraction from the dominant narrative of punishment. The first page boasted of the biggest prison programme in over a century, designed to 'protect the public through punishment and incapacitation of offenders'. The neurodiversity review was buried on page 17, serving as self-congratulatory PR rather than a genuine commitment to reform. Since Labour came to power, the rhetoric around prisons has softened, nodding to rehabilitation and systemic reform. But with plans for fourteen thousand new prison places, the commitment to punishment over real change remains clear.

The Danger of Remand

The government's attachment to the current system is especially troubling with remand numbers at a fifty-year high. Custodial remand, intended for those posing a threat, is increasingly used for non-violent repeat offenders due to inadequate community support for addiction, homelessness and mental illness. People on remand are at a higher risk of suicide but are denied access to the same mental health services as the general prison population. This was tragically underlined by the suicide of Andrew Shirley while held on remand at HMP Hewell in Worcestershire in 2021. Despite declaring his ADHD and paranoid schizophrenia – both of which significantly increase suicide risk – and hearing voices telling him to kill himself, he was placed in segregation without a mental health assessment or care plan.

Neurodivergence: Rhetoric Versus Reality

Appealing to 'neurodiversity' provides cover for injustice. Without a universally accepted definition, it can't be easily measured. With investigations into 'Environmental, Social and Corporate Governance' (ESG) at Deutsche Bank and Goldman Sachs underway, we're gradually becoming aware of 'greenwashing' as a front for corporate greed. As demonstrated by disgraced crypto-exchange founder Sam Bankman-Fried's much proclaimed 'effective altruism', flaunting ethical credentials can encourage trust and subsequent investment of capital. Enter the state's latest strategic distraction, 'neurobathing' – policies that appear to address mental health reform but lack real impact.

Centring neurodivergence is savvy; we're an ill-defined group with no united activism network and don't demand widespread accountability. The criminal justice system can say a lot and do little on a subject that doesn't yet leave a bad aftertaste. By contrast, public trust in the carceral system has been irreparably damaged on issues like race and violence against women. At a time when the Metropolitan Police is under massive scrutiny, a quick Google search of 'police neurodiversity' yields nothing but internal HR reforms. Public awareness and organised pressure on the CJS are lacking, leaving little demand for real change in how neurodivergent people in prison are treated.

Why Do So Many People with ADHD End Up in Prison?

ADHD has long been associated with bad behaviour. Historical literature framed ADHD-like behaviours as signs of deviance. After the 1870 Education Act mandated school attendance in the UK, children with ADHD stuck out more. In 1902 British paediatrician Sir George Frederic Still described children who struggled to pay attention as displaying an 'abnormal defect of moral control', meaning they failed to comply with society's standards. Arguably, failure to conform to whatever standards exist is what sends people to prison. The immoral child, Still said, sought instant gratification, lacked insight into long-term consequences and resisted punishment. So far, so ADHD.

Over time, the diagnosis evolved from 'badly built minds' (caused by the foetus absorbing insanity in utero, leading to 'partial moral dementia') in 1913,

» to 'hyperkinesis' in the 1930s,
» to 'minimal brain dysfunction' in the 1940s,
» and 'minimal brain damage' in the 1970s – all vague and stigmatising.

Papers like 'A Study of Minimal Brain Dysfunction Amongst Male Delinquent Drop-Outs' stoked fears of dangerous ADHD symptoms long before the diagnosis existed. Headlines today arguably perpetuate the stigma: 'ADHD Dad Sentenced for Murdering Four-Year-Old Daughter'; 'Raging ADHD Teen Went Berserk and Threatened to Kill Mum and Stepdad with Kitchen Knife'; 'Peterborough: Murderer Said ADHD Made Him Kill Partygoer'.

The growing number of neurodivergent people in prison reinforces the unconscious belief that they are inherently dangerous. By highlighting their prevalence without acknowledging systemic failings contributing to their incarceration, the government amplifies ADHD stigma and stirs up long-standing prejudices linked to race and class. In the absence of better information, if prison is for punishing wrongdoers, then it follows that many with ADHD are imprisoned because ADHD makes them do bad things. This moral framing is similar to that once applied to addiction – another issue of self-regulation that punishment cannot correct. Understanding the connection exposes the carceral system's failure to grasp ADHD as a neurobiological disorder rather than a moral failing.

Remember ASBOs?

When headlines about ADHD's increasing prevalence appeared in the early 2020s, I thought of the ASBOs (anti-social behaviour orders) introduced by Tony Blair in 1998, the same year ADHD became an official diagnosis in the UK. ASBOs issued to anyone aged ten or over imposed multiple conditions to prevent 'causing alarm or distress to other people'.

Being issued an ASBO as a young person was essentially a flume into the criminal justice system. Despite Home Office guidance suggesting ASBOs were primarily for adults, 40 per cent were given to under-eighteens. Worse still, no mental health or educational screening was required before issuing them, so untreated ADHD symptoms were punished as destructive behaviour.

ASBOs imposed petty restrictions like 'don't swear in public', but when breached they led to criminal records for children as young as ten. For adults, the penalties included up to five years in prison or an unlimited fine, while those under eighteen risked up to two years in a detention centre. It was like having incredibly strict parents, except any disobedience risked life-altering punishment. Many people, especially neurodivergent people, struggled to understand the terms of their ASBO. In 2005 thirteen-year-old triplets from Kent, each with severe developmental delay and ADHD, were handed restrictive ASBOs that they quickly breached resulting in two-year supervision orders. ASBOs disproportionately affected Black people and disadvantaged children with a history of abuse in high-crime neighbourhoods. At least a third of recipients had a mental illness, with one suicidal woman banned from visiting rivers, lakes and bridges.

Before ASBOs, parents of neurodivergent children struggled to access special educational support and were blamed for 'poor' parenting. The government didn't address the causes of the behaviours they sought to punish. We now know that a third of under-seventeen ASBO recipients had neurological or learning disorders, with 40 per cent likely to have been diagnosed with ADHD. There's a biological basis for the behaviour for which children with ADHD were unfairly punished. These children persisted in behaviours that gave instant dopamine feedback, regardless of punishment. ASBOs, however, linked ADHD symptoms to public safety risks, reinforcing stigma in the media.

No Catchy Acronym for Structural Inequality

The link between ADHD and prison isn't about inherent deviance but structural inequality and lack of support. People vulnerable due to race and class are more likely to be incarcerated, and ADHD compounds this vulnerability by impairing impulse control and emotional regulation, increasing the likelihood of behaviours that lead to arrest. Without diagnosis or support, these behaviours escalate, leading to the incarceration of those who might otherwise avoid behaviour deemed criminal. Once in 'the system', with no accommodations for their vulnerabilities, escape is nearly impossible.

In the UK, ADHD diagnosis waiting lists can stretch up to ten years. Without winning the postcode lottery or having the cash for private healthcare, many remain undiagnosed, making the cycle of crime, arrest, prison and reoffending far more likely. Poor educational outcomes are a major risk factor for criminality: 30 per cent of ADHD kids have learning difficulties, and 40 per cent face temporary exclusion from school, with 11 per cent permanently excluded.

This marks them as 'problems' – over 90 per cent of repeat offenders were excluded from school. Lack of stable employment pushes people towards illegal activity, and untreated ADHD exacerbates poor impulse control, making shoplifting or drunk driving harder to resist. Substance misuse, which lands many in prison, drops significantly once ADHD is treated. Given the likelihood of suffering with comorbid mental health issues or addiction (96 per cent of inmates) and poor access to services it's no surprise that ADHD people have more contact with the police, are younger at first arrest, and have higher risk of multiple convictions, with a two- to three-fold increased risk of later arrest, conviction and imprisonment. Due to low self-esteem resulting from constant criticism and overlap with oppositional defiant disorder – (ODD) a 'behavioural disorder that is characterised by a persistent pattern of disobedient, defiant and hostile behaviour towards authority figures' – clashes with the police become even more likely, further lubricating the path to prison.

While Brixton Prison may be 'out of sight, out of mind', the same cannot be said of the carceral system's foot-soldiers, whose sirens scream up and down Brixton Hill and who routinely stop people, particularly Black people, without reason. In the lead-up to the Brixton Uprising of 1981, more than a thousand young Black men were stopped in just one week. A lack of understanding of ADHD is compounded by the systemic racism at play in the police. Non-white people are more likely to be stopped, searched, charged and sentenced harshly. Neurodivergent people often have a heightened sense of justice – like an emotional allergy to injustice, like breaking out in hives – but one expressed through anger and kicking off.

When misinterpreted, neurodivergent behaviours make arrest more likely. For Black people with ADHD, hyperactivity may be interpreted as 'aggression' and taken to justify an escalation of force. Once in custody, non-white people are more likely to have mental health needs, less likely to have them met, and less likely to be identified with learning difficulties on entering prison. Despite this, research on the experiences of non-white neurodivergent people in the criminal justice system is virtually non-existent. In one report, only 3 per cent of those interviewed by Her Majesty's Inspectorate of Probation were Black.

Entering Prison with ADHD

In prisons, 80 per cent of ADHD goes undiagnosed. Even for
those with diagnoses, prison authorities can restrict prescriptions
like Ritalin. ADHD treatment is inconsistent – many are denied
medication prescribed by their GPs. The diagnosis itself is often
doubted – one boy had his diagnosis revoked and replaced
with three personality disorders. Another incarcerated person
explained, 'I've got ADHD, emotional psychotic personality
disorder, anxiety and personality disorder and PTSD. So, I came
to jail and straight away they said, "You're not having none
of your meds …" I'm getting phone calls from mental health
teams saying, "Have you took your meds?"' Others arrive with
diagnosed but unmedicated ADHD and aren't given information
about treatment options. Screening for ADHD before entering
prison could prevent this, but it's not done.

After years of advocacy by campaign group ADHD Liberty,
the City of London's police force became the first in the country
to trial screening detainees in May 2023. The long-term goal
is to create a pathway to allow diagnoses to be fast-tracked
under the NHS. Other police departments have agreed to trial
screenings, but there's no long-term commitment or funding.
Most participants are not assessed for neurodivergent conditions
at any stage in the CJS. ADHD is unusually treatable: 90 per
cent of ADHD patients respond to medication. So why has
nothing been done?

The stakes are high: ADHD adults have a significantly higher
risk of self-harm and suicide, particularly in their first weeks in
prison. Sarah Templeton warned the CJS that one of her clients,
an ADHD teen at HMP Lowdham Grange in Nottinghamshire,
posed a serious risk. He wasn't medicated and, tragically, died
by suicide. Medication aside, diagnosis might help people
understand their behaviour and empower them to access mental
health services. Crucially, underlying ADHD has to be addressed
before comorbid conditions can be treated successfully. ADHD
people often call their diagnosis 'life-changing' or say, 'It saved
my life.' I have said both, and find imagining my life without
a diagnosis painful. But, as a white-passing ciswoman from a

middle-class family, there are safety nets beneath safety nets. Many incarcerated people with ADHD have been systemically failed.

Breaking Point: Limits of Reform

There is an urgent need for reform in prisons to create a more humane environment and prepare us for systemic change. Changes can be made to mitigate the trauma that ADHD people experience in prison. However, we also need to reckon with how their experiences expose a system-wide flaw. Immediate adjustments – more outdoor time, vocational programmes, clearer instructions and active roles like garden work – could improve things. But these simply amount to rearranging deck chairs on the *Titanic*. Reforms for ADHD benefit everyone, so shouldn't we have a wider societal conversation about the function of prisons?

No Transparency

It's almost impossible to find out whether ADHD treatment is available in the UK carceral system. There is no comprehensive overview. What exists is dense, not designed for general audiences and offers conflicting statistics. The Tory government's 'prisoner interviews' in 2021 are the only source of insight into lived experience. They tell stories like that of 'Mr K', who disclosed his autism, ADHD and PTSD, but 'didn't think any staff were aware of his conditions, and if they were, they didn't mention them or do anything different to accommodate them'. Attempts to survey ADHD treatments available can only note the total lack of data available, especially for women and non-white inmates.

Fragile Futures: Young Offenders and Care

The situation is no better for young offenders. More than eleven thousand under-twenty-fives are held in Young Offender Institutions in England and Wales, with ADHD symptoms

present in 45 per cent of children in custody. Universal ADHD
screening in schools could prevent impulsive crimes like petty
theft, but this hasn't happened. Most incarcerated children have
multiple vulnerabilities and receive little support. Non-white
children are disproportionately represented in prison (48 per
cent of inmates). Children from care backgrounds, who make up
fewer than 1 per cent of the population, represent 54 per cent of
incarcerated youth.

Take Whitney (London, 26) who entered foster care aged eight
due to neglect and abuse. The second child in a large family,
she watched her siblings taken by social services one by one.
She was admitted to a series of foster homes and periodically
returned home. Alongside the helplessness of childhood abuse,
she 'suffered at the hand of the state': 'I never had a choice in my
situation – I was just a child, vulnerable and wanting to go back
to what I thought was a normal life with my mum.' By twelve
she had petitioned the court to return to her mother and nan. By
sixteen Whitney was finally diagnosed with ADHD after being
permanently excluded from multiple schools.

The feelings leading to Whitney's diagnosis should sound
familiar: a sense that something was off, that she didn't fit in,
was 'always angry', unable to sit still. She was constantly on the
verge of a meltdown, her brain racing at full speed. At school
other students avoided her, and teachers grew frustrated with her
constant disruptions. No adult advocated for her until she took
herself to the GP, which led to her ADHD diagnosis. Despite
this, she received little support, and her family didn't understand.

Some people will take Whitney's account in bad faith and use
it to support their own view that ADHD doesn't exist. Here is
what they will say: 'What do you expect? She grew up in and
out of care, has poor mental health and has experienced abuse
and significant trauma. Of course she can't concentrate.' Making
that case involves actively choosing to ignore what Whitney
herself is saying. She acknowledges that the comorbid mental
health difficulties that often come alongside ADHD are part of
what makes ADHD so difficult. She wrote her first suicide note
aged seven. CAMHS intervened soon after, and she was later
diagnosed with anorexia, complicating ADHD treatment.

The diagnosis answered 'a lot of questions', but support was lacking. Whitney saw CAMHS 'very infrequently'. When Whitney was in care, the state was meant to be fulfilling the capacity of 'parents', yet despite having the paperwork for years, nobody mentioned ADHD. Looking back, Whitney can see the 'clear indications' of ADHD in her care records and school reports. This is the tragedy: 'I believe this really could have changed my life if an adult professional or those involved in my care at the time noticed.' Indeed, if anyone had taken care.

Hope: Early Intervention

Intervention for ADHD children in Youth Offender Institutions could change life trajectories. A £1.3 million study conducted by King's College, London, gave two hundred young adults at three UK young offender institutes and prisons, Ritalin, leading to significant reduction in ADHD symptoms. Her Majesty's Inspectorate of Prisons noted that some participants 'experienced stability in their behaviour for the first time'. Incarceration as a child compounds the likelihood of reoffending – over two thirds of children do so within twelve months of release. Each offence tightens probation terms and reduces opportunities, making further offences more likely.

Often, as in Whitney's case, this cycle begins with permanent school exclusion. As a teenager, when she wasn't in care or at home, she was homeless. Determined to avoid homelessness again, she started dealing drugs. As a female drug dealer in trap houses, she felt the need to protect herself: 'If you were going to stab me, I was gonna stab you first.' She carried a knife, but she never used it.

Aged nineteen, Whitney received a suspended sentence for ten charges, including possession of bladed articles and malicious communication. Multiple breaches led to a two-month prison sentence, where she witnessed women trapped in repeat offending cycles, which terrified her, but the options for escape were slim: 'Women with convictions are pushed towards hairdressing and basic women-kind jobs. The ambition isn't great enough, and women aren't pushed out of their comfort zones.'

After leaving prison, Whitney took up boxing, which she credits for helping her stay out of trouble. Now she aims to become a boxing coach, providing young people with 'meaningful activity'. That sense of purpose, which prison denies, is crucial: 'I had so many emotions going on. I thought, I need an outlet – I can't keep fighting everyone; I can't keep fighting myself ... I need to invest my energy into something more positive.' Not everyone has Whitney's resilience, and the prison system does little to foster it.

Diagnosis Dilemma

Once incarcerated, ADHD diagnosis is unlikely due to understaffing and lack of awareness. Increasingly, people self-diagnose ADHD on arrival at prison, but waiting lists for formal diagnosis don't move. According to NICE guidelines, only a specialist psychiatrist can diagnose ADHD, and to be sent to the health wing, a person must be severely ill. Failing to take ADHD medication is more likely to result in solitary confinement due to being labelled a 'management problem' than recognition of specific needs. Even when someone reaches the health wing, diagnosis is complicated by the prison environment's stress which exacerbates ADHD symptoms. As multiple mental health disorders are overrepresented in prisons, there is a lot of noise to tune out.

Diagnosis also requires a medical history, often inaccessible to inmates. Frequent transfers between prisons lead to lost records and ADHD diagnosis requires evidence of 'functional impairment' in multiple environments, which is impossible to assess adequately in prison. Many prisoners can't provide childhood proof of symptoms, and some families are unwilling or unable to participate in the process.

In high-turnover remand prisons, many are released or transferred before their appointment. One study showed a 50 per cent non-attendance rate at an ADHD clinic due to symptoms like forgetfulness, as well as illiteracy and lockdowns. Taking the simple step of sending appointment letters as well as verbal reminders reduced non-attendance at appointments by 30 per cent, but this method became unsustainable as referrals increased. The prison system, prioritising security, doesn't account for learning difficulties – it's designed to protect the status quo.

Pills Behind Bars

NICE guidelines recommend stimulant medication as first-line treatment for ADHD, as it's fast-acting and has proven long-term benefits. The guidelines haven't been adjusted for custodial settings, but in prisons they are simply not met. Frustrated by the lack of transparency, I spoke to a friend who completed a psychology placement in a prison. 'ADHD wasn't really addressed at all,' she told me. ADHD medication is often not available, and prison drug culture complicates proper delivery. People may be bullied into giving up or selling their medication. Guards, too, may fail to distribute it properly. Ensuring proper distribution requires extra work for healthcare staff, and because amphetamines are controlled substances, concerns about misuse persist, though they're often overstated.

Amphetamines on Trial

Quick-release stimulants carry a high risk of misuse when snorted, but slow-release medications, like Concerta XL, show low misuse rates. A study on incarcerated adults treated with Concerta XL for twelve weeks showed significant reductions in fights, property damage, self-harm and drug use. Only 4 per cent of participants sought the maximum dose, indicating minimal drug-seeking behaviour for slow-release stimulants. Sedative antidepressants and antipsychotics pose higher misuse risks, yet they remain widely prescribed. No one really wants to be more 'awake' in prison.

Having never been in one myself, I emailed a friend who'd served time in two UK prisons. He confirmed that despite the robust trade in prescription medications, Ritalin was never offered, though sleeping pills, sedatives and heroin substitutes were common. When he arrived, he was only asked about suicide risk – there was no follow-up for ADHD or related needs. A caseworker noted that people with gang histories often mistrust ADHD medication, fearing it might dull them. On getting out, they'll return to environments in which they need to be keenly attuned to staying alive; being on edge can keep you safe.

ADHD in the Guard's Gaze

The rule-breaking behaviour and sometimes irascible nature of ADHD prisoners cause prison guards to view ADHD as a major complicating factor in correctional efforts. Faced with arbitrary rules, ADHD individuals frequently ask, 'Why?' The 'superpower' narrative common outside prison doesn't apply here. Spontaneity and whimsy aren't helpful in correctional settings.

Training in recognising ADHD in inmates for prison staff is limited, and there's little focus on how the condition presents differently across age and gender. The pandemic worsened staffing shortages, leaving 36 per cent of the prison workforce in the UK with less than three years' experience. While younger officers may be more open to mental health ideas, only senior staff can refer inmates for assessments, leading to many missed diagnoses.

Economically, diagnosing and treating ADHD is a no-brainer. Professor Philip Asherson from King's College Institute of Psychiatry, Psychology and Neuroscience estimates that an individual referral to specialist services costs £1,500 – a fraction of the cost of incarceration. As he argues, the cost-saving potential is obvious: diagnosing and treating ADHD could significantly reduce recidivism and save the UK government money in the long term.

ADHD in Justice: A Cycle of Misunderstanding and Unfair Trials

ADHD complicates every stage of the criminal justice process. In police interviews symptoms like emotional dysregulation, agitation and rapid speech can be perceived as guilt. Stress exacerbates these symptoms, making people with ADHD more likely to go off on tangents, appear evasive or repeatedly answer, 'I don't know.' This increases the likelihood of being held on remand before trial.

At trial, ADHD people are three times more likely to falsely plead guilty, often because compliance offers a way out of overwhelming situations. Neurodivergent people frequently have a heightened sensitivity to authority, but that doesn't mean they don't respect it. Rather, the fear of authority – rooted in years of punitive interactions – can lead to compliance as a survival mechanism. This isn't genuine agreement but an attempt to mitigate immediate discomfort, even at the cost of long-term consequences. While ADHD people might thrive in certain high-stakes environments, like fast-paced jobs or emergencies, the courtroom's rigid structure and adversarial nature present a different kind of high-stakes scenario – one that overwhelms rather than engages. A 2020 report from the Equality and Human Rights Commission found that neurodivergent defendants faced barriers to understanding and navigating the legal process, putting their right to a fair trial at risk. This led to inadequate or absent accommodations during hearings. The CJS expects active participation, but many prisoners don't even know they're entitled to provisions under the Equality Act. Courts may consider neurodivergent conditions during sentencing, but it's unclear to what extent. *Inside Time*, a national newspaper for prisoners, advises readers to seek expert advice on whether ADHD was considered in their sentencing, but it's unreasonable to expect neurodivergent people to advocate for themselves in a system stacked against them.

The court's failure to understand ADHD's impact on behaviour means many people don't receive appropriate accommodations, like extra time to process information, regular breaks or being allowed to hold on to written evidence while answering questions. During long, monotonous procedures, ADHD people might zone out and miss crucial details or fixate on irrelevant information. As ever, the risks of impulsivity and emotional dysregulation loom large. Someone with ADHD might blurt out an inappropriate response or fail to regulate their anger, which can be misinterpreted as guilt. Ironically, both ASD and ADHD are often associated with compulsive truth-telling, but NDs' communication styles can still make them appear suspicious. The criminal justice system's lack of understanding of ADHD is clear in the way it fails to consider how the disorder influences past behaviours.

ADHD in Captivity

Having ADHD as a child is difficult largely because of the lack of self-determination. I was constantly in trouble without understanding why, since I wasn't doing anything on purpose. ADHD interferes less with my adult life because I dictate its terms. I control my environment, take medication and use coping mechanisms. Crucially, no one forces me to do tasks I'm uninterested in, and I've developed ways to manage symptoms. If I were sent back to school, I have no doubt that once again I'd spend most of my time in detention. Still, I'm dependent on a structure of habits and rituals, liable to meltdown when life throws me off balance, and in my last house-share I wore noise-cancelling headphones most of the time.

In prison, though, people with ADHD lose control over the tools they need to manage their condition. Neurodivergent people struggle to acclimatise to prison's restricted environment, leading to further disruptive behaviour. They're expected to follow rules rigidly, without access to the autonomy that helps manage symptoms. The horror of solitary confinement, fluorescent lighting and constant yet erratic noise are features, not bugs, of the carceral system. For neurodivergent people they are particularly brutal, and require urgent change, but they are inhumane for everyone. You can always hear someone screaming. Around 40 per cent of ADHD individuals also have sensory processing disorder, making loud, bright or abrasive environments overwhelming.

The system is designed for punishment, not accommodation, so ADHD symptoms are intensified. Physical activity, a natural way to manage ADHD, is restricted. Following arbitrary rules becomes an insurmountable challenge when the brain is starved of dopamine, and there's not enough stimulation to keep it engaged.

Punished for Having ADHD

Difficulty following rules – diagnostic of ADHD – translates into perceived non-compliance in prison, leading to escalating punishments. Prison officers often interpret inattention as deliberate disobedience. ADHD's hallmark traits – extreme emotional changes, hyperactivity and impulsivity – can lead to aggression, property damage, self-harm and even arson.

About 60 per cent of young men with ADHD admitted to hospitals during incarceration are there due to injury or poisoning, compared to 40 per cent without ADHD. This underscores the violence and self-harm prevalent among ADHD prisoners, pointing to the urgent need for targeted support and staff training, rather than brute force. However, young prisoners report that physical restraint is the go-to response, rather than de-escalation. You don't have to agree with my politics – you might believe that physical force and harsher sentences are appropriate, but even if they were, pragmatically speaking, they don't work. This approach doesn't reduce the number of young people sent to prison, or lower recidivism.

ADHD people are eight times more likely to engage in aggressive incidents in prison. This 'difficult' behaviour, rather than being recognised as a response to an overwhelming environment, is punished – often through solitary confinement, which exacerbates ADHD symptoms. Placing someone with ADHD in solitary confinement is punishing them for the system's failure to accommodate their needs. They are punished in this way more than most.

Prison officers force compliance without flexibility. Even those who recognise the causal relationship between ADHD and rule-breaking may not take it into account when delivering sanctions. As one previously incarcerated person explained: 'I did have a few prisons officers ask me if I was ADHD. I had never been diagnosed with it back then so, at first, I didn't care. But after a few people raised that, I asked, "What do [you] do about that?" All of them just answered, "Nothing." They recognise what it is, yet their solution to deal with it is punishment.'

A study found that some staff view solitary confinement

as 'counterproductive' for ADHD prisoners, yet still deem it
'necessary to ensure equal treatment'. The 2022 Prison Reform
Trust report revealed that prisoners in segregation had only
thirty minutes a day for fresh air, showering and phone calls.
Some units still had no in-cell electricity.

The Revolving Door: Round and Round We Go...

ADHD undermines the rehabilitative trajectory prisons claim
to offer. It increases the risk of punishment and makes it
harder to engage in the limited educational and rehabilitative
programmes available. This failure to foster autonomy sends
a clear message: people with ADHD, already suffering from
low self-esteem, are seen as having no potential. They're just
'serving time', not expected to grow or improve. Reports note the
total lack of positive reinforcement from prison staff – without
which, behaviour change becomes nearly impossible for people
with ADHD.

While prisons theoretically offer a variety of therapies –
occupational, speech, music, yoga – vacancies in key roles render
them ineffective. As someone working in prisons said: 'We have
no speech and language therapist, despite their role in leading the
neurodiversity pathway. Therapy waiting lists are months long,
and one-on-one interventions are only for crises.'

Prison's Failed Promise of Rehabilitation

Reintegration into society is difficult for everyone, but especially
for people with ADHD. Prison doesn't address the underlying
issues that lead to incarceration, so, upon release, individuals
return to the same root causes – unresolved trauma, mental
health challenges, substance misuse – often with weakened
family ties and community connections. For people with ADHD,
rehabilitation should include being taught new skills and the
provision of continuity of care, but these are sorely lacking.

Low executive function makes it hard for people with ADHD
to meet probation conditions, even in terms of sheer information
retention. Frequent probation officer turnover doesn't help,

and many officers lack neurodiversity training. They often find, correctly, that ADHD people struggle with compliance, motivation and engagement. Worse still, due to the lack of joined-up services, the ADHD diagnosis often doesn't transfer from prison to the outside world. Many people leave with one week's worth of medication and then join the years-long NHS waiting list. If someone goes too long without medication, they must restart the diagnosis process, delaying treatment further. In the meantime, symptoms resurface, increasing the likelihood the newly released will violate probation, struggle with employment, or get lost in the benefits and housing systems.

Criminal convictions already make finding legal employment difficult. NICE guidelines recommend that people with ADHD receive a Care Programme Approach, which offers a multidisciplinary structure for complex cases. But low diagnosis rates mean few receive this support. Those who are diagnosed get a care-plan co-ordinator, tasked with identifying available services – an overwhelming job for individuals with low executive function who have been institutionalised and forced to take a passive role in their own care.

Rising rates of self-harm, suicide and sexual assault in prisons reveal that the dangers neurodivergent individuals face are the same dangers all prisoners face. However, ADHD increases vulnerability, making the conditions of the carceral system even more difficult to bear, creating a population in crisis.

A Drop in the Ocean: The Struggle for ADHD-Focused Initiatives in UK Prisons

There are few ADHD-specific initiatives in UK prisons, and those that exist struggle due to recruitment issues and vacant specialist roles. Most programmes that create lasting change – by providing alternatives to behaviour deemed criminal – focus on reintegrating people into society.

One such programme is the Clink Restaurant scheme, which opened its third location at HMP Brixton in 2014, training incarcerated people in hospitality. By May 2022 more than 2,500 people across twenty-five prisons had received certification. Participants in the Clink are 32 per cent less likely to reoffend. Fast-paced, stimulating environments like kitchens seem to suit people with ADHD. As nineteen-year-old Hayden said, 'The Clink supported me through significant struggles with ADHD. Now I'm employed as a kitchen porter and regularly see my young daughter.'

Another initiative, 'A Pond in Every Prison', introduced ponds, streams or wetlands in over half of UK prisons. Originally designed for young people at HMP Thorn Cross, Warrington, these were meant to help with ADHD and mental health issues by providing relaxation and focus. While the optics are appealing – who doesn't like a pond? – there's no substantive evidence that they alleviate ADHD symptoms, so it's hard to measure whether these kinds of interventions are truly effective.

Inside Time

Inside Time, the national newspaper for prisoners, reveals the confusion and frustration around ADHD management in prisons. One man sought advice on controlling nightly outbursts of rage, a symptom of his ADHD. Another asked if it was true that libraries were no longer a statutory right, as a prison guard had falsely told him – reading was his main strategy for coping inside. The newspaper is filled with creative strategies for surviving twenty-three-hour lockups and mental health breakdowns, exacerbated during Covid-19. For example, Marcus Martin, who was diagnosed with ADHD after spending twenty years in prison, now hosts Cre8tiveTV on prison network Wayout TV, an arts show demonstrating stress-management techniques incarcerated people can try, like painting with tea. It launched in 2022 and broadcasts to more than forty thousand people across sixty-three prisons in England and Wales.

Putting a Treadmill in a McDonald's Is Not a Health Initiative

The Conservative government's illusion of addressing neurodivergence in prisons, which I call 'neurobathing', involved appearing to take action while doing very little. The response to its own research into neurodivergence in the criminal justice system was full of vague promises quickly followed by distractions. Saying, 'We'll reform the system!' then pointing to a shiny new prison wing as proof of progress is the equivalent of putting a plaster on a broken leg, then high-fiving the doctor.

In August 2022 London's Pentonville prison, near King's Cross, launched the UK's first Neurodivergent Wing (NDW), housing forty-five men and five mentors, the first of its kind in England. This initiative, part of the government's national strategy, prioritises people with autism, championed by former justice secretary Sir Robert Buckland, who first publicly spoke about his daughter's diagnosis in 2013. Other prisons have also appointed neurodiversity officers and been accredited by the National Autism Society. However, the heavy focus on autism – mentioned twenty-seven times in the neurodivergent report – overlooks other conditions like ADHD (which is mentioned only fourteen times, suggesting they're still failing to grasp the rich complexity of neurodiversity). This reflects an increased societal comfort with autism, perhaps because it's less stigmatised and often linked to lucrative skills, such as those in the tech industry.

Even within secure psychiatric hospitals, where many neurodivergent people are detained, neurodivergence training is not mandatory and focuses almost exclusively on autism. Which is a limited approach, as more than half of people with autism also show ADHD symptoms, and two-thirds of people with ADHD have elevated levels of autistic traits.

Despite its limitations, many view Pentonville's Neurodivergent Wing as a step forwards. It provides a more supportive environment than mainstream prison conditions. At the time of writing, it's impossible to tell if the wing is a success, but officers point towards one incarcerated man's reduced rate of self-harm since being transferred as a positive sign. Staff at the NDW are specially trained in neurodevelopmental needs and trauma-informed care (unlike the rest of the prison) and the space is designed to be calmer and less overstimulating, with features like noise-absorption panels, earplugs, occupational therapy, yoga and even pet therapy. It also has a 'sensory room'

(not yet open) for up to three men, with 'underwater scenes of
fish projected onto the walls, soft mats on the floor, padded walls
and beanbags'.

It sounds very nice. Those forty-five men have their own
rooms. But though it provides a glimmer of hope, the rest of
Pentonville remains dire. Built in 1842 to hold 520 people in
single cells, the prison now houses more than 1,100, with 60
per cent of prisoners sharing a space originally meant for one.
The 2022 report revealed that more than half of Pentonville's
prisoners felt victimised by staff, and 44 per cent of new arrivals
felt unsafe on their first night, compared to 23 per cent in other
prisons. Since 2019 seven people have died by suicide. The
recommendation to provide 'decent and hygienic conditions,
including properly screened toilets and sufficient space for each
occupant',still hasn't been implemented.

The post-inspection report highlighted the NDW as a positive
step, praising the 'ambitious long-term vision *represented* by the
plan for a new unit intended to care for neurodiverse prisoners'
[italics mine]. However, the inspector noted that Pentonville had
seen 'more false dawns than most prisons', and its long history of
unmet promises casts doubt on the potential for true reform. In
2020 wheelchair users were denied fresh air, and 70 per cent of
people felt threatened by staff. Less than a quarter of prisoners
had access to meaningful work or education, and illicit drugs
were frequently smuggled in by drones. The inspector's blunt
conclusion: 'Pentonville cannot safely and decently care for its
current population.'

Pentonville prison, where insufficient use of body cameras
and limited footage retention undermines officer accountability,
operates, like all prisons, behind high walls and closed doors.
Yet, after a damning inspection report in 2022, Pentonville's
governor invited *Inside Time* to feature the NDW ('More Love to
Give'), where a an officer remarked, 'It doesn't feel like the same
prison.' Of course it doesn't – it's not. The forensic psychologist
behind the NDW hoped it would reduce bullying, violence,
anxiety and self-harm rates among neurodivergent men.

But What About Everyone Else?

Is the solution to an overcrowded, dangerous prison environment a small neurodivergence-friendly wing for just forty-five men? Or does this merely highlight the problems faced in the rest of the prison? Cynically, it could be seen as a gesture to distract from the system's inhumanity – a shallow 'neurobath'. The NDW, designed to be calming and free from overstimulation, might even isolate its inhabitants and leave them less prepared for life outside prison.

Following the scathing inspection report, the Prison Service deflected attention to the NDW, issuing vague statements about progress. Despite a new Labour government and small-scale efforts like neurodiversity managers in each prison and charities like ADHD Liberty stepping in, the deeper issue remains: universal ADHD screening still hasn't been implemented.

Sarah Templeton from ADHD Liberty notes that neurodiversity managers are 'bored', don't know their roles and are calling her charity for help. 'We're training one tomorrow from a big category A prison because they don't know what they're doing,' she explains. Prisoners (like everyone else) are often confused by the term 'neurodiversity' and don't understand what it encompasses. Advocacy groups are left scrambling to fill gaps created by inadequate government action.

The Labour government's Mental Health Bill, introduced in late 2024, aims to modernise mental health care. It proposes ending the use of police and prison cells for mental health crises, limiting detention for autistic people and those with learning disabilities to 28 days, and requiring personalised care plans for all patients. Labour's commitment to this bill, first introduced by Theresa May in 2017 but repeatedly delayed, signals potential for change, but despite growing government rhetoric about neurodivergence, actionable reforms for ADHD remain startlingly absent. Treatment in prisons is inconsistent, poorly monitored and deprioritised.

Like the general population, the prison population is both neurotypical and neurodivergent. The inability of the carceral system to meet the needs of neurodivergent people isn't a glitch – it's a feature of a system ill-suited for complexity. As Shon Faye argues in *The Transgender Issue*, as per Angela Davis's notion of the 'prison industrial complex': 'The normalisation of the trans prison will only lead to more trans people being incarcerated.' The same logic applies to neurodivergent people.

Hypersensitivity and the Neurodivergent Experience

Both ASD and ADHD are linked to hypersensitivity. During the pandemic, the experience of neurodivergent prisoners was like an overactive smoke alarm in a system already in flames. The lockdowns and isolation magnified the inherent harms of the prison environment. Did the public only show increased sympathy because lockdowns forced us to imagine the conditions of prisons? Does meaningful government action only happen when ministers have personal stakes, like a neurodivergent child? Are we only stirred to action by what personally affects us? The pandemic temporarily brought prisons into the public eye, but they are always present. Reforms framed as neurodivergence initiatives risk becoming justifications for expanding the prison system itself.

Neurodivergence Shatters the One-Size-Fits-All Prison System

The challenges faced by neurodivergent prisoners, particularly those with ADHD, reveal a much broader crisis. If half of incarcerated people are neurodivergent, then divergence becomes the norm. The UN has stated that neurodivergent children, many of whom enter the adult prison system, 'should not be in the child justice system at all'. If prison is failing such a large portion of its population, is it even fit for purpose?

Prisons house society's most vulnerable people, serving as proof of the carceral system's fundamental failure. This should constitute a call for rebellion. Given that 50 per cent of prisoners are neurodivergent and 96 per cent have comorbid mental health issues, Shon Faye is right: 'Prisons operate as containment facilities for the growing mental health crisis.'

Community-based diversion programmes could offer alternatives to incarceration, particularly for neurodivergent people and reoffenders serving short sentences. These programmes could save money, reduce recidivism and, most importantly, provide meaningful support to those caught in the criminal justice system.

Restorative Justice: A Promising Alternative

Restorative justice offers an alternative for people with ADHD who aren't deterred by punishment. This model focuses on repairing harm, allowing perpetrators to take responsibility and make amends. Studies show that restorative justice has a high victim satisfaction rate (85 per cent) and reduces recidivism by 14 per cent. For neurodivergent people, especially those with ADHD, it could provide a much-needed alternative to a criminal justice system that consistently fails them. For example, hate crime victims, many of whom are neurodivergent, rarely report such crimes – when they do, fewer than 2 per cent of perpetrators are prosecuted. Restorative justice gives victims a platform to be heard, and perpetrators the opportunity to confront their actions, creating a space for accountability and repair.

Angela Davis argues, 'To understand the social meaning of the prison today within the context of a developing prison industrial complex means that punishment has to be severed from its link with crime.' Consider drug offences, which disproportionately lead to Black people's incarceration despite their lower rates of drug use compared to white people. Imagine if every white person who had smoked weed or snorted cocaine (traces of which are regularly found in Parliament) was in jail – how quickly would incarceration be reconsidered?

A government report urges the criminal justice system to use 'soft skills' like empathy and listening. If rehabilitation were truly the goal, these skills would be prioritised, and prison staff would address immediate needs by simply asking questions and listening.

Prisons Don't Solve Crime

Prisons lock up people grappling with mental health issues, addiction, trauma and systemic inequality. High recidivism rates prove that prisons don't rehabilitate or reintegrate people into society; they exclude people temporarily, only to release them with fewer resources and compounded problems. If prisons aren't about justice or rehabilitation, they become about revenge.

People with ADHD expose the cracks in the carceral system because they can't conform. Instructions aren't heard or are forgotten. Frustration leads to impulsive destruction of property, and they're placed in segregation again. Depression kicks in due to understimulation. Cut off from physical activity, symptoms worsen and functionality is often extremely impaired by being incarcerated. ADHD's 'time blindness' troubles the idea of 'serving time' – we have a different sense of time to neurotypical people and are oblivious to linear state-controlled time. Dopamine inefficiency means that people with untreated ADHD do not have internal motivation. They are not able to consistently do something simply because they are told to.

ADHD people – with their inability to perform tasks they find meaningless and their drive towards meaningful work – have something to teach the prison system.

The prison system's failure to accommodate neurodivergence is a failure to accommodate human complexity. Awareness of neurodivergence should sound an alarm, not for prison reform, but for questioning why we rely on prisons at all. Prisons don't work for neurodivergent people – and they don't work for society. If we truly recognise human diversity, we must also recognise that our approach to justice can't be one-size-fits-all. We need to imagine systems of accountability and care that go beyond punishment.

SELF-COMPASSIONING

I DO NOT NEED TO SET THE BAR OUT OF MY OWN REACH

IT CAN BE HERE

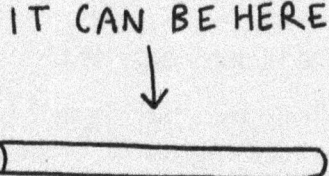

JUMP

WHeee

BECAUSE SMALL LEAPS LOOK EXCELLENT ON ME!

Self-Check Stoplight: Where's Your Energy At?

ADHD can take you through all levels of energy and focus, often in the same day. Use this guide to figure out where you are and what might help:

Red (Low Energy and Focus)

Brain feels like sludge? Low energy and can't get going? Try something restful or simple:

» Take a short nap or listen to a calming song.
» Go for a slow walk or stretch – something low effort but grounding.
» Tackle a super tiny task to build momentum – making tea counts.
» Find a heavy or gravity blanket or your softest hoodie, wrap yourself in it and cocoon.

Yellow (Medium Energy and Focus)

Some energy, but hard to focus? Here's what could help:

» Make a playlist to go along with this book.
» Try 'body-doubling' – work alongside someone, even virtually (YouTube) for motivation.
» Use a timer for short work bursts, like ten-to-fifteen minutes.
» Choose a nature-sound app to subtly occupy and stimulate your brain. I have Rainy Mood on all day.

Green (High Energy and Focus)

Feeling alert and ready? Go for it!

» Tackle bigger, tougher projects, or work on things you've been avoiding.

» Don't forget to reward yourself afterwards; keep the dopamine flowing!
» Momentum is key! Seize the energy to plan what you'll do next.

Chapter 10

The Dopamine Hunters: Addiction and ADHD

The Myth of Control

When Matthew Perry died, my social media timelines were flooded with clips from his *Newsnight* debate with Peter Hitchens on drug courts. *Friends* was the emotional white noise of my youth – a backdrop filled with unrealistic real-estate dreams and the wry humour of Chandler Bing. I'd always identified with Chandler's compulsive need to make people laugh, using jokes to diffuse tension that was reminiscent of his parents' divorce. Accepting Perry's death felt impossible, even as the updates poured in.

Curiosity led me to click on the *Newsnight* debate. Perry argued passionately for drug courts – mandating treatment over prison for non-violent first-time offenders – a move that drastically cuts reoffending rates. Baroness Meacher, a drug reform advocate, supported him, framing addiction as a health issue. On the other side of Jeremy Paxman sat Peter Hitchens, who condemned the courts as 'soft on criminals' and seemed to

be oddly pre-occupied with judges 'wearing tracksuit bottoms' –
a classist concern that left Perry, an American, baffled.

Peter Hitchens is essentially what you'd get if a sternly worded
'letter to the editor' became a person. ADHD denialism has
long been his crowd-pleaser. Twenty-three years ago, Hitchens
wrote his first article on ADHD and hasn't had a fresh take
since. In 2023, he asked in the *Daily Mail*: '[ADHD] has a
huge and powerful lobby which turns with fury on its critics
so I know this question will get me into loads of trouble but …
does ADHD even exist?' Classic right-wing move: conjure an
imaginary mob, weaponise scorn against a stigmatised minority.
Hitchens doesn't believe in dyslexia, opposed lockdown and
has a similar problem with abortion and same-sex marriage,
following an apparent pattern of disbelief in vulnerabilities
he hasn't personally experienced. On *Newsnight* Hitchens
asserted that addicts 'like taking drugs and don't want to stop',
a statement that is the rhetorical equivalent of covering your
own eyes and yelling, 'You can't see me.' Every year, millions
die because they can't stop. Few things irritate me more than
demands for 'objective truth' in these contexts. Hitchens
provided none himself, yet used it to undermine Perry, whose
relationship with his own experience was fraught. Such demand
feeds into the self-doubt many, especially neurodivergent people,
carry. Maybe it *is* all in our heads. Maybe we are just weak.

Science isn't on Hitchens's side. Addiction isn't about choice.
Perry acknowledged that 'the first drink is a choice', but after
that, the nature of choice changes. Addiction rewires the brain,
altering impulse control and decision-making processes. Brain
scans of addicts show long-term changes in the prefrontal
cortex – the very part that regulates executive function, already
compromised in ADHD. Addiction is a chronic, relapsing
disorder, marked by compulsive pursuit of rewards despite
escalating harm. Cravings become all-consuming. Control
is impaired, then lost. The brain's reward system is hijacked,
prioritising the substance above everything else. Even on a
fatal collision course, people with addiction are locked in
pursuit mode.

Hitchens's denial of the science behind addiction and

ADHD – despite overwhelming consensus – embodies how
society punishes vulnerability while glorifying self-reliance.
This harmful narrative dismisses the struggles of those who
fall outside the ideal of self-sufficiency, reinforcing stigma and
blocking compassionate interventions.

This chapter explores the intricate connection between ADHD
and addiction, examining how neurological, psychological
and societal factors intertwine to increase vulnerability among
neurodivergent people.

The Neurological Link Between ADHD and Addiction

ADHD is five to ten times more common among alcoholics than
in the general population. Having ADHD triples the risk of
substance misuse. The overlap isn't just predisposition – it's about
survival. People with ADHD often self-medicate to cope with
relentless internal chaos, making them vulnerable to substances
that promise quick relief. ADHD and addiction are biologically
linked; both disrupt behaviour and the brain's dopamine
pathways that control reward and pleasure. Understanding this
neurological overlap dispels the myth of 'choice' and opens the
door to proactive solutions.

Maia Szalavitz, who has both ADHD and autism and
struggled with cocaine and heroin addiction between the ages
of seventeen and twenty-three, provides a unique perspective.
In *Unbroken Brain* she frames addiction as a developmental
disorder, more similar to autism, ADHD and dyslexia than
to diseases like mumps or cancer. Her insights underpin this
chapter. Szalavitz argues that our approach to addiction mirrors
our treatment of neurodivergent disorders. Criminalising drug
use is akin to punishing repetitive autistic behaviours without
addressing underlying needs. Suppressing self-soothing behaviour
only heightens distress. Similarly, harsh drug policies may offer
quick 'solutions' but fail to address the distress that drives people
to seek refuge in drugs.

Neurodevelopmental disorders like ADHD and ASD make breaking free from addiction harder. Brain hyperconnectivity, a trait of ASD, can enhance memory but also lead to sensory overload and overlearning. Studies show that while the brain typically reduces synapses as it matures, autistic teens experience only a 16 per cent reduction compared to 41 per cent in neurotypical teens. This limited pruning reinforces overlearning and compulsive behaviours: overload creates a need to escape, while persistent connections amplify sensory experiences and emotional patterns, making it harder to break entrenched cycles.

The conditions share an inability to change behaviour through punishment alone, as the brain doesn't respond to negative reinforcement in the same way neurotypical brains might. As Szalavitz, a harm reduction advocate, asserts, hope emerges when learning is possible. With self-awareness and the right interventions, like structured routines, people with ADHD can adopt healthier patterns and reduce their risk of addiction – a point echoed by those now sober in this chapter.

Ideological forces shape how we judge people with addiction and ADHD. We judge those who lose control. Having empathy for people acting against their own best interests requires curiosity, imagination and the acknowledgement that some of your own advantages are systemic. Believing that our self-reliance and 'good choices' protect us fosters stigma, making it harder for people to seek help.

Addiction doesn't discriminate, but it's more dangerous for those who are disadvantaged because fewer resources and second chances exist. Szalavitz, found with 2.5 kilograms of cocaine but spared prison, attributes her leniency to being white, privileged and attending an Ivy League university.

Understanding the connection between addiction and ADHD reveals our societal insistence on framing issues of self-regulation as moral failings, solvable through punishment. It doesn't work.

Early Exposure: First to the Party, Last to Leave

Many first encounter addictive behaviours through seemingly harmless hobbies like video games or collecting Pokémon cards. But people with ADHD often start experimenting with alcohol and drugs earlier and more freely. This early exposure can quickly escalate into addiction because the adolescent ADHD brain is especially vulnerable to the rewiring effects of addictive substances. Children with ADHD are more likely to start drinking early – 40 per cent begin before the age of fifteen, compared to 22 per cent of children without ADHD. Most of the people I spoke to started experimenting with alcohol and drugs around the age of fourteen, well before their ADHD diagnosis.

Mary, a student and beautician, was diagnosed with ADHD aged forty-two but had her first drink aged five: 'I took a swig of sherry from the decanter in the front room and thought, "This is amazing."' By eighteen she had tried Ecstasy and immediately 'felt addicted'.

Sofia (Norwich, 24) diagnosed with ADHD at fifteen but never warned about addiction, had already fallen into it. The lack of early education meant she was blindsided when her misuse quickly escalated into dependency. She started drinking at twelve, blacking out by fourteen, and drinking at school by sixteen. She tried cocaine at fifteen and by seventeen was using pills and ketamine: 'My drinking was never gradual – I blacked out the first time I drank, and that pattern didn't stop until I got sober at twenty-one.' Impulsivity fuelled her addiction: 'I'd promise myself I'd stay sober, but the moment someone offered me a drink, I'd take it.' Once she understood herself more, sobriety became manageable: 'The meds help regulate my emotions, so I don't get as many urges to drink because my brain's under control.'

Early diagnosis is crucial to mitigating addiction risks. The first year at university, in a new environment with no established routine, is a flashpoint for people with ADHD – putting them at far greater risk than their neurotypical peers. Take Joel (Oxford, 34) a clinical trainee psychiatrist and recovering addict, who was diagnosed with ADHD at twenty-three while seeking help for addiction. He began using recreational drugs at fourteen and tried heroin in Laos at eighteen: 'I loved every drug I tried and immediately wanted more. I was fascinated by how they changed my experience of myself and of the world.'

I first met Joel when he was a fresher. I excelled at organising college events, getting freshers drunk while decorating rooms with tin foil and bypassing safety regulations. Several non-drinkers tugged at my sleeve and asked, 'What do we do?' Well, exactly, I thought, and hurried to set up sober alternatives while marvelling at their willingness to play board games – an activity I found abrasive and terrifying when sober at that age.

Joel stood out. Neurospicy people tend to unconsciously recognise each other; he had that slightly dazed look, like someone standing under a waterfall of information. He was razor-smart but chaotic – someone who might lose their shoes – and seemed surprised to find himself at lunch. We often hung out in a group of strays thrown together by pubs' early closing times, by our never wanting nights out to end. Looking back, I now realise that each of us was already grappling with at least one addiction, but I knew nothing then. I was twenty years old.

Ten years passed, and I didn't think about Joel. Until he published a piece on Vice about working for the *FT* while maintaining a heroin addiction. Learning he had been diagnosed with ADHD made my heart sink – I felt I should have seen it.

Listening to Joel's story now, it's clear that some of the pain he was trying to block out stemmed from undiagnosed ADHD. Emotional dysregulation and racing thoughts are characteristic, and Joel turned to alcohol to quiet his mind. He describes a 'restlessness and uneasiness, like I couldn't get peace'. People with ADHD often describe their minds as too noisy. As Joel put it, 'Alcohol quietened things down a bit.' At university, he used alcohol and self-harm to deal with baffling emotions. He couldn't concentrate and alcohol, then opiates, became his way to cope with the noise. 'I could just quietly get on with my studies,' he explained, or 'nod out' with a book when things got too intense. If Joel had known about ADHD, he could have had the self-awareness to put systems in place.

His friends supported him, but he felt isolated and different, trapped without the vocabulary to explain his experience. Instead, he rode the ADHD emotional rollercoaster, and his comfort in solitude turned into anxiety, pushing him to self-medicate with alcohol and ketamine. He would 'lose control' and do things that upset others, feeding his self-hatred. Eventually, his friends intervened, and the university drug services suggested he try sobriety.

Unaware of his co-occurring ADHD and addiction, Joel mistook brief abstinence for control. But when a friend was diagnosed with terminal cancer, ADHD's intense emotions overwhelmed him. Believing substances could 'eliminate emotions' – like rewiring a circuit board – he set about methodically numbing himself, but it left him feeling alienated, watching his friends connect emotionally while he felt on a separate plane.

More is More: Dopamine, Impulsivity and Time Blindness

Often called the 'pleasure neurotransmitter', dopamine plays a key role in our reward systems, driving not just pleasure but the desire itself. People with ADHD are vulnerable to addiction due to dopamine inefficiency – either low levels or poor uptake – leading to a restless search for balance. The pursuit of dopamine makes us swerve towards risk, cheap thrills and instant gratification. Addictive behaviours hijack the brain's dopamine pathways, making them irresistible. Chasing dopamine is like chasing a mirage – each hit provides fleeting relief but leaves us more depleted, deepening the cycle.

As Rachel (Winchester, 46) puts it, 'ADHD and moderation are hard to marry. You always want more of what makes you feel good. I simply don't have an off switch ... moderation can stay at home because I'm partying on.'

ADHD brains are driven by a restless, existential need for stimulation. It's not just boredom; it's a mental tap-dance, a compulsion to fill the void. Without stimulation, the mind of someone with ADHD is a starved beast. Once they get what they crave, there's a risk of binging. Dopamine doesn't create pleasure; it creates wanting. Addiction feeds a craving that keeps demanding more.

People with ADHD often continue dopamine-driven activities even when consequences worsen. This neurological overlap – impulsivity, sensitivity to rewards and dopamine dysregulation – explains why we're more prone to addiction. We're biologically predisposed and behaviourally wired for it. ADHD affects brain development – especially attention, impulse control and executive function – making it harder to foresee the long-term consequences.

I Scream, You Scream, We All Scream for D O P A M I N E

For people with ADHD, the brain's dopamine system is less responsive, which makes us particularly susceptible to addiction. Intense bursts of dopamine from substances like cocaine flood the brain, but, over time, natural production drops, leaving you wanting more. Chronic cocaine use reduces the number of dopamine receptors in the brain, and with ADHD we have fewer to begin with.

In the 1990s, psychology professor Kent Berridge challenged the notion that dopamine is linked to pleasure. He showed that 'wanting' and 'liking' are distinct brain functions. Addiction amplifies wanting without increasing liking, which explains why addicts crave more but enjoy it less over time. As Joel summarised: 'As addiction progresses, you want your drug more, but like it less.' Anyone who's ever been addicted to the chase, like shopping for something when 'only 1 left' pops up, knows it's about the moment of purchase, not the ownership. Gambling addicts rarely stop after winning the jackpot. Addiction is more about wanting than getting. The addicted person craves not just the substance but relief from the craving itself. Each time they give in, the cycle deepens, binding feelings of emptiness or loneliness to the external source of relief. The craving promises escape, but the escape guarantees it will return. You'll always need more.

I know the dopamine quest well. Growing up undiagnosed, I

tried hacking my brain with ridiculous amounts of coffee (now, medicated, I stop after two). By fifteen I'd grandiosely concluded there were seven ways to feel better: food, alcohol, drugs, sex, exercise, writing and intense experiences. Why not do all of them, all the time?

Young people with ADHD need to understand their brains to resist addiction. There's nothing wrong with hunting dopamine. Sure, managing it is a slog, but learning how can bring real joy.

Low dopamine drives us towards intense, high-stakes experiences. Matthew Perry's production company was called Anhedonia Productions – a fancy word for the emptiness that low dopamine causes. You feel nothing. Ice cream on a scorching day? Zilch. ADHD can drive this craving for intensity, which can lead to self-harm. Sofia nailed it: 'Using alcohol and other substances was the only way I could escape the madness in my brain. Once I started, I couldn't stop, constantly planning the next drink or drug, always terrified of running out.'

> Two main urges drive addiction in people with ADHD:
> » Quieting the brain: 'My brain is so busy all the time. Drinking shuts up the mean side of my brain and makes me feel unstoppable.'
> » Feeling weird: 'I felt different my whole life, but when people were drinking, I could be normal.'
> A third overlooked factor is ADHD's subjective sense of time, or 'time blindness'.

NOW
FOR EVER
ALWAYS

People with ADHD live in a state of now, for ever, and always. This warped sense of time fuels addiction – if you can't bear your feelings, drink or drugs offer quick relief. Now, I spend a few months sober each year. Initially, I panicked about how to change my mood. I miss the rush; without alcohol, the release is gradual, not instant.

Emotional regulation is another challenge. With time skewed, feelings seem eternal. ADHD's constant urgency makes it hard to trust that cravings will pass – they feel like tsunamis. The mantra 'this too shall pass' helps, but it's hard to believe.

Living in an eternal present becomes claustrophobic. When your mind ping-pongs between reacting to stimuli, dwelling on the past and anticipating possible futures, consequences become abstract, while the instant relief from substances feels overwhelmingly real.

In AA, Sofia learned to live in the moment: 'My ADHD brain lives in the future of events that haven't happened. Sometimes, I have to take things one minute at a time, but learning to live in the now helps when I have urges. When things get bad, I remind myself, "I'm just not drinking for this minute."'

Many people I spoke to grew up believing they had 'addictive personalities', a myth that obscured the link to ADHD. Even those diagnosed with ADHD weren't told about the addiction risks. They noticed their strong attachment to drinking, smoking or video games long before understanding their condition. ADHD was the missing piece that finally made sense and led to their recovery.

From a young age, I was told I had an addictive personality. Those waffle-biscuits stuck together with honey, *The Sims*. I found it very hard to start some things, and others, impossible to stop. Years after my diagnosis, understanding the dopamine-fuelled connection between ADHD and addiction reframed that morbid curiosity and sense of inevitability as empowerment.

Learning about dopamine should be part of holistic ADHD treatment. Dopamine inconsistency means we don't get the natural payoff from doing things we should, which normally motivates people to act. For those with ADHD, the need for a reward is amplified by low executive function, which makes even simple tasks seem monumental. Without knowing how dopamine works, it's hard to get ourselves going, so we turn to coffee, sugar or Instagram for quick dopamine hits – until they're not enough, and we seek more extreme solutions.

Self-Medicating: Quieting the Chaos, DIY Edition

Both ADHD and addiction involve attempts to align internal chaos with external realities, using external things to 'fix' feelings. We all do this to some degree – it's why God made cookie dough – but the problem starts when 'want' turns into 'need'.

People with ADHD are particularly prone to using substances to change how they feel. Without diagnosis or support, short-term relief often worsens long-term struggles, leading to our increased misuse of alcohol, caffeine, cigarettes, cannabis, cocaine or prescription meds.

Addictive substances can numb unruly emotions, temporarily stuff a hollow sadness, provide a hit of energy, lift you out of boredom, smudge feelings of alienation and mask inadequacy. They ease the way into parties and soften the landing once you're there. They help you climb out of mental stupor into the light for a while – like squashing a gnat buzzing around with guilt and anxiety between your finger and thumb.

Using the term 'self-medication' for ADHD is like saying you're 'freelance fire-fighting' when actually you set the kitchen on fire while trying to cook. You're trying to solve a problem, but the methods create more chaos than relief. Addictive substances hijack your reward system, offering temporary relief without addressing the cause. Everyone I spoke to discovered they had ADHD only after addiction took hold. The substances alleviated the chaos of living with ADHD. No one was offered services tailored to treat both ADHD and addiction.

For people with ADHD, nothing is just an activity – everything feels like a task. With an unreliable dopamine system, it makes sense to bribe yourself through the day. For Mary (London, 45), a single mother with ADHD, alcohol became her way of compensating for the constant mental effort required to manage work, parenting and the never-ending to-do list: 'I deserved it. It was getting home from work and the school run, starting dinner, opening that bottle of wine, and hearing that pop ... now I can relax.' This behaviour is common, and research suggests that women, especially those carrying the weight of domestic work, are more likely to use alcohol to cope, but for those with ADHD, the added layer of dopamine dysregulation makes it harder to unwind naturally. But the line between enjoying a glass of wine while cooking and being unable to make dinner without it is thin. Mary quit – she wasn't physiologically dependent but alcohol was the crutch she needed.

Bex (Worcestershire, 52) who started smoking cannabis at sixteen and used it daily into her late thirties, realised after her ADHD diagnosis: 'I needed cannabis to normalise my relax time. I didn't have the luxury of a diagnosis or proper meds. I saw it as a necessity, not an addiction.' Bex used cannabis as her nightly 'reward', but when life threw her curveballs – like the death of her father, and losing her job – it became her primary coping mechanism, eventually driving her into debt.

ADHD and bipolar disorder increase the addiction risk fivefold, because addiction is often driven by escaping the pain of living with either. People with ADHD don't talk about their drugs of choice in terms of getting high. Sometimes there's pleasure, even affection, for the anaesthetic that enables 'normal' function. But often it's about scaling the world down, trying to outrun yourself, or hungering for oblivion. For many, drinking quickly escalates into blackouts. At the end of it all, though, you're still you.

The difference between self-medication and addiction often depends on whether someone has other resources to meet their needs. People with ADHD often struggle to weigh risks, and without diagnosis, treatment or support it's hard to avoid self-medicating.

Social Masking and Liquid Courage

Eighty per cent of people with ADHD have at least one other
mental health disorder. Depression and anxiety, often rooted
in experiences of peer rejection, are tightly linked to substance
misuse, as self-medicating can 'hot-wire' the brain. Anxiety,
ADHD's shrill little companion, that brain monkey with a
miniature cymbal, is another major risk factor for addiction. The
stigma around ADHD, combined with inadequate mental health
support, pushes many towards substances for relief.

The stereotype of someone with ADHD as bubbly and
talkative isn't universal. Many of us swing between talking a
mile a minute and appearing mute. Even more struggle with
social skills, and feel overwhelmed, using substances to mask
social anxiety. At parties, the few times I've tried to stay sober,
people assumed I was overwhelmed or asked what was wrong.
Being hyperstimulated isn't 'normal'. In the UK, where alcohol is
the default social lubricant, being tipsy is more acceptable than
being awkward. This cultural norm can obscure the severity of
addiction, as self-medicating behaviour may be mistaken for
typical drinking habits, delaying help.

For Mary, drinking was survival. Although tipsiness could
make her feel 'comfortable', she hated small talk so 'felt a need
to get obliverated [sic]'. Clubbing, with its mix of intense sensory
stimulation and anonymity, dancing for hours by herself, seemed
like a better alternative, 'like being in the zone'.

Substance use becomes a constant amid mood swings and
the sensory volatility of ADHD. For people like Rachel, alcohol
masked the 'real' self society didn't see: 'I became the tequila-
shots girl, the I-want-to-be-liked girl.' She was masking struggles
from a world that didn't understand her needs. After graduation,
alcohol stayed her 'go-to when I was happy, sad, trying to be
fun Mum, or just trying to put on a happy face. To outsiders, I
didn't seem like an alcoholic, but I was having a crafty shot with
breakfast.'

Escaping a Racing Mind

Joel, who got clean at twenty-three after landing and losing his job at the *Financial Times*, felt he had to escape his own mind: 'Everyone else could slide into smooth conversations, while I played out a million scenarios in my head. I felt anxious, restless and couldn't sleep. It seemed pretty logical and humane to turn to opiates when I knew they meant I didn't have to put up with all of that.'

Opiates dulled his racing thoughts, easing insomnia and quieting social anxiety. He relied on self-harm as an emotional pressure valve. He was constantly afraid of saying something weird. He wasn't seeking a high; he wanted stability. But with undiagnosed ADHD, once he started, he couldn't stop. Eventually, the curiosity and wonder he felt about people were eclipsed by a sense of failure and shame as his addiction escalated. He hadn't heard of 'executive function', but its deficits – like constantly forgetting things – made him feel like he was 'constantly letting people down'. He began stealing food, spending all his money on heroin, and travelling to pharmacies that hadn't flagged him for buying codeine.

Sofia's story echoes Joel's. Self-harm was her first addiction, and she used substances to escape her brain. Following her mother's death, her substance use worsened: 'I felt depressed, out of control and in pain, so I drank. Then I had comedowns, which made it worse. And so the cycle continued.'

Substances amplify impulsivity and emotional extremes, especially with alcohol. Sofia self-harmed or attempted suicide whenever she drank or used drugs: 'I nearly died a couple of times, but I'm so grateful I didn't.'

The relentless mental noise of ADHD can drive a desperate search for anything that offers a reprieve, leading many to self-medicate in attempts to achieve fleeting moments of peace. Over time, the substances that initially provided calm end up creating an even louder chaos, reinforcing the cycle and deepening the sense of isolation.

Temporary Calm, Lasting Consequences

ADHD amplifies the need to 'take the edge off'. It makes your experience of the world volatile and intense. Nicotine helped Jay (Berkshire, 30) focus, while MDMA gave him the social ease he craved: 'I could feel the music, be present in conversations – my anxiety melted away.' This effect often leads people with ADHD to drugs resembling their medications, like cocaine, which can feel disturbingly familiar: 'This feels like meds, only fun,' one person shared.

Some people find that cannabis in conjunction with other coping mechanisms can restore balance, *as long as* they're honest with themselves and loved ones, maintain a strong support network, and seek 'good dopamine' from exercise, sunlight and laughter. But, especially for people with ADHD, the substance can't be the only crutch.

Managing Sleep and Energy Dysregulation

For many with ADHD, energy spikes at night are followed by lethargy in the morning. For some, alcohol drowns out repetitive thoughts, and hangovers can offer a break from the noise, making strategic excess a coping tool. (When you obsess over something negative, your brain lights up the same areas as if the negative event were happening all over again.) This need to silence the brain underscores why ADHD medication is crucial. Without it, people will find their own methods, and our culture pushes escape routes as much as it pushes goals.

Work addiction, another 'acceptable' form of self-medication, can block out trauma but eventually becomes its own prison. Joel's life as a heroin addict revolved around work. He used heroin 'to go to work, to stay at work', juggling methadone doses during lunch breaks. 'Physical sickness was never more than a few hours away, which was terrifying. I just wanted to do a good job at work, but managing a heroin addiction was immensely stressful.'

Towards a Compassionate Approach

Rat Park Revisited: Environment and Isolation

Addiction doesn't just result from exposure to drugs; it's the interplay of brain chemistry, genetics, environment and a complex emotional landscape. For people with ADHD, the 'laboratories' they grow up in are often hostile. Psychologist Bruce Alexander's 'Rat Park' experiment showed that rats in enriched environments were less likely to become addicted than those in isolation. Similarly, addiction in humans is often linked to emotional isolation and stress. Neurodivergent brains experience an amplified sense of reward and punishment, making the highs of addictive substances more euphoric and the lows of withdrawal more devastating. This creates a relentless cycle of dependency.

Reflect for a moment on how often children with ADHD are shamed at school, misunderstood as 'bad' or 'weird'. They face repeated rejection from teachers, peers and even family. The lifelong effects of bullying – often manifesting as emotional rejection – are compounded by isolation at home. For those with ADHD, this rejection and loneliness can lead to a sense of powerlessness, multiplied by there being no tangible proof of our difficulties. Add in difficulty maintaining relationships, poor mental health and financial instability, and it's easy to see how addiction becomes a coping mechanism. ADHD impairs the ability to assess risks and think long-term, so turning to addictive substances – whether for relief, escape or self-medication – often feels inevitable.

Breaking the Cycle: Positive Rituals and Community

Addiction thrives on ritual, with dopamine triggered by anticipation, not just the high. Addiction becomes a cycle of craving and disappointment, with each letdown fuelling the next chase. Repetition reinforces addiction, with routines around drug use becoming a source of comfort and dopamine release, alleviating anxiety. Specific cues – places, objects, people – become tied to cravings. Near the end of Joel's addiction, he'd accumulated two socks full of coins which he planned to spend on heroin. The jangling sound became part of the high: 'They were heavy. Noisy. Everything you'd want in a sock of coins ... As I walked through King's Cross, I could feel them thumping my flank. I could hear them jingling. I could feel the flutterings of anticipation of what I was about to do with them.'

Before twelve-step programmes, addiction often provides its own form of community – whether among people who've lost everything or those whose sensors can detect who else is interested in getting out of their skin. Recovery requires replacing these habits with healthier routines.

In twelve-step programmes, spirituality plays a major role. Mary learned in AA that she had been trying 'to fill a hole in my soul with material things'. For people with ADHD, staying motivated – especially without instant dopamine rewards – is tough, making community support vital. Addiction isolates, and connection is key to breaking its grip.

In recovery, Joel replaced old rituals with new ones. For years, he exercised, meditated and kept a daily journal. Today, he still exercises every morning – running, using gymnastics rings – almost without fail. His ADHD is still there, but now he manages it. Seven years ago, he would've laughed at the idea of a 'structured life', but now daily exercise makes him feel 'calmer, more content and focused'. Meditation helps him let go of intrusive thoughts, redirect his attention, and seek help when overwhelmed. 'That mindset – that I can always talk about something before I act – has slowed me down.'

Whatever it Takes to Feel Normal

As addiction progresses, the substance stops providing a high and becomes necessary just to feel normal. Dopamine rewires the brain so that only addiction-related behaviours hold value. This is termed salience attribution – where a false need outweighs real needs, making everything else irrelevant. Missing a family lunch becomes irrelevant compared to the risk of running out of your substance of choice. Mary stopped seeing friends who'd moved on with their careers and surrounded herself with people who drank and used drugs like her. 'I didn't want to talk to the mums at school. I'd wear sunglasses, a hood, and pretend to be on my phone.' Eventually, she became isolated: 'Towards the end, it was just me, YouTube and a bottle of wine.'

Long-term drug use reduces dopamine receptors in the brain, making normal activities less pleasurable and reinforcing addiction. At a certain point, you're chasing a high that's out of reach. Matthew Perry, for example, only stopped taking OxyContin when it no longer had any effect. ADHD, remember, already means fewer dopamine receptors, and long-term drug use worsens this deficit, creating a vicious cycle.

Authority Figures: Defiance and Distrust

For many people with ADHD, substance misuse is an original and a continuing 'fuck you'. After years of being told how to do things you can't do, or feeling perpetually 'not enough', addiction becomes a drawn out rebellion – the 'fuck you' stays around. Those who face multiple disadvantages often develop a deep mistrust of institutions, especially if they've had run-ins with the criminal justice system. While ADHD can drive people-pleasing in certain contexts, especially to avoid rejection, it can also manifest as defiance when the stakes feel completely unfair. People with ADHD tend to push back against authority figures, and addiction adds another layer of conflict.

Neurodivergent people often realise that they have an addiction problem when the boundaries they've put up themselves collapse. Maia Szalavitz recognised her addiction when she considered trading sex for heroin, a line she'd never imagined crossing. Joel's flimsy rules – 'no heroin before work' – soon collapsed, as did his control. Sofia's blackouts culminated in a series of terrifying incidents: her waking on her kitchen floor, bruised, with a broken hand and no memory of what had happened. The next time, she had no memory either, but she was burned and there was 'melted skin stuck to her electric stove'. The breaking point came after waking up in A & E, prompting her to seek help. At the time of writing, she has been sober for nineteen months.

Medication or Misuse?

The relationship between ADHD medications and addiction
has been controversial, especially regarding concerns of misuse.
However, research shows that treating ADHD with stimulant
medications significantly reduces the risk of addiction. Proper
treatment makes individuals far less likely to self-medicate with
substances. For long-term recovery, it's crucial to address both
ADHD and co-occurring disorders like addiction.

Stigma around ADHD and addiction often prevents people
from being honest with their doctors. This is problematic, as
treating ADHD alongside addiction is complex. Stimulants can
sometimes worsen other substance-use behaviours, like alcohol
misuse, so non-stimulant medications may need to be prescribed
and closely monitored. Unfortunately, clear treatment guidelines
for ADHD and substance-use disorders together are still lacking.

Stigma, coupled with scepticism around amphetamines, has
led many to mistrust ADHD medications, making them more
likely to self-medicate with alcohol or marijuana. This societal
reluctance to treat ADHD with appropriate medication directly
feeds into the addiction crisis.

Many devastating addictions could have been avoided with
early diagnosis and treatment. In *In the Realm of Hungry
Ghosts* Gabor Maté recounts the story of Remi, diagnosed
with ADHD later in life. His struggles with restlessness,
disorganisation and impulse control finally made sense. 'That's
me all over,' he admitted, slapping his forehead in recognition.
Diagnosed too late, Remi had already used cocaine since his
teens and switched to heroin in prison. Ritalin helped briefly –
'My mind isn't going off like a machine gun!' – and Remi
finally felt remorse for a stabbing he'd committed when high,
but he couldn't abstain from cocaine, and his prescription was
withdrawn. The diagnosis had come too late.

Diagnosis and Recovery

From Self-Disgust to Self-Awareness

Joel didn't seek an ADHD diagnosis. In a psychiatrist's office, he conceded that the signs were there – behavioural problems in primary school, explosive outbursts when bored. His undiagnosed ADHD fuelled his self-disgust, which in turn fuelled his addiction. Simple tasks like job applications or paying bills felt impossible, leading to a cycle of avoidance. Joel perceived himself as unreliable, hardened by impulsivity, never realising these behaviours were symptomatic of ADHD.

Joel's story reads like someone trying to drug the ADHD out of himself without knowing it. He felt like an outsider, lacking a 'manual for life' – a common experience among the neurodivergent. His diagnosis offered hope, shifting his perspective from self-hatred to self-compassion. He learned to create systems to support himself: 'Before, I just felt like I was a bad person. But I started to understand that some things are just harder for me than for others.'

Joel was prescribed ADHD medication but stopped taking it in rehab. He lived in a sober house where the owner viewed amphetamines as unacceptable within the twelve-steps. As Joel explained, 'There's no specific mention of amphetamine-based medications in the literature, but I've heard people equate them with recreational speed.' The tension between medical treatment and recovery programmes is common, especially regarding stimulant medications. In recovery, Joel reflected on the false promises of substance use. In his essay 'On Not Taking Cocaine in Colombia', he explains:

> The campaign waged by that craving voice boils down to a single message: it feels so good. 'Yes, it feels good,' I countered time and again, but it's a feeling I've felt a thousand times before. There is nothing new there. But ... nothing feels so good.
>
> And sadly, in a way that is true. Nothing can feel as good as that intense flash of euphoria. But it's such a bright flash that integral to it is the darkness that follows. One of the challenges

of recovery is to accept slow-burning pleasures instead. They
don't burn so brutally bright, but they leave you warm in their
wake, instead of in total darkness craving more light. When
you forgo the sublime intensity of narcotics, you need to find
excitement elsewhere.

Medication and the Twelve Steps in Harmony

Sofia's Twelve-step programme took a different approach. Early
on, she was told, 'Medication is separate from AA; only medical
professionals should advise on that.' Her medication played a
significant role in her recovery, helping her to manage being
overwhelmed and reducing addictive urges. She's been sober for
the longest stretch since aged twelve, and notices that without
her medication, 'the urge to drink or use increases massively'.

For Bex, who started smoking weed aged sixteen, five weeks
on ADHD medication led to a significant decrease in addictive
behaviours like internet shopping and gaming. She is now
working on reducing her cannabis use. ADHD medication offers
a critical pause – a moment where people can choose whether to
engage in addictive behaviour or not.

Mary was diagnosed with ADHD eight years into her
sobriety. For her, the diagnosis explained what she once thought
were personal failings. 'It wasn't just one big fuck-up: I was
undiagnosed, unmedicated and unregulated.' While she takes
ADHD medication, it's the twelve-steps that truly help her heal.
'The twelve-steps are my medication,' she says. 'Without them, I
would still feel that bottomless pit in my stomach.'

Unmasking

Rachel's diagnosis brought her self-awareness. Like many of
us, she first realised she had a problem during lockdown: 'I
was knocking back hand-poured gin and tonics like there was
no tomorrow, watching Boris push me further into a Covid
depression.' Alcohol became a quick fix for her dopamine
deficiency, giving her the confidence to be 'fun Rachel'. Every

social event became an excuse to drink: 'An afternoon street BBQ with neighbours? Let's have a drink. A summer picnic after school sports day? Let's have a drink. A morning coffee with friends? Well . . . if it turns into lunchtime, we could have a drink?' At a Christmas tree lights switch-on, she was unable to get an M&S mini bottle of wine to ease her overwhelm and became furious. That moment and a diagnosis made her realise that masking undiagnosed ADHD was part of the compulsion: 'Alcohol gave me what my brain couldn't [dopamine] and masked the undiscovered introvert in me . . . I don't actually like big social situations.'

Hitchens would demand 'objective proof', but in my experience and research, neurodivergent people are uniquely open to replacing their chosen substances with other addictive behaviours, like exercise or multiple non-alcoholic beverages. Of course, there are risks there too, but this openness challenges the conventional narrative of chronic relapse.

Through the interviews for this chapter, three generational shifts emerged: in how ADHD, addiction and alcohol are perceived. Many reflected on how different their lives could have been had they been diagnosed earlier. There was a sense of grief: what could their lives have been without the early misuse of substances?

At the time, I didn't question my role in getting freshers drunk. For Rachel too, growing up in the nineties meant falling into the grip of the drinking culture of the time: 'At fourteen, that's just what you did on a cold Friday night in a village outside Wolverhampton . . . you drank Diamond White, listened to Red Hot Chili Peppers on your Walkman and hung out with your mates on the fields.' Similarly, Mary began drinking at thirteen, which felt normal at the time: 'Everyone was doing it. It wasn't taboo. It was just very, very messy.'

Medication helps some people stay sober, but not everyone uses it. Joel has been sober for ten years without it. What matters most is self-awareness: understanding the risks of addiction that come with ADHD. Many people diagnosed young are careful when it comes to drugs because they know the risks. Take Josh – the one who liked chasing monkeys through jungle ravines in the employment chapter – for example: 'When unmedicated, I notice the greedy dopamine fiend in me in other areas, like sex. I am a reckless, fearless cliff-clambering thrill-seeker trapped in the body of a socially anxious nerd. But with drugs, I just don't take risks. Perhaps discovering psychedelics helped – extreme experiences that are nonetheless low risk. Whereas if I habitually used opiates, my drive for extremes could lead to a habit.'

What I heard repeatedly in my research was that the most dangerous peer pressure for neurodivergent people isn't about substances themselves – it's the pressure to mask. Constantly conforming to neurotypical expectations exacerbates ADHD's underlying issues, which pushes people further into addiction as they struggle to meet societal norms while managing their own riptide experiences.

NOT SLEEPING

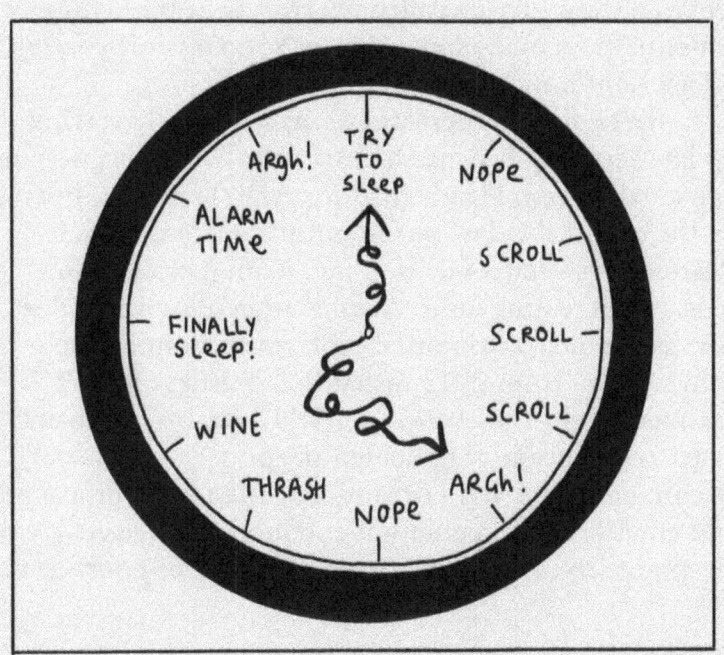

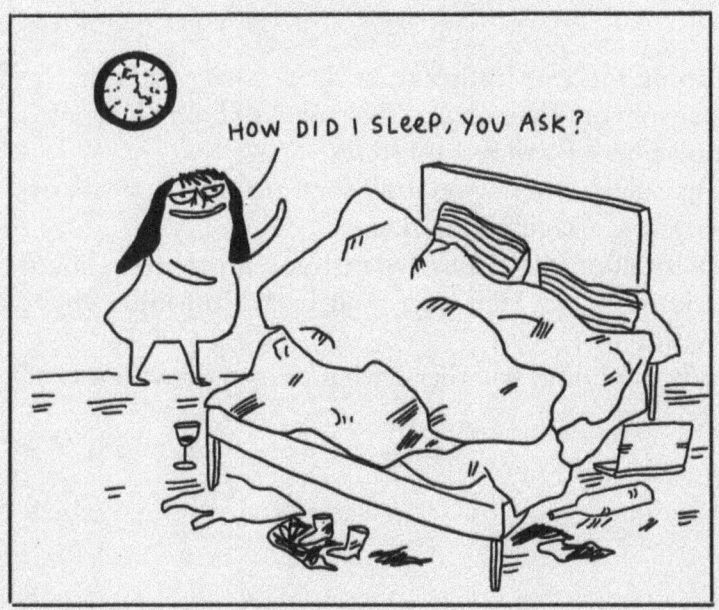

ADHD Sleep Looks Like:

- » **Delayed sleep phase syndrome:** staring at the ceiling, counting how many hours of sleep you'll get if you fall asleep right now.
- » **Revenge bedtime procrastination:** stubbornly staying up late scrolling because nighttime is your time, despite being exhausted. Heightened for ADHD people, because by the end of the day, our impulse control is shot.
- » **Restless legs syndrome:** tingling, itching or crawling sensation, creating an irresistible urge to move the legs.
- » **Anxiety-induced insomnia:** replaying a humiliating conversation from 2013 instead of drifting off.
- » **Frequent night-time waking:** ADHD brains are easily disturbed, causing fragmented sleep.
- » **Dream intensity:** vivid dreams due to sensory processing and emotional dysregulation extending into sleep.
- » **Sleep anxiety:** after repeated experiences of poor sleep.

What Helps:

- » Aiming for 'rest' rather than sleep (lower stakes).
- » Focusing on 'listening to the story' of an audiobook you've heard a thousand times.
- » Fancy sleep rituals you look forward to, e.g. a silk eye mask and weighted blanket.
- » Magnesium: eases muscle tension + promotes relaxation.
- » Melatonin: can help reset your body's off-kilter circadian rhythm.
- » Body doubling, whether with a person or with a bear.

Chapter 11

Social Media:
Advocating or Exploiting ADHD?

#ADHD: The Bitter and the Sweet

In a world where every click vies for our attention, social media platforms have become both our allies and our adversaries. Social media platforms are playgrounds of persuasive design, built on the premise that humans – like pigeons – will repeat any action immediately rewarded.

When people talk about ADHD now, they often aren't addressing clinical symptoms. Instead, they voice a broader unease – pressures from late capitalism, hustle culture, deteriorating mental health and scarcity. Articles on the 'pandemic brain' mirror ADHD symptoms as people search for reasons why they can't function. ADHD seems like a catchy answer rather than, say, 'The world is on fire.' What does it say about our times that people feel compelled to claim a neurodevelopmental disorder to validate their experience?

The flood of #ADHD content online offers some a sense of belonging but also undermines reality, often focusing on the privileged, who see ADHD as quirky or even a 'superpower' – not those struggling to keep a job. When neurotypicals use ADHD language for common frustrations, they dilute real challenges, much like white artists appropriating marginalised cultures and trivialising struggle.

Flattened Advocacy: The Influencer's Dilemma

Influencers play a numbers game – 'engagement' boils down to sheer eyeball count. Authentic advocacy aims for systemic change, but social media often reduces complex issues to quick likes and shares. While influencers may start with a mission to raise awareness, the system quickly commodifies their messages.

ADHD advocacy has evolved, but the attention economy – the incentivised competition for our limited focus and engagement – complicates this progress, often reinforcing stigma. Social media loves ADHD as a trending topic; influencers and culture warriors profit by stoking reactions, often simplifying ADHD to a caricature. Destigmatising ADHD requires more than positive narratives – it needs context that prevents it from becoming empty hype.

Still, that's no reason to write off social media advocacy. Many influencers create accessible, affirming content sorely needed by those who are underresourced or just coming to grips with ADHD. The pitfalls here belong to the platform, not the people using it.

ADHD as Clickbait

The #ADHD conversation is tangled in culture wars and oversimplified narratives. With billions of views on ADHD-related videos, platforms like Instagram and TikTok have diluted public discourse, promoting glossy versions of a disorder that can turn lives upside down. By March 2022, ADHD-related TikTok videos had amassed 2.4 billion views, yet a *Canadian Journal of Psychiatry* study revealed over half were misleading and lacking in scientific evidence.

By 2021 #ADHD was TikTok's seventh most popular health hashtag, underscoring the need to scrutinise platform-based health advice. Similar dangers arose with vape company JUUL's influencer-driven marketing, which led to a public health crisis.

ADHD content designed for mass appeal can be risky when tailored to make neurotypicals feel 'seen'.

Advocacy in the Algorithm: The Realities of ADHD Content

We need creators who make neurodiversity pop with candour and humour, building recognition and camaraderie. For ADHD users, social media visibility matters – especially for groups historically underdiagnosed – but it comes with pitfalls like self-diagnosis and oversimplified information. While online stories can't replace medical care, they provide support for those without access to professionals. Self-diagnosis isn't ideal, but when formal diagnosis isn't accessible, learning self-management techniques can be helpful.

ADHD is often dismissed as a trend or collective hyperfixation, yet the community defies debunked 'social contagion' theories – similarly used to target the trans community. Those pushing these theories aren't uncovering an epidemic; they're voicing discomfort with tech habits among young people.

For ADHD users, social media's quick dopamine bursts fuel intense interaction. We are most active later at night, post more impulsively, react more intensely and use saltier language. Unfortunately, stereotypes thrive here, flattening ADHD into a single narrative and overlooking intersectional layers of marginalisation. Social media has made space for authentic voices and nuanced advocacy, yet it's overwhelmingly white, and follower counts dip when race is discussed.

Opportunistic Treatments and Dubious Diagnoses

Social media promotes questionable ADHD 'treatments'. Ads push absurd tests like 'seeing dot patterns' or 'touching your ears'. Look out for language designed to make you feel exceptional – 'only people with ADHD can see X'. In the US, telehealth rules relaxed during the pandemic, and influencers were offered 'free' ADHD diagnoses for publicity – a slick way to market personal health. This content flourishes because, for many, platforms like TikTok have become the primary source of ADHD education, filling gaps left by a system that has rarely offered ADHD the attention it deserves.

#ADHD: The Bitter and the Sweet

Some creators reclaim social media as a space for real ADHD advocacy, breaking stereotypes and building community. Many ADHD people find reading difficult, making fast-paced video content essential. Key figures include:

Dani Donovan. Her visual storytelling maps complex ADHD experiences, like 'ADHD storytelling' (looping, apologetic), creating 'public art therapy' that resonates widely.

Richard Pink and Roxanne Emery (ADHD Love). TikTok stars, authors and app creators, their relatable videos use humour to dismantle myths, showing ADHD in positive relationship contexts without glamorising it.

ADHD Babes. Tired of being the only Black person at ADHD meet-ups, Vivienne Isebor launched ADHD Babes on Facebook and WhatsApp, building a community that addresses ADHD and the intersectional challenges of racism, sexism and ableism. Social media allowed them to expand, offering support without judgement or cost.

Jessica McCabe. Her 'How to ADHD' YouTube channel was pioneering, offering accessible content, connecting those feeling isolated.

Jesse J. Anderson. Author of *Extra Focus: the Quick Start to Adult ADHD*, he portrays ADHD as both challenging and creative, balancing awareness with uplift.

ADHD UK: Public Awareness

Led by Henry Shelford, the charity ADHD UK raises awareness and counters myths. Their protest against the *Panorama* documentary on ADHD made it the most complained-about episode ever. Shelford emphasises that no one 'catches ADHD on TikTok'; they recognise themselves. He critiques the 'superpower' trope, suggesting ADHD can be both a gift and kryptonite, depending on resources.

Navigating Digital Distractions: The ADHD Perspective

In the attention economy, content is currency – but for ADHD people, the stakes are higher. Digital platforms amplify hyperfocus or splinter it, making neurodivergent users uniquely vulnerable to persuasive design. Burnout hits harder and faster, often leading to impaired co-ordination and even injury. The attention economy's demands stress the need for inclusive design that considers cognitive differences.

As information velocity increases, ADHD users have had to adapt. Slow-focus activities like reading slip out of reach as Big Tech's ad-centric shifts feed instant, rapid content. My own approach shields me: no notifications, no YouTube, no auto-login. By reintroducing friction – manual logins, apps off my phone – I make my engagement intentional.

Like many ADHD people, I am never successful without being intentional. On good days, we time our social media use, employ apps to limit distractions, and stick to routines to curb impulsive scrolling. I batch social media interactions, hide my phone when it's too tempting and lock it away (in a kSafe) if I'm feeling click-y. My 'digital fortress' includes noise-cancelling headphones, privacy controls and ad-blockers – effective buffers. Increasingly, neurotypicals can benefit from such boundaries, helping them resist the siren call of endless feeds. Similar small survival tactics which emerged unconsciously now serve as a framework for resisting the attention economy – as I'll elaborate on in the next chapter. Watching my neurotypical boyfriend's reactive, unfiltered tech use, I suspect these strategies can help us all.

Morning Routine

I'm up with espresso no.1, opening
the curtains, turning on the sunset
lamp

My neurotypical boyfriend hits snooze

Second espresso in hand, I peel us oranges,
stretch vaguely, pack lunches, turn
on the lava lamp

                              He misses the orange segment I offer
                    because he's snuck his phone from under his
                              pillow. He's scrolling news stories and
                              pulling at his lip which is bleeding

I read him my list and he listens patiently,
glancing at Twitter. I ask about his day

                    I've got so much work to do, he groans, looking
                         through the emails that he's amassed overnight

I hand him a coffee and corral him into
word-puzzles on my phone until

                              He says fuck, fuck, fuck, I'm late!

I turn on *Moana* so that I can get dressed.

People with ADHD often use social media intentionally to
jump-start their brains; sometimes, I need that dopamine hit just
to get out of bed.

Neurodivergent people frequently re-watch the same shows
for comfort. Ambient entertainment reduces anxiety because we
know what's coming – a small rebellion against the attention
economy: it doesn't use me; I use it.

Yet we all know the tipping point when our actions disconnect
from our intentions – that's when the device shifts from tool
to trap. Being more susceptible to social media's addictiveness
makes us, when managing it well, more cautious.

Amber Versus TikTok

In the following pages, you'll see my experience of TikTok
interspersed with 'Pop-Up Alerts' – tiny info-bombs about its

design tricks and how they hijack our brains. Skip them, skim them or devour them at will.

1

Six weeks before my book was due, I joined TikTok. *(For literal-minded readers: I am about to behave unreasonably. TikTok made me do it. What follows is best interpreted as a joke.)* How else could I understand the attention economy? Was it sharing useful information or fuelling self-diagnosis? Was it imitating ADHD – or somehow infecting users with its strobing rhythms?

Marching into TikTok's firestorm felt manageable; after all, I'm a pro at handling my own attention. But nobody outsmarts TikTok; those who think they can haven't tangled with its algorithm. This book almost didn't get finished.

⚠ **Pop-Up**
Why is TikTok so irresistible?

Infinite scroll – a design that gives you an endless feed with no stopping points – magnifies time blindness. Engineer Aza Raskin regrets inventing it, admitting it keeps users on apps 50% longer. The average person now scrolls for two full days per month.

Number of followers: 5

2

At first, TikTok was a dream. In my pocket, I had a dopamine machine! For a week, it kept me from my usual compulsive habits. My overall screen time actually dropped because I wasn't hopping between apps; salty-sweet cravings vanished. Seeing mediocre videos with millions of likes, I felt on the verge of going viral. Happily, I posted my silly little videos – tips on writing a novel with ADHD, comparing my morning routine to a panda tumbling around, chaotic day-in-the-life montages about moving flats. Picture jump cuts, captions zipping across the screen, trending audio in the background – me talking fast, gesturing wildly or flopping onto a sofa mid-shot like I'd earned it.

When my boyfriend, Etienne, got home, I showed him an ethnicity filter that 'determined' I was 50 per cent Central African and 30 per cent Polynesian.

'What the fuck?' he said. Being accustomed to me narrating my latest hyperfixation, around and against Etienne, he smiled. I rambled about algorithms while he glazed over. 'It's better than zoning out with TV, right?' I asked, chopping tomatoes. 'It'll give me somewhere to put all my extra feelings!' I said.

Later, in bed, I added, confidently, 'Anyway, I won't get hooked; I'm not in it for the likes.'

His side-eye was brutal. 'If it makes you happy,' he said.

Number of followers: 12

3

Scrolling on TikTok felt like a never-ending summer day, a relief from the daily ADHD battle with motivation. TikTok's beauty filters instantly rendered me twice as attractive. I marvelled at how damaging it must be for teenage girls to think 'smoothness' at 100 or that the 'pretty baby' filter looks normal – and then used them myself.

'Maybe,' I thought, 'if ADHD is a problem, TikTok's the cure.' Tasks involving delayed gratification are tough for ADHD people, but TikTok offers on-ramps, like those filters, which make filming less daunting. Within minutes, I could make a video, likes floating up my screen like stars. How often do ADHD people get such fast positive reinforcement? Instagram felt curated, but TikTok was raw entertainment – a voyeuristic thrill. Rather than sell the myth of connection, TikTok offers discovery. The interactions are superficial, quick likes and comments. Like many ADHD people, I have more empathy than is helpful to me or anyone else, but on TikTok, my empathy was dialled down. I felt no responsibility for anyone.

'Can you watch *just* this one?' I'd ask Etienne as he worked on emails at 9 p.m.

'Fine,' he'd say, his lip tightening.

⚠ **Pop-Up**
Why do our feeds feel overwhelming?

Platforms like Twitter/X merge unrelated topics – political crises, cat memes, personal rants – into a single endless stream, known as 'context collapse'. The overload is calculated, allowing platforms like Facebook to profit from identity-driven content. Right now, eighty-one countries run disinformation campaigns on social media, turning 'context collapse' into a profitable enterprise. This manufactured chaos mirrors the strategy famously described by Steve Bannon as 'flooding the zone with shit' – a tactic designed to bury truth, which the Trump administration is currently perfecting.

Number of followers: 35

4

With five weeks to my deadline, TikTok flagged one of my videos, meaning that very few people would see it – I flew into a rage. I appealed repeatedly, obsessing over an urgent meme. Hours later, I was hyperfocused on perfecting a seven-second clip, syncing sounds. TikTok had fully pulled me under.

⚠ **Pop-Up**
When helpful designs turn manipulative

Persuasive design starts off convenient, like notifications to help organisation, but quickly becomes a trap. While some tech enthusiasts talk about 'nudges' to encourage positive behaviour, there are also 'dark nudges' encouraging deeper engagement than we intend. James Williams, co-founder of Time Well Spent, calls it 'adversarial design', like a GPS rerouting us into quicksand. The gap between perceived use and actual use widens as use increases. For ADHD users, this often fuels addictive patterns.

Oblivious, I was busy perfecting short clips, convinced I was on the cusp of going viral. I casually screen-shotted my follower count as proof of 'the journey'. I'd sent Etienne a TikTok, but he never replied. He suggested I begin tracking how many times I opened the app; I stopped when I hit fifty.

Number of followers: 43

5

Sunday, we walked through our neighbourhood, discussing Etienne's upcoming trip to Ukraine – he works for the Red Cross. In past relationships, I've inadvertently created drama for dopamine. Now, I don't need to. I'm proud of his work, but having an anxiety disorder and a boyfriend in war zones isn't ideal. While he talked, I kept stopping to take videos.

'What?' I said, 'I'm *listening*!' I opened the app to see one more like and my heart pinged.

ADHD thoughts leap towards the brightest thing, whatever delivers a dopamine hit. TikTok's quick fixes numb in seconds but can displace real, lasting sources of joy. It's a form of 'emotion-based coping' – a way to change how you feel in the moment – rather than 'problem-based coping,' which addresses the root and offers lasting relief.

⚠ **Pop-Up**
Power and inequity

Visibility is currency. Followers and engagement become monetisable assets. Those who opt out risk losing audiences or income. Meanwhile, sensational or divisive content is rewarded by algorithms, boosting harmful or simplistic takes. Marginalised voices rarely reach wide audiences; they end up giving attention without receiving it back.

I couldn't help thinking, this book will have to compete with Netflix, TV and TikTok. Soon, TikTok was everywhere: in the bathroom, on walks, making cyclists swerve.

Number of followers: 74

6

When I finally picked up my notebook, hoping for inspiration, I found it almost blank. Normally, I'd spill my feelings there, letting them mature over time and enrich my fiction later. Now, every thought went straight to TikTok.

Writing is lonely. You build a palace, and only a few people notice, usually just to ask if you've ever shagged someone on its balcony. On TikTok, there's immediate interaction. Crafting a video is faster, more gratifying than wrestling a sentence. I listened to podcasts on algorithm sensitivity while a little voice wondered if I was gaming the whole system. In my thought, I heard an echo of my male peers during undergrad, each set on 'winning' internet poker.

Attention spans multiple tasks through 'sampling'. TikTok broadens experience but drains depth. Overuse stunts deep thought, especially in young minds. It makes it hard to write.

Like any addict, I added guardrails: TikTok only at lunch, on the bus, before bed. One day, I forgot my medication and lost four hours in a TikTok haze. When Etienne came home, I punched the air: 'Two thousand likes!'

But jealousy crept in. My video of Etienne pushing a bookshelf had 15.3k views, while the videos featuring me barely broke a thousand. He laughed when he saw it. 'I'm blowing up!' He grinned.

'It's because of the song,' I muttered. '"Play that Funky Music, White Boy" in the background.' He watched it again.

'You are *very* white,' I said, sulkily.

Number of followers: 99

7

As my deadline loomed, I kept adding ideas to the book without cutting words. While my work structure collapsed, I was still managing to make three TikToks daily. Feeling defensive, I printed a thesis about TikTok at the library, which argued that dismissing people who find ADHD on TikTok overlooks those the system itself ignores.

'You see?' I said, brandishing the paper at Etienne, 'I'm already diagnosed, so criticising TikTok – where thousands recpgnise themselves – is gatekeeping!'

TikTok isn't a diagnostic tool; it's self-expression for those left out by the *DSM-V*. Dismissing neurotypicals' #ADHD interest misses a larger truth about today's world. Later, as Etienne slept – after gently telling me he minded TikTok less than my constant talk about it – I scrolled, ignoring videos pathologising everyday behaviours.

TikTok as a 'community of care' might sound far-fetched, but when engaged with consciously and deliberately – seeking out people who share your experiences, rather than simply reacting to the outrage and disgust the platform also thrives on – it can transform isolating struggles into collective narratives. For many, it's the only space where they can be completely honest about their daily lives and feel the rare, electrifying joy of someone responding, 'omg me too!' The algorithm shows you more of whatever you watch, so intentionality matters: by pausing before reacting, or deliberately engaging with content that enriches your experience, you can train it to be a tool for connection rather than conflict. Engaging in this way gave me a confidence I didn't know I needed and which many ADHD people lack. But there's a darker side to this platform, too.

> ⚠ **Pop-Up**
> *Attention hogs detected*
>
> Power in the attention economy depends on extracting, selling or profiting from our focus. Collective focus fuels influence,

> but the rich reap the rewards. During 2021's viral GameStop surge, small investors thought they'd beaten the system, until many lost their savings, while hedge funds walked away unscathed.

Despite my noble intention to enrich ADHD discourse, I found myself editing videos to be more provocative. In the attention economy, spotlight first; change later, right?

Number of followers: 150

8

What if TikTok had existed when I was fifteen, when ADHD resources were scarce? I'm glad it didn't. I'd have been less bored – and probably I'd have been famous – but like many ADHD people, I take the path of least resistance. I'd have watched hundreds of videos and thought I 'got it'. Managing ADHD is a lifelong practice, but TikTok fuels the myth that recognising yourself in content is enough – that the world will adapt.

I'd have loved beauty filters back then – as a way of erasing my face. Now, catching myself in the mirror after weeks of only seeing my TikTok reflection, I was shocked. I'd got used to myself glowing, permanently wearing false eyelashes. I'd started to feel like having ADHD was my primary identity, rather than being a writer. For many, this is liberating, but as a brand – a simplified, marketable version of oneself tailored for public consumption – it can harden into a boundary, displacing the understanding of other identities – especially for young people. Social media constructs 'Brand ADHD' by rewarding predictable content. A catchy ADHD video might get hundreds of thousands of views, while nuanced ones drop significantly. The algorithm favours oversimplified, trending content – essentially propaganda – for engagement.

The danger isn't TikTok but the lack of support making it a primary community source for so many. Watch #ADHD all you like – but remember, it's entertainment.

⚠ **Pop-Up**
Interference detected

The Depp v. Heard trial became a battleground for attention capital, where trending hashtags, constant social media commentary and bot-driven content amplified conflict for profit. Depp's resurgence followed a successful outcome in the US libel trial – a heavily publicised case where both parties gave evidence before a jury in filmed proceedings, generating widespread commentary. Depp's notoriety (amplified by a wave of tweets linked to inauthentic sources, reportedly tied to Saudi Arabia) preserved his fame, even boosting the 'Sauvage' campaign he fronted for Dior. Meanwhile, Heard lost work for being 'too noisy'. Here, 'noise' is information overload – a polluted attention economy.

Number of followers: 150

9

'Seriously?' Etienne asks.

I'm lying on the sofa, lost in TikTok. We've just moved, but I haven't unpacked. Absorbed in the loop, I mimic viral clips unconsciously. My latest refrain – 'Looking for a guy in finance. Six-five. Trust fund. Blue eyes' – has Etienne clenching his jaw each time, though he knows I'm not trying to annoy him.

Three weeks before my deadline, I start fixating on how perfect we'd be for 'reaction' videos. I used to hate neurotypical 'reaction' videos, with their voyeurism capturing neurodivergent behaviour like an ADHD safari – 'Watch how many times my girlfriend stims while we watch a movie!' As a kid, I was bullied for 'overreacting' – a trait now valuable in TikTok's attention economy. 'Why not make hay while the sun shines?' I mused defiantly, but cringed – when I get overwhelmed, it's not an act for views; it's a raw reaction that I can't control.

Later, restless, I mutter, 'I need my phone,' and consider smashing the kSafe where my phone is locked away. My mind keeps going back to Etienne's upcoming Kyiv work trip. Instead, I read about how 'The Umbrella Guy' made $65k reacting to edited Amber Heard trial clips. In the attention economy, reaction chains turn fleeting moments into endless loops, profitable for platforms and creators alike.

At the library, I 'swear off' TikTok for the day but decide desktop use is different. The likes were a sugary rush. When Etienne comes home, later, I hide my phone. He makes dinner as I nurse my sore thumb.

'How many likes would make you happy?' he asks.

'Three million?' I shrug. 'Whatever, I'm not in it for the likes.'

Number of followers: 151

10

When I heard about a possible TikTok ban, sharp anxiety hit. I hadn't realised how much I relied on it with Etienne's trip imminent. Normally, I'd schedule time with friends, but instead, I thought, I'll just work and TikTok.

With two weeks until my book deadline, my TikTok use climbed. Usually, I'd unwind with hours of TV in the background, but TikTok felt different – this was 'legitimate creative activity'. Plus, I could go viral any second.

On TikTok, I didn't think; I didn't feel much beyond occasional amusement. This isn't flow; it's absorption without substance, like a black hole. It made my head go quiet. It felt like a proxy ADHD medication, moving faster than my thoughts, creating paradoxical calm.

I hadn't smoked since my twenties, but I recognised the itch. 'Ten minutes,' I'd tell myself. 'Just five more.' Soon, I noticed that when my head was quiet, I lost the urge to write.

For many with ADHD, medication is the line between healthy engagement and compulsion. I saw how easily hyperfocus had taken over, echoing my interviewees talking about chasing satisfaction that remains elusive. ADHD users often lose control – and dignity – over time spent scrolling. Social media addiction is twice as likely in ADHD users; rapid, engaging content is harder to resist.

Number of followers: 188

11

But, oh, the simple reciprocity of posting a video and getting a like!

Normally, I struggle with things no one notices, tasks adults just do. But those TikTok hearts felt like affirmations. I stopped checking WhatsApp. Parasocial interactions – 'intimacy at a distance' – offer a comforting loop but can turn into a hollow alternative to real connection. TikTok's algorithm hooks ADHD vulnerabilities, creating a cycle that's hard to break. Likes and shares trigger dopamine release, reinforcing the habit. Even B. F. Skinner would have been hooked.

I tried Instagram instead – like switching from Marlboro Lights to Menthols out of health delusions. Even Twitter/X, where I looked for Trump's latest outrage, didn't scratch the itch. It was a warning flare about the sensation-seeking impulses TikTok had activated. Finally, I googled what I'd been avoiding: escalating attacks in Kyiv, where civilians were facing increasingly shortened response times to seek safety.

'This happens rarely,' Etienne kept telling me. 'I run really fast,' he said.

I went back to TikTok, watching a girl peel off a glycolic mask, audio turned up to hear every blackhead pop.

Number of followers: 199

12

The week before he leaves is always tense. He's patient, but there's a limit to how many times he can hear, 'But what if you die?'

Exasperated, Etienne's at his most French, puffing out air with a 'pfff'. Over the washing up, he mutters darkly to himself and thinks I don't understand.

While I scrolled TikTok, he wrapped up a call. Then he picked up my laptop and saw my open tabs: 'How to gain followers'; 'Best times to post on TikTok'.

He looked at me, waiting.

'Oh, so you can go to war zones for "research",' I said, making aggressive air quotes, as if the British Red Cross was merely a smokescreen for some sort of torrid affair, 'but I can't research TikTok for my book? TikTok is the real threat to our relationship?'

For a moment, I wished he'd just leave so I could scroll in peace. I pictured venting about him there, posting our juiciest fights – boyfriend in a war zone? Content gold. Ignoring this unflattering moment of clarity, I thought, Can't he let me have this one pleasure? 'You're jealous of TikTok!' I crowed.

He paused. 'I'm jealous of how much attention you're giving it,' he said.

'Well, now you know how that feels!'

We burst out laughing. I'd compared my need for TikTok to his for humanitarian work.

Later, staring at the kSafe, I whispered, 'That would've made a great TikTok.'

'Shut up,' he said, kissing me.

Clickbait is addictive – promising but rarely delivering. TikTok's 'hook' also drives addiction, with dopamine hits that always fall short. Why do we scroll for validation, knowing it's temporary? Is it the thrill of being seen, or just distraction?

I Was Shocked by the End!

To ease my TikTok withdrawal, I reached out to Hannah Rutherford (Bristol, 36) – a Twitch streamer late-diagnosed with ADHD. She calls TikTok 'the best and worst' for ADHD: 'It caters to hyperfocused learning. Right now, it's royal family lineages, cat videos, hoof videos, DIY hacks.' Platforms like TikTok offer endless variety, perfect for ADHD brains.

I want ADHD people to disrupt the attention economy. We're inconsistent, an unstable entity – our hyperfixations and aversions must vex the algorithm and fuck up its engagement

metrics. Could our surges in attention blow the system? I
pictured us blowing smoke in B. F. Skinner's face.

Hannah agrees – at first. Early on, the app 'didn't know
what I wanted', but as she curated her feed, it adapted. ADHD
influences TikTok use in two distinct ways, she says. First,
through tech-savviness: she actively curates her feed by marking
videos as 'not interested' – a feature designed to refine the
algorithm, and something I hadn't even thought to try. Second,
through ADHD traits like impulsivity and hyperfocus, which
can lead to either endlessly scrolling or obsessively engaging with
a specific niche of content. Users like Hannah who understand
their needs are less likely to get trapped.

I've never had a simple relationship with instant dopamine.
Resisting TikTok would've been strange. It's free, creative and
feels like you might get rich – it's designed to be addictive. But
having spent years managing impulses, once I acknowledged
what was happening, I had systems in place.

Eventually, TikTok's content pushed me away. An influencer
on a Bali swing said, 'TikTok got easier once I realised
everything is content.' Her butchering of Nora Ephron's
'everything is copy' was unsettling. Ephron turned pain into art;
'everything is content' fills space with filler.

In the gig economy, underpaid influencers hustle for
visibility, sometimes crowdfunding essentials. Chasing trends
seems glamorous until it's for your own survival. To get on
TikTok's creator programme, you need at least ten thousand
followers and to have accumulated a hundred thousand video
views over the previous thirty days. After that, the programme
promises $10,000 per million views, pushing spectacle for pay.
In practice, payouts depend on views and engagement, but
income is unpredictable, forcing creators to constantly chase
virality. It's dystopian: people in Florida stayed behind during
hurricane Milton to capture content for cash, while others
posted about not affording to comply with the mandatory

evacuation order. On TikTok, I watched a man bail water from a tent with a sawed-off plastic bottle. Caroline Calloway, a quintessential attention merchant, declared, 'I'm going to die,' then used the chaos to promote her next book. The *Spectator* later published her 'hurricane diaries'.

With ADHD, I'm wired for intense dopamine highs. Overusing TikTok is like binging on ultra-processed food: it hijacks satiety cues, reinforcing addictive patterns. Blaming yourself for binging on something engineered to be irresistible isn't helpful.

The key isn't cutting dopamine sources but adding sustainable activities to balance the hit – like time with friends. TikTok at lunch can bring joy, but it can't replace real connection. It should only replace time spent engaging with other candied dopamine-release systems (like Instagram).

Jessica McCabe coined the idea of a 'Dopamenu' to organise stimulation, like a diabetic managing sugar. 'Starters' (music, deep breaths) are quick hits; 'mains' require more engagement (reading, friends); 'sides' add extra value (podcasts alongside chores); and 'specials' (holidays) are lasting – anticipation also brings dopamine. Short-term fixes like scrolling are 'desserts' – tempting but unsustainable. Yet how many of us survive on sides and sweets alone?

To avoid hyperfixation and the binge–regret cycle, I need balance across the Dopamenu. If I'm going to drink, I need to exercise (because drinking is easier); if I'm going to use TikTok, I need to read (because TikTok is easier). It's not easy against an exquisitely engineered dopamine system, which is why kids, lacking media literacy, should be protected from it.

I still love TikTok. Life is hard – the bus smells, my socks get soaked in the rain. TikTok makes me happy, like a favourite snack. Recognising TikTok as a treat, I know what to do: delay the reaction chain by inserting a pause. I spent my twenties learning this 'pause' as a tool against impulsive behaviours.

TikTok warps time, which is dangerous for ADHD people,

whose time-sense is already liquid. A ten-second ASMR montage of someone leaving work, hitting the gym, meal-prepping and journalling before bed – all neatly time-stamped within two hours – can feel like a hate crime. Unless you're vigilant about remembering that you're consuming entertainment, these endless transformation videos become a cruel mirror of our executive dysfunction. For neurotypicals, the comparison stings; for us, it feels like this:

Now, I make videos offline, log on at set times, avoid checking for likes, and delete the app when not using it. Initially, I was filled with dread, but breaking the reaction chain soon broke TikTok's spell. Sporadic use made it boring; TikTok went from a house party I couldn't leave to one where, after walking a few blocks away, I felt a wincing sympathy for everyone still there, worsening their hangovers – not choosing to stay, but not quite leaving.

TikTok's addictive power lies in its algorithm: gamified points, endless content and short formats that make even dull videos seem worth the time. Shared trends can simulate connection, but the algorithm feeds impulses in unhealthy ways.

Reflecting on how ADHD makes us overshare, crave dopamine, have big feelings and tend towards addiction, I realise: if we're to disrupt the attention economy, neurotypicals need to see its effects on us – and understand they're next.

Ten Cognitive Tricks for Neurotypicals
Experiencing ADHD-like Symptoms

1. **Slice It Thin:** Don't stare at the whole elephant, just nibble an ear. Writing a report? Jot down the intro.
2. **Aim Embarrassingly Low:** 'Just ten minutes' feels way more achievable than 'finish by noon'. (Your brain loves easy victories.)
3. **Pretend Deadlines:** Your brain thrives on urgency (even fake urgency).
4. **Bribe Yourself:** Seriously. After each tiny milestone, do something briefly pleasurable (not scrolling).
5. **Hit Pause:** When spiralling, mentally press pause and shift focus to something nice and easy, like watering a plant or counting pencils.
6. **Ritualise It:** Predictability can beat paralysis. Schedule when you'll start, not when you'll finish.
7. **Noise-Cancel Your Life:** Headphones are magic. Or, scribble distractions on scrap paper, then ceremonially burn them.
8. **Clear Your Desk:** Or at least shove mess into a drawer you never open.
9. **Go Outside:** Walk around.
10. **Notice the Doomscroll:** Catch negative spirals mid-spin, yell 'stop', then point yourself back at the task. (Preferably before you end up googling 'do I have ADHD?')

ATTENTION ISSUES ARE NOT THE SAME AS ADHD
ATTENTION ISSUES ARE NOT THE SAME AS ADHD
ATTENTION ISSUES ARE NOT THE SAME AS ADHD
ATTENTION ISSUES ARE NOT THE SAME AS ADHD
ATTENTION ISSUES ARE NOT THE SAME AS ADHD
ATTENTION ISSUES ARE NOT THE SAME AS ADHD
ATTENTION ISSUES ARE NOT THE SAME AS ADHD
ATTENTION ISSUES ARE NOT THE SAME AS ADHD
ATTENTION ISSUES ARE NOT THE SAME AS ADHD
ATTENTION ISSUES ARE NOT THE SAME AS ADHD
ATTENTION ISSUES ARE NOT THE SAME AS ADHD

Oh wait ...

ATTENTION ISSUES ARE NOT THE SAME AS ADHD

Chapter 12

Unlikely Prophets

ADHD is often dismissed as a flaw – a short-circuit in a system that demands constant focus and seamless productivity. We're told our minds are sparking with faulty wiring, incapable of holding a steady charge of precious attention, let alone delivering it on demand. But what if, instead of a deficit, we possess an overabundance – attention that spills over and saturates overlooked corners of existence? Having explored how our way of life renders ADHD disabling in previous chapters, I'm feeling bold. It's time to stop viewing ADHD solely as a hindrance and start recognising it as a lens to reinterpret the world – one that uncovers hidden patterns and possibilities overlooked by conventional thinking. Maybe we're not malfunctioning; maybe we see the malfunction in a system demanding conformity. What if those of us navigating the world with ADHD are, in fact, unlikely prophets, revealing cracks in societal structures and offering new ways of living?

In a world equating worth with output, our wayward attention is a quiet rebellion – a refusal to reduce life's richness to spreadsheets. By reframing ADHD, we challenge the foundations of late capitalism's attention economy, opening space for empathy, creativity and a more humane way of being. If we're prophets, our first revelation might be that the value of attention lies precisely in its refusal to stay neatly within capitalism's boundaries.

Aroreretini: An Abundance of Attention

In Te reo Māori, there's a word – *Aroreretini* – meaning
'attention goes to many things'. It's a culturally resonant way
to describe ADHD, framing it as an abundance rather than
a deficit. Though not an official term, some people in New
Zealand use it to describe ADHD. Instead of pathologising
divergence, *Aroreretini* acknowledges the richness in attending
to multiple threads simultaneously. This aligns with Māori
values, where mental, physical, spiritual and social health
are interconnected – and offers a perspective that challenges
the Western narrative which labels our attention as lacking.
Perhaps our minds aren't faulty but finely tuned to a different
frequency – saturated rather than deficient. Embracing this
abundance can unlock creativity and innovation that challenge
the status quo.

I've seen this abundance in people like Hannah Rutherford,
the professional streamer who found community with fellow
'neurospicy' creators. Diagnosed with ADHD in her thirties,
Hannah realised her way of engaging – with games, her
audience, the world – wasn't a flaw but a feature. On her Twitch
channel, she lets her mind wander, and her viewers eagerly
follow. They pause mid-game to explore mythological references
or the etymology of a word. Her audience isn't there for a
scripted performance; they're there for the journey, tangents
and all.

Her approach challenges the traditional demands of the
attention economy, offering engagement built on genuine
curiosity. Hannah rejects the pressure to exaggerate for
attention. 'There's no point screaming and shouting on any
content platform,' she says. 'It just makes you look like a bit
of a dickhead, and it's emotionally draining.' Instead, she
builds connections through shared exploration, celebrating
the overlooked and unexpected. This subtly rebels against
an attention economy that demands we package ourselves as
marketable commodities. Embracing abundant attention fosters
genuine engagement over superficial consumption.

Most navigate the digital world through platforms designed

to manipulate and monetise focus. Google's algorithms don't necessarily serve us the most insightful information but prioritise who pays the most. Especially for those of us managing constant mental noise, this manipulation skews the pursuit of true understanding. (In this landscape, finding spaces that honour our way of thinking becomes an act of resistance.)

Elissa Schappell, the writer and artist, uses creativity as a shield against the attention economy. Engaged in the creative process, ADHD brains don't find flashy lures of persuasive design satisfying. 'They're making your brain jump from this to that, and our brains already do that, so we're not getting a hit from it,' she says.

Josh, another digital wanderer, uses Wikipedia as 'replacement therapy', immersing himself in topics like desert succulents and sea slugs, letting one curiosity lead organically to the next. Unlike profit-driven platforms, Wikipedia allows attention to roam unexploited. Embracing *Aroreretini* – letting attention go to many things – defies the narrowing demands of the attention economy. Platforms like Wikipedia, thriving on community contributions without ads, show that respecting wandering minds isn't idealistic – it works. It's one of the few platforms where attention to topics has held steady.

Being intellectually lost – even if it's due to forgetting or losing labels – pushes us to think differently, and in that lies the seed of true originality.

This heightened awareness is echoed by many within our community. As Josh put it:

> Living with ADHD has given me a kind of cynical clear-sightedness about the attention economy. I'm grateful for that. Billions are spent to capture our attention and influence our choices. We all know it, at least intellectually. It's become a talking point. But it's disturbingly common to meet people who haven't fully understood, who think it's something aimed at other people. Most will flat-out deny that marketing or propaganda works on them. They feel their tastes and political values float free of the bear traps ensnaring kids on TikTok or MAGA boomers. That's not a self-deception possible for me.

> You can't pretend you live in a world free of bear traps when you've spent so much time prying them off your leg, only to step straight into another.

If the attention economy narrows our focus, ADHD pulls it wide – forcing us to notice what others overlook and challenge what's presented as natural. Our struggles expose the tension between human needs and relentless demands for productivity.

Out of Sync: Defying the Grind

Capitalism thrives on uniformity, on cogs fitting neatly into the machinery of endless output. But those of us with ADHD don't fit this mould. Our attention is fluid and unpredictable. We're variables that can't be accounted for – glitches in the code – quietly disrupting capitalism's demand for sameness. ADHD makes us unlikely prophets against 'bullshit jobs' – roles that exist only to uphold meaningless systems. By exposing the absurdity of such tasks, we push for work that truly matters.

In economies that prioritise increasing productivity, people who struggle with attention, focus and self-regulation will always be undervalued. The stigma attached to ADHD often comes from our inability to function as interchangeable parts in an economy obsessed with growth. Big Tech sees us as tireless data generators, viewing time as an infinite resource to be mined. Finite things shouldn't be treated as commodities to be extracted. Surely we're beginning to learn that?

Sociologist John Holloway notes that while capitalism tends to absorb everything, cracks always emerge where new possibilities arise. The experiences of people with ADHD might represent those cracks – spaces where the system doesn't quite hold – making room for wild, imaginative change.

When the world doesn't accommodate us, we adapt. Our adaptive strategies highlight systemic flaws, not personal failures. While neurotypical individuals might endure the relentless pace until burnout forces a reckoning, we are keenly aware of the unsustainable demands placed upon us. We're accustomed to being overwhelmed and recognising the warning signs;

neurotypicals expect to process the onslaught of information at internet speed. We've heard the sirens all along.

Our struggles reveal the absurdity of valuing productivity over wellbeing. By not fitting in, we question a culture that sacrifices health for output. Consider how we approach tasks: the capitalist model prizes mono-tasking for efficiency, but our minds see connections others might miss. This isn't a lack of focus; it's a different type of engagement. In a society obsessed with quantifiable outcomes, perhaps it's the immeasurable qualities – like imagination and empathy – that hold true power to transform.

Embracing these so-called deficits sheds light on the rigid structures that fail many. We're not just nonconformists; we're exposing the system's limitations. The future may not belong to those producing the most per hour, but to those who imagine alternatives to a status quo marked by widespread burnout and socio-economic inequalities. Our discomfort with conventional productivity extends to an even more fundamental tension – our relationship with time itself.

Time Unbound: Finding Kairos in a Chronos World

If capitalism demands efficiency, our experience of time disrupts its rhythm. For those with ADHD, time isn't linear, it's elastic – a web of moments that loop, warp and spiral, defying straightforward narratives. Our perception of time refuses to tick along with the clock, as though it knows that life – real life – was never meant to fit into measured boxes.

The Ancient Greeks distinguished between two kinds of time: Chronos and Kairos. Chronos is sequential time – the schedules, deadlines, the monotonous procession of minutes and hours. It's the time capitalism thrives on, quantifiable and commodifiable. Kairos represents moments that rupture routine and leave lasting impressions. Before Chronos tightened its grip, communities understood time more fluidly, often aligned with natural rhythms.

Many with ADHD resonate more with Kairos than Chronos. One person shared, 'As ADHDers, we struggle with Chronos time. Knowing this lessened my guilt around time management.

When I'm on my own, I live in Kairos time. It gives me the
energy for time management when I need to align with society's
Chronos time.' Realigning with Kairos allows us to reclaim time
and let significant moments guide us.

Our natural rhythm often clashes with societal norms,
and that's not a flaw – it's an alternative way to engage
with life. In her book *Saving Time*, Jenny Odell argues that
Chronos embodies nihilism and determinism by suggesting a
predetermined future. Kairos, however, invites unpredictability
and creativity, opening possibilities. Especially in times
of environmental and social crisis, accepting reality while
embracing diverse potential outcomes is vital. If a system is built
to keep us distracted and unthinking, then irrationality – or
thinking at strange angles – is precisely what we need.

This divergence in experiencing time isn't unique to
ADHD; it reflects cultures that understand time as cyclical or
interconnected rather than strictly linear. Acknowledging these
alternative temporalities challenges the dominance of linear,
clock-bound time that capitalism enforces.

Constantly monitoring the clock, obsessing over each minute,
makes time slip through our fingers; it shifts attention from the
present to worries about the future or regrets about the past.
Capitalism encourages this state, keeping us desperate to escape
ourselves to 'engage' in ways that profit someone else.

I spent years paralysed by thoughts like, 'I will never live
this day again!' It happens less now, but the feeling still creeps
in – most recently during *Mamma Mia!*, when I turned to my
boyfriend, tears in my eyes, and whispered, 'I'll never be young
again.' Time is unruly. It leaps and twists, makes promises it
can't keep.

Being 'time blind' allows for different kinds of seeing. Time
becomes elastic. Trauma can trap us in loops, replaying moments
as if they had just occurred. Even without trauma, many with
ADHD experience a conflation of 'now' and 'not now'. Emotions
overlap; moments stack, and when I feel unmoored, I remind
myself, 'That was then, and this is now.'

Labelling time blindness as a deficit isolates it as an ADHD
problem. But time is relational; both neurotypical and

neurodivergent people are constrained by rigid time standards. Acknowledging that there are different ways of experiencing time isn't just compassionate – it's an act of collective self-preservation.

Our experiences expose the limitations of a society that values punctuality over presence, efficiency over empathy. Before the pandemic, many able-bodied people gave little thought to how those with disabilities navigate the world. When the shift to working from home proved beneficial for many, we extracted only the product – a simple solution to improve productivity. The deeper lesson – that flexibility and accessible structures are essential – was ignored. The rushed return to offices exposed this failure, showing a system still rooted in control and uniformity over adaptability and collective wellbeing, despite worker resistance and ongoing debates about flexibility.

Rejecting Chronos doesn't mean rejecting structure – it means seeking structures that honour our rhythms rather than erase them.

ADHD challenges the attention economy, which profits from erasing how we truly experience time and treats it as a stable, interchangeable commodity. I make time tangible, countering the illusion that the present moment is just a disposable link in an endless chain. Beyond time, structuring our lives in ways that resonate with ADHD experiences becomes essential for resilience.

Rituals for ADHD Resilience: Without Structure, There is No Creativity

As a kid, I fixated on how a tennis player bounced his ball three times before serving. He did it every time. My dad explained it as a mixture of luck and ritual. Watching the graceful arc of the serve, I didn't care how it worked, just that it did. I began creating my own private rituals – daily activities that structure attention. Rituals decide 'what comes next', easing the burden of constant decision-making.

Without The List, I'm adrift, constantly pestering others for cues as to what comes next. The List offloads the mental load of sequencing tasks, a function my executive brain struggles to automate. It's not just a coping mechanism, it's a personalised framework for freedom – a way to choreograph my life in harmony with my natural rhythms.

I

My life is entwined with The List – several pieces of paper clipped to cardboard, often the back of a notepad. Imagine being born without a skeleton and crafting an exoskeleton out of fierce intention, bright colours and paperclips. Unless I'm at a party or not responsible for myself – wallet, phone – I have The List. It's how I maintain dignity and agency, resisting the pull of the attention economy. It tethers me to the present and maps the nebulous terrain of future time. Without it, I don't know what the fuck is going on.

Crafted every weekend, The List spans one to three weeks, using a colour-coded system from my calendar. Blocks of time sport different hues – friends, family, tasks, work – everything is assigned a colour. The skewed sense of time that comes with ADHD makes it hard to tell if I've overcommitted, but I know if the pattern feels balanced.

The List is my permission slip to own my time according to the rhythm I choose. It's emphatically not about getting more done. On most Sundays, with four or five tasks like 'brush teeth', the empty space visually affirms my freedom: there's nothing else I 'should' be doing.

It's also my alibi. As a mixed-race woman with ADHD, depression and anxiety, I'm often perceived as hesitant or out of place. People feel the need to inform me that I'm doing something wrong. The List is proof – a living document – that I'm living on my own terms. It's fluid, adapting, bilingual; I'm always in the process of making it.

II

For neurotypical people, daily tasks like brushing teeth are automatic. For me, they require significant mental effort. My brain doesn't dole out dopamine for these mundane activities, but ticking them off does – The List helps bridge that gap. Through repetition and ritual, I've trained myself to automate certain tasks, minimising their drain on my limited executive function so I can write.

External scaffolding like The List lends structure, but because I have ADHD, it doesn't become internalised. Our coping mechanisms can be unhealthy or transiently brilliant. Remaking them is an act of creativity and true self-care.

The List is often met with scepticism. The gap between neurodivergent experiences and neurotypical expectations is wide. My friends regard it with reverence and resignation. (Nobody likes being a thing to be ticked off.) For someone with ADHD, a good day isn't about hitting milestones but managing obstacles, praying for luck and aiming towards where you want to end up. The shift requires empathy and a willingness to see the workings of someone else's experience.

III

By externalising my memory, The List reduces the cognitive load of living. Its first incarnation was scrawled on my arm – which I couldn't lose – to avoid detentions, a rare point my parents agreed on: both disapproved. Mum said the ink would give me cancer; Dad said it 'wasn't nice'. Given the alternative – detention for losing my homework diary – I chose my arm-list.

Throughout university the system evolved. There were daily lists, bullet points drawn as flowers. I wish I'd kept them all; I could paper an entire house with time. Such work is time consuming because it's creative – the tectonic-plate-moving kind of time in which I learned how to live.

Finding strategies that enable your unique way of processing the world takes time. My early attempts were chaotic. During my first year at university, my lists mixed 'write essay' with 'laundry' and 'buy marmalade'. Without my then-boyfriend's invention of the 'movable box' – non-essential tasks on Post-its that could be transferred to another day – I'd find myself paralysed, inconsolable, unable to go to the library because my photos remained unsorted. What lists leave out is equally important;

however urgent something feels, if it's not on my list, it has
to wait.

Ticking off tasks gives your brain a tiny hit of dopamine.
Learning to use lists as important stories rather than holy texts
is essential; it's easy to become hypervigilant about insulating
yourself from distractions. My father says, 'It's good to have
a plan, and the plan can change.' Marking out our lives with
routines that resonate with who we truly are matters. Within
this way of thinking, success resembles harmony – the concord
between our actions and what we care about.

Imagine playing an old record, with a few scratches and skips,
and finally getting the needle to settle in just the right groove.
When it does, the sound flows perfectly, filling the room, and
you can feel it resonate in your bones. The List is like that
needle finding its groove – it creates space for the music to play
uninterrupted, for everything to fall into place, even if just for a
little while.

IV

I don't cram The List with pointless things that stop me from
listening to the world. In *The Argonauts*, Maggie Nelson wrote
of leaving a space empty so that God could rush in. Take God to
mean whatever you like. For me, it's discipline allowing space for
magic, like I might write that day.

A friend suggested I publish The List here, as a mode of
defying the attention economy. Certainly, it serves as my
rebellion against its demands. Yet, I can't do that. What I can
offer is a new way of relating to time and productivity. This is my
offering – a way of holding space for possibilities while keeping
what is dear close. I used to think I was honing an organisational
system to stop letting people down. Now I realise I was crafting
a blueprint for living.

My internal world is busy. Even medicated, I produce less
work and function less consistently than most neurotypical
people. I decided long ago that my only metrics for success are
whether I'm writing and the state of my relationships.

The List is how I organise my worldview: how I exist in

relation to others, how I show up for the people I care about, how my writing grows.

Writing means you get to live multiple lives, both alone and when your work is read. Without The List I get paralysed about the order of things; I don't want to spend my life crying at the post office, where ADHD ensures I've inevitably forgotten a form, a stamp or the package itself. When you're writing, you're dealing with infinite possibility. That's where I want my freedom. The List allows me a relationship with time that is devotional. Understanding how I work enables me to be intentional in inhabiting my creative mind.

Yet, even the strongest rituals face challenges from outside forces, particularly when those forces are as invasive as digital technology.

Surviving the Scroll: ADHD in the Digital Landscape

Before I grasped the impact of surveillance capitalism, I was Big Tech's dream. I clicked without thinking, enticed by flashing lights and prompts. Small print? Loathed it. The danger became real when a year of researching ADHD turned my online world into an echo chamber of addictive, manipulative content designed to exploit my vulnerabilities.

Suddenly, algorithms bombarded me with questions I hadn't asked: what if I don't have ADHD? What if it's about gut health? Do I need magic mushroom dust?

What can they take when you have only £100 in your bank account?

Your peace of mind. Your agency. Your dignity.

Anyone seeking ADHD support online is steered towards productivity hacks and weight-loss tips – a perilous mix given our heightened risk of eating disorders. Despite avoiding diet content, it flooded my feed. Shunted into the intersection of wellness and ADHD, nearly all the creators were white. If this had been my first encounter, as a mixed-race woman, I might have felt ADHD wasn't 'for me'.

Surveillance capitalism hurts everyone, but ADHD amplifies this vulnerability. Targeted ads and personalised content latch on to our attention, wearing down our already impaired control. Ads trigger impulsive actions, and intense stimuli can lead to sensory overload and difficulty disconnecting. More than once, my boyfriend has gently pried my phone from my claws, relief washing over me only afterwards.

Critics link ADHD to capitalism's technological infrastructure, which heightens distractions through dopamine triggers and endless notifications. Overuse of technology can cause ADHD-like symptoms and exacerbate existing ADHD. But for the latter group, internal distractions often drown out external ones. Processing the 'real' world is overwhelming; navigating my own thoughts is a wild ride.

Paying attention looks different for neurotypical and neurodivergent brains, but without attention, nothing gets done. The neurotypical experience of tech overload chimes with aspects of ADHD, leading to phrases like, 'My brain has too many tabs open.' This common ground should foster mutual compassion. Our hard-won coping strategies can benefit everyone. While neurotypical methods don't always work for me, my techniques have helped neurotypical friends achieve better, more consistent results.

Scholar Jonathan Crary argues that capitalism has reshaped how we experience the world, making sustained focus nearly impossible as we're overwhelmed by new products, 'desires' and information. He suggests 'attention problems' occur when we medicalise 'issues caused by hyperindustrialization'. Recognising these forces allows us to shift from passive consumption to active resistance.

Once again, I'd like to challenge the idea that 'ADHD wouldn't exist without capitalism'. ADHD may be more disabling in a capitalist setting, but without medication I stumble, crash into things, get lost and neglect basic self-care. Writing feels like trying to sing with a head full of bees. Humans weren't designed to stare at screens for ten hours a day, but that doesn't explain why many of us struggle to sleep or miss bodily signals like hunger or pain.

Still, we don't experience attention independently of our environment. The spaces we inhabit shape our attention, guiding our perceptions and interactions. They're not passive backdrops; they direct the flow of our attention and construct our realities. Intentionally designing our social and digital spaces is key to nurturing collective attention and fostering empathy instead of anxiety.

Not having control over your attention isn't always bad. Free-floating attention, originally a psychoanalytic concept, can be creative and restorative, full of free association. It's entirely separate from the time burned up by our personal goals clashing with the objectives set by technology. Free-floating awareness eludes the attention economy's metrics – it's a receptive, liminal state, which ADHD brains spend more time in, making us more likely to be intuitive and in touch with unconscious material. Were our attention more narrowly focused, these riches would be lost. Big Tech wants shallow engagement, endless scrolling. No one on their deathbed has ever said, 'I wish I'd spent more time on TikTok.'

Even those resigned to surveillance capitalism's invasion of privacy are becoming more guarded with their attention, as if generosity leaves us at risk of being looted. It might seem more efficient to move through the world wearing blinkers, without the distraction of other people's needs.

But resisting this pull – redirecting our attention intentionally – is an act of defiance. By acknowledging and challenging Big Tech's manipulations, especially for those of us with ADHD, we begin to reclaim our agency.

Flow as Freedom

The attention economy fragments our focus, but people with ADHD often experience hyperfocus or its gorgeous cousin, flow – deeper, immersive, expansive engagement that makes the outside world fade away. Coined by psychologist Mihaly Csikszentmihalyi, 'flow' describes an optimal state where we feel and perform at our best. Having escaped an Italian prison camp during the Second World War, he sought a better system to make life more meaningful and discovered the joy of intrinsic rewards, like the satisfaction found in creativity. Observing artists, he noted their absorption in the process, completely indifferent to the outcome. Csikszentmihalyi critiqued Skinner's behaviourist approach, which reduced human actions to mere stimulus-response patterns (like little Albert) – flat-pack psychology, in his view. While Skinner graced *Time*'s cover in 1971, Csikszentmihalyi was at the University of Chicago, quietly redefining how we understand what makes life worth living.

For many with ADHD, flow isn't just enjoyable – it's essential. Flow requires focusing on a meaningful goal that's challenging but achievable. ADHD brains, driven by intrinsic interest, often find this engagement naturally. Research shows that those with ADHD often find satisfaction within, like autistic children learning for pure enjoyment, without external reinforcement. Flow liberates us from self-consciousness, rejuvenating our capacity to connect. The more we find it, the better we feel.

Expertise helps enter flow, but true immersion requires surrendering conscious control. Jazz guitarists in flow show reduced executive function activity, letting sensory processing take over. ADHD brains adept at surviving through finding flow might have an advantage here. Much of our attention is manipulated to provoke immediate reactions, such as with reaction videos, where we engage just to have our say. Resisting this cultural obsession with instant responses could lead to clearer thinking. There is freedom in not rushing to voice hastily formed opinions built from context-stripped facts. If everyone refrained from the hot take, we might listen more intently and act collectively.

ADHD experience shows the value of intentional attention. Instead of succumbing to endless notifications and the pressure to be perpetually 'on' we can choose where to direct our focus.

In a culture that often equates busyness with worth, slowing down and focusing deeply becomes a radical act. Our neurodivergent perspectives highlight the importance of setting boundaries and creating environments that nurture sustained attention. We remind others that stepping back from the barrage of stimuli and immersing oneself fully in a single pursuit is OK.

During the pandemic, friends who lived with a high pitch of anxiety fared better than the 'mentally well'. We were familiar with staying inside, defining 'enough' for ourselves. Through surviving, people with ADHD have grit. The variation and texture of experiences that make life with ADHD strange and beautiful aren't legible within a capitalist framework.

Even when well managed, ADHD makes the average day harder – a constraint that's sometimes hard to bear. As Miles describes, 'If everyone's brain is a little dog, people with ADHD have a golden retriever at the bottom of the stairs, and life is like balls coming down the stairs – and with ADHD, it's like all of the balls are coming down at once, and you can't pick which one you want, so you just miss all of them.'

Many, like Miles, long to feel like a 'proper human' or 'functional member of society'. This grief over what life without ADHD might look like is common, but as much as I sympathise, I also feel differently – on good days at least.

While writing this, on a retreat to the Catskills, I was determined to focus. Despite idyllic surroundings, no worries about feeding myself, and ADHD medication, I couldn't work. By day four of six, I snapped and accepted the inevitable. To concentrate, I built a makeshift fort out of chairs, cushions and duvets. I squirrelled inside with chocolate, water and chargers, draping a duvet over the top to block out the light – lamp glowing within. I had to physically narrow my tunnel of vision and render myself unable to move to force myself to do work I wanted to do.

On the other hand, the effort it takes to get to the desk means I don't leave it easily. The slog renders me profoundly grateful whenever circumstances align so I can write. I don't take anything for granted.

I wouldn't give up ADHD because I can't separate it from myself. That's because I've learned, most of the time, to give myself grace instead of measuring things by society's productivity standards, and that's made all the difference.

Reclaiming Attention: From Consumption to Creation

We've internalised the demands of the attention economy to a terrifying extent. For those with ADHD, trying to conform to hustle culture leads to dire mental health outcomes. The attention economy treats content consumption as currency, an exchange we experience in uniquely challenging ways.

To navigate this landscape, I create digital boundaries, resisting productivity tools that reinforce neurotypical standards. These tools often ignore our needs, shoving us into frames that crack on contact. Instead, I develop strategies that align with how my mind works, fostering self-compassion and countering the productivity vortex.

Online spaces can be important resources. In a keynote speech, Dani Donovan highlighted how ADHD communities offer support outside neurotypical feedback. When someone shares that they've finally cleared out the boot of their car after four years, fellow ADHD people celebrate them rather than judge. Unorthodox tricks that suit ADHD brains appear more on TikTok than in books – like K. C. Davis's tip (author of *How to Keep House While Drowning*) to store condiments in the fridge's vegetable drawers to avoid forgetting the veggies. These spaces remind us that care tasks are 'morally neutral' and that small wins are worth celebrating.

By subverting platforms designed to exploit us, we become unlikely prophets exposing Big Tech's hypocrisy, turning attention traps into tools for genuine connection. Dani's 'Anti-Planner', a flexible organiser for brains that don't fit traditional planners, benefits not just ADHD people but those with traumatic brain injuries, and veterans. ADHD people are accustomed to reduced executive function; those who acquire it have to adapt. After recovering from long Covid, a friend told me he finally understood what I meant by low executive function. Tasks that once seemed easy – like cooking 'simple' recipes – now felt insurmountable. First-hand experience bridged the gap between sympathy and understanding.

We need technologies that support us without eroding our agency – tools that honour our humanity instead of undermining it. However, the relationship between assistive technology and market forces is complex. American scholar Rosalind Picard's research into affective computing aimed to help autistic people interpret emotional cues, enhancing their quality of life. Dystopian twist: her technology was co-opted by surveillance start-ups, exploiting those it was meant to assist for advertising and market research. Similarly, tools designed for neurodivergent individuals have been repurposed as productivity monitors, prioritising commercial interests over our needs. This is why Big Tech's prescriptive solutions are harmful.

Communication is another challenge, especially when neurodivergent expressions clash with neurotypical expectations. I once used a plug-in to make myself sound more assertive by stripping excessive apologies from my emails – a trait common in ADHD. (The subtext was that it'd make me sound more like a man.) While it made my emails concise, they felt insincere. Why should we alter our communication styles to be taken seriously? ADHD people work hard to align with neurotypical norms, yet our emails are more likely to be dismissed as unprofessional or overly emotional. Bridging the gap between neurodivergent and neurotypical communication should be a two-way street, valuing deep, meaningful connections over mere efficiency.

Yet everything that makes having ADHD hard can enrich humanity if approached with empathy. Our heightened sensitivity breeds deep care; our impulsivity can mean generosity. Conversations with interviewees for this book were unguarded and sincere – like in one instance, someone sensed I was overwhelmed and shared a meme to uplift me. I noticed a readiness to change our minds without seeing it as weakness, a willingness to both alter the world and be altered by it – abandoning the self-first obsession of rugged individualism. Traits like overapologising aren't always flaws but signs of social sensitivity. Imagine our politics, our planet, if we valued these strengths.

Attention on Our Own Terms

David Foster Wallace's *This is Water* hinted at the kind of deliberate, inconsistent attention that neurotypicals could cultivate. He urged graduates to 'choose what you pay attention to' to avoid our 'natural default setting', which is the enemy, 'because the traffic jams and crowded aisles and long checkout lines give me time to think, and if I don't make a conscious decision about how to think and what to pay attention to, I'm gonna be pissed and miserable every time I have to shop'.

Deliberate attention means that even in a 'crowded, hot, slow, consumer-hell' moment, meaning can be found. By choosing what has value and what we care about, we can avoid the trap of 'worshipping' wealth or productivity, which only leads to dissatisfaction. Real freedom lies in attentiveness and caring for others, often in small, unnoticed ways.

Managing ADHD involves a radical reimagining of what a good day, week and life look like. It requires choosing where to get validation, rather than expecting it from socially conditioned places. It necessitates opting out of anxiety-fuelled comparison on social media. I spent years fighting the boom–bust cycle, but now I think of it like sped-up seasons, each phase needing different care.

Neurodivergence challenges the idea that humans are only 'productive' through mono-tasking. I need musical or video stimuli just to get out of bed. A neurotypical flowchart suggests attention flows from self to task to result. For ADHD minds, it's more prismatic, forceful and tidal. We don't default to binary thinking. Our thoughts say, 'Yes, but also …' and, 'The thing is …' leaving us open to more possibilities. Our comorbidities make us more attuned to complex layers of the world and what's going on in others' lives. Given the global rise of populism and divisive politics, inclusive, expansive thinking is essential – not 'either/or' but 'both and also'.

It's a running joke that we love parentheses due to the need to cram more ideas into a sentence. Neurotypical people like this less because 'this does not relate to that', whereas we know that, from the right angle, everything relates. Therein lies the chaos.

My sensitivity to minutiae – often rendering my experience of the world anew – has forced me to learn how to disengage from sensory input. In the attention economy, this becomes self-preservation against a system that manipulates us for profit and shapes public reactions, chipping away at intuition. It's not just one politician promoting misinformation but an entire system thriving on divided attention. We need a mutual alliance with neurotypicals, who are also under siege by this economy.

The Wisdom of the Gorilla: Seeing What Others Miss

Consider Daniel Simons's famous 1991 selective attention test, where participants watching a video counted how many times a group passed a ball. Halfway through, someone in a gorilla suit walked across the screen. Most participants didn't notice the gorilla. I found this astonishing; I couldn't track the passes because I was fixated on the gorilla. A friend who didn't see it said, 'What does this mean about me? That I could be attacked by a gorilla and not notice because I am committed to a menial task?' On the flip side, I'd felt dim for losing track of the ball. The fact that we see different things in the same situation is valuable and essential if we are to learn from each other. We have to stop ranking different modes of thinking and perception.

Cathy Davidson, Barack Obama's former education advisor, noted the overrepresentation of people with ADHD and dyslexia among successful innovators as a sign of adaptation: 'Unable to attune their attention to that of others, these people have had to invent workaround procedures which have enabled them to better perceive certain hidden faces of things.' This should be an advantage, as most peoples' attention being 'aligned on the returns of GDP growth' has meant 'that we have missed the gorilla of climate imbalance'.

Davidson's work supports the idea of ADHD people as unlikely prophets, exposing systemic flaws and challenging dominant narratives, from Big Tech's exploitation to climate inaction. By reclaiming our attention from systems that see us as mere data, ADHD minds pose a challenge to the attention economy, moving in ways it cannot fully grasp or tame. Where others might see disorder or inefficiency, I see an invitation to rewrite the rules – a covert rebellion, or perhaps a revolution. By choosing what deserves our attention, we affirm that the present is ours to shape, valuing connection, resonance and authenticity. What if, simply by honouring our own rhythm, we reveal that a different way of living was possible all along?

GETTING INTIMATE

Chapter 13

The Trojan Horse: An ADHD Manifesto

We are the Trojan horse within the fortress of the attention economy. Unseen, often underestimated, those of us navigating this attention-distorted world with inherent ingenuity carry the seeds of revolution. Our lived experiences don't just highlight the cracks – they are the catalysts for the profound transformation the world desperately needs. You, who have journeyed with me this far, understand that neurodivergent and neurotypical struggles are intertwined, and that people with ADHD are leading the charge. I know you can embrace this truth and push even further.

You may have noticed throughout this book that ideas sometimes pixelate and flash, or slow down and form quiet rock pools. Networks of thoughts branch, collide and germinate, growing hybrid plants in unexpected places. I've tried to rein myself in – to write in a style that stimulates neurodivergent readers while remaining accessible to neurotypical readers. Now, I write to you as one who instinctively understands that my observations aren't strictly linear but interrelated in a way that's true to life.

One of the strengths of having ADHD is the openness to changing your mind. As I've written and read, new ideas have folded into my work, so by the time I arrived at this final section, my mind was filled with origami animals. The book unfolded like an accordion, like a fan.

This chapter may be easier to consume for people whose

brains works like mine. If that's not you, remember: this is my mind after it's been organised, edited and proofread. Imagine it unfiltered. So take this as an experiment in empathy, a training session in the attention economy. If you have trouble following me, I ask you to dance – or, as Jenny Odell invites her readers, to 'take a walk'. Consider this manifesto an invitation to stroll, to challenge yourself, to pirouette, to leap, to explore.

Parentheses within parentheses do not cancel each other out. To argue against the attention economy with anything less than a mycelium-like structure would be to underestimate the task ahead. It relies on a network, but so do we. Embrace the tangents. Trust that you'll land on your feet – dishevelled maybe, but wide awake.

Priceless Focus: Why Attention Matters

Attention is uniquely ours and it is the faculty through which we experience collective life. It's like cells in an organism – distinct yet interdependent. It is fused with our perception. But what happens when our perception is manipulated and commodified?

Attention isn't fungible; it can't be permanently taken away. Is the attention you pay to a lover's mouth the same kind you pay to emails? Could you exchange one for another?

Our attention is unique to each of us, yet it's available only as something to be alienated – captured by consumer capitalism or submerged in the experiences we dive into passionately. However diverted it seems, our attention can always be reclaimed – and we don't have to put it into 'circulation' – we don't have to let it be commodified or fed into the attention economy for others to exploit.

People with ADHD naturally resist control and standardisation. Our brains are wired to disrupt the rigid systems defining productivity, time and attention in capitalist societies. This makes us ideal agitators of the status quo – with lived experience as our weapon. We've navigated these traps first-hand and developed adaptive strategies to share. Our unpredictability subverts these systems from within.

Beyond Economic Metaphors: Attention ≠ Time ≠ Money

I have to be honest: I've been using the term 'attention economy' for 308 pages, but it has never felt right. Does everything have to be an economy? Not everything is data to be mined or a resource to be extracted.

Philosopher Yves Citton suggests reimagining the attention economy as an 'ecology' – an 'ecosystem' we must nurture urgently to create ways of living that are both sustainable for the community and enriching for the individual. As social creatures, our existence depends on how thoughtfully we maintain the relationships that inform our surroundings and identity.

Viewing attention as a commodity reduces our cognitive and social engagements to mere transactions. ADHD is often framed in terms of 'deficit' and 'surplus', yet our interactions with the world are anything but linear. Economic metaphors dominate discussions about attention, suggesting we 'pay' for intellectual 'profits'. This transactional lens steers us towards efficiency and productivity at the cost of creativity and depth.

Metaphors help us express our private experiences of collective life – we're always giving up one thing for another. But if everything is understood in terms of a 'better return' and attentional 'efficiency', where is the room for art, for joy? This framing risks turning us into machines – optimised for output, doomed to plunder the earth until extinction. Roll out the red carpet for our AI overlords.

Rejecting the economic model of attention is urgent. Citton urges us to see attention as a 'transformative force', that shapes our goals. What we focus on determines what we value, challenging the myth of a purely 'rational' person and recognising that choices are influenced by communities.

Understanding attention as a creative act reveals its capacity to dynamically alter our experiences. It prompts us to ask: how should we direct our focus? What kind of collective do we wish to become?

This may sound strange coming from a person with ADHD, but though our attention is fragmented, that is not the problem. The real issue lies in our expectations and what we deem 'good' and 'important'. Moving away from static economic terms like 'values' – as if we were brands – can help align our lives with the intricate web that sustains us.

By nature, we resist the transactional, 'pay-for-productivity' logic that the attention economy holds sacred. This makes us unlikely infiltrators, bringing a way of living that rejects quantification and thrives on depth over efficiency.

Reaching Out

Attention is not a battery to be drained; it's the thread that connects us to each other and our environment. You can plug in to the relentless pursuit of growth that promises to destroy the habitat making life possible, or recognise attention – in its pure form – as connection. Our shared world will only be liveable if we attend to it.

Ultimately, we must shift our perception of attention from a commodity to be exploited to a relationship to be nurtured. The Latin root is 'attendere': 'ad' meaning 'to' or 'toward', and 'tendere' meaning 'to stretch'. So the literal translation is 'to stretch towards'. Attention is always reaching out. I understand the urge to isolate and primly repeat, 'I am focusing on myself.' Yet, whether you avoid your neighbour's eyes or not, life remains collective.

I used to dislike foxes in my Brixton neighbourhood – trotting around like furry little anarchists, attacking rubbish. But when my American friend Isadora encountered one for the first time, she was enraptured. She clutched my arm, as if too loud a breath might disturb this feral creature, and whispered, 'How magical.' Her attention transformed mine.

Attention is how I know I'm not alone. It connects me to loved ones, strangers, trees and so many ragged foxes. Holding these things in relation keeps us alive.

As neurodivergent individuals, we experience the overwhelming forces of the attention economy intensely. This heightened sensitivity makes us ideal agents of change. We can't pretend to live on a tranquil shore when we've spent so much of ourselves resisting the tides, only to be swept away again.

Time Isn't Money: Unpacking the Fungibility Myth

The idea that time is fungible – that it can be sliced into units and traded like currency – is rooted in colonialism and slavery. Enslaved labour was quantified as if time and goods, like sugar, held equal value. Historian Caitlin Rosenthal notes that this practice turned labour and commodities into 'standardised, free-floating, infinitely divisible' entities 'indelibly linked to human and ecological exhaustion'. This dehumanising perspective persists today, reinforced by the Benjamin Franklin adage 'time is money', pressing us to commodify every moment.

But time isn't a commodity; it's the cycle of sun and moon, a rhythm we inhabit rather than something we own or trade away. When we start viewing time as mere units to trade, we risk applying the same notion to our attention – treating it as a resource to be segmented and exploited. This paves the way for more aspects of our humanity to become fungible and commodified.

The whole point of infinite scroll is to keep us online longer because our time directly translates into their profit. We've accepted these artificial metrics, letting ourselves be treated like machines. But we aren't machines, and we must resist being exploited as if we are.

The push for productivity crushes creativity and drains life of its richness, rushing us through moments devoid of real satisfaction. It reduces life to a series of transactions.

As ADHD revolutionaries, we perceive time differently – not as a resource to be optimised, but as a fluid medium for creativity and connection. By rejecting capitalist metrics that commodify our time and attention, we challenge systems that profit from our very existence and reclaim the true worth of our experiences. Understanding time as personal and relational allows us to embrace concepts like 'Crip Time' – a recognition that time is adaptable, not a rigid structure to constrain us. This perspective alters how we see our place in the world and how we choose to spend our precious moments.

Embracing Crip Time: Time is Relational

ADHD's impact on time perception isn't fully understood, but a 2020 review confirmed that it does alter it. This might stem from challenges in working memory or inconsistent dopamine – the neurotransmitter tuning our internal clock.

An interviewee once cancelled a meeting, texting, 'I do not feel the master of my own time.' Her tone was tongue-in-cheek, but it reminded me of Frederick Winslow Taylor's 'Taylorism', an early twentieth-century strategy that pushed efficiency by breaking down tasks and ruthlessly monitoring workers, blurring the line between person and machine.

Today, time management – unless intentionally practised for personal needs – is a trap. It pushes us to produce more without profiting from increased productivity, while robbing life of depth. Mastering time often just means using it up faster.

Recognising ADHD's distinctive sense of time as an alternative perspective, rather than a flaw, is vital. Disability scholars and activists champion Crip Time, which reshapes our relationship with time by prioritising human needs over rigid schedules.

For example, if you have experience with disability or chronic illness, you know that linear time is a cruel myth. The effort to get out of bed can feel like jumping into a centrifuge; every plan has an asterisk, all plans are contingent. Time might be measured in pills or small victories, like reaching the bathroom.

Crip Time offers flexibility: on a daily level, it means flexibility and celebrating small achievements; on large scale, in challenging the norms around productivity, it opens the door for more inclusive policies like remote options. This benefits not just people with disabilities but also parents, caregivers and those who don't fit into a nine-to-five template, allowing all to contribute meaningfully. Companies with adaptable work policies often see happier, more loyal employees. Crip Time fosters solidarity among all human bodies, which eventually break down. Covid-19 drew our attention to this shared fragility.

During times when depression made washing my hair an event, I found Crip Time liberating. In a world not built for

ADHD, self-compassion isn't a 'nice to have' – it's essential. When I was younger, my approach was unhelpful and harsh. It went like this: if I lower my (unrealistic) standards, I'll become more unproductive, because at core I am lazy, selfish and weak. Over time, I learned that it's better to set goals that other people might think are tiny – like doll's-house furniture – and by meeting them, prove yourself to yourself every day. At the end of the year, you have a beautiful doll's house. Setting attainable goals and meeting them builds self-respect. Setting unreachable standards and failing daily proves nothing.

In my late twenties I began to understand the strength self-compassion requires. You have to ignore common wisdom about how to live. Accepting my idiosyncratic sense of time – where some days simply don't occur and I can't account for all my time as 'useful' – helped me reclaim time lost to shame and depression. ADHD means it takes me far longer to figure out how to do something than to actually do it. Trying to do things like neurotypical people, according to linear time, was punitive.

Society assumes that everyone perceives time the same way and can move through it at will. Embracing Crip Time disrupts that assumption. It draws from disability, queer and feminist movements, questioning demand for 'compulsory able-bodiedness' in capitalist societies.

Crip Time pushes for time that bends to human needs rather than squeezing them to the margins. Even benefit systems force people with disabilities out of normative time. Until recently, the London Transport Freedom Pass, which offers free travel for those unable to drive due to disability, restricted users until after 9.30 a.m., shutting many out of standard work hours. That this has changed gives us hope.

If I were naïve, I'd say that people should empathise with experiences they haven't had, but, instead, I'll point out that even the richest, fittest, most independent, rise-and-grind bro will experience some kind of disability. Understanding Crip Time isn't only altruistic – it's practical. In times of crisis – like global pandemics – flexibility becomes essential for everyone.

By challenging the notion of scarcity, Crip Time promotes a view that honours individual needs, community care and mutual support. With burnout prevalent even among neurotypicals, clearly there's a lesson to be learned: we must listen carefully to both our bodies and minds in a culture that encourages us to ignore them and push beyond their limits.

Attention as Earth Care

By aligning attention with ecological principles, we advocate for a more sustainable and interconnected approach to life. Treating attention as a commodity distracts us from our physical world, which we neglect, deepening environmental crises.

Attention not only connects us to each other, but also binds us to the earth. Although our individual lives end, time goes on; we are, in essence, gardening time for future generations. Understanding this requires stepping outside Chronos (clock time) long enough to see the glimmer of Kairos – the crucial opening between a doomed future and one we can still imagine, however uncertain its form.

These ideas are not new. They reflect a rejection of the rigid, clock-bound structures imposed by the industrial revolution, which alienated us from natural cycles. Indigenous worldviews, by contrast, embrace a cyclical, relational sense of time, rooted in the earth's natural rhythms and emphasising life's interconnectedness. In these cultures, time is defined by connections among people, their environment and events, rather than measured units. Oral traditions enrich this concept, with past wisdom living through elders' tales, weaving together past, present and future into a continuous narrative.

Neurodivergent people, as I discussed in Chapter 6, often perceive these connections more acutely due to our heightened sensitivity. Our unique processing styles allow us to see patterns others might overlook, and sense subtle shifts that signal larger changes in our environment. Our capacity to think outside convention helps us envision creative solutions to complex problems, including environmental challenges.

By recognising our attention as woven into an ecological web, we start to see our actions in a broader context. When we attend to nature, we become attuned to its needs and rhythms. This attentiveness can drive stewardship, conservation and a deeper appreciation for the planet that sustains us.

ADHD disruptors can unite with other marginalised thinkers – disability activists, indigenous groups and neurodivergent communities – who possess knowledge that can serve as a catalyst, to amplify a shared vision resisting systems that stunt human potential. Our inherent challenge to productivity-focused systems mirrors larger ecological and social justice movements opposing capitalist exploitation of people and the planet.

Directing attention towards our interconnectedness and ecological balance nurtures a deeper bond with the earth, a shift necessary for the planet's survival. Our ability to hyperfocus on what we're passionate about can fuel meaningful action and inspire collective efforts to protect and cherish our shared world.

The Need for Collective Action

The attention economy feeds on itself, reinforcing the idea that attention is scarce and demanding ever more content that seizes it. It is a self-perpetuating spiral which negatively impacts how we process information. Big Tech keeps us in dragonfly mode, zipping between things that glitter. By manipulating our attention, surveillance capitalism leads us to neglect our physical world. I've seen more photos of flowers on Instagram this month than I will see in ten lifetimes on earth. The filter bubble doesn't just limit how we perceive and interact with other humans.

I cried when I found out about the metaverse. I could imagine people giving up on the earth we have, because it's hard, and choosing to live in a virtual world instead. Most people won't have that choice. As a child, I asked my mother why the news only gave twenty seconds to the thousands who die in monsoon floods in India. She turned from the television and said, 'Because it happens every year.' Why are we pouring billions into virtual worlds – sustaining wealth for the few while extending the attention economy – but neglecting the one world we have?

I remember when the first tsunami hit Indonesia. I couldn't stop imagining the wall of water bearing down. On the weekends I saw my father, my recurring question was: 'What do we do if a tsunami comes?' My brother scowled in the front seat. But I asked again, seeking the comfort of a familiar refrain. Dad said we would hold hands and say, 'I love you,' and close our eyes. He lives in Vermont now. Last summer his doctor told him not to go outside. Wildfire smog had turned the sky over New York red. It smelled of burning timber. After five minutes, people said, it hurt to breathe.

We cannot hold the extent of the environmental crisis in our minds. It is too big; it is paralysing; we numb out. How can we sustain our focus without burning out? How can we attend to the world or even our local community with care, when caring hurts?

Reclaiming our attention from political and financial manipulation is a personal and collective act of defiance. This resistance defends our autonomy and challenges the systems that commodify our existence.

A Fresh Blueprint for Living

As the walls of old structures tremble, it becomes clear that we – who see time differently and scatter our attention like seeds – emerge as an unexpected force for renewal. We've been inside the gates all along. Once dismissed as liabilities, our experiences have become tools to help dismantle and rebuild a world more attuned to humanity's rhythms. The revolution is here, led by those who handle these complexities with innate resourcefulness.

Blending theoretical insights, personal stories and cultural critiques, this manifesto envisions a future where attention and time are reclaimed as sources of creativity, connection and harmony. Resisting the commodification of our minds means reclaiming our humanity, nurturing an attentiveness that enriches individual lives and collective wellbeing. Accepting ourselves and valuing our unique perspectives counters a society fuelled by inadequacy and scarcity. In doing so, we become radicals embodying abundance and contentment in a world built on unmet desires.

The assumption that one way of thinking is superior

silences those with lived experience. Accessing shared wisdom requires bridge-builders fluent in both worlds. Spider-Manning between associations makes perfect sense among people with ADHD. While neurodivergent people excel at forging lateral connections – inviting a richer, more inclusive understanding –for this book to be accessible to neurotypical readers, collaborative work had to occur.

Perhaps, finally, there's a collective will to implement ideas like taxing attention-seeking emails – a concept suggested by Bill Gates in 2004. Tim Wu argues that, throughout history, moments of 'collective disenchantment' with the attention industry have led to 'revolt', forcing the 'attention merchants' to 'revise their terms'. AI may accelerate this reckoning, threatening to burst the model – and our minds – with its capacity to generate endless content.

We must not underestimate the problem. Capitalism fuels the attention economy, and its efforts to snatch focus are infinite. We need sustainable forms of continual resistance that empower without depleting us.

Managing ADHD teaches humility about what we can realistically sustain – often through invisible work that quietly enriches our lives. Free from relentless pressure, all people produce better work aligned with their natural strengths and rhythms.

Shifting from hours to impact and quality creates more meaningful and inclusive labour practices, particularly for those with ADHD. Capitalism treats our lives as finite resources, relentlessly extracting productivity from us. ADHD's resistance to meaningless tasks defies a system intent on squeezing our existence into measurable units.

Conclusion: Giving Time to Time

I'm wary of the consumerist metaphor 'time well spent', though I admire some of its ideas. Productivity is still there, like grit under the skin. We don't have to use time efficiently. Time is relational. We inhabit it.

I end with the French phrase I like most: '*Il faut donner du temps au temps*,' which translates to, 'One must give time to time.'

Giving time to time means recognising the depth and richness of existence beyond capitalist constructs. Let us stretch towards one another, inhabit time together and nurture the connections that make life rich and sustainable. Our lives are short. Life is long.

TL;DR: How to Fight Back

This manifesto calls for a shift in how we view attention, time and productivity, fostering a more humane and connected world. Below are the core principles and actionable steps for neurodivergent (ND) and neurotypical (NT) people.

1. ADHD as a Force for Change

ADHD brings unique ingenuity to disrupt and transform the attention economy.

Actions:
ND: Embrace and share your perspective.
NT: Support and value diverse ways of thinking.
Everyone: Advocate for neurodiversity and challenge restrictive systems.

2. Attention is Connection

Attention is not a commodity but a connection to ourselves, others and the world, which has to be kept alive.

Actions:
ND: Protect your focus with nourishing activities.
NT: Prioritise full engagement over multitasking.
Everyone: Limit distractions and build deep connections.

3. Redefining Productivity

True productivity includes rest and enrichment, not just output.

Actions:
ND: Define success on your terms; prioritise wellbeing.
NT: Embrace and model balanced success metrics.
Everyone: Value contributions beyond economic gain and encourage real self-care.

4. Embracing Crip Time

Time is flexible and should accommodate diverse rhythms.

Actions:
ND: Honour your natural pace.
NT: Show patience and flexibility.
Everyone: Support varied timelines and productivity.

5. Collective Action and Community

Deep, real connections are essential.

Actions:
ND: Participate in supportive communities.
NT: Include and learn from ND voices.
Everyone: Build strong community bonds and collaborate on initiatives.

6. Resist Surveillance Capitalism

Reclaim your focus and protect your data.

Actions:
ND: Use strategies to protect your attention; limit exposure.
NT: Be critical of tech that manipulates your attention.
Everyone: Advocate for privacy and support ethical tech practices.

7. Attention and Ecology

Align attention with ecological awareness; recognise interconnectedness.

Actions:
ND: Engage with nature for grounding and inspiration.
NT: Adopt sustainable habits and educate others about environmental stewardship.
Everyone: Join initiatives that protect the environment; promote attentiveness.

Embrace these principles to reclaim attention, redefine time and build a society rooted in connection, creativity and sustainability. Stretch towards each other, inhabit time together and nurture meaningful connections.

AFFIRMING

Imagine yourself wrapped in a warm, amber-coloured orb of light. The glow is gentle, like late afternoon sun, just warm enough to feel comforting without overwhelming. This light surrounds you, steady and protective, softening all the noise outside your little sphere.

As you breathe, the light shifts in hue – maybe a soft gold or dusky lavender – adapting to whatever feels right in the moment. Within this orb, you're untouchable, focused and calm. Distractions bounce off its surface, unable to reach you, while you feel clear and steady inside, with only what you need drifting through. Breathe in, let the light fill you, and let it set a boundary for your energy, keeping you anchored and at peace.

Beyond Survival: ADHD Wisdom for Life

There are plenty of wonderful resources out there on meditation, the Pomodoro technique, exercise, continuous learning, etc. Here's distilled insight from twenty years:

Embrace Essentials
Most 'ADHD products' are trash. Essentials: gravity blanket, good noise-cancelling headphones, water bottle you love, pretty medication container you're less likely to lose. Have a charger in every port.

Habit-Stacking
Pair mundane tasks with enjoyable ones (e.g., podcasts while washing up). I do nothing without background audio – TV, rain sounds or audiobooks.

Templates and Lists
Create templates for repetitive tasks (packing, shopping) on your phone to save mental energy.

Accessible Tools
Leave tools, like an open laptop, visible to make starting easier. Hijack your own attention.

Sidle Up to Tasks
Approach tasks indirectly, like a crab. The more you stare them down, the bigger they seem.

Micro-Steps
Break tasks into tiny parts. When struggling, a friend still texts me, 'First thing: two feet on the floor.'

Realistic Routines
The best routine is what you can sustain. ADHD consistency differs from NT consistency – accept that.

'Done Now' Space
It's important to have somewhere you never mask. Create low-stimulation, comforting environments with talismans and soft clothes. Invest in lighting.

Transition Tools
Have engaging distractions (e.g., *Zelda*) to ease anxiety mid-transition.

Thank You, Next
Accept NT gifts like planners with gratitude; save energy explaining why you won't use them. Unless you choose violence, which is also fine.

Three-Minute Rule
Start a task for just three minutes to overcome inertia. Keep your promises to yourself.

Dessert First
Tackle the easiest task first. Do something you love and then suddenly switch your attention.

You are a Human Animal
Exercise doesn't have to be structured, but you need to move.

Find a Buddy
Work alongside someone – body doubling, even informally, helps.

Visualise Boundaries
Imagine a filter for external stimuli, creating a buffer for focus and emotional control. I picture myself in a sphere of light – warm, steady, translucent, defining my edges. It changes colour.

Use Mantras
Shift inner dialogue with affirmations that fit your mood.

Child-Like Self-Care
NTs telling us to take a relaxing bath gets very annoying. I find it easier to treat myself with care when I imagine I'm taking care of my own child.

Skip the Metrics
Unless you find it motivating, not everything needs tracking. Avoid obsessing over data (e.g., Fitbits) that fuels productivity anxiety. This work will not be graded!

Other People are Not You
A Post-it reminder: 'Do not compare your insides to their outsides.' Social media is heavily edited – take TikTok's '5-minute' chopped salad videos, for example, which would take me an hour in real life – which took me far too long to realise.

Daily Journalling
Jot down thoughts to clear mental clutter – talk to yourself on paper. I try to write down messages due to my urgent need to interrupt people – often by the end of the day they've lost their sheen.

Focus Apps and Playlists
Block distractions and create mood-matching playlists to set the day's rhythm.

Shortcuts Without Shame
Skip steps to simplify; having ADHD adds more steps by default.

Add Tech Friction
Introduce barriers to addictive tech to regain control.

Taste the Bittersweet
I recognise my level of distraction as the necessary counterpoint
to my ability to hyperfocus.

Silver Bullets Work for Us
Identify small changes that could greatly improve your wellbeing
(e.g., more socks).

And, finally, here are some things I remind myself of most days:

» You do not need to earn rest. You do not need to earn joy.
» Distraction is not a moral failing. I just don't want
  dickheads profiting off mine. The goal is practical
  self-direction.
» You have felt this way before and you have survived it.
» The worst-case scenario is always going to be exactly
  that. The worst-case scenario of a teddy bear's picnic is a
  bloodbath.
» Unless it's literally life or death, nothing is ever urgent.
  If somebody or something is trying to make you feel
  like something is urgent, they're trying to control you,
  financially or emotionally.
» Needing deadlines, gamification or pressure for non-
  interesting tasks is fine – it means you won't have a
  breakdown at forty and end up screaming, 'WHY DO I
  DO THIS JOB?'
» Nobody would ask a sprinter to run a marathon.
» You don't always know what you're learning during a
  side-quest.
» Self-flagellation is a false economy. Swear a lot, then get
  on with it.
» Often, how we talk or treat ourselves is harsher than any
  mistake.
» It helps to think of how, in action films, nobody gives up
  because there's only thirty seconds left.

Credits

Thank you to Rubyetc, who *got it*, instantly.

Thank you to the experts whose knowledge enriched my thinking, especially Andy Hargreaves and Sari Solden. And to the advocates, Dani Donovan, Henry Shelford, Jesse J. Anderson, Sarah Templeton and Stuart MacAlpine, who were so generous with their time.

Thank you also to everyone who bravely shared their experiences. One interviewee said, 'If I have to put up with the sh*t I've been given, I want to help as many people as possible know they're not alone!' To me, this felt like the very best of ADHD (compassion, grit) and an attitude worth cultivating. I hope reading this made you feel seen: Adam Bond, Alice O, Bex Connelly, Carla Jellema, Dusty Chipuara, Elissa Schappell, Hannah Rutherford, Ines Berges, James Nimno, Jay Harrison, Joel Lewin, Josh Hulbert, Kate Garner, Kit Griffiths, Mike How, Miles Spillman-Schappell, Nathan Gibbs, Rachel Derby, Rachel Idowu, Sofia Carlisle-Bel, Shauna Richardson, Teresa Howard, Vivienne Isebor, Whitney Clarke.

And finally, thank you to everyone who corresponded with me but who, sadly, I ran out of space to include in the book: Andrew J. McNair, Annie Werner, Catherine Dunkley, Catherine Wynne, Chris Merriman, Danny ABC, Emma Mahoney, Geoff Kewley, Graham Borland, Joanne O'Leary, Kelli Trapnell, Lianne Rollison, Lottie Fowler, Niamh Rasmussen, Nicola Carey-Shine, René Brooks.

Acknowledgements

To everyone who made this book possible: my agent Emma Paterson and the team at Dialogue, especially Hannah Chukwu – who didn't say no to a single crazy idea – and Eleanor Gaffney.

To my copy-editor, Ian Preece, and proof-reader David Bamford, for their patience.

To Tim Wu (*The Attention Merchants*) and Jenny Odell (*Saving Time* and *How to Do Nothing*), whose writing on attention changed how I thought about mine.

To Steve Silberman (*NeuroTribes*) and Nicolas Rasmussen (*On Speed: The Many Lives of Amphetamine*) whose expertise sent me down many wormholes.

To the Arts Council England for their generous support through DYCP funding, which enabled essential creative exploration, and to The London Library for giving me space and time to write.

To Isadora Spillman-Schappell, for reading all the drafts, and deciphering the mess ('So, what you're saying is . . .'). And to her mother, Elissa, whose brain made me like my own more.

To my parents, Dina Medland and Tim Medland, for giving me exactly the love, freedom and friction I needed to write this book.

To my friends, especially to Georgia Bird, who liked me before I was diagnosed or medicated.

To Etienne, for everything, always.

Notes

Introduction: ADHD in the British Media

12 *Brace yourself for a barrage of headlines* While not every article from this timeframe could be included, the selection aims to capture the overall trends and tone of media reporting.

12 *In March 2024 Work and Pensions Secretary Mel Stride claimed that 'mental health culture' had 'gone too far'* BACP, 'Secretary of State for Work and Pensions shows deep lack of consideration for mental health', BACP, 25 March 2024, https://www.bacp.co.uk/news/news-from-bacp/2024/25-march-secretary-of-state-for-work-and-pensions-shows-deep-lack-of-consideration-for-mental-health/

12 *'Sometimes we've got to be a little bit braver and say to those young people, "You are not disabled, you can go to work ... we're going to support you."'* Hatton, Ben, 'Lee Anderson plays down "poverty nonsense", saying 1970s was "real poverty"', *Independent*, 3 October 2023, https://www.independent.co.uk/news/uk/lee-anderson-conservative-party-europe-manchester-facebook-b2423190.html

13 *Over the past two years, referrals to specialists and self-diagnoses have spiked, with the reported 400 per cent increase in adults seeking diagnoses since 2020.* ADHD Works, 'Questions you might be afraid to ask about ADHD: Answered', https://www.adhdworks.info/blog/questions-you-might-be-afraid-to-ask-about-adhd-answered

14 *I THOUGHT I'D GIVEN BIRTH TO A DEVIL CHILD* Hohler, Emily, 'I thought I'd given birth to a devil child', *Sunday Telegraph*, 15 December 1996.

14 *In 1991, for the first time, a five-year-old boy successfully sued the Sun for libel.* 'The *Sun* pays libel damages to boy aged 5', *Independent*, 24 May 1991.

14 *'Terror Tot Jonathan Hunt was last night dubbed Britain's naughtiest kid after wrecking his parents' home, cutting off his own ear, and killing the cat.'* '*Sun* pays libel cash to boy, 5; Jonathan Hunt', *The Times*, 24 May 1991.

15 *The court found the journalist had portrayed him as 'wilfully naughty'* Ibid.

15 *articles warned, 'Children with Attention Disorders Can Destroy a Family.'* Packer, Amy, 'Life with my kid in the corner', *Daily Express*, 1 December 1999.

15 *Headlines cautioned of 'The Criminal Gene'* Jones, Steve, 'The criminal gene', *Daily Telegraph*, 27 April 1996.

16 *MOTHER'S HYPER HELPER* 'Mother's hyper helper', *Daily Express*, 10 November 1994.

16 *'My Son was "Like a Cabbage"'* Sharon, Howard, 'My son was "like a cabbage"', *Independent*, 1 April 1995.

16 *'Ritalin Made My Son a Demon'* Browne, Anthony, 'Ritalin made my son a demon', *Observer,* 9 April 2000.

16 *Opinion pieces polarised ADHD kids into being either 'ill' or 'naughty', 'sick' or 'bad', with medication presented as another binary – either a 'wonder drug' or a 'chemical cosh'* 'Wonder drug or chemical cosh', *Daily Mail*, 24 April 1995.

17 *Lucas Lawson, a nineteen-year-old American, had died after crushing and snorting pills.* 'How a wonder drug turned into a menace', *Daily Mail*, 9 April 1996.

17 *CHILDREN'S DRUG IS MORE POTENT THAN COCAINE* West, Jean, 'Children's drug is more potent than cocaine', *Observer*, 9 September 2001.

17 *'Children's Drug is More Potent Than Cocaine' proclaimed the* Observer Ibid.

17 Daily Mail *described ADHD as a 'fashionable' disorder, with stories of kids trading pills dubbed 'Vitamin R' in playgrounds.* 'How a wonder drug turned into a menace'.

17 *One columnist even wrote, 'Have you come to accept the fact that your work ambitions and dreams may never be realised?', suggesting that ADHD was merely an alibi for personal failure.* Furnham, Adrian, 'Nobody's fault – but especially not your own', *Daily Telegraph*, 1 February 1999.

18 *With increased awareness came a backlash of articles like 'Are We Creating a Generation of Addicts?'* Thomson, Alice, 'Are we creating a generation of addicts?', *Daily Telegraph*, 3 November 2000.

19 *the* Daily Mail *lumped ADHD with 'trans issues', appearing to mock both as symptoms of 'politically correct' overreach and dismissing ADHD as a 'modern malady' born of indulgent parenting.* Sarler, Carol, 'Pity poor Zach, a five-year-old victim of the politically correct gender identity industry', *Daily Mail*, 22 February 2012.

19 *ARE WE TURNING CHILDREN INTO DRUGGED ZOMBIES?* Orr, Deborah, 'Are we turning children into drugged zombies?', *Independent*, 22 July 2003.

20 *some newspapers seemed to yearn for its return, publishing earnest letters explicitly putting ADHD forward as an opportunity to ask, 'Should We Let Teachers Smack?'* 'Should we let teachers smack?', *Daily Mail*, 8 August 2000.

20 *NOBODY IS CALLED BAD ANY MORE. OR A BIT THICK. THEY HAVE ADHD OR MILD BEFFBURGER'S SYNDROME …* Routledge, Paul, 'It's not ADHD … He's a very naughty boy', *Daily Mirror*, 26 June 2009.

20 *'These diagnoses give parents an excuse for failed parenting', wrote Paul Routledge in the* Daily Mirror, *where he repeatedly returned to this argument over the years. In one column, he recalled his father's belief that the 'medical intervention' needed for behaviour problems was 'a bloody good hiding'.* Ibid.

20 *Psychologist Aric Sigman once called for a return to smacking, blaming ADHD on working mothers and daycare.* Morrison, Blake, 'Aric Sigman: The "just say no" dad', *Guardian*, 19 September 2009, https://www. theguardian.com/lifeandstyle/2009/sep/19/aric-sigman-parents-control

20 *In his view, 'the medicalising of civil disorders ... deflects any apportionment of blame'* Driscoll, Margarette, 'Parents too scared to say "no" are raising a spoilt generation', *Sunday Times*, 13 September 2009, https://www.thetimes.com/article/parents-too-scared-to-say-no-are-raising-a-spoilt-generation-00bnzbq8bkr

21 *The letter concluded, tongue-in-cheek, that ADHD only emerged in medical journals after such practices were banned.* Burke, V., 'Six of the best', *Daily Mail*, 17 June 2003.

21 *ARE THESE CHILDREN REALLY ILL OR ARE THEY JUST NAUGHTY?* 'Are these children really ill or are they just naughty?', *Daily Mail*, 25 March 1997.

21 *'£10,000 Wrecking Spree of the Little Devil Aged Four'* '£10,000 wrecking spree of the little devil aged four', *Daily Mail*, 12 July 2000.

21 *Under sensational banners like 'The Curse of Kids' Cocaine', articles contained misinformation, claiming Ritalin was addictive, required ever-increasing doses and led to suicide.* 'The curse of kids' cocaine', *Daily Mail*, 13 May 2000; *see also* 'Mothers who use cocaine', *Daily Mirror*, 28 September 2013.

22 *They harped on about the uncertainty of long-term side effects – standard for any new drug – with little evidence.* Derbyshire, David, 'Ritalin may have "long-term" side effects', *Daily Telegraph*, 12 November 2001.

22 *'one in seven children will be on such behaviour-controlling medication as Ritalin by 2007'* 'I was an addict at four', *Daily Express*, 2 January 2001.

22 *Amid the scare stories were 'success' tales of mothers who 'took control' by weaning their kids off Ritalin* Macrae, Fiona, 'Fish oil "calms children better than Ritalin"', *Daily Mail*, 20 June 2006.

22 *Only omega-3 fatty acids have shown even mild effectiveness in alleviating ADHD symptoms, particularly hyperactivity and inattentiveness, but the benefits are modest and over time come with a hefty price tag.* Richardson, Alexandra J., 'ω-3 fatty acids produce a small improvement in ADHD symptoms in children compared with placebo', *BMJ Mental Health*, 15:46 (2012), https://doi.org/10.1136/ebmental-2011-100523

22 *FAT MUMS ARE LINKED TO HYPER KIDS* 'Fat mums are linked to hyper kids', *Daily Mirror*, 3 November 2007.

22 *But headlines like 'Fat Mums Linked to Hyper Kids', or claims that women who 'Load Up on Candy and Burgers', seemed to suggest that ADHD was caused by maternal choices.* Ibid; De Graaf, Mia, 'Women who load up on candy and burgers during pregnancy "more likely to have a child with ADHD"', *Daily Mail*, 18 August 2016.

23 *'Disease Behind the Tantrums'* Derbyshire, David and Highfield, Roger, 'Disease behind the tantrums', *Daily Telegraph*, 9 September 2004.

23 *ever-growing ADHD 'epidemic' feeding the public's fears.* 'Anti-tantrum drug almost killed my son', *Daily Express*, 30 March 2004.

23 *ADHD ADVICE SECRETLY PAID FOR BY DRUG COMPANIES* Foggo, Daniel, 'ADHD advice secretly paid for by drug companies', *Sunday Telegraph*, 9 October 2005.

24 *'Ritalin Nation'* 'Ritalin nation', *Sunday Telegraph*, 16 October 2005.

24 *'Would You Rather Be Smarter, Sexier and More Successful? Soon, Wonder Drugs Could Transform You into the Person You Really Want to Be.'* 'Would you rather be smarter, sexier and more successful? Soon, wonder drugs could transform you into the person you really want to be', *Sunday Times*, 12 January 2003.

24 *CHILDREN BEHAVING BADLY ARE RAKING IN £170M A YEAR* 'Children behaving badly are raking in £170m a year', *Daily Mail*, 30 January 2006.

24 *'How the Culture of Blame Has Made Victims of Us All'* Persaud, Raj, 'How the culture of blame has made victims of us all', *Daily Telegraph*, 22 January 2005.

24 *'We Want a Mansion Say Family of Ten on £32,600 in Benefits'* 'We want a mansion say family of ten on £32,600 in benefits', *Daily Express*, 17 April 2006.

24 *'Kicked Out of School 38 Times (But, Guess What, it's Not His Fault)'* UK tabloid newspaper, 4 February 2006.

24 *'Gratification culture' became a stand-in for ADHD, tied to low-income families and giro cheques.* 'Why there's chaos in our schools: Bad parents are to blame for the pupils from hell', *Daily Express*, 28 May 2004.

25 *Ross, labelled a 'yob', was photographed rolling what 'appeared to be a marijuana joint'. The article included a photo of one friend holding a BB gun and another holding a rock behind his back, captioned: 'Yob: Mate Hides Rock Behind Back.'* Disley, Jan, 'Gun yob at play', *Daily Mirror*, 27 August 2005.

25 *IT'S NOW A CASE OF RULE BRATANNIA* Routledge, Paul, 'It's now a case of Rule Bratannia', *Daily Mirror*, 27 October 2006.

25 *'£20,000 Benefits So This Father of Seven Can Keep His Children in Video Games ... and Pay His Huge Booze Bill'* Ballinger, Lucy, '£20,000 benefits so this father of seven can keep his children in video games and pay his huge booze bill', *Daily Mail*, 5 May 2010.

25 *'Scrounger Mum on £20,000 Wants More'* 'Scrounger mum on £20,000 wants more', *Daily Express*, 29 October 2007.

25 *Little Johnny is never badly behaved. He has Attention Deficit Hyperactivity Disorder. I do not believe ADHD exists. It's a medical fake, nothing more than a cloak for inadequate parenting. Little Johnny runs riot because his mum (and his dad, in the unlikely event that he is around) does not give him the firm environment in which to grow.* Routledge, 'It's now a case of Rule Bratannia'.

26 *THE BOY THEY CALL CHUCKY* 'The boy they call Chucky', *Daily Mirror*, 12 September 2005.

26 *Headlines like 'Surviving Teens from Hell' told tales of sons mugging their mothers with knives* 'Surviving teens from hell', *Daily Express*, March 2005.

26 *'My ADHD Son Is Out of Control. If He Was a Dog I'd Put Him Down.'* Reilly, Rachel, '"If my son was a dog, I'd have him put down": Mother whose son suffers from ADHD says she is fed up of her daily, violent battles with him', *Daily Mail*, 22 May 2013.

26 *These claims oversimplified complex issues, framing correlation as causation.* Neil, Beth, 'Ritalin: Should we dish out the chill pill to kids?', *Daily Mirror*, 19 June 2007.

27 *CHEMICAL STRAITJACKET* Feltz, Vanessa, 'Scandal of using drugs to replace parenting', *Daily Express,* 31 July 2007.

28 *'chemical babysitter'* Ibid.

28 *One article cited a 'Conservative Party study' claiming Ritalin was overprescribed, even to children under a year old – evidence I haven't been able to find.* Ibid.

28 *SCHOOLCHILDREN COULD BE GIVEN 'SMART DRUGS' IN A BID TO BOOST BRAINPOWER* Clark, Laura, 'Schoolchildren could be given "smart drugs" in a bid to boost brainpower', *Daily Mail,* 19 September 2008, https://www.dailymail.co.uk/news/article-1058391/ Schoolchildren-given-smart-drugs-bid-boost-brainpower.html

28 *'Parents Give Children Ritalin at Exam Time'* Clark, Laura, 'Parents give children Ritalin at exam time', *Daily Mail,* 29 May 2007.

29 *'Fear for Smart Pill Generation'* 'Fear for smart pill generation', *Daily Mail,* 18 August 2008.

29 *'Schoolchildren Could Be Given "Smart Drugs" in a Bid to Boost Brainpower'* Clark, 'Schoolchildren could be given "smart drugs" in a bid to boost brainpower'.

29 *Simultaneously, another genre of articles criminalised parents for medicating their children while suggesting ADHD could be 'cured' by a walk Daily Mail,* 25 October 2008.

29 *IT'S NOT ADHD, SIR, IT'S IN MY GENES* Dalrymple, Theodore, 'It's not ADHD, Sir, it's in my genes', *Daily Telegraph,* 1 October 2010.

29 *'ADHD "Caused By Genetic Faults"'* Adams, Stephen, 'ADHD "caused by genetic faults"', *Daily Telegraph,* 30 September 2010.

29 *'It's Not ADHD, Sir, it's in My Genes'* Dalrymple, 'It's not ADHD, Sir, it's in my genes'.

29 *'Naughty Boy Syndrome Is Genetic'* 'Naughty boy syndrome is genetic', *Daily Express,* 30 September 2010.

30 *'If further research provides conclusive proof of these findings, I will believe it is a brain disorder ... Until then, I will continue to believe that bad parenting is to blame.'* Routledge, Paul, 'Sick or poor parenting', *Daily Mirror,* 1 October 2010.

30 *'Everyone under nineteen seems to have ADHD. It seems to be infectious.'* Fagge, Nick, 'Judge's scorn for "hyperactive" thugs', *Daily Express,* 2 April 2010.

30 *'Did Our Greatest PM Have ADHD?'* Dobbs, Michael, 'Did our greatest PM have ADHD?', *Daily Express,* 2 October 2010.

30 *Rory Bremner described his 'butterfly brain' in 2011, admitting to ADHD still attracted curiosity and scepticism, like confessing belief in UFOs.* Bremner, Rory, 'My "butterfly" brain is a blessing and a curse', *Daily Express,* 7 June 2011.

30 *'Kids Don't Need Pills, They Need Parenting'* Furedi, Frank, 'Kids don't need pills, they need parenting', *Independent,* 13 August 2013.

30 *'Hyperactive or Just Hype'* Cooper, Charlie, 'The irresistible rise in ADHD diagnoses: Hyperactive or just hype?', *Independent,* 24 August 2013.

30 *'Doctors Too Ready to Diagnose ADHD'* 'Doctors "too ready to diagnose ADHD"', *Independent,* 6 November 2013.

30 *Under Boris Johnson (2019–22) neurodivergence occasionally surfaced in policies like the National Disability Strategy, which aimed to improve*

access to public services, but critics called it scattershot with little appetite for addressing entrenched social inequalities. 'Briefing Paper: National Disability Strategy', The Neurological Alliance, August 2021, https://www. neural.org.uk/wp-content/uploads/2021/08/ NA-briefing-paper-National-Disability-Strategy.pdf

31   *'bladed fidget spinners'* Farhoud, Nada, 'Dangerous bladed fidget spinners so sharp they can puncture eyes and flesh', *Daily Mirror*, 2 August 2017.

31   *Media coverage mirrored the past but with a twist: occasional nods to the fact that women have ADHD too, or advocating the therapeutic benefits of activities like ping-pong.* Stoppard, Miriam, 'Why playing ping pong is great for the brain and could help prevent dementia', *Daily Mirror*, 5 May 2017.

31   *'ADHD is a brain disorder, not a label for poor parenting, say scientists'* Bodkin, Henry, 'ADHD is a brain disorder, not a label for poor parenting, say scientists', *Daily Telegraph*, 16 February 2017.

31   *FORGETTING WHERE YOU'VE PARKED YOUR CAR COULD MEAN YOU HAVE ADHD* Benyon, Lucy, 'It's not just children! Forgetting where you've parked your car could mean you have ADHD', *Daily Mail*, 11 September 2017.

31   *IS YOUR WARDROBE CRAMMED? IT COULD BE A SIGN YOU'VE GOT A NEW MEDICAL DISORDER* Waters, Jo, 'Is your wardrobe this crammed? It could be a sign you've got a new medical disorder', *Daily Mail*, 10 September 2018.

32   *ADHD was attributed to geniuses – from Leonardo da Vinci to Beethoven* Pinkstone, Joe, 'Did Leonardo da Vinci suffer from ADHD?' *Daily Mail*, 24 May 2019; Knapton, Sarah, 'Leonardo da Vinci may have suffered from ADHD, expert claims', *Daily Telegraph*, 24 May 2019.

32   *'Brother's an Evil Monster'* 'Brother's an evil monster', *Daily Star*, 20 June 2022.

32   *'Twisted Bruv & Sis Couple Get 35 Years'* Lawton, Jerry, 'Twisted bruv & sis couple get 35 years', *Daily Star*, 13 March 2019.

32   *Yet, while demand for diagnoses overwhelms the NHS – with waiting lists stretching up to ten years in some areas – articles centring ADHD dominate public discourse.* ADHD UK, 'ADHD UK's report into NHS ADHD assessment waiting lists', October 2023, https://adhduk.co.uk/ nhs-adhd-assessments-waiting-lists-report/

32   *'Reading this Column May Be a Sign You Have ADHD'* Tutty, Sonja, 'Reading this column may be a sign you have ADHD', *The Times*, 9 October 2022.

32   *'Why Do So Many Comedians Have ADHD?'* Maxwell, Dominic, 'Why do so many comedians have ADHD?', *The Times*, 4 August 2022.

32   *'Number of People Seeking ADHD Diagnosis Soars Since Lockdown'* Donnelly, Laura, 'Number of people seeking ADHD diagnosis soars since lockdown', *The Times*, 22 October 2022.

32   *'The ADHD Self-Diagnosis "Industry" Offering a Quick Fix That Doesn't Exist'* Dunbar, Polly, 'The ADHD self-diagnosis "industry" offering a quick fix that doesn't exist', *Daily Telegraph*, 10 February 2023.

32   *'No, You Don't Have ADHD'* Rudra, Pravina, 'No, you don't have ADHD', *New Statesman*, 2 November 2022.

33   *'I Can't Persuade My ADHD Son to Stop Smoking Cannabis'* Byron,

Tanya, 'I can't persuade my ADHD son to stop smoking cannabis', *The Times*, 6 December 2021.

33   *'I Was Diagnosed with ADHD at 47. I Cried from Relief'* Duguid, Stacey, 'I was diagnosed with ADHD at 47. I cried from relief', *The Times*, 5 December 2021.

33   *'I Was Diagnosed with ADHD at 37. This Is My Story'* Brown, Kat, 'I was diagnosed with ADHD at 37. This is my story', *The Times*, 10 April 2021.

33   *By 2022 the first parliamentary debate on ADHD assessment hinted at growing recognition, with politicians acknowledging the 'lack of understanding about what ADHD actually is' and the 'complete lack of data on ADHD care'* Colburn, Elliot, 'Autism and ADHD assessments', UK Parliament, 6 February 2023, https://hansard.parliament.uk/commons/ 2023-02-06/debates/183A24F1-C943-4D2E-8238-4B03AF11D715/ AutismAndADHDAssessments

34   *'Please ... No Adult ADHD Diagnoses'* Burchill, Julie, 'Why I'm sceptical of the ADHD epidemic', *Spectator*, 5 February 2023, https://www. spectator.co.uk/article/why-im-sceptical-of-the-adhd-epidemic/

1. Beyond the Headlines: The Realities of Diagnosing ADHD

36   *Around half of ADHD kids struggle with fine motor control – using scissors, joined-up writing, tying shoelaces.* NeuroLaunch editorial team, 'Understanding fine motor skills in ADHD: Challenges, strategies, and support', NeuroLaunch, 4 August 2024, https:// neurolaunch.com/ fine-motor-skills-adhd/

36   *During his session with Prince Harry, Maté claimed ADHD was both curable and a 'normal response to normal stress'.* Tingle, Rory and Lockhart, Alastair, ' "I felt different to the rest of my family – and my mum felt the same": Prince Harry opens up on his "broken home" upbringing saying parents rowing in front of children "is not a good idea" – but FAILS to mention William once in 90min toxic trauma chat', *Daily Mail*, 4 March 2023, https://www.dailymail.co.uk/news/article-11820279/Prince-Harry-talks-toxic-trauma-expert-Gabor-Mate.html

37   *ADHD adults are five times more likely to attempt suicide, with one in four women considered at such risk.* Constance, Lilly, 'Study: Nearly one in four women with ADHD has attempted suicide', *ADDitude*, 5 January 2021, https://www. additudemag.com/adhd-in-women-suicide-risk/

38   *Attention deficit hyperactivity disorder (ADHD) is a neurodevelopmental disorder characterised by persistent patterns of inattention, hyperactivity and impulsivity that interfere with daily life and functioning.* DSM-V describes ADHD as 'a persistent pattern of inattention and/or hyperactivity-impulsivity that interferes with functioning or development'. American Psychiatric Association (ed.), *The Diagnostic and Statistical Manual of Mental Disorders*, fifth ed. (Washington, DC: American Psychiatric Association, 2013); CDC defines ADHD as 'one of the most common neurodevelopmental disorders or childhood' characterised by 'inattentive', hyperactive-impulse' or 'combined' presentation of symptoms. CDC, 'About Attention-deficit/hyperactivity disorder (ADHD)', CDC, 23 October 2024, https://www.cdc.gov/adhd/about/?CDC_AAref_Val=https:// www.cdc.gov/ncbddd/adhd/facts.html

39 *'ADHD is not a disorder of knowing what to do; it's a disorder of doing what you know.'* Barkley, Russell, 'The important role of executive functioning and self-regulation in ADHD', https://www.russellbarkley.org/factsheets/ ADHD_EF_and_SR.pdf

39 *Brain-imaging scans* Positron emission tomography (PET) scans.

39 *Furthermore, it's technically classified as a mental health disorder in diagnostic manuals.* ICD-11: World Health Organization (ed.), *International Classification of Diseases Version 11* (Geneva: World Health Organization, 1993) and *DSM-V;* American Psychiatric Association (ed.), *The Diagnostic and Statistical Manual of Mental Disorders,* fifth ed. (Washington, DC: American Psychiatric Association, 2013).

39 *Roughly 80 per cent of ADHD people have at least one additional mental health condition, such as major depressive disorder, bipolar disorder or PTSD.* Torgersen, T., Gjervan, B. and Rasmussen, K., 'ADHD in adults: A study of clinical characteristics, impairment and comorbidity', *Nordic Journal of Psychiatry,* 60:1 (2006), pp. 38–43.

39 *Half of us have an anxiety disorder.* Van der Meer, Dennis et al., 'Anxiety modulates the relation between attention-deficit/hyperactivity disorder severity and working memory-related brain activity', *World Journal of Biological Psychiatry,* 19:6 (2018), pp. 450–60, https://pmc.ncbi.nlm.nih.gov/articles/PMC5581282/

40 *In 1980, the* DSM-III *introduced the term attention deficit disorder (ADD), recognising both inattention and hyperactivity, and allowing for diagnoses with or without hyperactivity.* Barkley, Russell A., *Attention Deficit Hyperactivity Disorder: A Handbook for Diagnosis and Treatment* (New York: Guildford Press, 1991); Demazeux, Steeves and Singy, Patrick (eds), *The DSM-5 in Perspective: Philosophical Reflections on the Psychiatric Babel* (New York: Springer, 2015).

42 *'Think you've got ADHD? You might not, but you may still need help.'* Palaniswami, Paari, 'Think you've got ADHD? You might not, but you may still need help', *Sydney Morning Herald,* 23 February 2023.

42 *90 per cent of adults with ADHD also have a psychiatric disorder.* Ginsberg, Ylva, Quintero, Javier, Anand, Ernie, Casillas, Marta and Upadhyaya, Himanshu P., 'Underdiagnosis of attention-deficit/hyperactivity disorder in adult patients: A review of the literature', *The Primary Care Companion for CNS Disorders,* 16:3 (2014), 15 June 2014, https://www.ncbi.nlm.nih.gov/pmc/articles/PMC4195639/

42 *Diagnosing ADHD first is key since treating secondary disorders alone isn't effective.* NICE, 'Attention deficit hyperactivity disorder: Diagnosis and management', NICE, 14 March 2018, https://www.nice.org.uk/guidance/ng87

44 *ADHD is often overdiagnosed in white children and underdiagnosed in children of colour due to biased, white-centred diagnostic models.* Clark, Nicole, 'No one's ever talked to me about this before', *New York Times,* 24 May 2001, https://www.nytimes.com/2021/05/24/style/adhd-online-creators-diagnosis.html

45 *'Culturally,' she says, 'the expectation is punitive rather than supportive.'* Ofori, Morgan, 'UK's black children "face cultural barriers" in accessing help for autism and ADHD', *Guardian,* 31 March 2024, https://www.theguardian.com/education/2024/mar/31/uk-black-children-cultural-barriers-accessing-help-autism-adhd

47 *In theory, patients in England have the 'right to choose' their mental healthcare provider if wait times are excessive, but charity ADHD UK notes that this policy, introduced in 2018, is still 'relatively new' and poorly understood by GPs and patients alike.* 'Right to choose (NHS England)', ADHD UK, https://adhduk.co.uk/right-to-choose/

47 *pilot scheme removing access to autism and ADHD assessments for adults, citing the need to 'stem the flow' of referrals.* YDRF, 'North Yorkshire and York Health and Care Partnership are removing access to autism and ADHD assessment and diagnosis for adults in North Yorkshire and York in new pilot', York Disability Rights Forum, 26 March 2023, https://ydrf.org.uk/2023/03/26/autism-and-adhd-assessments-to-be-refused/

47 *The NHS simply can't handle the recent spike in ADHD diagnoses, with waiting lists stretching up to ten years according to ADHD UK.* ADHD UK, 'ADHD UK's report into NHS ADHD assessment waiting lists', https://adhduk.co.uk/nhs-adhd-assessments-waiting-lists-report/

47 *Covid-19 sparked a new awareness of ADHD, but simultaneously strained the resources needed to treat it.* Harris Green, Hannah, 'When it comes to adult ADHD, the US medical system is falling behind', *Guardian*, 8 July 2023, https://www.theguardian.com/society/2023/jul/08/adult-adhd-us-medical-system-tiktok-demand

48 *the BBC's* Panorama *aired* Private ADHD Clinics Exposed, *hitting every tired trope that frames ADHD as a controversy rather than a serious condition.* 'Private ADHD Clinics Exposed', *Panorama*, BBC One, 15 May 2023, https:// www.bbc.co.uk/programmes/m001m0f9

48 *Yet Smith argues the real issue isn't overdiagnosis, but decades of underdiagnosis and an NHS system designed before ADHD was properly understood.* Smith, Mike, 'Is it really too easy to be diagnosed with ADHD?', *Guardian*, 17 May 2023, https://www.theguardian.com/commentisfree/2023/may/17/nhs-psychiatrist-adhd-underdiagnosis

48 *The episode became the most complained-about* Panorama *broadcast in history, even surpassing the one about Princess Diana.* Shelford, Henry, head of ADHD UK, interview with author.

48 *In May 2023, the BBC defended the documentary, claiming it followed editorial guidelines – it said that it did not seek to question the legitimacy of the condition or its impact but believed that it sparked vital debates on private ADHD diagnoses and care standards, and was clearly in the public interest.* BBC, 'Panorama: "Private ADHD Clinics Exposed"', approach to the programme, BBC One, 15 May 2023', BBC, 22 May 2023, https:// www. bbc.co.uk/contact/complaint/panoramaprivateadhdclinicsexposed

49 *He called for updated NICE guidelines, as current ones require only an 'appropriate, qualified practitioner' without defining a minimum training standard. He also pushed for national ADHD wait time targets and dedicated funding. ADHD isn't 'rising' – it's finally being recognised. As Smith put it, 'A tiny fraction of people in the UK take stimulant medication, the gold standard treatment – far fewer than the 2–4 per cent of adults who likely have the condition.'* Smith, 'Is it really too easy to be diagnosed with ADHD?'.

50 *'You can't "overdiagnose" a condition. What you can do is misdiagnose it – mood disorders can mimic ADHD, or they may actually be*

secondary to undiagnosed ADHD.' Walters, Meg and Pantony, Ali, 'I'm a doctor and this is what I think about GPs "over-diagnosing" ADHD', *Glamour*, 9 April 2024, https://www.glamourmagazine.co.uk/article/adhd-over-diagnosis-doctor-interview

52   *By twelve, the average ADHD kid has heard twenty thousand more negative remarks than their neurotypical peers.* 'Prioritize praising your child with ADHD', CHADD, https://chadd.org/adhd-news/adhd-news-caregivers/adhd-weekly-prioritize-praising-your-child-with-adhd/

2. The Attention Economy

56   *ADHD was discussed as a pathology of late capitalism in 2011, seen as a by-product of hypermediated consumer culture by some cultural theorists and critics.* Fisher, Mark, *Capitalist Realism: Is There No Alternative?* (London: Zero Books, 2009).

56   *Fredric Jameson did so when he called 1980s postmodern culture 'schizophrenic', reducing a serious mental health condition to an abstract critique of identity fragmentation.* Jameson, Fredric, 'Postmodernism, or, the cultural logic of late capitalism', *New Left Review*, 1:146 (1984).

57   *'Your attention is holy, it is the soil seeding itself.'* Lockwood, Patricia, *No One Is Talking About This* (New York: Riverhead Books, 2021).

57   *'What information consumes is rather obvious: it consumes the attention of its recipients.'* Simon, Herbert A., 'Designing organizations for an information-rich world', in *Computers, Communications, and the Public Interest* (Baltimore: Johns Hopkins Press, 1971), pp. 37–72.

58   *Michael Goldhaber popularised the term, declaring attention more valuable than money in the digital age.* Goldhaber, Michael H., 'The attention economy and the net', *First Monday*, 2:4 (1997), https://doi.org/10.5210/fm.v2i4.519

58   *She critiques the financial sector's obsession with* value extraction *and argues for a system that appreciates* value creation *instead.* Mazzucato, Mariana, *The Value of Everything: Making and Taking in the Global Economy* (New York: Allen Lane, 2018).

59   *Cultural panic about distraction has existed since the days of Saint Augustine.* 'Late have I loved you, O Beauty so ancient and so new, late have I loved you! And behold, you were within, and I was in the external world and sought you there, and in my unlovely state I plunged into those lovely created things which you made. You were with me, but I was not with you. The lovely things kept me far from you, though if they did not have their existence in you, they had no existence at all.' Saint Augustine, 'Confessions', *Book X*, Chapter 27.

59   *Even nineteenth-century novels were feared to promote 'superficial' and 'debased' attention.* Thain, Marion, 'Distracted reading: Acts of attention in the age of the internet', *DHQ: Digital Humanities Quarterly*, 12:2 (2018).

60   *Arthur Charles Nielsen paid families to install 'black boxes' in their homes to track what they tuned into on the radio – much like today's cookies.* Wu, Tim, *The Attention Merchants: The Epic Scramble to Get Inside Our Heads* (New York: Alfred A. Knopf, 2016).

62   *Effecto is an app which has been widely criticised for luring users into a quiz designed to make sure everyone scores high on ADHD traits – there's no 'none' option.* 'Effecto App', Better Business Bureau, https://www.bbb.

org/us/ca/san-francisco/profile/mental-health-services/effecto-app-1116-945598/ complaints?page=2&utm

62 *By the time users realise it's a glorified mood tracker, cancellation is neither quick nor easy.* Holden, Sophie, 'Effecto Scam App! Please read!', Google Play Help, 15 August 2024, https://support.google.com/googleplay/thread/291017744/ effecto-scam-app-please-read?hl=en

62 *By the time users realise it's a glorified mood tracker, cancellation is neither quick nor easy.* All of Effecto's ads mention ADHD (as shown in the Meta Ad library), but on their actual page it is listed as a mood tracker. *See* What in the ADHD? (@WhatintheADHD), 'Effecto App for ADHD: Is it Legit? (Bad Ad Review)', YouTube, 18 December 2023, https://www.youtube.com/ watch?v=oS5760OvlYw

63 *These are the 'attention merchants' that legal scholar and author Tim Wu warns us against.* Wu, *The Attention Merchants.* This evolution is his mapped out at length in his book.

63 *'race to the bottom of the brainstem'* Harris, Tristan, 'How technology is hijacking your mind – from a magician and Google design ethicist', *Thrive Global*, 18 May 2016, https://medium.com/thrive-global/how-technology-hijacks-peoples-minds-from-a-magician-and-google-s-design-ethicist-56d62ef5edf3

63 *Calloway now sells skincare explicitly branded 'Snake Oil' in a playful nod to her grifter reputation, cleverly repackaged for the attention economy.* 'Caroline Calloway: The snake oil set', Caroline Calloway, https://carolinecalloway.com/products/snake-oil-set?variant=40204433162286

64 *Companies like Listerine planted anxieties with slogans like 'Halitosis Makes You Unpopular', using behaviourist psychology to shape behaviour.* Watts, Linda S., George, Alice L. and Beekman, Scott, *Social History of the United States: The 1920s* quoted in Wu, *The Attention Merchants.*

64 *'from 4.5 to over 16 million households'* Wu, *The Attention Merchants.*

64 *'I hate television. I hate it as much as peanuts. But I can't stop eating peanuts.'* Welles, Orson, *New York Herald Tribune*, 12 October 1956. Reproduced in Andrews, Robert, *The Columbia Dictionary of Quotations* (New York: Columbia University Press, 1993), p. 900.

65 *'Without selective interest, experience is an utter chaos,'* James, William, *The Principles of Psychology*, vol. 1 (New York: Henry Holt, 1890).

65 *'information velocity'* Williams, James, *Stand Out Of Our Light: Freedom and Resistance In The Attention Economy* (Cambridge: Cambridge University Press, 2018).

65 *'Technologists build products meant to persuade people to do what we want them to do ... we call these people "users", and, even if we don't say it aloud, we secretly wish every one of them would become fiendishly hooked.'* Eyal, Nir, *Hooked: How to Build Habit-Forming Products* (New York: Portfolio, 2014).

68 *As American writer Grafton Tanner notes, these strategies shift blame from platforms back onto users, reinforcing the neoliberal ideals that fuel the runaway growth of the attention economy and prioritise individual responsibility over systemic change.* Tanner, Grafton, 'Digital detox: Big tech's phony crisis of conscience', *LA Review of Books*, 9 August 2018, https://lareviewofbooks.org/article/digital-detox-big-techs-phony-crisis-of-conscience/

70 *He claims tech 'undermines our capacities for reflection and self-regulation', framing what he sees as neurotypical weaknesses – traits which are also symptoms of ADHD – with a heavy dose of moral judgement. His idea of 'epistemic distraction' reads like a roll call of ADHD traits. He says it leads to 'impulsivity' and 'wantonness'.* Williams, Stand Out Of Our Light.

3. Education: What is School for?

73 *By April 2021, students had missed over half of their scheduled classroom days.* Major, Lee Elliot, Eyles, Andrew and Machin, Stephen, 'Pupils lost a third of their expected learning during COVID, with Wales and Scotland even further behind', LSE, 7 July 2021, https://blogs.lse.ac.uk/covid19/2021/07/ 07/pupils-lost-a-third-of-their-expected-learning-during-covid-with-wales-and-scotland-even-further-behind/

73 *By summer 2022, the number of 'severely absent' children – those missing more than half their school days – had doubled.* 'Lost and not found', The Centre for Social Justice, https://www.centreforsocialjustice.org.uk/library/lost-and-not-found

74 *Over a third reported improved performance in reading, writing and mathematics; a quarter even noted better relationships with family and peers.* Shah, Ruchita, Raju, V. Venkatesh, Sharma, Akhilesh and Grover, Sandeep, 'Impact of COVID-19 and lockdown on children with ADHD and their families: An online survey and a continuity care model', *Journal of Neurosciences in Rural Practices*, 12:1 (2021), https://www.ncbi.nlm.nih.gov/pmc/articles/PMC7846322/

74 *We all want children in school – those who don't attend face higher risks of legal trouble later on – but pushing them back into a broken system is a missed opportunity.* 'English schoolchildren are still missing months of classes', *The Economist*, 20 April 2023, https://www.economist.com/britain/2023/04/20/english-schoolchildren-are-still-missing-months-of-classes

75 *In the US, advertisements are everywhere in schools – even plastered on lunch trays and bathroom walls.* Hari, Johann, *Stolen Focus: Why You Can't Pay Attention – and How to Think Deeply Again* (New York: Crown, 2022).

75 *Citton advocates for an 'attention ecology'* Citton, Yves, *The Ecology of Attention* (Cambridge: Polity, 2017).

75 *Today, anxiety has replaced submission as the dominant emotional response – heightened by the constant feedback loops of technology.* Davies, William, 'The reaction economy', *London Review of Books*, 45:5, 2 March 2023, https://www.lrb.co.uk/the-paper/v45/n05/william-davies/the-reaction-economy

75 *we've created systems addicted to extrinsic rewards, leaving children in a state of perpetual anticipation – not of discovery, but of judgement.* Ibid.

75 *When post-pandemic absenteeism spiked, the government responded by doubling down on tests, reducing breaks and sticking to a rote curriculum.* Although several countries, like Wales, and some US states, including California, have either started to roll back tests or abandoned large-scale testing entirely, that hasn't stopped the rest of us.

76 *In his TED Talk, Sir Ken Robinson, educational theorist, criticised how*

schools separate the 'academic' from the 'non-academic'. Robinson, Ken, 'Do schools kill creativity?' TED, February 2006, https://www.ted.com/talks/sir_ken_robinson_do_schools_kill_creativity?subtitle=en

77 *Lacking the resources to properly support these students, schools frequently resort to exclusions or part-time timetables – strategies that function more as blame than as support.* Allan, Suzanne, 'My teen went five years without full-time education', BBC, 27 June 2023, https://www.bbc.co.uk/news/uk-scotland-66019138; Brierley, Louise, 'Rugby mother battles for school place for son with ADHD', BBC, 20 April 2023, https://www.bbc.co.uk/news/av/uk-england-coventry-warwickshire-65327162

77 *Children with ADHD are a hundred times more likely to be permanently excluded from school than their neurotypical peers.* O'Regan, F., 'Persistent disruptive behaviour and exclusion', *ADHD in Practice*, 1:1 (2009), pp. 8–11.

77 *In the UK, 46 per cent of excluded students have ADHD, and nearly half of ADHD students have been excluded at least once.* 39 per cent of children with ADHD have been excluded for a fixed term; 11 per cent of excluded children with ADHD having been excluded permanently. 'Children and Families Bill', UK Parliament, 2012–3, https://publications.parliament.uk/pa/cm201213/cmpublic/childrenandfamilies/memo/cf96.htm

77 *These exclusions increase their risk of criminal behaviour – 49 per cent of male and 33 per cent of female prisoners were once excluded from school.* UK ADHD, 'ADHD and exclusion in schools', https://www.ukadhd.com/adhd-and-exclusion-in-schools.htm

79 *Race on the Agenda (ROTA) ran seminars across London, gathering insights from five hundred participants from communities of colour.* Nea, Barbara, 'Attention deficit/hyperactivity disorder and London's Black, Asian and Minority Ethnic communities – a discussion paper', Race on the Agenda, October 2013, https://www.rota.org.uk/sites/default/files/webfm/adhd_and_bame_communities_in_the_uk_-_a_discussion_paper_november_2013.pdf

79 *They wished schools had responded to their educational needs instead of simply labelling them.* Ibid.

81 *The most important factor in a student's success is the quality of their teacher.* Fullan, Michael and Hargreaves, Andy, *Call to Action: Bringing the Professionals Back In* (Oxford: Learning Forward, 2016).

81 *Sixty-nine per cent of primary and 78 per cent of secondary school teachers find their workloads unmanageable.* EB News, '78 per cent of secondary teachers think workload is unmanageable', *Education Business*, 4 October 2018, https://educationbusinessuk.net/news/04102018/seventy-eight-cent-secondary-teachers-still-think-workload-unmanageable

81 *Over half say their job has a negative effect on their mental or physical health.* Teacher Wellbeing Index 2023 (London: Education Support, 2003), https://www.educationsupport.org.uk/media/0h4jd5pt/twix_2023.pdf

83 *students with ADHD want to 'be treasured for the gifts they bring to the classroom, not demeaned for failing to do things the same way as everyone else'.* Knowles, Trudy, *The Kids Behind the Label: An Inside Look at ADHD for Classroom Teachers* (Toronto: Pearson Education Canada, 2006).

86 *Learning comes from curiosity and connection, not compliance.* A

good resource on what a neurodiverse classroom looks like is Howkins, Liz, '"Slant: won't work for SEND students, so what does?', ADHD Foundation 13 September 2021, https://www.adhdfoundation.org.uk/2021/09/13/slant-wont-work-for-send-students-so-what-does/

87 *Similarly, Estonia's education system, rated the best in Europe by the OECD, emphasises problem-solving, critical thinking and digital literacy from an early age* Sylvester, Rachel, 'Estonia's curriculum is one of the best – what can it teach us?', *The Times*, 21 November 2024, https://www.thetimes.com/uk/education/article/estonias-curriculum-is-one-of-the-best-what-can-it-teach-us-l56hmdxq0

90 *'a slow walk to madness or death'* Weale, Sally, '"It's been tumultuous": Covid-19 stress takes toll on teachers in England', *Guardian*, 14 December 2020, https://www.theguardian.com/education/2020/dec/14/covid-stress-takes-toll-on-teachers-in-england

93 *'centre lessons around broad understandings and essential questions – ones that transcend specific topics and tie learning together'* Southeast Michigan Stewardship Coalition, 'Getting the big idea: Concept-based teaching and learning', *Transforming Learning Environments through Global and STEM Education*, 13 August 2013, https://semiscoalition.org/wp-content/uploads/Getting-the-Big-Idea-Handout.pdf

95 *ADHD students need relevant, hands-on experiences that engage their strengths.* Ibid.

4. Gendered Expectations: 'Maybe You Should Try Harder'

99 *'A high-functioning, overachieving woman, constantly bordering on burnout, was seen as fine. As long as I didn't burn out, no one cared that maybe I was functioning but not fine.'* Ayres, Zoe (@ZJAyres), 'A high-functioning, overachieving woman, constantly bordering on burnout, was seen as fine …', X, 21 September 2023, https://x.com/ZJAyres/status/1704853563254657073

99 *boys' symptoms are flagged, while girls' symptoms – often showing up as anxiety or physical complaints such as headaches – are dismissed.* Almekhlafi, Kayla and Jain, Sonia, 'Unveiling gender disparities in ADHD: A literature review on factors and impacts of late diagnosis in females (2010—2023)', *Journal of Women's Mental Health*, 1:1 (2024), pp. 9–21, https://openaccesspub.org/womans-mental-health/article/2125

99 *In the UK, ADHD is underdiagnosed in girls, who are three times less likely than boys to receive a diagnosis despite comparable prevalence.* 'Out of 14.6 million UK children under 18 years, it is estimated that 423,000 girls in the UK under age 18 have ADHD but are three times less likely than boys to be diagnosed and supported'. Lloyd, Tony, Brown, Megan and Lock, Amy, *A Call to Action: The Majority of Women with ADHD are Being Left Behind* (Liverpool: ADHD Foundation, 2021).

101 *This social conditioning fosters an external locus of control in many women with ADHD.* Girls with ADHD also tend to lose their internal locus of control sooner than girls without ADHD. Moore, Elaine A., *The Amphetamine Debate* (Jefferson: McFarland & Co, 2010), p. 53.

102 *For women with ADHD, societal expectations around femininity, self-control and domesticity create a constant, unspoken pressure to embody qualities that don't come naturally, which leads to isolation and higher*

rates of anxiety and mood disorders. 'Robison et al. (2008) looked at gender differences in ADHD symptoms, psychological functioning, physical symptoms, and treatment response. They found that women were rated as more impaired on every measure of ADHD symptoms. Women were also found to score higher on rating scales for anxiety and depression as well as experienced greater emotional dysregulation compared to men.' Attoe, Darby E. and Climie, Emma A., 'Miss. Diagnosis: A systematic review of ADHD in adult women', *Journal of Attention Disorders*, 27:7 (2023), pp. 645–57. Drawing from Robison, Reid J. et al., 'Gender differences in two clinical trials of adults with attention-deficit/ hyperactivity disorder: A retrospective data analysis', *Clinical Psychiatry*, 69:2 (2008), pp. 213–21.

105 *Nearly half of women with ADHD also experience premenstrual dysphoric disorder (PMDD), a severe, clinically recognised mood disorder distinct from PMS.* 'One 2021 study in the *Journal Of Psychiatric Research* found that women with ADHD have a much higher risk of PMDD (premenstrual dysphoric disorder, a severe form of premenstrual syndrome or PMS) at 45.5% prevalence compared with 28.7% in non-ADHD women.' Noyce, Eleanor, 'Women with ADHD may experience different hormonal changes during their periods – here's how', *Stylist*, 2023, https://www.stylist.co.uk/fitness-health/wellbeing/women-with-adhd-hormones-periods/798359

106 *Child psychiatrist Donald Winnicott may be the patron saint of ADHD mothers with his 1950s concept of the 'good enough mother'.* Winnicott, D. W., *Playing and Reality* (New York: Penguin, 1971).

109 *Many girls with ADHD are first treated for symptoms of other conditions, and it's not uncommon for them to be prescribed antidepressants before ever being evaluated for ADHD.* For example, 14 per cent of girls with ADHD are prescribed antidepressants before being evaluated for ADHD, compared to only 5 per cent of boys. Attoe and Climie, 'Miss. Diagnosis: A systematic review of ADHD in adult women'.

111 *WOMEN IN THEIR 20S AND 30S DRIVE RECORD SURGE IN ADHD PRESCRIPTIONS AMID ROW OVER WHETHER CONDITION IS BEING OVER-DIAGNOSED* Ely, John, 'Women in their 20s and 30s drive record surge in ADHD prescriptions amid row over whether condition is over-diagnosed', *Daily Mail*, 6 July 2023.

113 *'Always Be Optimising'* The phrase 'Always Be Optimising' is borrowed from Jia Tolentino's essay 'Always Be Optimizing' in *Trick Mirror* (New York: Random House, 2019).

114 *'Given access to enough amphetamine, any rat, monkey, or man would eventually self-destruct.'* Rasmussen, Nicolas, *On Speed: The Many Lives of Amphetamine* (New York and London: New York University Press, 2008).

116 *'It goes from "I have a messy desk" to "I'm messy" to "I'm bad and that means I shouldn't let myself go out into the world."'* Solden, Sari, interview with author. These ideas are also in her books.

5. Family Dynamics: Reimagining What Family Can Be

122 *Studies show that couples with a child with ADHD are almost twice as likely to split before their child turns eight.* Wymbs, B. T., Pelham, W.

E., Jr., Molina, B. S. G., Gnagy, E. M., Wilson, T. K. and Greenhouse, J. B., 'Rate and predictors of divorce among parents of youth with ADHD', *Journal of Consulting and Clinical Psychology*, 76:5 (2008), pp. 735–44, https://www.ncbi.nlm.nih.gov/pmc/articles/ PMC2631569/. Parents of youth diagnosed with ADHD in childhood (22.7 per cent) were more likely to divorce by the time their children were eight years old than parents of youth without ADHD (12.6 per cent). *See also* Gray, D. E., 'Coping over time: The parents of children with autism', *Journal of Intellectual Disability Research*, 50:12 (2006), pp. 970–6, https://onlinelibrary.wiley.com/doi/10.1111/j.1365-2788.2006.00933.x. In this study, a database of 172,299 parent couples was examined, of which 2,457 had a first-born child diagnosed with ADHD. Their results over the period considered (1990 to 2007) showed that ten years after the child's birth, parents of children who had been diagnosed with ADHD were 75 per cent more likely to have divorced.

125 *Studies show ADHD kids view their parents as 'demanding and power-hungry', while parents feel 'more power-assertive and less warm'.* Graves Hammerness, Paul, *ADHD* (Santa Barbara: Greenwood, 2008).

125 *Mothers, especially, report more 'stressful', 'demanding' and 'exhausting' interactions.* Perez Algorta, Guillermo et al., 'Maternal ADHD symptoms, personality, and parenting stress: Differences between mothers of children with ADHD and mothers of comparison children', *Journal of Attention Disorders*, 22:13 (2018), pp. 1266–77, https://www.doi.co.uk/10.1177/1087054714561290

126 *'I sometimes feel like there's all this chatter about ADHD and how to help people with it ... but no acknowledgement' of the 'frazzled' neurotypical parents who must guide every step of the day.* @hotterthanhades, 'To be sick and tired of parenting a kid with ADHD?', Mumsnet, 24 June 2023, https://www.mumsnet.com/talk/am_i_being_ unreasonable/4834706-to-be-sick-and-tired-of-parenting-a-kid-with-adhd

126 *'ADHD doesn't make someone an arsehole. Only arseholes do that.'* @LookingForFreeDoughnuts, 'ADHD=/=arsehole.', Mumsnet, 15 June 2023, https://www.mumsnet.com/talk/am_i_being_unreasonable/4827971-adhd-arsehole>

127 *Your child's ADHD behaviour may have any of the following beneficial effects: it may garner Attention for her; it may get others to make Accommodations for her; it may help her Avoid certain situations; it may help her Acquire something she wants; and it may Antagonise others for doing things she does not like. Any one of the five As can increase the frequency of ADHD behaviour.* Wiener, Craig, *Parenting Your Child with ADHD: A No-Nonsense Guide for Nurturing Self-Reliance and Cooperation* (Oakland: New Harbinger, 2013).

129 *Gabor Maté emphasises the importance of building ADHD children's self-esteem through 'unconditional positive regard' – essentially, unconditional love. Maté focuses on 'long-term development' over 'short-term obedience', suggesting that self-regulation can be nurtured by prioritising a child's wellbeing over behavioural goals. He states, 'The cost of getting a child to school on time is secure attachment ... the world will teach her the necessary lessons if she is helped to become open to learning.'* Maté, Gabor, *Scattered Minds: The Origins and Healing of Attention Deficit Disorder* (Toronto: Vintage Canada, 2019).

129 *'Better a patient person than a warrior, one with self-control than one who takes a city.'* Proverbs 16:32, The Bible, https://www.biblestudytools.com/proverbs/16-32.html

130 *'If my parents had kind of collaborated with her …' Asher shook his head, 'If they try to understand you, that's all that needs to happen,' he said.* Glean, Asher (@AsherGlean), TikTok, 18 July 2023, https://www.tiktok.com/@asherglean/video/7257160332924308763

130 *Undergraduates with ADHD often describe their childhoods as filled with feelings of 'difference', 'isolation' and a 'craving for understanding'.* Bertin, Mark, *The Family ADHD Solution: A Scientific Approach to Maximizing Your Child's Attention and Minimizing Parental Stress* (New York: St Martin's Griffin, 2011).

130 *The most common descriptors for their experience are: 'stupid', 'lazy', 'useless', 'selfish' and 'broken', leaving them feeling that their 'real' selves are persistently 'bad'.* Kendall, Judy, Hatton, Diane, Beckett, Ann and Leo, Michael, 'Children's accounts of attention-deficit/hyperactivity disorder', *Advances in Nursing Science*, 26:2 (2003), pp. 114–30, https://journals.lww.com/advancesinnursingscience/abstract/2003/04000/children_s_accounts_of.4.aspx

132 *91 per cent of parents of ADHD kids feel stressed or worried about their child's life, and over 60 per cent say family activities are disrupted.* Davies, Beverly, *How to Help Your Child with ADHD* (Torquay: White Ladder Press, 2012).

135 *ADHD often runs in families – if a parent has ADHD, their child's risk increases threefold.* Bertin, *The Family ADHD Solution.*

138 *Psychologist Dr Sharon Saline's 'Five Cs' – self-Control, Consistency, Compassion, Collaboration and Celebration – are parenting essentials for ADHD families.* Saline, Sharon and Markham, Laura, *What Your ADHD Child Wishes You Knew: Working Together to Empower Kids for Success in School and Life* (New York: TarcherPerigee, 2018).

143 *Children with two or more ACEs (adverse childhood experiences) are twice as likely to be diagnosed with ADHD.* Walker, Courtney S., Walker, Benjamin H., Brown, Dustin C., Buttross, Susan and Sarver, Dustin E., 'Defining the role of exposure to ACEs in ADHD: Examination in a national sample of US children', *Child Abuse and Neglect*, 112 (2021), https://doi.org/10.1016/j.chiabu.2020.104884

143 *For a family dealing with ACEs, the explanation of ADHD may seem neater, but if ADHD-like symptoms are danger flares, or pleas for help, diagnosis and medication won't work.* Brown, Nicole, 'Associations between adverse childhood experiences and ADHD diagnosis and severity', *Academic Pediatrics*, 17 (2017), pp. 349–55, http://www.doi.org/10.1016/j.acap.2016.08.013

6. The Neurodivergent Alliance: Autism and ADHD

146 *Roughly 3 to 4 per cent of the general population has ADHD. But, within the autistic community, 40 per cent to 70 per cent also meet ADHD criteria.* Hours, Camille, Recasens, Christophe and Baleyte, Jean-Marc, 'ASD and ADHD comorbidity: What are we talking about?', *Frontiers in Psychiatry*, 13 (2022), https://doi.org/10.3389/fpsyt.2022.837424

146 *Similarly, 20 per cent to 50 per cent of those with ADHD meet the criteria*

for autism. Rusting, Ricki, 'Decoding the overlap between autism and ADHD', *Spectrum*, 7 February 2018, https://doi.org/10.53053/KCZY8213

147   *'a rare form of childhood psychosis'* Kanner, Leo, *Childhood Psychosis: Initial Studies and New Insights* (London: John Wiley & Sons, 1973).

148   *'Not everything that steps out of line or is unusual is inferior,'* Silberman, Steve, *NeuroTribes: The Legacy of Autism and the Future of Neurodiversity* (New York: Avery, 2016); Sheffer, Edith, *Asperger's Children: The Origins of Autism in Nazi Vienna* (New York: W. W. Norton & Co., 2018).

148   *In 2013, the* DSM-V *folded Asperger's into autism spectrum disorder aiming to remove hierarchies but simultaneously sparking debate over the loss of a label that had brought clarity and community for some.* Smith, Daniel, 'Call a kid a zebra', *London Review of Books*, 38:10, 19 May 2016, https://www.lrb.co.uk/the-paper/v38/n10

148   *However, after those books were published, documents surfaced showing Asperger directly referred children to euthanasia programs where they were killed.* Czech, H. Hans, 'Asperger, National Socialism, and "race hygiene" in Nazi-era Vienna', *Molecular Autism*, 9:29 (2018), https://doi.org/10.1186/s13229-018-0208-6

148   *Under Nazi rule, human worth was tied to economic output, with disabled people dehumanised as 'life unworthy of life'. Children with autism, epilepsy and most likely ADHD became test subjects for mass extermination.* '[Alfred] Hoche and penal law expert Karl Binding ... co-authored a book in 1920 called *The Liberation and Destruction of Life Unworthy of Life.* ... They described disabled people as *Lebensunwertes Leben* ("life unworthy of life"), calling them "useless eaters" and "human ballast" who consume precious resources without repaying their debt to society. Ending the lives of these "empty human husks" – who were not even aware of the misery that they inflicted on others – was not only a socially beneficial act, Hoche and Binder claimed, it was the most compassionate thing that could be done under the circumstances.' Silberman, *NeuroTribes*.

149   *Until relatively recently, doctors weren't much better – making parents feel hopeless by likening the condition to 'terminal illnesses' and comparing autistic children to 'animals'.* Silberman, *NeuroTribes*.

149   *'stroke victims'* Dunlop, Marilyn, '"Odd duck" behavior in families perhaps caused by brain disorder', *Toronto Star*, 17 February 1989.

149   *'the plague of those unable to feel'* Juan, Stephen, 'The cruel, heartless victims of Asperger's; Only human', *Sydney Morning Herald*, 19 July 1990.

152   *'I can see her in there,'* Silberman, *NeuroTribes*.

153   *Redefining 'neurodiversity' meant coining terms like 'neurotypical' (thanks to pioneering advocates like Neurodivergent K and sociologist Judy Singer in 1998) to challenge the idea that the majority defines 'normal'.* Singer, Judy, 'Neurodiversity: The birth of an idea', thesis (Sydney: University of Technology Sydney, 1998).

153   *'the master's tools'* Lorde, Audre, 'The master's tools will never dismantle the master's house', in *Sister Outsider: Essays and Speeches* (Berkeley: Crossing Press, 2007), pp. 110–4.

154   *One institution in America – the Judge Rotenberg Educational Center*

in Massachusetts – still uses electric shocks in ABA therapy. Ruhalter, Kana and Rath, Arun, 'Electric shock therapy is still allowed in one Mass. treatment facility. Advocates say change is long overdue', GBH, 11 September 2023, https://www.wgbh.org/news/local/2023-09-11/electric-shock-therapy-is-still-allowed-in-one-mass-treatment-facility-advocates-say-change-is-long-overdue

154 *'The "experts'" explanation for failing to make me a "tidy", "appropriate", "good girl", obedient and compliant Autistic was my severe impairment, low IQ, my inability to learn, or, as Løvaas might have said (and something a doctor actually said), my lack of human dignity.'* Sequenzia, Amy, 'My thoughts on ABA', Autistic Women and Nonbinary Network, 11 February 2015, https://awnnetwork.org/my-thoughts-on-aba/

155 *'compliance-based society'* Winter, Jessica, 'The argument over a long-standing autism intervention', *New Yorker*, 12 February 2024, https://www.newyorker.com/science/annals-of-medicine/the-argument-over-a-long-standing-autism-intervention

155 *'with an aggravated sense of injustice and a deep desire to tell the absolute truth'* Taylor, Louise, 'Greta Thunberg is far from the only neurodivergent climate activist – many who see the world differently also want to change it', Conversation, 23 October 2023, https://theconversation.com/greta-thunberg-is-far-from-the-only-neurodivergent-climate-activist-many-who-see-the-world-differently-also-want-to-change-it-210492

156 *'If the emissions have to stop, then we must stop the emissions. To me that is black or white. There are no grey areas when it comes to survival.'* Thunberg, Greta, 'Almost everything is black and white', Declaration of Rebellion, Extinction Rebellion, Parliament Square, London, 31 October 2018.

7. Cultural Mythology: Amphetamines and the American Dream

162 *'American Dream'* A hallucination of the Depression invented by historian James Truslow Adams in his popular book *The Epic of America* (1931).

162 *only half of Americans born in 1980 earn as much as their parents.* Chetty, Raj, Grusky, David, Hell, Maximilian, Hendren, Nathaniel, Manduca, Robert and Narang, Jimmy, 'The fading American dream: Trends in absolute income mobility since 1940', *Science*, 356:6336 (2017), pp. 398–406, https://rajchetty.com/wp-content/uploads/2021/04/the-fading-american-dream.html-charsetutf-8

162 *The result was a blurring of personal failure and systemic flaws, as amphetamines slotted neatly into the demands of soldiers, students, truck drivers and dieters alike.* Rasmussen, Nicolas, *On Speed: The Many Lives of Amphetamine* (New York: New York University Press, 2008).

164 *In fact, untreated ADHD increases the risk of substance misuse.* Multiple studies have shown that 'children with ADHD who remain untreated are more likely to abuse drugs than children with ADHD who receive medical treatment'. Moore, *The Amphetamine Debate*, p. 6.

166 *Cerebral became TikTok's third-largest advertiser, using marketing tactics straight out of Purdue Pharma's playbook – the company infamous for fuelling America's opioid crisis through aggressive promotion of OxyContin.* Fox Cahn, Albert, 'The looming addiction crisis fuelled by AI', *Business Insider*, 13 July 2023, https://www.businessinsider.com/

ai-adderall-targeted-advertising-opioid-crisis-cerebral-purdue-pharma-2023-7?r=US&IR=T
See also Van Zee, Art, 'The promotion and marketing of OxyContin: Commercial triumph, public health tragedy', *American Journal of Public Health*, 99:2 (2009) pp. 221–7.

166 *There are fewer than ten doctors per hundred thousand young patients, and nearly half don't accept insurance, meaning that patients have to pay out of their own pocket.* Chan, Wilfred, '"The worst it's ever been": Mysterious US Adderall shortage puts ADHD patients at risk', *Guardian*, 30 January 2023, https://www.theguardian.com/society/2023/jan/29/adderall-shortage-us-adhd-ritalin-drugs

167 *Globally, ADHD affects about 5 per cent of the population, but in the US that figure is 10 per cent, with some states – Louisiana, Kentucky, Alabama, Mississippi, West Virginia – reporting rates closer to 15 per cent.* 'State-based prevalence of ADHD diagnosis and treatment 2016–2019', CDC, https://www.cdc.gov/adhd/data/state-based-prevalence-of-adhd-diagnosis-and-treatment-2016-2019.html

167 *ADHD is much more readily diagnosed and medicated in the US than in the UK, where teenagers are nearly fourteen times less likely to receive medication.* Sax, Leonard, 'Comparison', https://www.leonardsax.com/comparison.htm

167 *teens with ADHD are 62 per cent more likely than their peers to have car accidents within their first month of driving.* 'ADHD and car accidents: When is the driver at fault?', Avrek Law, 2023, https://www.avrek.com/blog/adhd-and-car-accidents-is-it-your-fault/

168 *'adrenaline-like effects'* Rasmussen, *On Speed.*

168 *'definite drive to accomplish as much as possible' and a 'subdued' emotional response* Bradley, Charles, 'The behavior of children receiving benzedrine', *The American Journal of Psychiatry*, 94 (1937), pp. 577–85, https://doi.org/10.1176/ajp.94.3.577

169 *the idea of students gaining an unfair advantage deterred SKF from marketing Benzedrine as a neuroenhancer.* Moore, *The Amphetamine Debate*, p. 5.

169 *'heavily drugged, fearless and berserk'* Kennedy, Robert M., *The German Campaign in Poland, 1939*, Department of the Army Pamphlet No. 20–255 (Washington, DC: Department of the Army, 1956), http://www.ibiblio.org/hyperwar/USA/DAP-Poland/index.html; Ellis, L. F., *The War in France and Flanders, 1939–1940* (London: HMSO, 1954), http://www.ibiblio.org/hyperwar/UN/UK/UK-NWE-Flanders/index.html; Weinberg, Gerhard, *A World at Arms* (Cambridge: Cambridge University Press, 1994); newspaper source quoted in Sargant, William, *The Unquiet Mind: The Autobiography of a Physician in Psychological Medicine* (Boston: Little, Brown, 1967), pp. 45–7.

169 *'Blitzkrieg was guided by methamphetamine. If not to say that Blitzkrieg was founded on methamphetamine.'* Andreas, Peter, 'How methamphetamine became a key part of Nazi military strategy', *Time*, 7 January 2020, https://time.com/5752114/nazi-military-drugs/

170 *'drug to inspire the fighting spirits'* Rasmussen, *On Speed.*

170 *Winston Churchill personally recommended Benzedrine for use by British military personnel.* Ibid.

170   *'operational fatigue'* Ibid.
170   *the sailor who consumed five inhalers within forty-eight hours, didn't eat or sleep then hurled himself through a plate-glass window.* Ibid.
170   *'on top of things and able to carry on [their] duties without rest' really they were 'making all sorts of mistakes'* Pugh, James, 'The Royal Air Force, bomber command and the use of benzedrine sulphate: An examination of policy and practice during the Second World War', *Journal of Contemporary History*, 53:4 (2018), pp. 740–61, https://www.jstor.org/stable/26537417
172   *'Artificial stimulation eventually becomes unpleasant.'* Rasmussen, *On Speed.*
172   *'The Adderall Workout'* Giacobbe, Alyssa, 'The Adderall workout', *New York Magazine*, 20 May 2016, https://nymag.com/article/2016/05/the-adderall-workout.html
172   *'amphetamine-tinged stone-collecting craze'* Rasmussen, *On Speed.*
173   *'Benny has made me see a lot. The intensifying awareness naturally leads to an overflow of old notions, and voila, new material wells up like water, forming at the brim of consciousness. Brand new water!'* Kerouac, Jack, letter to Ginsberg, 1945, quoted in Charters, Ann (ed.), *Jack Kerouac: Selected Letters, 1940–1956* (New York: Penguin, 1996).
173   *'gin and hot water to blunt the pain and ... Dexedrine to blunt the gin'* Didion, Joan, *Slouching Toward Bethlehem*, reissue ed. (New York: Farrar, Straus and Giroux, 2008).
174   *After a brief spike in methamphetamine injections, the UK's amphetamine use began to decline.* Rasmussen, *On Speed.*
174   *'Speed is anti-social, paranoid-making ... a plague in the whole dope industry.'* Ibid.
174   *'I don't care if it's horse piss ... it's the only thing that works.'* Ibid.
174   *By the mid-1960s, around one in twenty Americans had an amphetamine prescription, with nearly half also using illicit speed – around ten million people.* 'Equal to the entire combined populations of New York and Philadelphia at the time.' Gibson, Campbell, 'Population of the 100 Largest Cities and Other Urban Places in the United States: 1790 To 1990', US Census Bureau, 1998, http://www.census.gov/population/www/documentation/ twps0027.html
174   *'I turned into a pair of eyeballs and ears.'* Rasmussen, *On Speed.*
176   *In some, up to 10 per cent of children were on stimulants to 'make them easier to handle'.* Hinshaw, Stephen P. and Scheffler, Richard M., *The ADHD Explosion: Myths, Medication, Money, and Today's Push for Performance* (Oxford: Oxford University Press, 2014).
176   *By 2007 ADHD diagnoses among poor children rose 59 per cent in states under No Child Left Behind, compared to under 10 per cent for wealthier children.* Black, non-Hispanic children and white, non-Hispanic children are more often diagnosed with ADHD (12 per cent and 10 per cent, respectively), than Hispanic children (8 per cent) or Asian, non-Hispanic children (3 per cent). Healy, Melissa, 'The ADHD explosion: A new book explores factors that have fueled it', *Los Angeles Times*, 25 February 2014, https://www.latimes.com/science/sciencenow/la-sci-sn-adhd-explosion-book-authors-20140225-story.html
179   *Up to a third of US college students use stimulants to boost academic*

performance. 'Peer-reviewed journal articles started reporting that as many as a fifth, a quarter, or even a third of all college students in the United States take stimulants to help with midterms, finals or term papers.' Hinshaw and Scheffler, *The ADHD Explosion*, p. 61.

180   *Professors see this all the time – students faking symptoms, taking too many pills, spiralling at the health centre.* Jacobs, Andrew, 'The Adderall advantage', *New York Times*, 31 July 2005, https://www.nytimes.com/2005/07/31/education/edlife/the-adderall-advantage.html

180   *'If you don't take them, you're at a disadvantage.'* Ibid.

182   *'Elizabeth, with her Adderall.'* Schwarz, Alan, 'Workers seeking productivity in a pill are abusing ADHD drugs', *New York Times*, 19 April 2015, https://www.nytimes.com/ 2015/04/19/us/workers-seeking-productivity-in-a-pill-are-abusing-adhd-drugs.html

184   *'passive rebellion against the competitive consumerist social order, the unconscious and private equivalent of the collective factory slowdown'* Rasmussen, *On Speed.*

8. (Paid) Employment Versus (Invisible) Labour

187   *A review by the Attention Deficit Disorder Association found that ADHD people are 60 per cent more likely to be fired, 30 per cent more likely to face ongoing job struggles, and three times more likely to quit impulsively.* ADDA editorial team, 'Impact of ADHD at work', ADDA, 24 July 2023, https://add.org/impact-of-adhd-at-work/

197   *ADHD UK reports that only 43 per cent of ADHD Personal Independence Payment (PIP) claims succeed, compared to an overall average of 53 per cent.* 'PIP health conditions', Benefits and Work, https://www.benefitsandwork.co.uk/personal-independence-payment-pip/pip-health-conditions/claim-pip-for-adhd

197   *'£300m Bill for Handouts'* Graham-Brown, Daisy, '£300m bill for handouts: Spending on disability benefits for people claiming to have ADHD shoots up 41,000 per cent within a decade', *Daily Mail*, 13 April 2024, https://www.dailymail.co.uk/news/article-13305357/spending-disability-benefits-adhd-rise-decade.html

197   *But these benefits are essential services, funded by taxpayers, reflecting the long-overdue recognition of psychiatric disorders and ADHD's frequent comorbidities – many claimants have multiple disabilities.* 'In 2023, there were 52,989 PIP claimants with ADHD listed as their main disabling condition. This makes it the fourteenth most common condition to get an award of PIP for out of over 500 conditions listed by the DWP.' 'PIP health conditions', https://www.benefitsandwork.co.uk/personal-independence-payment-pip/pip-health-conditions/claim-pip-for-adhd

197   *In early 2024 more than twenty thousand people were waiting for assistance, a number that quadrupled throughout the year: by December, the list had grown to 25,063.* Pring, John, 'Access to Work waiting-list climbs again, despite DWP claims', Disability News Service, 29 February 2024, https://www. disabilitynewsservice.com/access-to-work-waiting-list-climbs-again-despite-dwp-claims/

198   *Force people off benefits so they 'don't grow up thinking they can't work'. He says, 'If you are not disabled, you can go to work,'* Hatton, Ben, 'Lee

Anderson plays down "poverty nonsense", saying 1970s was "real poverty"', *Independent*, 3 October 2023, https://www.independent.co.uk/news/uk/lee-anderson-conservative-party-europe-manchester-facebook-b2423190.html

202 *'mentioned [...] he has ADHD' but doesn't have a diagnosis. 'I'm sceptical [but] ADHD might help explain the problems with his performance. What should I do?'* O'Toole, Vicki, 'Dear Vicki: Our engineer blamed a performance issue on ADHD. I'm sceptical, but what should I do?', *Irish Independent*, 8 April 2024, https://www.independent.ie/business/in-the-workplace/ dear-vicki-our-engineer-blamed-a-performance-issue-on-adhd-im-sceptical-but-what-should-i-do/a1408279680.html

202 *'Meet the Professional Victim Who's Made £35,000 from Over 100 Disability Complaints.'* Sears, Neil, 'Meet the professional victim who's made £35,000 from more than 100 disability complaints accused of "making a career out of tribunals"', *Daily Mail*, 2 February 2024, https://www.dailymail.co.uk/news/article-13039435/professional-victim-money-disability-complaints.html

9. Prison: Crime and ... Revenge?

210 *In the last thirty years the UK prison population has risen by 80 per cent* Ministry of Justice, *Prison Population Projections: 2022 to 2027* (London: Ministry of Justice, 2022).

210 *the largest in Western Europe without any corresponding reduction in violent crime* Prison Reform Trust, *Prison: The Facts* (London: Prison Reform Trust, 2019), https://prisonreformtrust.org.uk/wp-content/uploads/old_files/ Documents/Bromley%20Briefings/Prison%20the%20facts%20 Summer%202019.pdf

210 *'We take prisons for granted but are often afraid to face the realities they produce.' Prisons are both 'present' and 'absent', seemingly 'disconnected from our own lives'.* Davis, Angela Y., *Are Prisons Obsolete?* (New York: Seven Stories Press, 2003).

210 *over 40 per cent of adults are convicted of another offence within a year* Ministry of Justice, 'Proven Reoffending Statistics Quarterly: January to March 2020', in *Prison: The Facts*.

210 *for ADHD adults that rate is one third higher* Children and Adults with Attention-Deficit/Hyperactivity Disorder (CHADD), 'Go directly to jail, do not pass "Go" ...', CHADD, 3 September 2017, https://chadd.org/adhd-weekly/go-directly-to-jail-do-not-pass-go/

211 *ADHD prevalence inside UK prisons is estimated as ten times higher than outside.* Campbell, Denis, 'One in four UK prisoners has attention deficit hyperactivity disorder, says report', *Guardian*, 18 June 2022, https://www.theguardian.com/society/2022/jun/18/uk-prisoners-attention-deficit-disorder-adhd-prison

211 *Calls for ADHD screening in the carceral system date back to 2009* Hill, Amelia, 'All prisoners to be tested for ADHD', *Guardian*, 27 December 2009, https://www.theguardian.com/uk/2009/dec/27/adhd-prisons-mental-health-crime

211 *treatment reduces criminal behaviour by 32 per cent in men and 41 per cent in women* Lichtenstein, Paul, Halldner, Linda, Zetterqvist, Johan, Sjölander, Arvid, Serlachius, Eva, Fazel, Seena, Långström, Niklas and Larsson, Henrik, 'Medication for attention deficit-hyperactivity disorder

and criminality', *New England Journal of Medicine*, 367:21 (2012), https://www.doi.org/ 10.1056/NEJMoa1203241

211 *Untreated ADHD in prisons still costs the UK justice system £11.7 million annually.* Young, Susan, González, Rafael A., Fridman, Moshe, Hodgkins, Paul, Kim, Keira and Gudjonsson, Gisli H., 'The economic consequences of attention-deficit hyperactivity disorder in the Scottish prison system', *BMC Psychiatry*, 18 (2018), https://doi.org/10.1186/s12888-018-1792-x

211 *From March 2020 until February 2021 85 per cent of people in UK prisons spent twenty-three hours a day locked in 3-metre-by-2-metre cells, meeting the UN definition of torture.* Allison, Eric, 'Treatment of UK prisoners during Covid meets UN definition of torture', *Guardian*, 20 July 2022, https://www.theguardian.com/society/2022/jul/20/ treatment-of-uk-prisoners-during-covid-meets-un-definition-of-torture

211 *Studies show that half of people with ADHD have experienced depression and they're four times more likely to have generalised anxiety disorder.* Kuntz, Leah, 'ADHD and generalized anxiety disorder: Hand in hand?', *Psychiatric Times*, 14 December 2021, https://www.psychiatrictimes. com/view/adhd-and-generalized-anxiety-disorder-hand-in-hand; Dodson, William, 'The ADHD–depression link: Symptom parallels and distinctions', *ADDitude*, 7 April 2024, https://www.additudemag.com/ adhd-depression-link-symptoms-diagnosis-treatments/

211 *'I also have ADHD, so the lockdown has affected that. I told them I was suicidal. The senior officer stood there when I slit myself, and instead of helping me, ran to get healthcare for himself because I had hepatitis at the time.'* User Voice and Queen's University Belfast, *Coping with Covid in Prison: The Impact of the Prisoner Lockdown* (London: User Voice, 2022), https://www.uservoice.org/wp-content/uploads/2022/08/User-Voice-QUB-Coping-with-Covid.pdf

211 *'experiencing thoughts that they would "be better off dead"'* Ibid.

212 *'penalises people whose condition is marked by failure to change when punished'* Szalavitz, Maia, *Unbroken Brain: A Revolutionary New Way of Understanding Addiction* (New York: St. Martin's Press, 2016).

212 *One study suggests that 74 per cent of incarcerated people with ADHD have a substance misuse disorder characterised by persistence despite negative consequences.* Young, S., Sedgwick, O., Fridman, M., Gudjonsson, G., Hodgkins, P., Lantigua, M. and Gonzales, R. A., 'Comorbid psychiatric disorders among incarcerated ADHD populations: A meta-analysis', *Psychological Medicine*, 45:12 (2015), pp. 2499–510, https://www.doi.org/10.1017/S0033291715000598

212 *In July 2021 the Tory government published an independent review of neurodiversity in the criminal justice system (CJS), identifying ADHD as an area of high impact.* ADHD Foundation, *ADHD in the Criminal Justice System Roundtable* (London: Takeda, 2022), https://www. adhdfoundation.org.uk/wp-content/uploads/2022/06/Takeda_ADHD-in-the-CJS-Roundtable-Report_Final.pdf

212 *'protect the public through punishment and incapacitation of offenders'* Ministry of Justice, *Prisons Strategy White Paper* (London: Ministry of Justice, 2021), https://assets.publishing.service.gov.uk/media/ 61af18e38fa8f5037e8ccc47/prisons-strategy-white-paper.pdf

213 *Despite declaring his ADHD and paranoid schizophrenia – both of which*

significantly increase suicide risk – and hearing voices telling him to kill himself, he was placed in segregation without a mental health assessment or care plan. 'Andrew Shirley: Inquest finds failures at HMP Hewell amounting to neglect caused death', INQUEST, 20 January 2023, https://www.inquest.org.uk/andrew-shirley-inquest

214 *'abnormal defect of moral control'* Still, George, 'Some abnormal psychical conditions in children: Excerpts from three lectures', *Journal of Attention Disorders*, 10:2 (2006), pp. 126– 36, https://www.doi.org/10.1177/1087054706288114

214 *'A Study of Minimal Brain Dysfunction Amongst Male Delinquent Drop-Outs'* Tarnopol, L., 'Delinquency and minimal brain dysfunction', *Journal of Learning Disabilities*, 3:4 (1970), https://www.ojp.gov/ncjrs/virtual-library/abstracts/delinquency-and-minimal-brain-dysfunction

214 *'ADHD Dad Sentenced for Murdering Four-Year-Old Daughter'* News24, 'ADHD dad sentenced for murdering four-year-old daughter', News24, 21 May 2015, https://www.news24.com/life/wellness/body/condition-centres/adhd/about-adhd/adhd-dad-sentenced-for-murdering-four-year-old-daughter-20150521

214 *'Raging ADHD Teen Went Berserk and Threatened to Kill Mum and Stepdad with Kitchen Knife'* Naylor, Martin, '"Raging" ADHD teen went berserk and threated to kill mum and stepdad with kitchen knife', *Derby Telegraph*, 26 January 2023, https://www.derbytelegraph.co.uk/news/local-news/raging-adhd-teen-went-berserk-8068986

214 *'Peterborough: Murderer Said ADHD Made Him Kill Partygoer'* BBC News, 'Peterborough: Murderer said ADHD made him kill partygoer', BBC News, 21 January 2022, https://www.bbc.co.uk/news/uk-england-cambridgeshire-60047881

215 *In 2005 thirteen-year-old triplets from Kent, each with severe developmental delay and ADHD, were handed restrictive ASBOs that they quickly breached resulting in two-year supervision orders.* Nixon, Judy, Hodge, Nick, Parr, Sadie, Willis, Ben and Hunter, Caroline, 'Anti-social behaviour and disability in the UK', *People, Place and Policy*, 2:1 (2007), pp. 37–47, https://www.doi.org/10.3351/ppp.0002.0001.0005

216 *At least a third of recipients had a mental illness, with one suicidal woman banned from visiting rivers, lakes and bridges.* Burney, Elizabeth, 'Out with yobs', *CJM*, 67 (2007), https://www.crimeandjustice.org.uk/sites/crimeandjustice.org.uk/files/09627250708553201.pdf

216 *We now know that a third of under-seventeen ASBO recipients had neurological or learning disorders* 'ASBOs ill suit special needs', *The Times*, 15 November 2005, https://www.thetimes.com/article/asbos-ill-suit-special-needs-tzf6zd6m3n9

216 *with 40 per cent likely to have been diagnosed with ADHD* Hunter, Caroline, Hodge, Nick, Nixon, Judy, Parr, Sadie and Willis, Ben, *Disabled People's Experiences of Antisocial Behaviour and Harassment in Social Housing: A Critical Review* (Sheffield: Sheffield Hallam University, 2007), https://disability-studies.leeds.ac.uk/wp-content/uploads/sites/40/ library/hodge-ASBO-Final-Report.pdf

216 *In the UK, ADHD diagnosis waiting lists can stretch up to ten years.* ADHD UK, 'ADHD UK's report into NHS ADHD assessment waiting lists', https://adhduk.co.uk/nhs-adhd-assessments-waiting-lists-report/

216 *In the UK, ADHD diagnosis waiting lists can stretch up to ten years.*
   Wareham, Sophie, 'ADHD waiting times "crisis" as patients face seven-
   year wait for NHS diagnosis', *Big Issue*, 27 December 2021, https://www.
   bigissue.com/life/health/adhd-nhs-diagnosis-waiting-times-crisis/

216 *30 per cent of ADHD kids have learning difficulties, and 40 per cent face
   temporary exclusion from school, with 11 per cent permanently excluded.*
   'ADHD and exclusion in schools', UK ADHD Partnership, https://www.
   ukadhd.com/adhd-and-exclusion-in-schools.htm

217 *This marks them as 'problems' – over 90 per cent of repeat offenders were
   excluded from school.* Revolving Doors, *New Generation: Preventing
   Young Adults Being Caught in the Revolving Door* (London: Revolving
   Doors Agency, 2020), https://t2a.org.uk/wp-content/uploads/2020/05/
   RDA_NGP_Young-adults-in-the-revolving-door_For-screen-002_0.pdf

217 *96 per cent of inmates* Robins, Jon, 'ADHD critically under-diagnosed
   in prisons, says report', The Justice Gap, 21 June 2022, https://www.
   thejusticegap.com/adhd-critically-under-diagnosed-in-prisons-says-report/

217 *ADHD people have more contact with the police, are younger at first arrest,
   and have higher risk of multiple convictions, with a two- to three-fold
   increased risk of later arrest, conviction and imprisonment.* Young, Susan,
   Gudjonsson, Gisli H., Goodwin, Emily J., Jotangia, Amit, Farooq, Romana,
   Haddrick, David and Adamou, Marios, 'Beyond the gates: Identifying
   and managing offenders with attention deficit hyperactivity disorder in
   community probation services', *AIMS Public Health*, 1:1 (2014), pp. 33–42.

217 *'behavioural disorder that is characterised by a persistent pattern of
   disobedient, defiant and hostile behaviour towards authority figures'*
   'Oppositional Defiant Disorder', The Good Schools Guide, https://
   www.goodschoolsguide.co.uk/special-educational-needs/types-of-sen/
   oppositional-defiant-disorder

217 *In the lead-up to the Brixton Uprising of 1981, more than a thousand
   young Black men were stopped in just one week.* Taylor, Diane, 'Frontline
   tactics', *druglink*, July/August 2006, https://www.drugwise.org.uk/wp-
   content/uploads/Frontline-tactics.pdf

217 *For Black people with ADHD, hyperactivity may be interpreted as
   'aggression' and taken to justify an escalation of force.* Revolving Doors,
   Revolving Doors Neurodiversity Policy Position (London: Revolving
   Doors Agency, 2022), https://revolving-doors.org.uk/wp-content/uploads/
   2022/09/Revolving-Doors-neurodiversity-policy-position.pdf

218 *In prisons, 80 per cent of ADHD goes undiagnosed.* ADHD Foundation,
   ADHD in the Criminal Justice System Roundtable.

218 *Even for those with diagnoses, prison authorities can restrict prescriptions
   like Ritalin.* 'ADHD in UK prisons "critically underdiagnosed"',
   Inside Time, 27 June 2022, https://insidetime.org/newsround/
   adhd-in-uk-prisons-critically-underdiagnosed/

218 *'I've got ADHD, emotional psychotic personality disorder, anxiety and
   personality disorder and PTSD. So, I came to jail and straight away
   they said, "You're not having none of your meds . . ." I'm getting phone
   calls from mental health teams saying, "Have you took your meds?"'*
   User Voice, *Neurodiversity in the Criminal Justice System* (London: User
   Voice, 2021), https://www.uservoice.org/wp-content/uploads/2021/07/
   Neurodiversity-in-the-Criminal-Justice-System.pdf

218 *Others arrive with diagnosed but unmedicated ADHD and aren't given information about treatment options.* Campbell, 'One in four UK prisoners has attention deficit hyperactivity disorder, says report'.

218 *After years of advocacy by campaign group ADHD Liberty, the City of London's police force became the first in the country to trial screening detainees in May 2023. The long-term goal is to create a pathway to allow diagnoses to be fast-tracked under the NHS. Other police departments have agreed to trial screenings, but there's no long-term commitment or funding. Most participants are not assessed for neurodivergent conditions at any stage in the CJS.* Sarah Templeton, founder of The ADHD Liberty charity, campaigns on the link between undiagnosed ADHD and the CJS. She advocates for ADHD screening to be carried out on every prison induction wing and has people who work for the police and have ADHD on her side. I have interviewed her for this book. Here is her website: https://www.adhdliberty.org/

218 *Screening for ADHD before entering prison could prevent this, but it's not done.* User Voice, *Neurodiversity in the Criminal Justice System.*

218 *90 per cent of ADHD patients respond to medication.* Cortese, Samuele, 'Regional analysis of UK primary care prescribing and adult service referrals for young people with attention-deficit hyperactivity disorder: From little to very little', *BJPsych Open*, 6:3 (2020), https://www.doi.org/10.1192/bjo.2020.28

219 *'didn't think any staff were aware of his conditions, and if they were, they didn't mention them or do anything different to accommodate them'* HMICFRS, *Neurodiversity in the Criminal Justice System: A Review of Evidence* (London: His Majesty's Inspectorate of Constabulary and Fire & Rescue Services, 2021), https://www.justiceinspectorates.gov.uk/cjji/wp-content/uploads/sites/2/2021/07/Neurodiversity-evidence-review-web-2021.pdf

219 *More than eleven thousand under-twenty-fives are held in Young Offender Institutions in England and Wales* Representing 14 per cent of the total population in custody. Davies, Miranda, Hutchings, Rachel and Keeble, Eilís, *Growing up Inside: Understanding the Key Health Care Issues for Young People in Young Offender Institutions and Prisons* (London: Nuffield Trust, 2023, https://www.nuffieldtrust.org.uk/research/growing-up-inside-understanding-the-key-health-care-issues-for-young-people-in-young-offender-institutions-and-prisons

219 *ADHD symptoms present in 45 per cent of children in custody* Young, Susan and Harpin, Val, 'The challenge of ADHD and youth offending', *Cutting Edge Psychiatry in Practice*, 2 (2012), pp. 138–43.

221 *'experienced stability in their behaviour for the first time'* 'New study to tackle ADHD in young prisoners', King's College London, 2016, https://www.kcl.ac.uk/archive/news/ioppn/records/2016/october/new-study-to-tackle-adhd-in-young-prisoners

221 *Incarceration as a child compounds the likelihood of reoffending – over two thirds of children do so within twelve months of release.* Ibid.

222 *Increasingly, people self-diagnose ADHD on arrival at prison, but waiting lists for formal diagnosis don't move.* Ibid.

222 *'management problem'* All quotes here are from an interview with Ines

Berges, forensic social worker at West London Mental Health NHS Trust, Department of Social Work.

223 *The prison system, prioritising security, doesn't account for learning difficulties – it's designed to protect the status quo.* Chaplin, Eddie et al., 'Prisoners with attention deficit hyperactivity disorder: Co-morbidities and service pathways', *International Journal of Prisoner Health*, 18:3 (2022), pp. 245–58, https://doi.org/10.1108/IJPH-03-2021-0020

223 *The guidelines haven't been adjusted for custodial settings, but in prisons they are simply not met.* Young, Susan et al., 'Failure of healthcare provision for attention-deficit/ hyperactivity disorder in the United Kingdom: A consensus statement', *Frontiers in Psychiatry*, 12 (2021), https://www.frontiersin.org/journals/psychiatry/articles/10.3389/fpsyt.2021.649399/full

223 *Only 4 per cent of participants sought the maximum dose, indicating minimal drug-seeking behaviour for slow-release stimulants.* Young, Susan et al., 'Identification and treatment of offenders with attention-deficit/ hyperactivity disorder in the prison population: A practical approach based upon expert consensus', *BMC Psychiatry*, 18 (2018), https://doi.org/10.1186/s12888-018-1858-9

224 *The pandemic worsened staffing shortages, leaving 36 per cent of the prison workforce in the UK with less than three years' experience.* Bancroft, Holly, 'Fears prisons could be run by gangs as thousands of guards quit', *Independent*, 13 September 2023, https://www.independent.co.uk/news/uk/home-news/prisons-hmp-jail-officers-daniel-khaliffe-b2410020.html

224 *diagnosing and treating ADHD could significantly reduce recidivism and save the UK government money in the long term.* 'ADHD treatment "may reduce risk of criminal behaviour"', BBC News, 22 November 2022, https://www.bbc.co.uk/news/health-20414822

225 *'I don't know.'* Young, S., Sedgwick, O., Fridman, M., Gudjonsson, G., Hodgkins, P., Lantigua, M. and González, R. A., 'Co-morbid psychiatric disorders among incarcerated ADHD populations: A meta-analysis', *Psychological Medicine*, 45:12 (2015), pp. 2499–510, https://www.doi.org/10.1017/S0033291715000598

225 *At trial, ADHD people are three times more likely to falsely plead guilty, often because compliance offers a way out of overwhelming situations.* HMICFRS, *Neurodiversity in the Criminal Justice System: A Review of Evidence.*

225 Inside Time, *a national newspaper for prisoners, advises readers to seek expert advice on whether ADHD was considered in their sentencing, but it's unreasonable to expect neurodivergent people to advocate for themselves in a system stacked against them.* 'Defendants with hidden disabilities don't get fair trials, says watchdog', *Inside Time*, 15 June 2020, https://insidetime.org/newsround/defendants-with-hidden-disabilities-dont-get-fair-trials-says-watchdog/

225 *Someone with ADHD might blurt out an inappropriate response or fail to regulate their anger, which can be misinterpreted as guilt.* 'ADHD & criminal justice: Understanding the iceberg', Communicourt, 12 October 2022, https://www.communicourt.co.uk/news/adhd-criminal-justice-understanding-the-iceberg/

227 *About 60 per cent of young men with ADHD admitted to hospitals during*

incarceration are there due to injury or poisoning, compared to 40 per cent without ADHD. Davies et al., *Growing up Inside.*

227 *ADHD people are eight times more likely to engage in aggressive incidents in prison.* Young, Susan and Thome, Johannes, 'ADHD and offenders', *World Journal of Biological Psychiatry*, 12:S1 (2011), pp. 124–8, https://www.doi.org/10.3109/15622975.2011.600319

227 *They are punished in this way more than most.* Buadze, Anna, Friedl, Nadine, Schleifer, Roman, Young, Susan, Schneeberger, Andres and Liebrenz, Michael, 'Perceptions and attitudes of correctional staff toward ADHD: A challenging disorder in everyday prison life', *Frontiers in Psychiatry*, 11 (2021), https://www.doi.org/10.3389/fpsyt.2020.600005

227 *'I did have a few prisons officers ask me if I was ADHD. I had never been diagnosed with it back then so, at first, I didn't care. But after a few people raised that, I asked, "What do [you] do about that?" All of them just answered, "Nothing." They recognise what it is, yet their solution to deal with it is punishment.'* Revolving Doors, *Revolving Doors Neurodiversity Policy Position.*

228 *'counterproductive' for ADHD prisoners, yet still deem it 'necessary to ensure equal treatment'.* Buadze et al., 'Perceptions and attitudes of correctional staff toward ADHD: A challenging disorder in everyday prison life'.

230 *Participants in the Clink are 32 per cent less likely to reoffend.* UK Government, *Thousands of Prisoners Trained to Become Cooks* (London: UK Government, 2022), https://www.gov.uk/government/news/thousands-of-prisoners-trained-to-become-cooks

230 *'The Clink supported me through significant struggles with ADHD. Now I'm employed as a kitchen porter and regularly see my young daughter.'* Ibid.

230 *Another initiative, 'A Pond in Every Prison', introduced ponds, streams or wetlands in over half of UK prisons.* 'A pond in every prison', *Inside Time*, 1 September 2020, https:// insidetime.org/comment/a-pond-in-every-prison/

230 *One man sought advice on controlling nightly outbursts of rage, a symptom of his ADHD.* Watson, Caroline and Kirk, Richard, 'Inside health', *Inside Time*, 3 May 2022, https://insidetime.org/information/inside-health-19/

230 *Another asked if it was true that libraries were no longer a statutory right, as a prison guard had falsely told him – reading was his main strategy for coping inside.* 'Library no longer a statutory right?', *Inside Time*, 1 July 2016, https://insidetime.org/mailbag/library-no-longer-a-statutory-right/

230 *It launched in 2022 and broadcasts to more than forty thousand people across sixty-three prisons in England and Wales.* Leapman, Ben, 'On-screen winner!', *Inside Time*, 3 May 2022, https://insidetime.org/comment/on-screen-winner/

231 *In August 2022 London's Pentonville prison, near King's Cross, launched the UK's first Neurodivergent Wing (NDW), housing forty-five men and five mentors, the first of its kind in England.* Leapman, Ben, 'More love to give', *Inside Time*, 1 November 2022, https://insidetime.org/comment/more-love-to-give/

231 *more than half of people with autism also show ADHD symptoms, and two-thirds of people with ADHD have elevated levels of autistic traits.*

Szalavitz, *Unbroken Brain: A Revolutionary New Way of Understanding Addiction*, p. 55.

232   *'underwater scenes of fish projected onto the walls, soft mats on the floor, padded walls and beanbags'* Leapman, 'More love to give'.

232   *Built in 1842 to hold 520 people in single cells, the prison now houses more than 1,100, with 60 per cent of prisoners sharing a space originally meant for one. The 2022 report revealed that more than half of Pentonville's prisoners felt victimised by staff, and 44 per cent of new arrivals felt unsafe on their first night, compared to 23 per cent in other prisons.* Gregory, Julia, '"Cramped relic": Urgent action needed to "save lives" inside overcrowded Pentonville prison, campaigners warn', *Islington Citizen*, 19 October 2022, https://www.islingtoncitizen.co.uk/2022/10/19/urgent-action-save-lives-pentonville-prison/

232   *The recommendation to provide 'decent and hygienic conditions, including properly screened toilets and sufficient space for each occupant', still hasn't been implemented. The post-inspection report highlighted the NDW as a positive step, praising the 'ambitious long-term vision represented by the plan for a new unit intended to care for neurodiverse prisoners' [italics mine]. However, the inspector noted that Pentonville had seen 'more false dawns than most prisons'* Her Majesty's Inspectorate of Prisons, *Report on an Unannounced Inspection of HMP Pentonville* (London: Her Majesty's Inspectorate of Prisons, 2022), https://www.justiceinspectorates.gov.uk/hmiprisons/wp-content/uploads/sites/4/2022/10/Pentonville-web-2022.pdf

232   *In 2020 wheelchair users were denied fresh air, and 70 per cent of people felt threatened by staff.* Bentham, Martin, 'Pentonville prison condemned by inspector for failing to let inmates in wheelchairs go outside', *Evening Standard*, 10 December 2020, https://www.standard.co.uk/news/london/pentonville-prison-inspector-wheelchair-report-b220598.html

232   *The forensic psychologist behind the NDW hoped it would reduce bullying, violence, anxiety and self-harm rates among neurodivergent men.* 'Pentonville neurodiversity unit set to open', *Inside Time*, 26 July 2022, https://insidetime.org/newsround/pentonville-neurodiversity-unit-set-to-open/

234   *'The normalisation of the trans prison will only lead to more trans people being incarcerated.'* Faye, Shon, *The Transgender Issue: An Argument for Justice* (London: Penguin Books, 2021).

234   *'should not be in the child justice system at all'* 'Justice for children', United Nations, https://violenceagainstchildren. un.org/content/justice-system

234   *'Prisons operate as containment facilities for the growing mental health crisis.'* Faye, *The Transgender Issue*.

235   *Studies show that restorative justice has a high victim satisfaction rate (85 per cent) and reduces recidivism by 14 per cent.* UK Parliament, 'Written evidence from the Restorative Justice Council (RJC)', https://committees.parliament.uk/writtenevidence/109062/pdf/

235   *'To understand the social meaning of the prison today within the context of a developing prison industrial complex means that punishment has to be severed from its link with crime.'* Davis, *Are Prisons Obsolete?*

10. The Dopamine Hunters: Addiction and ADHD

240 *On the other side of Jeremy Paxman sat Peter Hitchens, who condemned the courts as 'soft on criminals' and seemed to be oddly pre-occupied with judges 'wearing tracksuit bottoms' – a classist concern that left Perry, an American, baffled.* BBC *Newsnight*, 'Matthew Perry debates drug courts with Peter Hitchens – BBC Newsnight', YouTube, 16 December 2013, https://www.youtube.com/ watch?v=CDtIZZiySgA

241 *'[ADHD] has a huge and powerful lobby which turns with fury on its critics so I know this question will get me into loads of trouble but . . . does ADHD even exist?'* Hitchens, 'It has a huge and powerful lobby which turns with fury on its critics so I know this question will get me into loads of trouble but . . . does ADHD even exist?'.

241 *'like taking drugs and don't want to stop'* Zurcher, Anthony, 'Is addiction a fantasy?', BBC News, 17 December 2023, https://www.bbc.co.uk/news/ blogs-echochambers-25422399

242 *ADHD is five to ten times more common among alcoholics than in the general population. Having ADHD triples the risk of substance misuse.* 'ADHD triples risk of substance abuse – but it doesn't have to', Rehabs UK, 4 April 2024, https://rehabsuk.com/blog/ adhd-triples-risk-of-substance-abuse-but-it-doesn-t-have-to/

242 *In* Unbroken Brain *she frames addiction as a developmental disorder, more similar to autism, ADHD and dyslexia than to diseases like mumps or cancer.* Szalavitz, *Unbroken Brain*.

244 *But people with ADHD often start experimenting with alcohol and drugs earlier and more freely.* Magon, Rakesh and Müller, Ulrich, 'ADHD with comorbid substance use disorder: Review of treatment', *Advances in Psychiatric Treatment*, 18:6 (2012), pp. 436–46, https://www.doi.org.uk/ 10.1192/apt.bp.111.009340

244 *Children with ADHD are more likely to start drinking early – 40 per cent begin before the age of fifteen, compared to 22 per cent of children without ADHD.* 'ADHD triples risk of substance abuse – but it doesn't have to'.

255 *For people with ADHD, the 'laboratories' they grow up in are often hostile. Psychologist Bruce Alexander's 'Rat Park' experiment showed that rats in enriched environments were less likely to become addicted than those in isolation. Similarly, addiction in humans is often linked to emotional isolation and stress.* Szalavitz, *Unbroken Brain*.

256 *This is termed salience attribution – where a false need outweighs real needs, making everything else irrelevant.* 'Burst discharges (phasic firing) of dopamine-containing neurons are necessary to establish long-term memories associating predictive stimuli with rewards and punishers.' Wise, Roy A. and Robble, Mykel A., 'Dopamine and addiction', *Annual Review of Psychology*, 71 (2020), pp. 79–106, https://doi.org/10.1146/ annurev-psych-010418-103337

258 *'That's me all over,' he admitted, slapping his forehead in recognition. Diagnosed too late, Remi had already used cocaine since his teens and switched to heroin in prison. Ritalin helped briefly – 'My mind isn't going off like a machine gun!'* Maté, Gabor, *In the Realm of Hungry Ghosts: Close Encounters with Addiction* (Toronto: Vintage Canada, 2008).

259 *The campaign waged by that craving voice boils down to a single message:*

it feels so good. 'Yes, it feels good,' I countered time and again, but it's a feeling I've felt a thousand times before. There is nothing new there. But ... nothing feels so good. And sadly, in a way that is true. Nothing can feel as good as that intense flash of euphoria. But it's such a bright flash that integral to it is the darkness that follows. One of the challenges of recovery is to accept slow-burning pleasures instead. They don't burn so brutally bright, but they leave you warm in their wake, instead of in total darkness craving more light. When you forgo the sublime intensity of narcotics, you need to find excitement elsewhere. Lewin, Joel, 'On not taking cocaine in Colombia', *RecoveReads*, 19 May 2023, https://recovereads.com/2023/05/19/on-not-taking-cocaine-in-colombia/

11. Social Media: Advocating or Exploiting ADHD?

266 *By March 2022, ADHD-related TikTok videos had amassed 2.4 billion views, yet a* Canadian Journal of Psychiatry *study revealed over half were misleading and lacking in scientific evidence.* Williams, Camille, 'TikTok is my therapist: The dangers and promise of viral #MentalHealth videos', *ADDitude*, 31 March 2022, https://www.additudemag.com/tiktok-adhd-videos-self-diagnosis-support/

267 *We are most active later at night, post more impulsively, react more intensely and use saltier language.* Guntuku, S. C. et al., 'Language of ADHD in adults on social media', *Journal of Attention Disorders*, 23:12 (2019), pp. 1475–85, https://www.doi.org/10.1177/1087054717738083

273 *Right now, eighty-one countries run disinformation campaigns on social media, turning 'context collapse' into a profitable enterprise.* 'Industrialized disinformation: 2020 global inventory of organized social media manipulation', Programme on Democracy and Technology, https://demtech.oii.ox.ac.uk/research/posts/industrialized-disinformation/

273 *Persuasive design starts off convenient, like notifications to help organisation, but quickly becomes a trap.* Lewin, Joel, Field, Matt and Davies, Emma, 'Investigating the impact of "dark nudges" on drinking intentions: A between groups, randomized and online experimental study', *British Journal of Health Psychology*, 29 (2024), pp. 272–92, https://doi.org/10.1111/bjhp.12698

273 *'adversarial design'* Williams, *Stand Out Of Our Light.*

276 *thesis about TikTok at the library, which argued that dismissing people who find ADHD on TikTok overlooks those the system itself ignores.* Locke, Toby Austin, 'In the cracks of attention: ADHD, vernacular anthropologies, and communities of care on TikTok', *Teaching Anthropology*, 12:1 (2023), pp. 23–35.

278 *The Depp v. Heard trial became a battleground for attention capital, where trending hashtags, constant social media commentary and bot-driven content amplified conflict for profit.* Who Trolled Amber?, Tortoise media, 2024, https://www.tortoisemedia.com/listen/who-trolled-amber

278 *Meanwhile, Heard lost work for being 'too noisy'. Organised accounts tweeted at all companies associated with her – 'this brand supports domestic violence against men' – losing her a L'Oréal campaign. Warner Bros. reduced her role and banned her from the media for the sequel to* Aquaman.

282 *Users like Hannah who understand their needs are less likely to get trapped.* Hannah prefers exploring the 'For You' page for fresh

content, unlike others who might seek a more controlled and 'safe' feed, highlighting how personal preferences and ADHD traits affect user experience.

283 *'I'm going to die,'* Millar, Brittany, 'Controversial influencer Caroline Calloway says she's "going to die" in Hurricane Milton for refusing to evacuate', *Independent*, 10 October 2024, https://www.independent.co.uk/life-style/caroline-calloway-hurricane-milton-tiktok-insta-b2626995.html

12. Unlikely Prophets

288 *'attention goes to many things'* 'Join us in the search for an MRI marker of ADHD', Mātai, https://www.matai.org.nz/adhd

288 *This aligns with Māori values, where mental, physical, spiritual and social health are interconnected* De Stigter, Giorgi, 'Aroreretini – Attention deficit disorders (ADD & ADHD)', Georgi de Stigter, 15 October 2023, https://georgids.com/2023/10/15/aroreretini-attention-deficit-disorders-add-adhd/

289 *It's one of the few platforms where attention to topics has held steady.* Hari, *Stolen Focus: Why You Can't Pay Attention – and How to Think Deeply Again*, p. 28.

290 *'bullshit jobs'* Graeber, David, 'On the phenomenon of bullshit jobs', *Strike!*, August 2013, https://strikemag.org/bullshit-jobs/

290 *Sociologist John Holloway notes that while capitalism tends to absorb everything, cracks always emerge where new possibilities arise.* Holloway, John, *Crack Capitalism* (London: Pluto Press, 2010).

291 *'As ADHDers, we struggle with Chronos time. Knowing this lessened my guilt around time management. When I'm on my own, I live in Kairos time. It gives me the energy for time management when I need to align with society's Chronos time.'* @chained_changeling, 'Theory: Sense of time, chronos vs kairos', Reddit, 2024, https://www.reddit.com/r/adhdwomen/comments/18m7qfn/theory_ sense_of_time_chronos_vs_kairos/

292 *In her book* Saving Time, *Jenny Odell argues that Chronos embodies nihilism and determinism by suggesting a predetermined future.* Odell, Jenny, *Saving Time: Discovering a Life Beyond the Clock* (New York: Random House, 2023).

298 *'attention problems' occur when we medicalise 'issues caused by hyperindustrialization'* In the 'ongoing crisis of attentiveness, in which the changing configurations of capitalism continually push attention to new limits and thresholds, with an endless sequence of new products, sources of stimulation, and streams of information, and then respond with new methods of managing and regulating perception'. Crary, Jonathan, *24/7: Late Capitalism and the Ends of Sleep* (New York: Verso, 2013).

298 *Humans weren't designed to stare at screens for ten hours a day, but that doesn't explain why many of us struggle to sleep or miss bodily signals like hunger or pain. See* Glossary. Interoception is the sense that helps you understand and feel what's going on inside your body.

300 *Expertise helps enter flow, but true immersion requires surrendering conscious control.* Csikszentmihalyi, M., *Flow and the Foundations of Positive Psychology: The Collected Works of Mihaly Csikszentmihalyi* (Dordrecht: Springer, 2014).

300 *In a culture that often equates busyness with worth, slowing down and focusing deeply becomes a radical act.* Odell, Jenny, *How to Do Nothing:*

Resisting the Attention Economy (New York: Melville House, 2019).

302 *Dani Donovan highlighted how ADHD communities offer support outside neurotypical feedback.* Donovan, Dani, 'ADHD storytelling and bridging the gap between clinical knowledge and lived experience', *Annual International Conference on ADHD 2023*, 30 November 2023.

302 *'morally neutral'* Davis, K. C., *How to Keep House While Drowning: A Gentle Approach to Cleaning and Organizing* (New York: Simon & Schuster, 2022).

303 *'choose what you pay attention to' to avoid our 'natural default setting', which is the enemy, 'because the traffic jams and crowded aisles and long checkout lines give me time to think, and if I don't make a conscious decision about how to think and what to pay attention to, I'm gonna be pissed and miserable every time I have to shop'.* Foster Wallace, David, *This Is Water: Some Thoughts, Delivered on a Significant Occasion, about Living a Compassionate Life* (New York: Little, Brown and Company, 2009).

305 *'Unable to attune their attention to that of others, these people have had to invent workaround procedures which have enabled them to better perceive certain hidden faces of things.'* This should be an advantage, as most peoples' attention being 'aligned on the returns of GDP growth' has meant 'that we have missed the gorilla of climate imbalance' Davidson, Cathy N., *Now You See It: How the Brain Science of Attention Will Transform the Way We Live, Work, and Learn* (London: Viking Press, 2011).

13. The Trojan Horse: An ADHD Manifesto

308 *'take a walk'* Odell, *How to Do Nothing*.

308 *Our attention is unique to each of us, yet it's available only as something to be alienated – captured by consumer capitalism or submerged in the experiences we dive into passionately.* Citton, Yves, *The Ecology of Attention*.

308 *'circulation'* Ibid.

309 *Philosopher Yves Citton suggests reimagining the attention economy as 'ecology' – an 'ecosystem' we must nurture urgently to create ways of living that are both sustainable for the community and enriching for the individiual.* Ibid.

311 *'standardised, free-floating, infinitely divisible' entities 'indelibly linked to human and ecological exhaustion'* Rosenthal, Caitlin, *Accounting for Slavery: Masters and Management* (Cambridge: Harvard University Press, 2018). This book explores the history of time and labour quantification, linking it to systemic exhaustion.

311 *'Crip Time'* Kafer, Alison, *Feminist, Queer, Crip* (Bloomington and Indianapolis: Indiana University Press, 2013).

312 *ADHD's impact on time perception isn't fully understood, but a 2020 review confirmed that it does alter it.* Mette, Christian, 'Time perception in adult ADHD: Findings from a decade – a review', *International Journal of Environmental and Public Health*, 20:4 (2023), https://www.mdpi.com/1660-4601/20/4/3098#

312 *Disability scholars and activists champion Crip Time, which reshapes our relationship with time by prioritising human needs over rigid schedules.*

Kafer, *Feminist, Queer, Crip.* 'Rather than bend disabled bodies and minds to meet the clock, crip time bends the clock to meet disabled bodies and minds.'

313 *'compulsory able-bodiedness'* McRuer, Robert, *Crip Theory: Cultural Signs of Queerness and Disability* (New York: NYU Press, 2006).

314 *With burnout prevalent even among neurotypicals, clearly there's a lesson to be learned: we must listen carefully to both our bodies and minds in a culture that encourages us to ignore them and push beyond their limits.* Adapted from Samuels, Ellen, 'Six ways of looking at crip time', *Disability Studies Quarterly*, 37:3 (2017).

314 *Indigenous worldviews, by contrast, embrace a cyclical, relational sense of time, rooted in the earth's natural rhythms and emphasising life's interconnectedness.* Cajete, Gregory, *Native Science: Natural Laws of Interdependence* (Santa Fe: Clear Light Publishers, 2000); Yunkaporta, Tyson, *Sand Talk: How Indigenous Thinking Can Save the World* (New York: HarperOne, 2020); Wall Kimmerer, Robin, *Braiding Sweetgrass: Indigenous Wisdom, Scientific Knowledge, and the Teachings of Plants* (Minneapolis: Milkweed Editions, 2013).

314 *Our unique processing styles allow us to see patterns others might overlook, and sense subtle shifts that signal larger changes in our environment.* Brown, Thomas E., *Attention Deficit Disorder: The Unfocused Mind in Children and Adults*, rev. ed. (New Haven: Yale University Press, 2006).

315 *The attention economy feeds on itself, reinforcing the idea that attention is scarce and demanding ever more content that seizes it.* Zuboff, Shoshana, *The Age of Surveillance Capitalism* (London: Profile Books, 2019).

317 *moments of 'collective disenchantment' with the attention industry have led to 'revolt', forcing the 'attention merchants' to 'revise their terms'* Wu, *The Attention Merchants.*

Bringing a book from manuscript to what you are reading is a team effort.

Dialogue Books would like to thank everyone who helped to publish *Attention Seeker* in the UK.

Editorial
Hannah Chukwu
Adriano Noble
Eleanor Gaffney

Contracts
Stephanie Evans
Sasha Duszynska Lewis
Isabel Camara

Sales
Megan Schaffer
Kyla Dean
Dominic Smith
Sinead White
Georgina Cutler-Ross
Kerri Hood
Jess Harvey
Natasha Weninger-Kong

Design
Nico Taylor
Sara Mahon
Sasha Egonu
Luke Applin

Production
Amanda Jones

Publicity
Corinna Zifko

Marketing
Emily Moran

Operations
Rosie Stevens

Finance
Chris Vale
Jonathan Gant

Audio
Dominic Gribben

Copy-Editor
Ian Preece

Proofreader
David Bamford